A
Hard
Rain
Fell

University Press
of Mississippi
Jackson

A
Hard
Rain
Fell

SDS
and
Why
It
Failed

David
Barber

www.upress.state.ms.us

The University Press of Mississippi is a member of the
Association of American University Presses.

∞

Library of Congress Cataloging-in-Publication Data

Barber, David, 1950–
   A hard rain fell : SDS and why it failed / David Barber.
      p.   cm.
   Includes bibliographical references and index.
   ISBN-13: 978-1-934110-17-1 (cloth : alk. paper)
   ISBN-10: 1-934110-17-5 (cloth : alk. paper)
1. Students for a Democratic Society (U.S.)—History.
2. New Left—United States—History. 3. College
students—United States—Political activity—History.
I. Title.
   LA229.B25 2008
   378.1'98—dc22
                                    2007021107

British Library Cataloging-in-Publication Data available

To my wife, Lisa,
and my daughters,
Emily and Laura.
With all my love
and gratitude.

Contents

Acknowledgments

I want to begin by acknowledging something that must be apparent to anyone who reads through these pages: I am quite clearly an interested party in this history. I was a participant in the struggles of the 1960s and have, since that time, attempted to make sense of that era. From that standpoint, I must acknowledge all the activists, too numerous to mention, who, in a variety of ways, opened my eyes to the realities of race, sex, and empire in the United States. I've lost contact with most of these people, but I hope that they will find that the lessons they taught me long years ago live on through this book.

I began this project in graduate school, and I completed most of it after September 2001. For all people of goodwill, these post-9/11 years have been extraordinarily difficult. I owe a deep debt of gratitude to fellow graduate students who shared my concerns and fears during these hard years: Kim Davis, Hilary Anne Hallet, Michael Meloy, Kelly Hopkins, George Jarrett, Toby Green, Monica Fitzgerald, Chris Rodriguez, Christina Bueno, and Lia Schraeder. Rene Francisco Poitevin, Michelle Young, Jaime Anderson, and Kye Epps all renewed my faith at an important time.

For help in my understanding of writing as a craft, I am indebted to Bill Bonds, Blanche Weisen Cook, and Bill Issell. Alan Taylor's incisive criticisms of my writing were particularly helpful. Colin Palmer allowed me to do a very early version of what would become a part of my first chapter, despite the fact that the paper I proposed to him did not quite fit the assignment he'd given me.

Although he disagreed passionately with some of my conclusions, Noel Ignatiev still had the courage and integrity to support my project. As editor of the critical whiteness studies/activist journal *Race Traitor*, Noel accepted and published my overly long article, " 'A F***g White Revolutionary Movement' and Other Fables of Whiteness." That article was an early draft of parts of the first and fourth chapters of this book. Jama Lazerow and Yohuru Williams also gave me important help, forcing me to sharpen my argument as I prepared a chapter for their forthcoming book on the Black Panther Party.

I am also indebted to those individuals who read and commented on individual chapters and drafts. Elizabeth Montgomery expressed an early interest in my project, thoroughly read my entire dissertation, and tirelessly improved its language. Phil Rubio was a constant support and champion, and never hesitated to read and challenge my work, despite his own pressing needs to be writing his own dissertation. Louis Segal, an adjunct instructor who in a more just society would be a tenured professor, strongly validated my work, as did Norma Smith, Lucy Barber, Lisa Materson, and Margie Ferguson.

James Lowen, reading for the University Press of Mississippi, offered me important direction for improvement. Most of all, I am indebted to him for pushing me to interview more individuals from that time. Perhaps he was trying to tell me that one of the greatest rewards for a historian of the recent past is to speak with people who have helped shape history. And this was indeed a great pleasure for me. I can't begin to thank the people who allowed me to speak with them: Chude (Pam Parker) Allen, Bo Burlingham, Kathleen Cleaver, Lewis Cole, Rev. Walter Coleman, Carl Davidson, Bernardine Dohrn, Lynn French, Noel Ignatiev, Martin Kenner, Mike Klonsky, Julius Lester, Russ Neurfeld, Carl Oglesby, and Mark Rudd. Mark was a tremendous help in the final year of this project, and had the great courage to read, question, and engage with me around what must have been difficult material for him. Chude Allen, one of the few "heroines" of this book, pushed me again and again on my third chapter, and greatly strengthened my work.

I thank my dissertation committee members for their guidance and support. Waldo Martin underlined the significance of what I was attempting and fully believed in its value. Ruth Frankenberg provided both helpful criticism and warm support for my dissertation, and her help was invaluable. Clarence Walker, my dissertation adviser, has contributed immeasurably to this project. Clarence's insights have vastly strengthened this book.

I also give warm thanks to my colleagues here at my new academic home, the University of Tennessee at Martin. In particular, Catherine Ann Carls repeatedly helped with spur of the moment problems I confronted with my manuscript. David Coffey, our department chair and all-around wonderful person, fostered an extremely supportive atmosphere and helped with my revisions of a troubled introduction. James Feiser provided an extensive critique of parts of my work and influenced its final shape.

I want to thank Seetha Srinivasan, the University Press of Mississippi's director. Seetha actively sought out the work of an unknown scholar, and I am indebted to her for her courage, commitment, and good judgment.

I owe special thanks to David Roediger. David closely read my manuscript and argued that I needed to be more generous with the New Left, acknowledging more fully the difficulties of the battle New Leftists were attempting to wage. I have done my best to change my book in the direction David has indicated. As a New Leftist myself, I was part and parcel of all the errors, and shortcomings, and, yes, failures of the New Left. It is one thing to acknowledge this. It is another thing to understand that those failings had deep consequences. I hurt people, in very real, material ways. I did things that I am not proud of having done. Any harshness that remains in this book, any lack of charity toward the New Left, has as much to do with my own inability to reconcile my past with my ideals as it has to do with the New Left.

I want to also acknowledge several people for their ongoing support and love. Mary Isham has for some time past been a continual source of wisdom and courage to me, as she is to all who know her. My step-mother Jess Barber has stayed with me through thick and thin, and my mother- and father-in-law, Helen and Fred Robinson, have provided immeasurable love and support for my family and myself over some difficult years.

My eight-year-old twin daughters, Emily and Laura, in waking up early *every* morning to share my work hours with me, in laughing and shouting and crying, in continually asking if I'd finished my book yet, and in giving me their beautiful love, and allowing me to love them, unreservedly, have given me more strength than they can know. I hope that when they are old enough to read this book, they will find a value in it that compensates them for the times I was too absorbed in my work to give them my full attention.

Most of all I am indebted to my wife, Lisa Robinson. I was already in graduate school when we married. At the time, we knew that pursuing graduate school, raising children, and facing the uncertainty of the academic job market would be a hard road. Neither of us, I think, understood just how hard it would be. Without her constant and untiring work and her love for me, this book simply would not be.

—David Barber
June 2006

A
Hard
Rain
Fell

Introduction

Why the New Left Failed

The only thing that white people have that black people need, or should want, is power—and no one holds power forever. White people cannot, in the generality, be taken as models of how to live. Rather, the white man is himself in sore need of new standards, which will release him from his confusion and place him once again in fruitful communion with the depths of his own being. And I repeat: The price of the liberation of the white people is the liberation of the blacks—the total liberation, in the cities, in the towns, before the law, and in the mind.

—James Baldwin, *The Fire Next Time*, 1963

I begin this book at the end of my story.

May 4, 1970. After exchanging rock, bottle, and tear gas volleys with student antiwar protesters, a contingent of eighty Ohio National Guardsmen on the campus of Kent State University turned their backs on demonstrators and began moving away from the charged scene. To the students, spread out over a field and parking lot, the Guardsmen appeared to be retreating as they marched away, up "Blanket Hill." When the Guardsmen reached the crest of the hill, however, about twenty of them spun on their heels, lowered their M1 carbines, and began firing. Students reacted slowly. Many at first believed that the troops were shooting blanks. But then, as bullets crashed into trees, and auto windshields, and people, reality set in:

A girl was screaming. "They're not using blanks. They're not using blanks." Another student fell over, dead. A student collapsed to the ground, hit. Suddenly, after about 30 seconds, the shooting stopped. We got up and looked around. One girl was lying on the ground, holding her stomach. Her face was white. There were others, lying on the ground. Some moved, some didn't.

The whole area was one of panic. We heard a girl crying hysterically. "Get an ambulance, get an ambulance," others were shouting. A guy picked up one girl and held her in his arms. The front of her was covered with blood. "She's dead," he was shouting. "She's dead. I know she's dead."[1]

In the thirteen-second fusillade, four students, the closest of them almost a football field away from the Guard, died where the Guardsmen's bullets found them. Another nine students were wounded, one of them paralyzed for life.

On the following day, the *Washington Post* reported that "tens of thousands of college students, marched, heard speeches, burned buildings and flags, smashed windows and barricaded roads yesterday to vent their outrage at the widened war in Indochina and the killing of four youths at Kent State University."[2] Over the next several days and weeks, between four and five million students participated in the largest student strike in American history, shutting down nearly 600 of the nation's college campuses, burning down or bombing more than two dozen college Reserve Officers' Training Corps (ROTC) and military research facilities, and compelling U.S. president Richard Nixon to cut short the United States' latest escalation of the Vietnam War, the U.S. invasion of Cambodia.

Today, few people alive at the time clearly remember these events, and those born subsequently know nothing more than the name, Kent State, if they know that. People remember so little of this time because the greatest antiwar protest in American history is the end of a story, not the beginning. It is the end because the movements that spawned this giant protest were defeated at the end of the 1960s. The forces that engendered racism and war in America won out over the social movements that opposed them.

In this book I aim to trace the history of one of those social movements, the white New Left, from 1965 to May 1970. At their best, the young white New Left activists sought to spearhead the antiwar movement, ally with the black freedom movement, and fundamentally reorient American values. In tracing this history, my ultimate goal is to uncover the reasons for the New Left's collapse and defeat, the basis for May 1970 being the end of a story, rather than the beginning.

More than any other organization, Students for a Democratic Society (SDS) represented the trajectory of the white New Left and the white student movement of the 1960s. SDS began its work in 1960 with 250 members, tapping into the inspirational and moral power of the civil rights movement and slowly mobilizing a northern white student constituency. By April 1965, when it organized the first national demonstration against the war in Vietnam, SDS membership had reached 2,500. Less than six months after that demonstration, SDS membership had quadrupled to

10,000. By April 1968, the month of Martin Luther King Jr.'s assassination and of the Columbia University rebellion, 35,000 people called themselves SDS members. In the wake of these events, SDS membership took a qualitative leap, reaching somewhere between 80,000 and 100,000 by the time of 1968's presidential election.[3] Yet eight months later SDS split at its June national convention, and, for all intent and purposes, it ceased to have an independent national existence by the end of 1969.

Undoubtedly, a wide variety of factors contributed to the white New Left's collapse. Government repression against the New Left certainly played a significant role in the collapse. However, repression is only successful to the extent to which it can play upon the internal shortcomings of a movement. On a superficial level, SDS collapsed when it splintered into factions. But the white New Left always contained within itself a range of understandings and practical divisions. I contend that even the factions that emerged in SDS's last dramatic year—the lead-pipe and bomb-wielding Weatherman (Revolutionary Youth Movement I, or RYM I), the Marxist-Leninist jargoning Revolutionary Youth Movement II (RYM II), and the arch enemy of both these factions, the Old Left Progressive Labor Party (PL)—operated within a single broad ideological consensus. The New Left's ultimate failure hinged on its inability to break decisively from that framework, a framework that held in a variety of forms to traditional American notions of race, gender, class, and nation.

The New Left failed because it ultimately came to reflect the dominant white culture's understandings of race, gender, class, and nation. While all these elements are inextricably intertwined, race is the key element in understanding the trajectory of the New Left. Pushed by the black movement, white New Leftists struggled to come to grips with their own white upbringing. But the young white activists of the 1960s never succeeded in decisively breaking with the traditional American notions of race. The New Left's failure fully to come to terms with its own whiteness finally doomed its efforts.

Prior to Black Power, white radicals in SDS simply assumed that they would lead the struggle for social change in the United States. As late as mid-June 1966, SDS's national secretary, Paul Booth, was proclaiming that "SDS has been the most creative and relevant factor on the Left." But Booth could make such a claim only if he viewed the predominantly black Student Nonviolent Coordinating Committee (SNCC) as a particular in the constellation of the American political universe—as the representative of American blacks or of the "struggle in the South" rather than of broader efforts for social change. SNCC's projects, which included the Freedom Rides, the Mississippi Summer Project, the Mississippi Freedom Democratic Party challenge, as well as early and clear positions against the Vietnam War, repeatedly shook the nation and inspired, challenged, and educated SDS. In marginalizing this history, Booth revealed the full extent to which white racial blinders shut out America's social realities, even to those young activists working to alter those realities. Within days of Booth's claims, however, SNCC raised its greatest challenge to white ideology: the call for "Black Power." Black Power decisively shifted the course of the struggle for social change in the United States and forced young white radicals to interrogate the meaning and implications of their own identities as young white people.[4]

In the first place, Black Power activists demanded that white New Leftists organize in the white community against white racism. This demand upended SDS's white liberal, charitable, and paternalist thought and practice. SDSers could no longer "help" black people. On the contrary, SNCC activists emphatically told young whites that blacks did not want or need their help; rather than feeling good about helping others, white activists had to take responsibility for the racism in themselves and in their communities. Thus, SNCC's black activists began to define the role of young whites. For serious New Leftists, this marked a real revolution. Whites had always had the power to define their own role and the role of others—the power, in Toni Morrison's words, to "narrate the world."[5] More than anything, this power to define underwrote an assumption of the "normality of whiteness." That is to say, the power to define appeared as a human power, as something natural to white people. But, of course, it was not that. Power was (and is) a social construction, a relationship in which whites had power because blacks did not. SNCC's challenge, and the intensifying black social struggle that accompanied it, compelled New Leftists to see their power not as natural or raceless but as inextricably intertwined with whiteness. It compelled them, in short, to examine their own racialization, their own whiteness.

In a February 1967 paper titled "In White America: Radical Consciousness and Social Change," SDS national secretary Greg Calvert reflected a part of the new consciousness dawning in SDS:

> We owe SNCC a deep debt of gratitude for having slapped us brutally in the face with the slogan of Black Power, a slogan which said to white radicals: "Go home and organize in white America which is *your* reality and which only you are equipped to change." . . .
>
> The liberal reformist is always engaged in "fighting someone else's battles." His struggle is involved in relieving the tension produced by the contradictions between his own existence and life-style, his self-image, and the conditions of existence and life-style of those who do not share his privileged, unearned status. . . .
>
> The problem in white America is the failure to admit or recognize unfreedom. . . . Only when white America comes to terms with its own unfreedom can it participate in the creation of a revolutionary movement.[6]

Calvert's metaphor of being slapped suggests the shock of SNCC's challenge. Moreover, even Calvert's title reflected a changed understanding of the world and SDS's place in it. Until SNCC called for Black Power, no "white Left" existed in a place called "white America."

If the New Left was part of a revolution in the 1960s, then, here was its content: white Americans began to understand themselves as racialized subjects and not as models for other, nonwhite peoples to emulate. For the first time, a core of whites in America began to examine critically that which they had always assumed as natural—their own whiteness.

Nonetheless, the New Left proved that it could sustain this kind of self-reflection and practice only so long as the black movement was capable of continually prodding it. Repeatedly, SDS, both on the national and local levels, found itself focusing on racial issues in the wake of important black struggles; just as repeatedly, SDS placed race on the back burner when black organizations faltered or when the black social movement paused to catch its breath. For example, Berkeley SDS convened "Black Power Day" within a few weeks of the September 1966 black rioting in San Francisco. In their prospectus and propaganda for the event, SDS leaders expressed a clear appreciation for the historical significance of Black Power and a clear understanding of the tasks that the black movement placed upon white radicals: "The change in the Negro Movement from 'civil rights' and 'integration' to the organization of black people into an independent power bloc, may be the most significant development for change in America in decades.... White radicals should create the best possible platform, within the white population, for Black Power advocates and the activists in this growing movement."[7] But if, in October 1966, Bay Area New Leftists could view the transition from civil rights to Black Power as possibly the "most significant development for change in America in decades," they could not maintain that vision for very long, and could not apply it practically or consistently. By late November, Northern California regional SDSers apparently had found other, "most significant" developments upon which to focus their energies. In a circular inviting people to the SDS national conference, the regional leaders made no clear reference to any conference discussion or workshops on the white Left's relation to the black struggle.[8]

The struggle between two opposing understandings of race defined the New Left's trajectory and ultimately defined its demise. In those periods when the black movement was particularly strong and particularly clear in its own understandings, white New Leftists came to understand race in ways that few whites had ever been able to understand it in the past. During those times, New Leftists sought a new practice that would break with the privilege of race. At the same time, white national culture's traditional ideology of race continually pulled at and distorted these new understandings.

By the end of the 1960s, as the black movement came under a concerted government attack, the New Left had reverted to mainstream American understandings of race: most frequently ignoring the black struggle; subsuming it under the "more important" class struggle; or assuming a "more revolutionary than thou" posture toward the black movement. True, the New Left had modified these mainstream understandings to make them compatible with the narrative of struggles in which it had participated; but the basic understanding was still a traditional one in which activists no longer questioned their white racial identity, assumed that it was natural, and took on the "leading role" that that identity always conferred on white people.

In short, the New Left failed not because it radically separated itself from America's mainstream, the claim of a number of important historians of the period. Rather, it failed because it came to mirror that mainstream, and in mirroring traditional American racial attitudes, it ceased to represent a Left.

Some historians, following Doug Rossinow's powerful study, have begun to emphasize the importance of "authenticity" in trying to understand the New Left's rise and fall.[9] According to this interpretation, students doubted their authenticity and refused to understand themselves as real agents of social change. Consequently, they cast about for one or another revolutionary vanguard—China, Vietnam, the Third World, the black struggle, the working class—and made their own struggle subordinate to these vanguard struggles. The more fervently they raised these external vanguards, championed "other people's struggles," the more thoroughly did they alienate ever larger segments of their own constituency. But while this emphasis on authenticity is important, it is only half the story. Yes, students during the 1960s quested after authenticity. But the question is, "Why?" I argue that white students failed to see themselves as authentic agents of social change because of their whiteness, their white privilege.

Whiteness is an extraordinarily powerful ideological construct, extraordinarily seductive—tellings whites they are the best, the brightest, the most humane, the most deserving. Moreover, this seductive construct is reinforced with real power and wealth.

To be sure, this belief in white superiority is unfounded. Somewhere, in the recesses of their souls, those promoting and benefiting from white supremacy know the false foundation of their privileged lives. If white youth quested after authenticity in the 1960s, they did so because black social struggles brought the lie of whiteness out into the open for them. The struggle for authenticity, at its root, was simply the struggle to comprehend and purge themselves of the lie of whiteness.

Whiteness was not only discomforting, however; it was also comforting, it was the known, hence, secure. Attacking privilege promised liberation—liberation from a false sense of self—but it also profoundly threatened white youths' existing sense of self, however uncomfortable that existing sense was. Hence, young white activists were repelled by white privilege even as they were drawn to it. Their trajectory through the 1960s had this ambivalence at its core. Young white students strove to purge from themselves white identity's false foundation, while at the same time striving to hold on to that identity. Black struggles, Vietnam, Cuba—all informed and offered the prospect of liberation. But as the closest of those struggles, the black struggle, waned, the safety of whiteness became more alluring.

Chapter 1, "The New Left and the Black Movement, 1965–1968," traces SDS's relationship to the black struggle through the most tumultuous years of the black movement's existence: Black Power's proclamation, the great urban rebellions of 1967, the Black Panther Party's rise to prominence, and Martin Luther King Jr.'s assassination. More than at any other time in SDS's brief life, these were the years that SDS's young white activists were challenged to understand their own racialization and, in bits and pieces, slowly began to see the "constructedness" of their own identities.

I follow the same basic line of inquiry for each of the other areas of my study: the New Left's understandings of class, nation, and gender. In Chapter 2, "The New Left and the American Empire, 1962–1968," I explore how SDS came to understand the United States as an empire. Here, the Vietnam War's brutality—so greatly at odds with the United States' stated aims in Southeast Asia—served as the driving force in uncovering the real basis of U.S. policy. As the United States escalated its violence and terror against Vietnam, in seeming contradiction to its role as Free World leader and even its own short-term interests in the region, New Leftists saw with ever sharper clarity the outlines of a great empire protecting itself in Vietnam. Meetings with Vietnamese and Cuban revolutionaries reinforced the vision that the needs of American empire drove the Vietnam War. Equally important, meetings with Third World revolutionaries gave New Leftists a sense of the "enemy" as profoundly human and as struggling for the positive goal of self-determination. In meeting with the "other," though, New Leftists also gained a counterpoint for understanding themselves and the culture in which they lived. More than anything, this sense of self—as a constructed, cultural self and not a "natural" self—drove the New Left forward in its quest to understand empire.

Two things prevented the New Left from fleshing out its understanding of empire. First, New Leftists had a most difficult time understanding that America's domination of other nations was central to the internal life of the United States—to its social, economic, and political structures. Empire, New Leftists consistently believed, happened outside the United States. Capitalism happened inside the United States. Attempts at drawing up a class portrait of the United States foundered again and again on this distinction. Second, while leading New Leftists themselves acknowledged the black movement's significance in opening up a skepticism concerning the United States' good intentions in the world, New Leftists almost wholly ignored that movement's intellectual work on empire: the thinking and practice of W. E. B. DuBois, Malcolm X, the Black Panthers, and SNCC. To the extent that SDSers paid attention to Malcolm, or to the Panthers' Eldridge Cleaver or Huey Newton, they invariably stressed the black movement's "thuggery over its theory," in Errol Henderson's apt characterization.[10] This failure undermined the New Left's ability to get a clear picture of the United States or of the world. Discounting black intellectual work on empire cut off the New Left from ideas far older and more deeply rooted than its own thinking. Just as important, this failure to respect black intellectual work maintained an imperial division of labor: intellectual work here, for whites; practical work there, for black people. Still, by mid-1968 the New Left had made significant inroads into understanding empire, and the possibility existed for the New Left to push beyond its limitations.

Chapter 3, "The New Left and Feminism, 1965–1969," examines how the New Left received the social struggles of white women; how that struggle opened new vistas for the New Left, particularly female SDSers; and how, simultaneously, the pull of traditional American gender relations distorted those new understandings and kept them within the orbit of white male domination. Feminist historians and contemporary documents offer ample evidence that the white New Left retained a traditional American gendered division of labor and held to traditional male values—competitiveness, careerism, manipulativeness, and so forth. While men were arguing and making grand theory and policy, women did what at the time was called "shit work"—they made the coffee, typed the letters, ran the office, cooked the food, and kept the men satisfied. If women attained any status in the white New Left, at least prior to the late 1960s, they attained it through their connection to men.[11]

However, following in the wake of a self-assertive Black Power, female New Left activists increasingly recognized and rejected this traditional gendered division of labor and the values that underwrote that division, particularly as it became clear that New Left men were well satisfied with the sexual status quo. When, for example, SDS and women's liberation activist Marilyn Salzman Webb sought to address a January 1969 counterinaugural demonstration in Washington, D.C., on the role of women in the movement, pandemonium broke out in the audience, with men jeering and catcalling: "Take it off!" "Fuck her!" "Take her off stage! Rape her in a back alley!"[12] In the wake of such events and of the attitude revealed in those events, women quit the New Left and condemned it for its failure to transcend the gendered norms of the society it was supposedly in revolt against.

While the strength of the black struggle compelled white New Leftists to begin to see how race shaped not only the broader society but also New Left culture itself, white women's struggles did not have the power to fundamentally challenge male New Left understandings of gender roles. By and large, New Left males accepted the "naturalness" of those proscribed roles without examination. When women demanded that the New Left examine its gender roles, the men in the New Left rejected that demand in characteristic fashion: support for black liberation and opposition to the Vietnam War were the movement's main priorities; the movement could not be diverted to address women's secondary concerns. Just two months after the counterinaugural fiasco, for example, SDS interorganizational secretary Bernardine Dohrn articulated the dominant New Left criticism of the women's movement: the women's movement was "bourgeois, unconscious or unconcerned with class struggle and the exploitation of working women"; moreover, it ignored the pressing needs of the black liberation movement and the Vietnamese struggle.[13] It was no accident that in the male-dominated New Left, a female SDS leader would be the person who would most forcefully articulate this criticism of the women's movement.

In short, the New Left refused to examine gender seriously, and, in refusing that examination, it continued to uncritically accept as natural U.S. society's definitions of gender. Those women who rose to prominence within the New Left were in general women who could "out-macho" men.[14]

White women's critiques of the New Left were themselves unexamined in their racialization: contrary to how women articulated their criticisms, their critiques were not of "men" in general but of white men specifically. Certainly, the black movement was severely constrained by its understanding and implementation of gender roles. But the gender roles in the black movement and community were different than the gender roles in the white movement and white society. Black men, for example, simply did not assume that their voices would be heard by American leaders; white men not only assumed that their voices would be heard, but expected that their voices would affect policy. Consequently, white male leadership roles most often centered on verbal or theoretical prowess.[15] While not discarding verbal skills, black leadership roles had a much larger practical component—the ability to organize or to act. Especially since the ability to organize—to relate to people, to understand their problems, to guide their activities—contains characteristics more typically "female," black women had access to leadership roles that the white New Left denied white women. When Casey Hayden and Mary King—both white women working within SNCC—drafted their original memo on the role of women in the movement, they were thus unable to appreciate black women's reluctance to take up the women's issue. Hayden and King and other white women had indeed been marginalized in SNCC's southern organizing, confined to the office, and given secondary or auxiliary roles. But this marginalization occurred at least in part because they were white and not only because they were female. In contrast, black women in SNCC played leading roles in a number of SNCC organizing projects.[16] Thus, while the male-dominated New Left refused to acknowledge the significance of women's voices in the movement, white women, developing a critique of the New Left's sexism, themselves failed to fully appreciate that they were speaking not for women in general but for white women specifically. In consequence, like the New Left in general, white women's liberationists tended to conceive of their struggle as the most significant struggle. Said one activist: "The most serious problem for the moment is not the war, the draft, the presidency, the racial problem, but our own problem."[17]

Chapter 4, "The New Left Starts to Disintegrate," and Chapter 5, "Reasserting the Centrality of White Radicals," take these separate elements—race, empire and class, and gender—and tie them together through the last tumultuous months of SDS's existence. Chapter 4 plays out the struggles between Old Left understandings of race, gender, and empire and New Left understandings in the period between the end of 1968 and the fall of 1969. During these years, an Old Left sect, PL, sought to take over SDS. At the heart of PL's program stood the Old Left notion that black nationalism was a diversion from the all-important class struggle. To save SDS from PL's clutches, SDS leaders were compelled to strengthen their ties to and understanding of black nationalism. The U.S. government's repressive campaign against black nationalism added urgency to this task. Thus, by the spring of 1969, SDS, for the first time, clearly articulated a mission for itself that corresponded with the one that SNCC had laid down three years earlier: that SDS would organize white communities against racism.

To be sure, SDS's position was fraught with contradictions. Particularly as the government's repression intensified against the black movement, SDS's increasingly obvious factions threatened to depart from this antiracist mission along two complementary paths: the side that would become the Weatherman faction tended toward condemning all whites as sold out to privilege and as wedded to counterrevolution, racism, and imperialism. Condemning whites as sellouts, however, obviated the need for organizing them against racism. That task was an impossible one. Those who were to follow RYM II, on the other hand, tended to negate the significance of white privilege and began to emphasize the "objective," class unity of whites and blacks. Challenging racism thus became secondary to organizing white communities against capitalism and the bosses. As repression intensified against the black movement, as it could exert less and less influence in the New Left, SDS's tendencies became more pronounced. In the summer of 1969, in a decisive blow to the black movement, both RYM factions rejected working with the Panthers in a campaign that would have forced SDS to take the politics of black self-determination out into racist white communities.

Simultaneously, both RYM factions, each in its own way, continued to try to define and contain the threat that the women's liberation movement posed to the New Left. Weatherman refused to acknowledge the independent significance of women's struggle against oppression. Like PL, which insisted that women's oppression could only be combated as part of the "class struggle," Weatherman insisted that it could only be taken on as part of the anti-imperialist, antiracist struggle. Insofar as women's oppression constrained women from taking on race and empire, Weatherman thought it needed to be dealt with. But women's oppression, in Weatherman's view, had no real independent significance. RYM II did slightly better. It demanded that male chauvinism and supremacy be taken on in the movement, but failed to define the movement's male physiognomy.

Chapter 5 analyzes RYM factions from mid-October 1969 to the great upheaval of May 1970. As the antiwar movement began to peak in November 1969, SDS's factions increasingly isolated themselves from this mass movement. Weatherman did so by determining that mass demonstrations were irrelevant and that only violence mattered. Indeed, Weatherman went so far as to declare that at the nation's largest antiwar protest in history, the issue was not the war but was violence—that is, whether the antiwar movement would take up violence against the U.S. government. RYM IIers, on the other hand, isolated themselves by increasingly ducking behind Marxist dogma: only the united proletariat, black and white, could bring down imperialism. The key task for revolutionaries was not mobilizing masses of new people against the war, but was building the foundations for a revolutionary Marxist-Leninist party of the working class in the United States.

During this same period, a large part of the women's movement—many of those closest to the New Left—irrevocably broke with SDS's factions. SDS had never dealt squarely with the problem of women's oppression, but as the women's movement continued to grow in strength, SDS, and then both its factions, more and more elaborately crafted women's liberation to accord with the needs of the factions' white male leaders. Weatherman, while condemning the women's movement as racist, imperialist, and bourgeois, nevertheless established its own program of women's liberation: smashing monogamy. That this program freed men from all responsibility to women and created an environment of sex on demand for the faction's male leaders did not go unnoticed by the women's movement. RYM II's male leaders, on the one hand, effectively sabotaged the efforts of the faction's female members to deal with male supremacy. On the other hand, RYM II men increasingly cast their entire leadership in terms of theoretical clarity on the nature of the class struggle in the United States. Naturally, this "Marxist-Leninist" leadership reframed the "women's question" in ways that continued to make indispensable their own, white male leadership. Women did not have a chance in this male intellectual environment, and women's movement partisans understood this as well. In the face of this continued male intransigence, women exited the New Left, and the positions of separatist radical feminism were reinforced.

Both SDS factions continued to distance themselves from the black movement and continued to define that movement in terms that accorded with their own white understandings. Weatherman, most egregiously, disparaged the Black Panthers in the name of an imaginary black leadership that did not exist in the social lives of black people themselves. Less than six months after SDS had declared the Panthers the vanguard of the black revolution, at least one sector of Weatherman was working to define the Panthers as "revisionist," that is, as having departed from the revolutionary path. At the same time, it began casting about for a new, revolutionary black vanguard that would more adequately meet the needs of the revolution, as Weatherman was defining that revolution. Although RYM II did not so hypocritically abandon the Panthers at the height of the government repression, abandon them they did. Whereas Weatherman betrayed the Panthers in the name of the black revolution, RYM II abandoned them in the name of the proletarian revolution. The forms were different; the content was the same.

When Richard Nixon overtly extended the Vietnam War into Cambodia at the end of April 1970, and when National Guard troops killed four students at Kent State on May 4, 1970, the student movement reached its peak with the largest demonstrations in U.S. history. SDS, which could have coordinated the demonstrations, provided an educational focus for the participants, and linked the war to racism, was dead. Its leaders—both factions—had scuttled SDS in the name of what they saw as a clearer revolutionary vision.

This is the story that I will tell.

My story is a history of SDS and the white New Left. I believe, however, that it is possible to offer a history of a white group and avoid a white-centered history. With SDS especially, this has not been done.[18] Even when we read histories of the 1960s as an era, SDS or the New Left often winds up in the center of the story. I have understood the 1960s, in contrast, as a tremendous upheaval, a storm, or a series of storms. The eye of those storms, decidedly, was an international movement against colonialism, white supremacy, and imperialism. Within the United States, people of color, and in the first place, black people, constituted the storm's center. A New Left emerged in the United States—and in the old centers of empire in Europe—as a tail to those storms. That is to say, to switch metaphors, that the New Left was the dependent variable in this history. The New Left did not lead the great changes taking place, but followed in their wake. Moreover, as part of the social order under attack—white, male, American society—the New Left constantly found its understandings shaped by the old. Whatever thinking and action emerged from the New Left, then, emerged out of this contradictory foundation.

I have tried to show the New Left in this light. Consequently, I have devoted some effort to portraying the struggles waged by black people, by the Vietnamese, and by women in the United States in the mid and late 1960s, and the thinking that guided those struggles. We simply cannot understand the New Left outside this context. Moreover, in making the effort to describe these struggles, I hope that I adequately convey a sense of the tremendous social upheavals that drove white radicals to try to reenvision their world, and which made them passionate about the changes they sought.

Histories of the New Left break down into two basic schools. A traditional liberal school came to the fore at the end of the 1980s and into the 1990s. Represented by scholars and former activists like Todd Gitlin, Maurice Isserman, and Tom Hayden, this liberal school argues that the New Left uncritically followed in the wake of the Black Power movement, substituted rage for reason, and collapsed when this rage alienated mainstream Americans.[19] A second, radical school is not so consolidated as is the liberal school, and has not offered a coherent model for understanding the New Left's collapse. Nevertheless, scholars like Doug Rossinow and, more recently, Ron Jacobs, Jeremy Varon, Max Elbaum, and Dan Berger champion precisely that which the liberal school condemns: the New Left's relation to Black Power and Third World revolution.[20] In contrast to the radical school, I argue that while the New Left certainly professed in words a solidarity with SNCC and the Panthers, in its deeds, white New Leftists never accepted the real demands that black activists placed upon them. The black nationalism that SDS leaders followed was a black nationalism that SDSers themselves created. Organizationally, the Panthers and the Vietnamese both counseled against the paths that SDS's main factions took beginning in the summer of 1969. This argument also answers the liberal school of interpretation: the New Left did not uncritically follow the black nationalist movement; indeed, on virtually every practical question, white radicals refused to follow the black movement. Hence, the New Left failed not because it was too radical in its support of the black nationalist movement but because it was not radical enough.

Chapter One

The New Left and the
Black Movement, 1965–1968

Until mid-1965, the black-led civil rights movement operated within a fundamentally liberal framework: racism was an aberration; it was something particular to the South; and it was untrue to the foundation and principles upon which Americans had constructed their freedom. Through nonviolent moral suasion, civil rights activists would touch the hearts of their opponents and win a place for themselves in the great American system.[1] Its liberal ideological foundation notwithstanding, the civil rights movement was an activist movement, and that activism had two important consequences: first, civil rights movement activism broke the Joseph McCarthy era–imposed years of quiet. In so doing, the black movement opened up social activism's possibilities for other strata of the population. The New Left, then, found its inspiration, its earliest training, and its earliest recruitment as the northern wing of the southern-based black civil rights movement. But if the black movement's ideology was liberal, so, too, was the ideology of the New Left that followed in its wake. With a liberal ideology guiding it, an ideology that posited the integration of blacks in the American framework as its ultimate goal, white New Leftists had no reason to question their own racial identities. On the contrary, if the battle was for integration, young whites were among those with whom blacks would be integrated. They were not the racialized ones; they were part of the American mainstream; they were normal.

A second consequence, however, flowed from the civil rights movement's activism: that activism continually tested its guiding liberal ideology, its liberal explanation of racial phenomena, against America's social realities. By winning major civil rights legislation in 1964 and 1965 and successfully overturning de jure segregation in the United States, the civil rights movement completed its liberal reform agenda.

All people were now equal before the law. And yet black people continued to face seemingly insurmountable obstacles to social progress. In short, the black movement had tested the liberal hypothesis on race relations and found it wanting. Another ideology was needed to explain this failure, to explain the ongoing oppression blacks experienced in the United States. Black Power was that ideology: a colonial system of white supremacy—both structural and ideological in nature—defined American life and history. Malcolm X, and before him, W. E. B. DuBois, had already outlined the basic elements of this worldview. And SNCC, founded by the young blacks who had carried out 1960s sit-ins for lunch-counter integration, had, through practical experience, rediscovered this worldview by mid decade.

Thus did black people come to challenge American liberal ideology and the racial identities on which that ideology rested. Since black racial identity was central to the formation, development, and existence of white racial identity, however, blacks could not challenge their place in America's racial hierarchy without calling into question white racial identity.[2]

But for whites to apprehend their own racialization was not a simple process. As the black movement waxed and waned from 1966 to mid-1968, some individual white activists sought to take seriously the burgeoning black struggle's demands on white activists and attempted to develop a new sense of self and a new sense of community. But the New Left as a whole could maintain a focus on the significance of the black struggle only so long as that struggle remained in the very center of national consciousness: the demand raised for Black Power in 1966, a summer of rioting in 1967, black student struggles in 1968 and 1969. SDS's appreciation for the black struggle and, consequently, its appreciation for white activists' own racialization rapidly went from cold to hot and back again. More often than not, SDSers took the black movement's style over its substance and interpreted the movement's main demands on white activists in ways that left white racial identity intact, if somewhat discomforted.

In June 1966, as civil rights marchers crossed the state of Mississippi in a "March Against Fear," the movement came to a decisive crossroads. On the evening of June 16, SNCC chairman Stokely Carmichael addressed a crowd of marchers and local residents in Greenwood. Having just been released from jail, Carmichael angrily told the rally: "This is the 27th time I have been arrested. I ain't going to jail no more! I ain't going to jail no more! ... We want Black Power!" "What do we want?" Carmichael called. "Black Power!" came back the response. "What do we want?" "Black Power!"[3]

It was an electrifying slogan. Most important, Black Power represented not just SNCC's experience but the experience of masses of black people in the South and in the North. As if to punctuate Carmichael's cry, urban rebellions swept the nation in the weeks following the march: Omaha, Chicago, and Cleveland in July

1966; Brooklyn in August; Milwaukee, Dayton, Ohio, Waukegan, Illinois, Benton Harbor, Michigan, and Jackson, Mississippi, in early September; and San Francisco and Oakland in late September and early October.[4]

In the fall of 1966, Carmichael authored a number of widely circulated articles in which he clarified the meaning, significance, and origin of Black Power. In these articles, and in speeches he gave at the time, he laid out a stinging indictment of the United States and of the prospects for liberal reform and integration. Two factors defined the lives of black people, Carmichael asserted: "they are poor and they are black." Blacks constituted a colonial people living within the borders of the United States. A powerful few exploited this colony and all the U.S. colonies, stretching "from Mississippi and Harlem to South America, the Middle East, southern Africa, and Vietnam." Racism originated in the need to hide and rationalize this exploitation. Consequently, Carmichael averred, "for racism to die, a totally different America must be born."

Rather than face this reality, Carmichael argued, white society preferred to talk about "integration." Even at its best, however, integration could only mean that a few blacks who had made it could leave the ghetto and its impoverished people behind. Worse, he continued, integration was "based on complete acceptance of the fact that *in order to have* a decent house or education blacks must move into a white neighborhood or send their children to a white school. This reinforces, among both black and white, the idea that 'white' is automatically better and 'black' by definition inferior. This is why integration is a subterfuge for the maintenance of white supremacy." Carmichael indicted America as a colonial power; tied together Latin America, South Africa, Vietnam, and the plight of black people; and labeled integration an instrument for maintaining white supremacy.

What were the practical implications of this anticolonial analysis of race, asked Carmichael. On the one hand, for a variety of reasons, black people needed to organize themselves, independently of whites. Psychologically, "only black people can convey the revolutionary idea that black people are able to do things themselves." Because they did not understand this psychological reality, friendly whites actually had "furthered white supremacy" without realizing or wanting it. But in insisting that blacks be free to organize themselves independently of whites, black people did not seek to deny white friends and allies. They only sought the right to choose who were their friends and who were their enemies. Moreover, Carmichael insisted, black people "cannot have the oppressors tell the oppressed how to rid themselves of the oppressor."

On the other hand, white supporters had to take a different role, a role that they had been reluctant to take up until then: they needed to "go into their own communities—which is where the racism exists—and work to get rid of it." Instead of going into black communities and preaching nonviolence there, white organizers should be going into white communities and teaching white people the value of nonviolence. The possibility of a real coalition between poor blacks and poor whites, Carmichael argued, depended upon the work of white organizers; blacks could help white activists in this task, but this was the responsibility of whites.[5]

Speaking in October before a predominantly white crowd of 13,000 at the Black Power Day Conference in Berkeley, California, Carmichael argued the same line in still sharper fashion.[6] Whites, Carmichael stated, needed to "move inside their *own* community and start tearing down racism *where in fact it does exist! Where it exists!*" White people lived in Cicero, Illinois, where Martin Luther King Jr. had recently been stoned; whites prevented black people from living in that community; and whites forced blacks to live in ghettos. Could the white organizer "be a man who's willing to move into the *white* community and start organizing where the organization is needed[?] Can he do that? (Shouts and applause)."[7]

SNCC, Carmichael continued, was raising fundamental questions about the United States. Indeed, to those who suggested that blacks simply wanted a piece of the American pie, Carmichael answered: "The American pie means *raping* South Africa, *beating* Vietnam, *beating* South America, *raping the Philippines, raping every country you've been in.* . . . *I don't want any of your blood-money*—I don't want it! Don't want to be *part* of that system! And the question is how do *we* raise those questions. . . . (Great applause. 'Go ahead. Bravo.')." America had become the wealthiest country in the world, Carmichael explained, by plundering the rest of the world. America's youth could stop this plunder and start creating a genuinely humane community only by moving into and transforming the white community, he argued. Black people were already building the kind of movement that would humanize America. "The challenge," Carmichael concluded, "is that the white activist has failed miserably to develop the movement inside of his community. . . . Can we find white people who are going to have the courage to go into white communities and start organizing them?"[8]

Thus did the black movement's most militant sector challenge white liberalism and white radical activists.

On the surface, SDS's National Office responded immediately, clearly, and unequivocally in support of SNCC's turn to Black Power. Within a week of Carmichael's first Black Power speech, SDS issued a statement supporting SNCC. Written by former SDS president Todd Gitlin, the statement affirmed that SDS supported more than SNCC's simple right to choose Black Power as its direction: SDS "welcomed" and "supported" SNCC's new direction. Black Power, SDS argued, was both a "strategy for social change and a mode of organization." When the United

States was understood as an "essentially racist culture," then this strategy and mode of organization made sense. White society discriminated against and exploited blacks as a group. Consequently, blacks "must act as a group in order to challenge their condition." Moreover, although white society discriminated against blacks, it insisted that blacks "seek their salvation in integration—that is, in accommodation to the dominant social values, under white leadership." Thus SDS affirmed the wisdom of black people organizing black people on black terms.

But what of the charge, SDS asked, that any Black Power strategy would fail given the fact that blacks were a minority? Responsibility for such a failure would lie not with SNCC, SDS answered, but with "those whites who fail to build white movements that can at some point ally with the black movement for common goals." White critics therefore must understand and take up their true task: "organizing primarily among the powerless, the disenfranchised, the dependent whites," building up their power in a variety of spheres—community organizations, unions, professional associations. Only on such a foundation, SDS argued, would it be possible for white activists to build a real coalition with poor blacks and reconstruct American life with new, more humane principles.[9]

Yet SDS's national position failed to define explicitly the content of whites organizing whites: that whites must be organized against racism. Even if that position was implicit, the national statement glossed over three realities: first, divergent local SDS and New Left understandings of SNCC and Black Power; second, SDS's three-year-old nationwide commitment to building an "interracial movement of the poor"; and third, and most important, SDS's long-standing self-conception as the vanguard for social change in America.

Outside of the National Office, local chapter and project understandings of the turn to Black Power were uneven and weak on the crucial point of antiracist organizing. Indeed, the majority of New Leftists failed to appreciate Black Power's imperative for antiracist organizing in the white community. Radical historian and well-known New Leftist Staughton Lynd, for example, took what would become a fairly representative position on Black Power's implications for white activists. Said Lynd: "What SNCC is saying is: 'Blacks should be organized by blacks, and what white organizers do is something for white organizers to decide.'"[10] Several years later Lynd would look back on the turn to Black Power and see in it the origins of the white radical determination to focus on antidraft work. According to Lynd, white civil rights movement veterans "wanted to retain a politics of daring, but wanted to get away from the role of . . . auxiliary to a radicalism [whose] center of gravity was in other people's lives." White radicals sought after something "which would have the same spirit, ask as much of us, and challenge the system as fundamentally as had our work in Mississippi."[11]

In short, Lynd did not appreciate that SNCC's Black Power demand defined not just the work of black activists but white activists' work as well. Neither did Lynd understand that the battle against racism and for the liberation of black people was not auxiliary to white radicals, but stood at the very center of their work. The battle against racism was central because it was the battle to get white people to understand their own racialization; that is, it was the battle to understand the structure of the society in which whites lived, to understand privilege, and to understand class. If whites did not understand their racialization, they would have to believe that their condition, relative to black people, was natural. Understanding their own racialization was the prerequisite to understanding the social relationships of their society.

Second, SDS had a long-standing commitment to building precisely the kind of movement that Black Power ideology called into question, that is, an "interracial movement of the poor." Since 1963, SDSers had been organizing in both white and black urban communities throughout the North with the organization's Economic Research and Action Project (ERAP). Old-guard SDSers had founded ERAP in self-conscious imitation of SNCC's work in the South, and SNCC's intellectual leadership had inspired and shaped the project's organizing style and content. However, long before Black Power, as early as the fall of 1963, SNCC's black activists were already arguing that whites should be organizing in the white community. Thus, when SDS leaders Tom Hayden and Todd Gitlin first proposed ERAP at the September 1963 SDS National Council meeting, they were already being pushed to orient the project toward poor white organizing.[12] Although SDSers seemed receptive to that charge and sought to establish the first ERAP project in a poor white community in Chicago, they nevertheless resisted following the black nationalist lead and actively sought to send white student organizers into black communities. Years later Tom Hayden acknowledged that both he and Carl Wittman, Hayden's coauthor on ERAP's main theoretical document, "An Interracial Movement of the Poor?," had fashioned ERAP at least in part as a response to Malcolm X's growing influence in the civil rights movement. The two young white men were eager, in Hayden's words, "to prove that at least some whites weren't 'devils'" and that "an integrationist perspective stressing common economic interests could still work."[13]

From its earliest days, then, ERAP bore an equivocal relationship to the black nationalist tendency then rising within the civil rights movement. While SDSers agreed in theory on the necessity for white activists to be organizing poor white people, this equivocal relationship to Malcolm's leadership and SNCC's growing black nationalism pushed them into a practical disunity with the notion that blacks should organize blacks. By 1966, the majority of ERAP efforts, including both Hayden's Newark project and Wittman's Chester, Pennsylvania, project, were in black communities.[14]

Wittman's Chester project became ERAP's first success story and the model for future organizing efforts.[15] Yet between 1964 and 1966, Chester's black community leaders, like black leaders across the United States, transformed their consciousness from liberal civil rights consciousness to Black Power consciousness. Concomitant with that change, Chester's ERAP project evolved into a chapter of the Congress of Racial Equality (CORE), a national civil rights organization that also made the transition to Black Power. In an open letter to ERAP penned in the fall of 1965, Donald Jackson, Chester CORE's chair, vehemently denounced ERAP's white arrogance. Jackson maintained that all the problems of black people "have their roots in American racism," and that racism was "a tool of economic exploitation, a means to political power, and a system of psychological gratification." But ERAP had never really come to terms with that truth, argued Jackson. Consequently, white ERAPers continued to organize in black ghettos, bringing with them a baleful influence: they reinforced "dependency patterns among blacks"; introduced "alien goals into the black struggle"; presumed the superiority of white people's view of black problems to black people's view of those problems; recklessly and inhumanly trifled "with black individuals, persons who are the most psychologically vulnerable"; and stifled the "development of independent black organizations . . . the only realistic safeguard for black people against white society."[16] In short, Jackson denounced ERAP organizers for retaining the common white belief in white intellectual superiority and for implicitly disbelieving in the ability of blacks to organize themselves. Eight months before Black Power, militant black activists were publicly challenging the right of white organizers to come into the black community and calling them on the unexamined assumptions of their whiteness.

Even those projects located in white communities, however, failed to take up the Black Power challenge that whites organize whites against racism. The largest ERAP effort aimed at poor whites, Chicago's Jobs or Income Now (JOIN), had some success in creating alliances with black groups, but prior to 1967 did not explicitly make antiracist organizing a central tenet of its work. Instead, JOIN activists sought to organize people by trying to help them with their "immediate problems." By so focusing their work, JOIN organizers hoped to gain people's trust while at the same time raising larger questions about the nature, organization, and power relations of the society. One of JOIN's leading organizers, Mike James, described the general organizing rap he used in the summer of 1966:

Ya know, workers in factories and the men in the mines back home [in Appalachia] had a tough time of it. They found that the only way they could get any justice was by getting together in a group that had some power. . . . If you ain't got money, the welfare, these landlords who charge high rents for rotten places, and these slave labor hiring halls all push you around. If you're poor your kids gotta go to that Stewart school, while the rich kids over by the lake got that fancy Brenneman. . . . It's just like in the mines. The only way that people from the south, the little guy, is going to get any justice is by sticking together, forming a strong union and getting some power to make the welfare, the landlords, the cops, the schools and the stores respect us.[17]

Thus, two months after Carmichael first publicly demanded Black Power, JOIN organizers were not yet defining racism as a principal problem confronting white people. At bottom, JOIN's SDS organizers were unable to understand that race was not simply something that affected black people, or a problem that originated among white people, but was itself a central part of white people's identity and oppression. Consequently, JOIN organizers sought to organize Appalachian whites against their own oppression without drawing any necessary connection between these southern whites and black people.

While SDS quickly affirmed its support for Black Power, that support did not yet include any searching analysis of Black Power's implications for ERAP. White organizers continued to operate in black communities, despite the wishes and the protest of black leaders; and white organizers continued to organize in white communities without placing antiracist struggle at the center of that work.

Still, a more important obstacle stood in the way of SDS's ability to appreciate Black Power's significance to white activists: SDS members' long-held belief that SDS stood as the center of social change in the United States. On any number of levels, this view accorded with the traditional self-conceptions of most white Americans. Prior to the 1960s, the power that whiteness held over people in the United States lay in its unexamined, or seemingly natural, character.[18] Few people questioned the notion that white people were the "normal" Americans, while blacks and Latinos were somehow special cases, if they were Americans at all. This view of what was "normal" and what was particular carried over into social activism. Black people might have a particular fight against racism, but whites, unencumbered by any particular racial distinctions, would lead the struggle for social change on more universal grounds.[19]

As race invisibly shaped the individual white activist's consciousness, so it shaped the collective New Left's consciousness. Even in the face of the civil rights movement's growing power and the national and international controversy that it generated, SDS persisted in seeing its actions as the central work for social change in the United States. At SDS's December 1965 national conference, for example, national secretary Paul Booth and former national secretary Lee Webb delineated the elements that would forge a "radical politics" in the United States: "It will be on the bedrock of the demands of the poor for an income, Negroes for an end to racism and economic discrimination, students and faculty for control over their own universities, that this movement will be built.... Their demands will rock the very foundations of the domestic concensus [sic] on which our foreign policy rests. This attack ... will announce the beginnings in this country of a real movement for a democratic society."[20] The Montgomery bus boycott, the black student sit-in movement of 1960, the Freedom Rides, Albany, Birmingham, Selma, the Mississippi Freedom Summer, the Mississippi Freedom Democratic Party, the numerous martyrs of the civil rights movement, and the destruction of de jure segregation in the United States: in the eyes of SDS leaders, these signal events did not "announce the beginnings ... of a real movement for a democratic society." They were simply battles against racism. Evidently, the real movement for a democratic society would wait on New Leftists and the kinds of coalitions that they might forge.

In short, SDS envisioned a division of labor in the struggle for social change. Black people and the civil rights movement would be responsible for the struggle against racism—apparently a black problem—and would be a single element in SDS's radical coalition. SDS would be responsible for everything else. Working through ERAP, SDS would mobilize the urban poor, which included both blacks and whites; working on campuses, SDS would mobilize students and faculty; and working through the antiwar movement, SDS would bring these disparate elements together and build a radical movement.[21]

Even as SNCC turned self-consciously to black nationalism and revolution, SDS leaders continued to marginalize SNCC, making it only a single element of the national work of social change. In an open letter to SNCC sent two weeks prior to Carmichael's call for Black Power, SDS's national secretary, Paul Booth, sought to defend SNCC from escalating liberal attacks. But he did so in a characteristic manner. Liberal criticisms, Booth argued, really represented a larger and deeper problem—"the relation of the liberal community to movements for social change." In contrast, SDS had taken a better approach to SNCC: "We have followed SNCC's evolution for years, learning from it, adapting its approaches in our own organizing efforts, and acting as allies when called upon to assist the struggle in the South. And as SNCC and the movement in which you work have taken more explicitly political approaches to organizing, we have welcomed this as a sign of the strength of those movements, and as evidence of real possibilities for social change."[22] By identifying SNCC with "the struggle in the South," Booth continued to view SNCC within SDS's framework of social change. SNCC's principal base of operation indeed may have been the South, but even in 1965 and early 1966 SNCC clearly identified itself as an organization that represented the aspirations of black people throughout the nation. Moreover, the civil rights struggle in the South repeatedly had shaken the nation and affected the world. Harlem in 1964 and Watts in 1965 had already announced that the black struggle transcended "the South." Finally, by "welcoming" what SDS discerned as SNCC's increasingly "political" approach to the struggle, SDS positioned itself as an elder and wiser sibling, approving a younger sibling's growing maturity. Even as SNCC's black nationalist turn shook the nation anew, SDS held tightly to its self-perception as raceless and to white activists' centrality in the process of social change.

Nevertheless, SNCC's call for Black Power did open new possibilities of understanding for white activists. First, with Black Power's rise, references to the "white power structure" and "white radicals" appeared in New Left discussions for the first time, even if such references continued to coexist with notions of building a racially undifferentiated radical movement. By speaking of a "white power structure," SDSers began to break with traditional interpretations of class, and began to cast the black struggle in anticolonial terms. More important, by calling themselves white radicals, New Leftists displayed an embryonic understanding of their own racialization. Even a single year earlier white leftists had called themselves simply "radicals," or "leftists" or "New Leftists." As such, they envisioned for themselves the widest possible roles in the creation of a new society. In contrast, black people first had to overcome the barriers of race in order to achieve their humanity. Unracialized, "raceless" radicals had no such obstacles in front of them and thus could stand fully in the forefront of the struggle for a humanized world. Now, as white radicals, their options had narrowed markedly; they could no longer enter black communities and expect to be welcomed in an unequivocal fashion. Now, for the first time, however uncomfortably they acknowledged the fact, other people were defining the nature of social change.

Second, some New Left activists quickly grasped this significance. Robin Brooks, a white professor of history at Spelman College, for example, appreciated that Black Power had the potential for shaking up the New Left's worldview. In his coverage of a July 1966 Atlanta speech by black poet and dramatist LeRoi Jones, Brooks offered *New Left Notes* readers their first full analysis of Black Power. Jones's speech, reported Brooks, had argued that blacks "were a captive people, brought here against their will." Their liberation demanded two things: a recovery of their own culture and an identification with the anticolonial revolutions going on in the world. On the first score, blacks were a spiritual people, whereas white culture, Western culture, represented "a debased and dying materialism ... devoid of spirituality." Blacks "would not be free until they threw off this culture and resumed their heritage." In addition, Black Power was part of the "struggle of colored peoples all over the world" against "the West, led by white America." This was a struggle that would not be conducted nonviolently;

indeed, Jones, following Frantz Fanon, saw revolutionary violence as a key to the process of ennobling the oppressed. And, Brooks added, "some day the colored majority of the world's people would confront their oppressor."[23] Brooks offered SDS members a strikingly new, and far more violent, vision of social change. Certainly, it was a vision that seemed to accord more closely with the contemporary racial scene than did the nonviolent vision with which most SDSers entered the movement.

Moreover, following Jones's argument, Brooks accurately perceived that Black Power threatened the self-identification and activity of white liberals and radicals. Black Power, Brooks explained, stripped away one of the main ways in which liberals justified their own behavior: "their sense of benevolence. If we cannot help the Negro to attain equality, with our money—and with our lives, if need be—what can we do? What does the social worker do when he has no more clients?" Black Power similarly confronted white radicals. What were young men and women who had risked their lives during the Mississippi Freedom Summer to do now that they could "no longer participate in the councils of their former black comrades"? Brooks reported that Jones refused to answer that question. Nevertheless, Brooks gave his own answer to the question, as he understood the answers that Malcolm and SNCC had already given: "Don't tell us about how this world is being run and misrun ... we know. If you have something to say, tell it to your white brothers. Set up Freedom Schools for the white liberals and for the white racists; talk to the lily-white trade unionists and to the politicians who are drafting colored boys to die in Viet Nam for the democracy they don't have here." Here was a clear understanding of what black activists were asking white activists to take on.

What if revolution broke out before these antiracist Freedom Schools had had time to work? In that case, Brooks argued, white radicals needed to follow the lead of the few French Algerians who sided with the Algerian struggle: disrupt the morale of the forces of repression, impede the counterrevolution, even blow up "power plants and police stations." "Black and white together" had not had this content in the early New Left and civil rights movements.

Brooks concluded his analysis of Black Power by insisting that the times through which they were passing were unique. With conscientious work and "the help of Black Power and the Viet Cong," white radicals might "manage to accomplish the miracle. If we do, then we may have entitled ourselves to some share, in keeping with our real merits and numbers, in the reconstruction of a world in which love and nonviolence prevail. But there are no short cuts. That is what LeRoi Jones, in his own way, may be telling us."[24] In contrast to rhetoric that all too often inflated SDS's role in the struggle for social change, Brooks interjected a rare note of humility and proffered a model of change in which whites were not the center of social action. On the contrary, Brooks suggested that they were in the rear and would have extremely difficult work to do if they were to play any significant role at all.

Anne Braden, a white Louisville civil rights activist with nearly two decades of experience in the struggle, was another activist who grasped Black Power's meaning for young whites.[25] At the time, Braden was working with the Southern Student Organizing Committee (SSOC), SDS's fraternal organization in the South. Like SDS activists, SSOC activists were attempting to set up ERAP-type projects in the South and were taking the same approach to white community organizing that Staughton Lynd was advocating: "What white organizers do is something for white organizers to decide." Indeed, Braden saw this position as the "prevalent" New Left interpretation of Black Power, and she protested against it. Certainly, Braden argued, blacks should be organizing blacks. But organizing white communities required black organizers as well as white organizers. Moreover, organizing white communities demanded a commitment to organizing against racism, from the very start. White activists could only focus on the "oppression" of poor whites, separate from their relationship to black people, at their own peril, Braden warned. One well-known organizing experience had already demonstrated the dangers of such an approach. Saul Alinsky had successfully organized poor whites against their own oppression in Chicago's "Back-of-the-Yards" movement. That very movement of poor whites, however, later became the "backbone of a movement to keep Negroes out of that part of Chicago."

Thus, while black self-organization and its corollary of "black consciousness" might be historical necessities, Braden continued, "the last thing in the world we need is 'white consciousness.'" "As a matter of fact," she added, "we already have 'white consciousness,' with all the evil and destruction that indicates. What we need to do is tear it down." Consequently, white organizers had to reach white people and to convince them of racism's evils, and of the meaning of racism to their own lives, *from the very beginning.*"[26]

Third, on a practical level, too, some SDS chapters struggled to understand Black Power's significance. Three SDS chapters—the Berkeley, Stanford, and University of Nebraska, Lincoln chapters—took Black Power seriously enough to organize major conferences on the subject. All three conferences occurred at the end of October 1966, and campus activists understood their purpose in similar ways. At Berkeley and Stanford, SDS members sought to provide a venue at which proponents of Black Power could present their views, raise money to support SNCC, win a wider understanding of Black Power among whites, and "motivate whites to organize whites." Black Power, one Stanford SDSer noted, "had something positive to say to the white community and to white radicals in particular."[27] At Lincoln, 900 people attended the Black Power Conference, whose aim was to win "a clearer understanding of the country's most serious internal problem" and dispel the racist slanders cast against Black Power by national media and politicians.[28]

But such events, and the insightful thinking of people like Brooks and Braden, were as yet only the smallest part of SDS's activities and understanding. Indeed, as Black Power fell from the national headlines, most SDS leaders and members returned to more comfortable and familiar notions of themselves and their activities. In November 1966—less than six months after Carmichael's call for Black Power— Allen Jehlen, a Boston SDSer, felt sufficiently emboldened to launch the first direct attack on Black Power to appear in *New Left Notes*. Jehlen's critique was in fact not a new response to Black Power but the traditional Old Left response to black nationalism: class, as most of the Old Left traditionally defined it, trumped race. Black people's real enemy was the greedy exploiter, or the labor aristocrat, and not the average white worker. Racism was "false consciousness" for the majority of white workers.

Specifically, it was a mistake, Jehlen claimed, for black radicals to attack "white society as a whole." True, "most" whites were strongly prejudiced against blacks, but this did not mean that most whites would oppose improved living conditions for blacks. Much smaller groups of whites—slumlords, employers, skilled craft unions, branches of governments, and boards of education—were really responsible for the actual conditions black people faced. White "suburbanites" would not rally to support slumlords because, Jehlen argued, "the great majority of white suburbanites have no interests, real or perceived, in maintaining bad housing conditions for Negroes."[29] Thus, Jehlen reduced racism to a "bad idea" for most white suburbanites.

In arguing his position, however, Jehlen undercounted the actual numbers of whites who fitted into the categories that he had named as having interests in black exploitation. Moreover, he had failed to assay the connections that these slumlords, employers, craft union members—and a host of sectors that he had not named—had with white suburbanites: all these sectors drained resources out of the ghetto, and those resources reappeared in the suburbs as schools, roads, and social infrastructure benefiting the white suburbs. Jehlen also overlooked the power differential that existed between suburb and ghetto and that resulted in governments subsidizing highway construction serving the suburbs, for example, over urban mass transit. On a still larger scale, Jehlen could not see that if the white suburbs had been created in relation to the black community on a material level, then the white suburban identity had followed suit—that white suburban identity also defined itself in relation to the identity of the ghetto.[30]

But SDS leaders discounted Black Power in still more significant ways than such direct opposition. For example, they did not deem the meaning and implications of

Black Power important enough for serious discussion at SDS's December 1966 national meeting; most characteristically, they returned to their older notions of an "interracial movement of the poor" and SDS's central role in constructing that movement.

In its original plan for SDS's December 1966 national conference, SDS leaders projected workshops on four topics: the labor movement, "developing a Third Party," campus organizing, and community organizing. In the community-organizing workshops, SDS leaders proposed discussions that Black Power concerns certainly affected, particularly discussions of poor whites.[31] Nevertheless, if SDS's original June 1966 statement on Black Power had more than a passing significance to SDS, if Black Power truly represented "a strategy for social change and a mode of organization" that correctly reflected the needs imposed by a racist culture upon black people, and if Black Power represented a significant challenge to white radicals, then SDS would have taken a far more explicit approach to Black Power than it actually did. Indeed, SDS projected discussions on the labor movement and on third party organizing, neither of which had a fraction of the impact that the black movement and Black Power had on SDS.

Moreover, in its December convention issue of New Left Notes, SDS featured an article by Todd Gitlin, "On Organizing the Poor in America." Gitlin, of course, had authored SDS's Black Power resolution six months earlier. Here, however, Gitlin resurrected the old SDS line of subsuming blacks under the rubric of "the poor" and discounted the Black Power demand that white organizers directly challenge racism in the white communities. Gitlin began by retracing SDS's ERAP history and summarized the original reasoning behind ERAP's strategy: "the civil rights movement was numerically in need of allies; . . . that the situation of Negroes was primarily economic and required economic solutions; that the more radical people in the Negro movement were becoming aware of these facts; that the most natural allies for Negroes, therefore, were whites whose condition closely resembled that of Negroes . . . poor whites." If this was the thinking that lay back of ERAP's origin, Gitlin offered no update of white community organizing based upon SNCC's criticisms and demands. In a footnote to his article, Gitlin did acknowledge SNCC's insistence that the responsibility for organizing poor whites lay with white radicals. But Gitlin was less forthcoming in discussing the other side of SNCC's understanding: that blacks should organize blacks. Indeed, the former SDS president made no mention of ERAP projects in black communities, like Newark. Instead, Gitlin smuggled black people into his vision by seeing them as poor—and not black, or only incidentally black—as in the pre–Black Power SDS manner. Gitlin discussed police brutality, for example, as though it were an issue that came out of poor communities, and not the black community specifically. In urban slums, this Harvard graduate explained, the police were "an occupying army"; occupying armies eventually generate resistance, frequently violent resistance. "In American circumstances, the sporadic violent revolts—'riots'—are usually fruitless, though they have proved at least embarrassing," Gitlin observed.

Moreover, Gitlin assessed the "situation of Negroes" as "primarily economic." Of course, this ran counter to Carmichael's characterization of blacks suffering as a consequence of two factors: that they were black and that they were poor. Most striking of all was Gitlin's paternalism: "the more radical people in the Negro movement were becoming aware" of the truth that had already been revealed to ERAP organizers and architects.

On the key point of organizing white communities against racism, Gitlin offered an ambivalent message. Basing his arguments on JOIN's efforts in Chicago, Gitlin claimed that when organizers cited the civil rights movement's unity as an effective means for attaining goals, they were able to "dismantle, or at least submerge, the racism and privatism of the poor white." Poor whites, Gitlin argued, may not have had a traditional sense of class consciousness, but they did have a "populist" consciousness: they did see the "little people" versus the "big people" and the poor against the rich. This populist consciousness, Gitlin asserted, "may be compelling enough to overpower even Southern white racism." While he could not guarantee this outcome pending more and greater organizing efforts among poor whites, Gitlin nevertheless took some "comfort in knowing that the 'interracial movement of the poor' was still a live idea."[32]

The deeper notions that a few SDSers had developed in the immediate wake of Black Power—that racism had shaped the lives of whites as surely as it had the lives of black people, that racism had allied whites with the oppressors of black people and people of color throughout the world, that white activists were not the center of the struggle for social change, and that blacks played a leading role both in defining the nature of social change in America and in themselves struggling for that change—Gitlin had left all these notions behind.

Thus, by the end of 1966 SDS was well on its way to resuming its pre–Black Power vision of social change. It would not be until the summer of 1967 that black social motion would once again compel SDSers to reexamine their understanding of social change and their own identities as white activists. Indeed, as the first Black Power summer faded from memory, other SDSers joined Gitlin in direct or indirect repudiations of Black Power. First, SDS activists simply forgot Black Power and race as having any significance to their work. At the April 1967 National Council meeting, for example, discussions of race played no significant role in defining SDS activities. (To be sure, Vietnam had by this time become a predominant concern for SDS activists, but this concern for Vietnam did not exclude deepening the white New Left's understandings of racism. SDSers chose to downplay their relation to the most significant social movement within the United States.) Second, some activists directly repudiated the demands that black activists were making on them.

PL, a faction that was growing in significance within SDS, became in this period the Old Left standard bearer in its response to Black Power. According to PL, the United States had two fundamental classes: a tiny ruling class and an immense, multiracial working class. Race (and empire) had no reality outside of this class construct. Black people were simply superexploited workers, and racism was merely a trick that the ruling class foisted on the working class in order to keep it divided and powerless. Only the ruling class had any material interest in the degraded condition of blacks and other nonwhite peoples. White workers had no short- or long-term stake in racism or in imperialism. Unfortunately for PL, since the United States' social realities—and the reality of race, in the first place—continually ran up against and contradicted these basic tenets, PL could sustain itself only through dogmatism, sectarianism, and the "discipline" of its members.

As prospects for the "long, hot summer" of 1967 approached, PL intensified its attack on Black Power analysis. In a June 1967 *New Left Notes* article, for example, PL activist and Chicago SDSer Earl Silbar sought to negate the black nationalist content of the riots in 1966. Silbar began by warning SDS members that "the government and the mass media ... have been preparing to instigate race wars this summer." In pursuit of this end, Silbar argued, the media was falsely portraying the previous summer's "rebellions" as race riots. However, those rebellions had not been race riots, but part of a class war. To prove this, Silbar asserted that blacks had "fought cops, bayonets and tanks." "This is a race riot?" he asked rhetorically. "Yes, if cops are a separate race!"

According to Silbar, the media portrayed the rebellions as racial for two reasons: first, the media sought to whip up white workers' racial fears "and divert their energies and pent-up hatreds from their worsening job conditions" and bosses. It was all the more important to whip up these fears, Silbar added, "because of organized workers' evident determination to fight for decent wages and human conditions" in the face of government efforts to enlist their support for the war in Southeast Asia. Second, the media portrayed the rebellions as racial in order to pit "white against black worker" and thereby "crush the militant opposition of black people to the war, its draft and oppressive ghetto conditions in a sea of blood."[33]

To a certain extent, Silbar and PL were pushing the same strategy as Gitlin and the ERAP advocates of the interracial movement of the poor, only casting that strategy in more classical Marxist language. Like Gitlin, PL would not effectively challenge white working-class racism; it would simply deny that that racism had any real basis. It would also seek to convince white workers to align with blacks on the basis that blacks were fighting the same class enemies that white workers themselves fought. PL thus sought to cover up white workers' long history of helping to construct segregated labor and housing markets and educational and public facilities. The answer to black people's problems, PL argued, lay not with Black Power but with uniting with the white working class and fighting for socialism.

Even mainstream and respected SDSers took similar tacks. At the June 1967 SDS national convention, SDSers Bob Gottlieb, Gerry Tenney, and Dave Gilbert offered the main theoretical document, "Toward a Theory of Social Change in America." In their view, blacks and other racial minorities, together with the permanently unemployed and underemployed, constituted an "underclass." As "the most deprived class in America," the underclass was "one of the centers of radicalism" in the nation and had "been the first to bring forth demands for control and radical change." But, continued the three SDSers, the underclass was removed "from the sources of power—the centers of production" and therefore could not single-handedly alter American social relations. For that, it would need to ally with the working class.[34] Like PL, these veteran SDSers saw black freedom as contingent upon the ability of blacks to ally with white workers.

SDS was an organization that prided itself on its "nonideological ideology." By nonideological ideology, SDSers simply meant that they would attempt to derive a theory of social action from the realities of social struggle, rather than imposing a theory on that social reality. This was particularly important to an organization that began its active life at a time when the Left in the United States had been laid low and when social motion originated not with workers but with black people. Thus, it was all the more striking that Gottlieb, Tenney, and Gilbert, and SDS generally, chose not to explore the theoretical and practical implications of Black Power, something new and challenging in America's social and political landscape, but returned instead to a reworked Marxist theory of class struggle as the path to social change in the United States. Evidently, in the absence of an immediate and compelling black social activism, SDS would have a hard time retaining any self-critical vision of its racial identity or any realistic understanding of America's social realities.

Exactly six weeks before assassins took his life, Malcolm X forecast that blood would flow in 1965 in America's cities as it never had before.[35] Six months after his death, the black community of Watts in Los Angeles confirmed Malcolm's prediction when blacks took to the streets in the largest racial riot since 1943. By the time police and National Guardsmen subdued the August rebellion, 4,000 people were in jail; 34 people were dead, most killed by the police; hundreds more had been injured; and rioters had destroyed $35 million in property.[36] Malcolm, of course, had no crystal ball when he spoke in January 1965, nor did he need one. He simply was an attentive observer and committed partisan in the battle then going on for black freedom. Blood would flow in 1965, Malcolm argued, because the conditions that had made it flow in 1963 and 1964 still existed in 1965.[37]

And it continued to flow after 1965. While the summer of 1966 had no single rebellion whose intensity compared to that of Watts, nevertheless black rebellions increased in their extent across the breadth of the nation, with over forty disorders and riots. During the following summer of 1967—the media dubbed it "the summer of love" after San Francisco's hippies scene—black rebellions increased in both number and intensity: 150 cities reported disorders and riots in that year, nearly four times the number of cities than the previous year. In the largest of these rebellions, black communities in Newark and Detroit both erupted within days of each other. In Newark, over a score of people died, and rioters destroyed more than $10 million in property. In Detroit, police arrested 7,200 people. Police, National Guard, and army troops killed thirty-one people; altogether, forty-three people died in the riot, with property losses totaling approximately $40 million.[38]

Newark's rebellion could not help but affect SDS. Since 1963, SDS had run the Newark Community Union Project (NCUP), an ERAP project, with white ERAP staffers living in the heart of Newark's black community. Less than two weeks after Newark's rioting ended, white ERAPer Eric Mann recounted the uprising to SDS members. "The riots," Mann reported, "were probably the most popular action that has ever been taken in this community." As he walked down the street on which he lived during the riot, he was reminded of a block party: "People were laughing, kids were walking around with new clothes, with new toys. People had a lot of food in their homes, and television sets. The primary demands were quite obviously economic and psycholgical [sic], not political. It was the idea that 'we did it,' that 'we screwed all those stores that were taking advantage of us' and also that we got some of the things we wanted and needed."[39] If Mann did not see anything political in black people avenging themselves on those who had exploited them, fellow NCUP staffer Steve Block interpreted events differently. "Black consciousness has been heightened," Block reported. The notion "of Black Power and black unity now really seem to make sense and to be important."[40]

NCUP staff person and SDS founder Tom Hayden also understood the riot's political implications. Newark's rioting, argued Hayden, represented "the assertion of new methods of opposing the racism that politics, nonviolence and community organization have failed to end." Although these new methods did not yet amount to revolution, Hayden continued, the fact that blacks had chosen this new path was significant. Intransigent white American racism was teaching blacks "that they must prepare to fight." Slowly, then, the conditions "for an American form of guerrilla warfare based in the slums" were building, and the riot signaled that process. Although both liberals and conservatives might condemn the riot and its implications for America's future, Hayden maintained that the riot was nothing less than people making history. True, said Hayden, it was a

> primitive ... form of history making. But if people are barred from using the sophisticated instruments of the established order for their ends, they will find another way. Rocks and bottles are only a beginning, but they cause more attention than all the reports in Washington. To the people involved, the riot is far less lawless and far more representative than the system of arbitrary rules and prescribed channels they confront every day. . . .
>
> Men are now appearing in the ghettos who might turn the energy of the riot to a more organized and continuous revolutionary direction. . . . They understand that the institutions of the white community are unreliable in the absence of black community power. They recognize that national civil rights leaders will not secure the kind of change that is needed. They assume that disobedience, disorder, and even violence must be risked as the only alternative to continuing slavery.[41]

Thus, Hayden forecast revolution as one possible issue of the nation's contemporary social problems. And this was not revolution as metaphor. This was revolution as Malcolm depicted it: bloody and violent.

Five days after the rioting ended in Newark, Detroit exploded, even more violently. The riot raged for an entire week and ended only after officials had called in nearly 10,000 National Guardsmen and 2,700 U.S. Army paratroopers.[42] And while the riots in Detroit and Newark were the largest and most costly, major disturbances involving numerous arsons and allegations of sniper activity as well as rock, bottle, and Molotov cocktail throwing occurred in scores of U.S. cities.[43]

This unprecedented black social protest profoundly influenced SDS. Some SDSers saw an imminent revolution springing from the ghetto rebellions. In early August, SDS's National Interim Committee (NIC), for example, met and debated the question of how SDS was to relate to the uprisings. One NIC member urged that "SDS should work to organize students into unions where they could then initiate revolution on the campus and take off from there." Other NIC members argued that "SDS's main course of action should be to get students off the campus and into the ghettos, black and white, and to lead students into actively preparing people for revolution." One of the advocates for this position insisted that the "United States's great slave population"—black people—had recognized that they never would become real citizens of the nation. Consequently, "they must now set out on the lonely course left to them—armed struggle." But a variety of peoples—poor whites included—had a stake in this. "When and if these groups ever united with the black revolutionaries, who are now slowly forming to ignite fires of change in this great land of slavery, then we will witness the second American Revolution."[44]

In Chicago, JOIN organizers Mike James and Bob Lawson announced that their job was "to try to explain [to their white constituencies that the] black rebellions ... [were] not ... race riots, but ... [were] class wars." They hoped that by so doing, they could channel the frustration of poor whites against "the real oppressors" rather than against the "niggers." The two JOIN organizers acknowledged that they could not guarantee the success of their mission. Nevertheless, James and Lawson complained, JOIN was one of the few projects nationally that was even attempting to build poor white constituencies "that can relate and be related to, by blacks." Moreover, the situation was urgent, the two white organizers argued. Those white radicals who, for whatever reason, thought that they could not be organizing poor whites should "begin to build guerrilla forces (white black panther parties for self-defense). Whites must begin to move, to act now so that black people will not be isolated and crushed, and so a radical movement can begin to develop in America."[45]

Thus, some SDS members and leaders responded to the summer's upsurge of black social motion with ever more dramatic readings of the situation. The United States, it seemed to them, teetered on the edge of a revolution. For the first time, a variety of SDS members began suggesting that white radicals take up arms against the state.

New Leftists also produced somewhat less dramatic, but seemingly no less radical, reassessments of the contemporary social struggle. These new readings of social struggle were apparent in the struggles occurring at the 1967 Chicago Labor Day weekend convocation of the National Conference for a New Politics (NCNP). Coming at the end of the summer's urban upheavals, this combination of 2,000 white liberals, New Leftists, and black activists could not help but produce a volatile weekend in which the relationship between whites and blacks would take center stage and in which activists would contest the meaning and content of social change in the United States.

White leftists and liberals had initiated the NCNP in the hopes of drawing together the main social movements of the day—the antiwar, civil rights, and Black Power movements. The unification of social movements would have benefited the overall struggle for social change in the United States, but unification of social movements is not a simple process of addition. Black activists at the NCNP believed that historically white social movements—the populists and the labor movement most clearly—used blacks as bodies in battles that lower-class whites fought against white elites. As soon as these white-led movements won some form of accommodation with the elites, however, they forgot their black allies.[46] For now, in the wake of what one SNCC activist termed "the high-tide of black resistance," black activists were in no mood to set themselves up for another fall. If there were to be unity of the black and antiwar movements, it would come on black terms, or it would not come at all. Consequently, black delegates to the NCNP issued thirteen demands to the convention, including the demand that the convention cede to blacks, who constituted one-sixth of those in attendance, 50 percent of the votes. Said SNCC's James Forman to the assembled delegates: "There can be no new concept of politics, no new coalitions, unless those of us who are the most dispossessed assume leadership and give direction to that new form of politics. If this does not happen, we are going to see the same old liberal-labor treachery of very rich white folks and Democratic-party-oriented whites and Negroes trying to determine what they can do for us."[47] Another of the demands called for the immediate creation of "white civilizing committees ... in all white communities to civilize and humanize the savage and beast like character that runs rampant throughout America." Black radicals once again were insisting that white radicals take responsibility for the racism in white communities. After an acrimonious debate, the convention narrowly acceded to the black caucus demands.

While the summer of 1967 deeply affected white New Leftists, the greater part of the New Left took from that summer not the demands of the black movement but the black movement's militancy. Indeed, SDS activists entered the fall of 1967 intent on escalating the movement's militancy and taking the movement "from protest to resistance," in the words of a popular internal slogan of the day. On campuses and in demonstrations, white radicals sought to block, attack, or destroy symbols of the nation's war effort: draft boards, armed forces recruiters, recruiters for corporate munitions makers, induction centers, the Pentagon.

In the San Francisco Bay Area, for example, debates rent the antiwar movement as it planned a week of antidraft activities, "Stop the Draft Week." A leader of the Resistance, an antidraft group, characterized the discussions as splitting "between the traditional pacifists who envisioned the usual kind of sit-in ... and radicals, mainly SDS people, vicariously intoxicated by the summer riots, who spoke at first clearly, but with increasing vagueness of violent confrontation with the power structure."[48] Frank Bardacke, a leader of the radicals and subsequently indicted for the Draft Week activities, recalled that "our idea was highly influenced by the Black Power people."[49] Ultimately, the radicals seized the initiative, and on the final day of the action 10,000 demonstrators marched on the Oakland induction center, outnumbering and confronting the police, creating chaos in the city, and giving white radicals a taste of the urban rebellions they modeled their behavior on. One SDS participant described the action: "Trash cans and newspaper racks were pulled into the streets. Writing appeared on walls, on sidewalks: 'Free Oakland,' 'Che Lives,' 'Resist,' 'Shut It Down.' Soon, unlocked cars were pushed into the intersections, along with large potted trees and movable benches. The sanctity of private property, which had held white students back from this kind of defensive action before, gave way to a new evaluation." Police lines moved toward the crowds to disperse them, and the radicals obliged by getting onto the sidewalks and then converging on the streets again, behind the police lines. Demonstrators again and again surrounded outnumbered police, demoralized them, and made them ineffective. Word of the tactic spread rapidly among the demonstrators, "who were beginning to feel and even act somewhat like urban guerrillas."

> For the first time demonstrators, unarmed, saw police lines retreat in front of them. It was our first taste of real victory. . . . We had taken and held downtown Oakland. . . . We had seen the cops back away from us. . . . Not only the sanctity of property, and the sanctity (invulnerability) of cops had been destroyed that day; we had established new goals, new criterion [sic] for success in what were clearly the early battles of a long, long war.[50]

Summarized Bardacke: "We finally had ourselves a white riot."[51]

On the following day, October 21, 1967, and on the other side of the continent, New Leftists again broke from traditional models of protest at the Pentagon. Radicals at the Pentagon demonstration, like their counterparts in Oakland, wanted and did take the demonstration beyond the liberal "witness" politics that had dominated the movement in the past. Led by SDS and Yippies, between 5,000 and 10,000 demonstrators, "unwilling," in the words of one activist, "to commit a humiliating form" of civil disobedience, broke through lines of baton- and tear-gas-wielding troops, knocked down cyclone fencing, and camped themselves for the night in uneasy, but victorious, ranks on the Pentagon's lawn.[52]

On college campuses as well, antiwar, anti-ROTC, antidraft, and antirecruiting actions took on a far more militant tone. At the University of Wisconsin, Madison, demonstrators battled police after the latter brutally arrested students seeking to block access to Dow Chemical Company recruiters. After absorbing police charges and numerous volleys of tear gas lobbed at them, students finally fought back with rocks, bricks, and whatever else they could throw. Students broke one police officer's nose and another's leg in the melee.[53] Madison activist Paul Buhle would later liken the action to the Watts riot.[54] At Brooklyn College, 1,000 students battled police in a demonstration to oust navy recruiters.[55] Similar battles against war recruiting raged at the University of Illinois and at Oberlin, while Columbia SDSers led street battles at a New York City visit by Secretary of State Dean Rusk.[56]

Antiwar work also took on a more audacious character. For example, Columbia University SDSers confronted New York's Selective Service chief, Colonel Paul Akst, in ways that would have been unimaginable a year earlier. As the colonel addressed an audience of Columbia students in early February 1968, half-a-dozen SDSers, dressed in army fatigues and carrying fifes and drums and toy guns, entered the rear of the auditorium, "stomping, yelling, shouting, singing chaotically." When heads turned to see the commotion, an SDS activist seated in the front row rushed the podium and tossed a lemon-meringue pie in the colonel's face. Similar escalations of militancy occurred on scores of campuses.[57]

SDS's interorganizational secretary, Carl Davidson, summarized all these changes in the temperament and militancy of the movement. "The recent confrontations on our campuses between radical students and recruiters from the military and the war industries demonstrate the beginnings of a new phase of struggle within the antiwar movement." The level of student resistance, Davidson claimed, was "almost without precedent in the history of the American university." Whereas in the spring, antirecruiting sit-ins had occurred on college campuses as acts of "moral witness" against the war, the fall's actions had taken on the quality of "Tactical Political Resistance." Davidson saw four main reasons for this transformation: the continuing war against the Vietnamese; increasing government repression; a more sophisticated analysis of the university's role as part of and servant to American imperial society; and finally: "The black ghetto rebellions this summer fundamentally altered the political reality of white America, including the white left. The black liberation movement has replaced the civil rights and antipoverty movements, revealing the utter bankruptcy of corporate liberalisms [sic] cooptive [sic] programs. The events of this summer marked not only the possibility, but the beginning of the second American revolution."[58] Thus, in the fall of 1967 white New Leftists succeeded in breaking through their own "hang-ups" about the sanctity of property and the necessity for nonviolence. Destroying property and fighting the police were no longer taboo, as such actions had been in the past. While other factors undoubtedly played into this change in movement sensibilities, black social action in the summer of 1967 had set the example and tone of militancy that white New Leftists followed: black people in the streets had legitimized rock- and bottle-throwing tactics, had first destroyed property, and had fought the police. Davidson and other New Leftists implicitly, and in some cases explicitly, acknowledged this. For the most part, however, such acknowledgments were of limited value to the black movement. Black activists had demanded that white radicals organize against racism in the white community. SDS had largely ignored this demand and maintained a vision of white radicals organizing on whatever terms they themselves deemed relevant. The New Left's new militancy, however, too often stood in the same relation to black social motion as rock and roll did to rhythm and blues, or white jazz to black jazz: it was unable to transcend being an expropriation—a "rip-off"—and unable to mount a serious self-conscious attempt at acknowledging the white radicals' relationship to the black movement. Its imitation of black assertiveness acknowledged the strength of the black movement, but in a fashion designed not to enhance that strength but to use that power to address its own immediate, white, concerns.

Consequently, from the fall of 1967 to the assassination of Martin Luther King Jr., SDS chapter activity consisted overwhelmingly of antidraft, antiwar, and anti-recruiting work. SDSers had done this work before, true, but never with the fervor and militancy with which they now approached their work. In comparison, only a handful of SDS chapters conducted any concerted activities or campaigns around issues of university racism. In the late winter of 1968, when state troopers in Orangeburg, South Carolina, murdered three black students and wounded sixteen others in a nonviolent desegregation struggle, apparently only one SDS chapter mobilized to protest the shootings.[59]

By the early spring of 1968, most SDS members and leaders had been unable to develop any deep analysis of their relationship to the black struggle and of their own racialization. But actual events were unfolding that would force SDS to confront these questions squarely. Above all, four phenomena compelled SDS to assess and reassess its understanding of and relationship to the black social movement: escalating repression against the black movement, Martin Luther King Jr.'s assassination, the emergence of the Black Panther Party for Self-Defense, and militant black student demonstrations.

On August 25, 1967, with the fires of Detroit and Newark still smoldering, J. Edgar Hoover initiated the Federal Bureau of Investigation (FBI) Counterintelligence Program (COINTELPRO) against the organized black movement. In a secret FBI memo, Hoover himself articulated COINTELPRO's objectives: to "disrupt, misdirect, discredit or otherwise neutralize" the black movement; to set black nationalist groups against each other; and to alienate black and white support from the black nationalist struggle. Hoover also found it particularly important that the FBI prevent the rise of a "messiah," "someone who could unify, and electrify, the militant black nationalist movement." In practical terms, the FBI orchestrated a harassment, arrest, and assassination campaign against SNCC and against what was then a local Oakland-based black group, the Black Panther Party for Self-Defense, as well as other local black nationalist organizations.[60]

Between July 1967 and February 1968, various police agencies arrested SNCC's new chairman, H. Rap Brown, no less than six times on a variety of charges, and imposed over $250,000 in bail bonds on Brown.[61] In October 1967 in Oakland, a police campaign of harassment against Black Panther founder and minister of defense Huey P. Newton culminated in a shoot-out that left one police officer dead and Newton seriously wounded and under arrest. By early March 1968, SDS leaders were beginning to realize that this repression seriously threatened the black movement's viability and demanded SDS's immediate attention. Equally important, COINTELPRO's intensity forced SDS to reassess its sense of self and its sensibilities about race.

In an unsigned March 1968 front-page article in *New Left Notes*, "Attack on Militants—The Man Moves Hard: Where Are We?" SDS offered a self-critical look at its lack of effort in countering the growing repression against the black struggle. "There is a new and qualitative change in Federal court actions," the article reported. "It is clear that the Man has decided to jail militant black leaders before next summer." The article continued by reeling off the various dates and places that Rap Brown had been busted and concluded by asking: "Will our silence insure that Rap and the black people of this country are imprisoned and killed?" Or, on the contrary, would white leftists make it clear through word and deed that "we are supporting our black brothers in every way possible."[62]

In the context of this growing repression and the self-critical attitude that it engendered, *New Left Notes* two weeks later published "Learn the Lessons of U.S. History," by Noel Ignatin. In two closely argued pages, "Learn the Lessons" decisively challenged SDS's dominant vision of the black struggle's significance, of white-black relations, of white ERAP-type organizing, and, implicitly, of white identity.

Ignatin began his article by characterizing the ERAP, Old Left, and PL style of organizing whites: "Find the issues which immediately affect the people we are trying to reach, and which they feel most keenly. Organize around these issues and, as the people are drawn more into struggle in their own interest, they will come to see, with our help, who are their friends and enemies. Specifically, coalitions between poor white and black will develop from each fighting for his own 'self-interest,' and coming to see that there is a common enemy, the rich white man." But, he argued, white supremacist thinking, and the material privilege on which it rested, would not allow such an approach to work. According to Ignatin, the nation's elite had made a deal with white workers: if the workers would support the rulers in their "enslavement of the non-white-majority of the earth's population," then the elite would reward them with "a monopoly of skilled jobs, education, and health facilities superior to those of non-whites." Moreover, white workers would occasionally be allowed to enter the ranks of the elite, and they would be accorded "social privileges and a whole series of privileges befitting" their white skin. Ignatin then succinctly summarized his viewpoint: "White supremacy is a deal between the exploiters and the exploited, at the expense of the rest of the exploited." "Self-interest" coalitions were bound to fail "if the self-interest of the whites means the maintainance [*sic*] of white supremacy and the white-skin privilege."

All the nation's great labor struggles, Ignatin continued, had foundered on the shoals of racial privilege. DuBois had so argued concerning the labor struggles of the Reconstruction period. C. Vann Woodward had shown that during the populist era, whites had opted for white supremacy over class solidarity. And, added Ignatin, in the 1940s the Congress of Industrial Organizations (CIO) had halted its organizing effort in the South, opting for accommodation with New Deal liberals rather than taking up the task of jointly organizing white and black southern workers.

Ignatin's analysis was not entirely new. W. E. B. DuBois, whom Ignatin credited in "Learn the Lessons," had said much the same thing in his masterwork, *Black Reconstruction*. And Carmichael's Black Power analysis implicitly had said as much. What was new about Ignatin's argument was that it was coming from within the white New Left and combating the traditional white Left formulations that had managed to overlook white privilege. Real solidarity with black people, Ignatin was saying, would require something more of whites than simply lining up against the rich.

> Solidarity between black and white requires more from the white than a willingness to "help the Negroes up if it doesn't lower us any." It requires a willingness to renounce our privileges, precisely to "lower ourselves" in order that we can all rise up together. If anyone says that it will be difficult to get the whites to renounce their privileges, I readily concede the difficulty—whoever said it would be easy to make a revolution? But is [*sic*] anyone thinks it is possible to skip this renunciation and to build coalitions between blacks and whites who want to maintain their privileges, I will point to 1877, 1904 and 1940, and say that if this task is not tackled and achieved, we will see the same thing over again.[63]

In the face of the overwhelming majority of New Leftists who had seized upon Black Power as a means of taking up struggles against the war as legitimate "white" struggles and who had consigned struggles against racism to an ancillary position in the struggle for social change, and of the smaller number of New Leftists who had taken up organizing the white poor but also made race and racism something external to that process, Ignatin threw down the challenge: if the white Left failed to confront white supremacy, failed to confront white privilege, then it could not contribute to significant social change in the country.

Ignatin's "Learn the Lessons" appeared in the *New Left Notes* number that SDS had prepared to coincide with its March 1968 National Council meeting in Lexington, Kentucky. At Lexington, SDS passed a far more significant and thoughtful resolution on race than the one it had passed over a year and a half earlier after SNCC's turn to Black Power. The resolution began by expressing concern over the prospects of government suppression of the black movement in the face of the summer's expected unrest. However, the resolution's real strength lay with its analysis of racism. Racist culture, the resolution argued, was not only black people's enemy but white people's enemy, too. Racism was a ruling-class ideology that encouraged white people to identify with their rulers and that maintained a system that stood against their interests as human beings. Moreover, nearly two years after SNCC's turn to Black Power, SDS finally declared that

> we have a special responsibility to fight racism among our own white population. In the context of that struggle against racism in the white population, we will be able to aid the struggle for black survival and for black liberation in every way we can.
>
> Finally, we recognize that racism insinuates itself into both our personal and our political attitudes. We are determined to fight it in our personal lives as we fight all the aspects of a racist culture that the system attempts to inject into us.[64]

At last SDS publicly committed itself to organizing whites against racism and recognized in collective form that racism shaped and distorted SDS's own vision. Thus, SDS members took their first real step toward recognizing their own racialization as whites in America. Although this was a real advance for SDS, it was by no means the New Left's settled position. Staughton Lynd called SDS's response the "politics of guilt": "During the last year SDS has been reverting to the . . . politics of middle-class self-flagellation. . . . Since the spring of 1968 National Council meeting SDS has asked white people again to play the role of auxiliaries to other people's radicalism."[65]

Nevertheless, in the face of developing historical events, Lynd's position was in retreat within SDS. This would become apparent with the assassination of Martin Luther King Jr. The reaction of black people to King's assassination was massive and instantaneous. Major disturbances broke out in over 100 cities, and government officials called out 75,000 National Guardsmen to suppress the riots. In the days that followed, 39 people died, 2,500 suffered injuries, and rioters destroyed untold amounts of property. In Washington, D.C., seventy fires raged simultaneously, and a pall of smoke hung over the city. Troops surrounded the White House and Capitol. Before the rioting had ended, black youth had looted and destroyed property within two blocks of 1600 Pennsylvania Avenue.[66]

Across the country, tens of thousands of white and black students responded to the assassination in actions led by SDS and by coalitions of SDS and black student organizations. In Boston, for example, 20,000 students rallied on the Boston

Commons in a memorial for King. On the following day, 13,000 students demonstrated in front of Boston's city hall demanding that the police and the National Guard "be kept out of the ghetto"; teams of white students leafleted campuses and white neighborhoods in support of the demand. In Austin, Texas, 1,300 students rallied in memory of King, marched on the statehouse, entered it en masse, and continued their demonstration inside the capitol building. Similar actions occurred in communities and on campuses across the nation.[67]

If the ghetto rebellion in the nation's capital crowned the black response to King's assassination, then the struggle at Columbia University represented the height of the white student protest that followed King's death. Two days after the assassination, SDS leader Mark Rudd shocked Columbia's respectable community when he disrupted a university-sponsored memorial for King. Rudd stood up in the middle of liberal Columbia vice president David Truman's eulogy and denounced the hypocrisy of an administration that would pay tribute to King while paying its predominantly black custodial staff a pittance, displacing black tenants who lived on university-owned real estate, and aggressively encroaching on surrounding black neighborhoods.[68]

Writing less than a year after the rebellion, Rudd acknowledged that the first "push to whites" at Columbia came from King's assassination, "which spurred SDS on to greater militancy." The second push came from Columbia's black students. According to Rudd, the Student Afro-American Society (SAS) had been "mostly a cultural or social organization" prior to King's assassination. Following King's death, however, SAS began "to make political demands." Most important, SAS lined itself up with the demands of Harlem activists who had campaigned against Columbia's plans to build a university gym facility in Harlem's Morningside Park. Not only would the facility snatch up another portion of Harlem's limited green spaces, but the original proposal contained an insulting concession to the community: community members would be given access to a special portion of the facility through a rear door.

On April 23, less than three weeks after King's death, a joint SDS-SAS rally and demonstration escalated into a Columbia building occupation after demonstrators ripped down fences enclosing the gym construction site. While the building occupation began as a joint SDS-SAS action, before the first evening was out, black students had asked the white students to leave. Rudd admitted that SAS based its decision, at least in part, on SAS's evaluation of SDS's lack of militancy and determination. Nevertheless, SAS's own resolve deeply affected SDSers, who proceeded to seize and occupy five more buildings over the next several days. Rudd would later admit the centrality of the black students—and Harlem—for the rebellion. SDS's occupation, Rudd confessed, "itself hinged on that of the blacks, and the overwhelming presence of the black students and Harlem itself in proximity forced us to keep the image of the real world—away from which middle-class white students can so easily slip—clear and bright in our own minds. Because of the blacks, we recognized the immediacy and necessity of the struggle: Vietnam is far away, unfortunately, for most people, and our pain has become diffuse and dull."[69]

The anger that King's assassination evoked among both white and black students and especially among black people living in inner cities across the nation spurred the New Left's militancy. But King's assassination also raised fundamental questions about the ideology of whiteness. By recognizing a distinctive "middle-class white student" mindset, Rudd and the New Left were beginning to recognize the "constructedness" of their own worldview. Hitherto, most of the New Left had uncritically accepted its own standpoint as unracialized and "natural." Now, some significant portion of the New Left was beginning to examine these assumptions.

Two days after King's assassination, on the same day that Mark Rudd disrupted David Truman's memorial speech for King, Oakland, California, police killed eighteen-year-old Black Panther "L'il" Bobby Hutton and seriously wounded Black Panther minister of information Eldridge Cleaver. The intensifying government repression against the Panthers, coupled with the group's powerful vision of social change, would constitute yet another important impetus in SDS's quest for self-definition.

The attack on Hutton and Cleaver was the most extreme action to date against the Panthers. At the time of the attack, *New Left Notes* was able to report that over the previous eight months, "pictures and descriptions of Panther leaders" had been "widely distributed to police." In January, San Francisco police had broken down Cleaver's door without a warrant and searched his apartment. In February, Oakland police had done the same thing at Panther chairman Bobby Seale's apartment and arrested Seale and his wife. In late March, also without a warrant, San Diego police broke into and searched the home of the party's local organizer. Moreover, police had been continually harassing Panthers over an extended period of time. In Oakland itself, Oakland police had killed five unarmed black youth under eighteen years of age in the single month of March. In addition, *New Left Notes* reported, the mass media had been carrying out "a campaign of slander" against the Panthers. "This systematic political persecution of the Black Panther Party MUST BE RESISTED," insisted *New Left Notes*.[70]

Merritt Community College students Huey Newton and Bobby Seale founded the Panthers in Oakland in 1966. The group first drew national attention with its patrolling of the black community to deter police harassment. Openly carrying shotguns, then legal under California law, teams of Panthers would follow police patrols through Oakland's black community. When the police stopped a black person, the Panthers would jump out, observe the police, and provide legal advice to the person being questioned. Oftentimes better versed in California law than the police, the Panthers frustrated the police, both through their command of the law and through their refusal to be intimidated. In October 1967, the Panthers were thrust into the national limelight when police shot and jailed Newton in a shoot-out that left one Oakland police officer dead. Subsequently, the Panthers, working together with other black nationalist organizations, including SNCC, raised the cry of "Free Huey!" in black communities across the country. The Panthers again achieved national recognition when California's legislature sought to close the loophole in its laws that allowed carrying weapons openly. Determined to protest the bill, two dozen Panthers descended on the capitol, weapons in hand. Surrounded by press as they strode onto the capitol grounds, the Panthers in the bustle and confusion accidentally entered a wrong door that opened directly into the assembly chambers.[71] Police arrested the Panthers, but the image of young armed black revolutionaries disrupting California's legislature reverberated through the nation's black ghettos. At about the same time, paroled convict and celebrated radical journalist Eldridge Cleaver joined the Panther ranks and also added to the group's growing visibility. Young blacks in cities across the country raced to take up the Panther banner and found Panther chapters.[72]

Cleaver especially influenced the New Left. As a journalist for the slick left-liberal magazine *Ramparts* and as the author of a best-selling collection of essays, *Soul on Ice*, Cleaver drew powerful portraits of the Panthers. In a famous *Ramparts* piece following his April 1968 bust, for example, Cleaver described his first meeting with the Panthers. The Panthers had taken responsibility for security for Malcolm X's widow, Betty Shabazz, during her visit to San Francisco. Twenty armed Panthers escorted Shabazz to *Ramparts'* office for an interview with Cleaver. The sight of the armed black men, all with black leather jackets, black berets, and light-colored turtleneck shirts, halted traffic and brought a contingent of San Francisco police to the scene. Cleaver described for his *Ramparts* readers the ensuing confrontation as one of the policemen—"a big, beefy" fellow—stepped forward and challenged the Panthers.

This was the most tense of moments. Huey stopped in his tracks and stared at the cop. . . .

Huey walked to within a few feet of the cop and said, "What's the matter, you got an itchy finger?"

The cop made no reply.

"You want to draw your gun?" Huey asked him.

The other cops were calling out for this cop to cool it . . . but he didn't seem to be able to hear them. He was staring into Huey's eyes, measuring him.

"O.K.," Huey said. "You big fat racist pig, draw your gun!"

The cop made no move.

"Draw it, you cowardly dog!" Huey pumped a round into the chamber of the
shotgun. "I'm waiting," he said, and stood there waiting for the cop to draw. . . .

I was thinking, staring at Huey surrounded by all those cops and daring one of them
to draw, "Goddam, that nigger is c-r-a-z-y!"

Then the cop facing Huey gave it up. He heaved a heavy sigh and lowered his
head. Huey literally laughed in his face and then went off up the street at a jaunty pace,
disappearing in a blaze of dazzling sunlight.[73]

This was heady stuff for white (and especially male) New Leftists frustrated with their
inability to stop a system they deemed unjust. The Panthers' mystique, their rapid
growth throughout the country, and the government's mounting repression against
them all drew the New Left's admiration, support, and, increasingly, emulation.

Particularly under Newton's and Cleaver's leadership, the Panthers developed
a sophisticated analysis of American society. Malcolm, Marx, Mao, Fanon, and,
especially, the actual experience of blacks in the United States shaped the Panther
theory and program. As with SNCC, the Panthers saw blacks in America as an
internal colony and self-consciously aligned themselves with the world anticolonial
revolution. And, like SNCC, the Black Panther Party was an all-black organization.
Unlike SNCC, however, the Panthers were Marxists, with a class analysis of black
society and of American society that blended Marx and Malcolm. Finally, because
the Panthers began as a black nationalist organization, they did not share the same
concern with white domination manifested by SNCC, which had to fight its way to
black nationalism against the resistance and "guidance" of friendly white liberals.[74]

On a general level, the Panthers did not challenge white radicals in the same way
as SNCC had; that is, the Panthers did not explicitly urge white radicals to organize
white communities against racism—at least not prior to the summer of 1969. On
the contrary, they presented to New Leftists a more comforting assessment of white
activism than did SNCC. In his pre-Panther book, *Soul on Ice*, for example, Cleaver
praised "a generation of white youth" in rebellion from their racist history. These
white youth, he insisted, were "truly worthy of a black man's respect."[75] For New
Leftists insecure about their relation to black people and hesitant to pursue Black
Power's implications for whites, such praise was indeed welcome.

Even on a more official plane of Panther policy, however, the Panthers gave far
more latitude to the New Left than did SNCC. In a widely reprinted and circulated prison interview that Newton gave in the summer of 1968, he demanded two
things of white radicals. First, white radicals needed to give complete support to the
Panther ten-point program. But the Panther program said nothing concerning the
role of whites in the revolution, and Newton himself left the meaning of complete

support for the Panther program undefined. Second, Newton insisted that white radicals attack the police in the white community when black radicals were attacked in the black community. Explained Newton: "When something happens in the black colony—when we're attacked and ambushed in the black colony—then the white revolutionary students and intellectuals and all the other whites who support the colony should respond by defending us, by attacking the enemy in their community. Every time that we're attacked in our community there should be a reaction by the white revolutionaries, they should respond by defending us, by attacking part of the security force." Here was a vision that was more in line with the New Left's understanding of itself as "revolutionary" than was SNCC's demand on SDS. White activists could avoid the seemingly tedious—and at times really dangerous—work of serious organizing in white communities against racism so long as they were willing to periodically shout "Off the Pig" in public.[76]

But if the Panthers were less demanding of white radicals in the party's general attitude toward them, in its specific efforts at working with the New Left, the Panthers made more concrete demands upon SDS than did SNCC. These specific demands had an implicit content that pushed white radicals to organize in their own white communities against racism—just what SNCC had asked of them.

In their first national contact with SDS, for example, the Panthers sought an alliance around Cleaver's 1968 Peace and Freedom Party presidential campaign. To secure Cleaver's candidacy, the Peace and Freedom Party, organized by white left-liberals, had endorsed the entire Panther program—Newton's precondition for the Panthers' cooperation. Perhaps chastened by the NCNP experience the previous fall, Peace and Freedom's white leftists understood correctly that a unified program for social change in the United States had to have the approval of the black community and its militant representatives. Possibly to push Peace and Freedom still farther to the left, or simply to give the campaign a national presence that only SDS had, Cleaver sought SDS's alliance in the campaign. Specifically, Cleaver proposed that Carl Oglesby, one of SDS's most important leaders, run as Cleaver's vice presidential candidate.[77] Oglesby refused to make the decision on his own and referred Cleaver's request to SDS's executive committee, NIC. In this first formal discussion of SDS's relation to the Panthers, SDS rejected Cleaver's offer. SDS's rejection itself took a characteristic form and foreshadowed the development of a significant tendency in SDS—Weatherman.

Newly elected SDS interorganizational secretary Bernardine Dohrn publicly reported SDS's decision to the membership two weeks after the meeting. Dohrn opened her report with a quotation from Newton's prison interview: white radicals had to choose their friends and their enemies, and, having made that decision, put it into practice "by attacking" the police. She then acknowledged that the Panthers' "existance [*sic*] and growth ... has [*sic*] posed the question of black/white revolutionary movements in clear, immediate, and real form." For those still not familiar with the Panthers, she sketched a favorable summary of their politics: the Panthers self-consciously saw themselves as organizing the "field niggers," Malcolm X's term for the most downtrodden working-class and unemployed blacks; they were "revolutionary nationalists," inveterate opponents of both black capitalism and nonrevolutionary cultural nationalism ("pork-chop nationalism" as the Panthers described it); they were anticapitalist; they were willing to ally with white radicals in pursuit of "tactical necessities"; and they were seeking to use Cleaver's Peace and Freedom Party candidacy as a means of promoting Panther "politics and organization." Nevertheless, she declared, SDS rejected Cleaver's proposal for Oglesby's candidacy, insisting that while SDS respected the Panthers' alliance with the Peace and Freedom Party, "alliances made by us must be evaluated on our own terms."

The white and the black movements, Dohrn explained, had "different levels of consciousness," and these different levels dictated different strategies. Oglesby's candidacy would commit SDS to an alliance not only with the Panthers but also with the white left-liberals in Peace and Freedom and would involve the "vehicle of electoral politics." And, she continued, since SDS had numerous differences with the Peace and Freedom Party, Oglesby's candidacy ran the risk of misrepresenting SDS. Thus, SDS leaders rejected the alliance because of Peace and Freedom's association with it and because they believed that electoral politics were inappropriate for the level of consciousness in SDS's white constituency.

How, then, would SDS continue to develop a relation with the Panthers? Dohrn argued that SDS was seeking "to develop not exclusive or opportunistic alliances, but solid political relationships based on common experiences and goals." SDS sought to build alliances "not on least common denominator politics" but on clear recognition of differences as well as similarities. Thus, said Dohrn, SDS thought that there were stronger means available for promoting a Panther-SDS alliance than the methods that Cleaver had proposed. These means included SDS nationally promoting the Panthers in SDS chapters, joint speaking tours by Panther and SDS leaders, and "the development of Defense and Self-Defense organizations." In any case, Dohrn recognized the Panthers' growing influence nationally and suggested that SDS needed to be in close communication with the Panthers, linking up with their programs and issues "when—and as long as—our political perspectives are similar."

Dohrn closed her report in a telling fashion. SDS would reject the Panthers' concrete leadership but do so by one-upping the Panthers' revolutionary rhetoric. Said Dohrn: "The main point is: the best thing that we can be doing for ourselves, as well as for the Panthers and the revolutionary black liberation struggle, is to build a fucking white revolutionary mass movement, not a national paper alliance. Building a white Left movement from the ground up means we need the Panthers and black radicals there—at the ground level."[78] Dohrn's piece was infused with this inflated sense of self-importance. SDS—not the Panthers, not the black liberation movement–knew what was best for the entire movement. "Building a white Left movement from the ground up means we need the Panthers and black radicals there–at the ground level." And the Panthers and the black radicals needed to know their place in this greater scheme of things.

As Cleaver understood, however, no necessary contradiction stood between SDS's "building a fucking white revolutionary mass movement" and Cleaver's presidential campaign. On the contrary, the value of the campaign lay in its ability to reach out to millions of people with a radical program and analysis of American society, something the Left in the United States had not been able to undertake seriously since Eugene Debs's campaigns in the early twentieth century. Radicals waged such campaigns not to win elections, but primarily to reach out to and organize new people into the social change movement.

Apparently, this was not militant enough for SDS. Moreover, by starting her report with a quote from the jailed Newton, Dohrn threw back at the Panthers their own militance. Newton had said to attack the police. If very few SDSers were ready for this, still, pumping their fists in the air and declaiming against the police were far more in keeping with the SDS leaders' developing self-image than was working on an election campaign. We will cooperate with you, Dohrn was saying, but on the level that we choose, on a level of militance that we deem really revolutionary. This would not be the last time that SDS would reject the Panthers' leadership using the same "more revolutionary than thou" posturing.

In rejecting the Panther proposal, however, SDS was doing more than simply rejecting the Panthers' leadership: it was rejecting the same demand that SNCC had made on white New Leftists. The Panther proposal to take up its electoral strategy was only a practical form for the demand that white activists go into white communities and organize against the racism of those communities.

After SDS published Dohrn's piece, Cleaver, Cornell's SDS chapter, and California's Peace and Freedom Party all requested that SDS reconsider Cleaver's proposal.[79] SDS's NIC, already having spent considerable time discussing the proposal when it was first broached, spent an additional two days going over the question. Again, SDS rejected Cleaver's request. In this second rejection, SDS leaders listed a number of concerns about Oglesby's running, most of which Dohrn had already raised. One new concern centered on the divisions within the black movement: some SDS chapters had relationships with SNCC, while others had relationships with the

Panthers. NIC members expressed the fear that allowing Oglesby to run with Cleaver would cast SDS nationally with the Panthers in this struggle internal to the black movement.

To be sure, this was a serious consideration, demanding serious thought. But whatever the real problems that might have arisen from SDS's electoral cooperation with the Panthers at a time when black liberation forces were divided, NIC also made clear that Dohrn had already articulated the main basis for rejecting Oglseby's candidacy: electoral work was not militant enough for SDS. The militant and widely publicized demonstrations at the Democratic Party's National Convention in Chicago only weeks earlier had demonstrated, NIC claimed, "that young people in this country are not necessarily caught up in the bullshit that is the American electoral process, that young people are willing and able to 'vote with their feet' in the streets of America. This is where the potential for a real functional relationship will be built. This is where the makings of an insurgent cross-strata youth movement lie. This is the one place where both black and white radicals are being forced to take their case." One further factor characterized NIC's second Cleaver/Oglesby discussion. Even the positive arguments for allowing Oglseby's candidacy centered on SDS. For example, NIC believed that an Oglesby candidacy might serve as a recruiting tool for SDS.[80] However, NIC did not make any effort to see Cleaver's proposal from the standpoint of how strengthening Cleaver's candidacy might benefit the black movement.

Following NIC's rejection of his proposal, Cleaver then asked that SDS send representatives to meet him and discuss the Oglesby candidacy face to face. Cleaver was unable to convince these representatives that Oglesby's candidacy would advance the movement, a third strike against the Panthers' leadership.[81]

On almost every level, the New Left's history had been one of following the lead of the black movement: SDS had followed the civil rights movement into activism, into community organizing, "from protest to resistance," and from resistance to "revolution." Yet SDS, while following the black movement's practical leadership, could never appreciate its intellectual leadership and always jealously guarded its own vision and, ultimately, the resources accruing to it out of its white privilege.

In *Soul on Ice*, Cleaver had developed an interesting psychological characterization of blacks and whites: from the times of slavery, it had been necessary for the male slave owner to characterize the male slave as mindless, as all brawn and no brains—the "supermasculine menial" in Cleaver's words. The male slave owner, who did no physical work, had to characterize himself as having an intellect that suited him to the job of running the plantation and running the lives of those on it—the "omnipotent administrator." According to Cleaver, these same basic psychological traits held into the present, and in the movements for social change. On a psychological level, these roles defined what was revolutionary for blacks and for whites. For blacks, the task was to recover the mind. And, argued Cleaver, the Panthers embodied that recovery. Black people would lead their own liberation. On the other hand, whites had to recover their bodies and, by implication, respect black people's minds.[82] In choosing the Panthers' militancy over their electoral strategy, SDS chose the black body over the black mind, or, what was the same thing, they chose the white mind over the black mind. It was what the white Left in the United States had always done.

The challenge, the demand black radicals made to white activists that they organize white communities against racism, struck at the very core of New Leftists' identity. While Carmichael had suggested that white activists' failing had to do with a lack of courage—and certainly, in the South especially, organizing against racism in white communities took real courage—the real failing centered on white activists' inability to consistently and deeply appreciate their own racialization. Inevitably, a white activist would fail to challenge a white community's racism—and raise the ire of that community—if he or she approached whites as a saved person might approach sinners. The sin was not external to the organizer; if the organizer wanted to facilitate a community's dealing with its racism, he or she could do so only by laying open how race had shaped and continued to shape his or her own thinking and identity. Leading an entire community against racism then involved taking that community through the same process of recognizing racially constructed identity that the organizer was going through. This was the fear that white organizers hesitated before. As James Baldwin had explained it as early as 1963, white racial identity was a trap. American society had raised young whites to believe in the superiority, in the innately unclouded and universal nature of their vision and identity. To take on racism, young whites had to acknowledge to themselves that they had as much to learn—indeed, more to learn—about the nature of the society in which they lived as they had to teach; that they were not the people that fate had miraculously crafted to lead society to salvation but were, so long as they held to their white identities, a part of the problem.[83]

Chapter Two

The New Left and the
American Empire, 1962–1968

By 1965—the year that the Lyndon Johnson administration decisively escalated the United States' war against Vietnam—SDS leaders were beginning to conceive of the United States as an empire. More than anything, the United States' brutality in Vietnam would push increasing numbers of young white activists to this understanding. But a whole host of events and struggles stood behind Vietnam and provided the indispensable context within which activists could comprehend this American empire. In the first place, the black struggle made anti-imperial struggles comprehensible to New Leftists. Africa's anticolonial revolutions, especially, resonated with New Leftists schooled in the civil rights struggle. It was difficult not to see the connection between black people struggling against segregation in the southern United States and black people struggling against apartheid in South Africa. And that connection, coupled with the United States' practical support for the apartheid government, raised troubling questions for SDSers. Second, the United States' Cold War rhetoric, its self-proclaimed role as "leader of the Free World," stood in sharp contrast to the actual support that the United States gave to anti-Communist dictators the world over. In particular, the United States' duplicity toward Cuba's successful popular revolution against dictator Fulgencio Batista underlined this contradiction and helped open New Leftists to alternative accounts of the Cold War. Third, in meeting directly with Cuban and Vietnamese revolutionaries, SDSers came away with a very different vision of the "the enemy" than the one presented by U.S. government leaders. These meetings at once humanized the Cubans and Vietnamese and made more credible their narratives of the United States–Third World relationship.

Still, even as New Leftists were discovering the reality of an American imperialism, they could not wholly escape traditional notions of their own national identity. This manifested itself in two particularly characteristic ways. First, even the best New Leftists consistently failed to take seriously the theoretical work analyzing U.S. imperialism that came out of the black community and the anticolonial revolution more generally. SDS leaders either ignored or were unaware of the intellectual work of W. E. B. DuBois, Malcolm X, and, most immediately, SNCC. In failing to embrace this theoretical work, however, SDS deprived itself of important insights on the character of the U.S. empire and especially of how that empire shaped U.S. domestic life, culture, ideology, structure, and even the personal identities of its citizens. This failure also perpetuated a part of the U.S. empire's division of labor and thus undermined SDS's attempts at understanding and battling imperialism.

Second, SDS's developing vision of the United States as an empire coexisted with attempts at a class analysis that almost entirely ignored imperialism. Indeed, in the same fashion that New Leftists long understood racism as only affecting black people and disconnected racism from their own experience, New Leftists by and large saw imperialism as something external to the United States, as what the United States did abroad, and not something that wholly shaped the internal life of the country. Slowly, and especially as the United States escalated its war against Vietnam, SDSers came to understand that this was a false vision and, however imperfectly, sought to recast their understanding of empire and nation. But this remained a battle, with powerful forces inside and outside of SDS continually undermining SDS's attempts at comprehending the American empire.

In July 1962, with fewer than 1,000 members scattered across the nation, SDS drafted the first real American New Left manifesto, the Port Huron Statement. Most memorably, the Port Huron Statement articulated the alienation that growing numbers of youth were experiencing within American society and the roles they were being called upon to play by that society: "Loneliness, estrangement, isolation describe the vast distance between man and man today. These dominant tendencies cannot be overcome by better personnel management, nor by improved gadgets, but only when a love of man overcomes the idolatrous worship of things by man." As the antidote to this alienation, the statement sought to promote new values, insisting that a truly human society would hold "men" as "infinitely precious and possessed of unfulfilled capacities for reason, freedom, and love."

Of the Port Huron Statement's 25,000 words, approximately one-fifth were devoted specifically to trying to comprehend the United States' place in the world.

At its best, the statement described, and rejected as false, America's traditional Cold War narrative:

> When we were kids the United States was the wealthiest and strongest country in the world ... an initiator of the United Nations that we thought would distribute Western influence throughout the world. Freedom and equality for each individual, government of, by, and for the people—these American values we found good, principles by which we could live as men. ...
>
> The proclaimed peaceful intentions of the United States contradicted its economic and military investments in the Cold War status quo.

But this critique fell short on two counts: first, it did not draw any explicit connection between the United States' international role and the alienation it so strongly described and condemned. And second, it simply juxtaposed the United States' Cold War rhetoric with its Cold War practice. The statement did not claim that the contradiction stemmed from anything necessary in America's social constitution. On the contrary, the Port Huron Statement saw the negative aspects of U.S. policy flowing out of a generalized failure of America's leadership to stay abreast of the times, and not from any self-conscious pursuit of U.S. interests as perceived by U.S. leaders. Indeed, so closely tied to liberalism were most SDSers in 1962 that the Port Huron Statement's language closely echoed President John Kennedy's Cold War rhetoric. For example, Kennedy complained that under Eisenhower the United States was passively reacting to the world's anticolonial upsurge rather than "marching at the head of this world wide revolution, counseling it, helping it come to a healthy fruition."[1] Echoing Kennedy's liberal critique, the Port Huron Statement argued that "although mankind desperately needs revolutionary leadership, America rests in national stalemate." U.S. goals were "ambiguous and tradition-bound instead of informed and clear, its democratic system apathetic and manipulated rather than 'of, by, and for the people.'"[2]

The irony was that when Kennedy pledged the energy of a new generation to the cause of freedom, he was looking to establish more firmly precisely the kind of hegemony that SDSers would come to unequivocally reject. Even as SDS was drafting the Port Huron Statement, Kennedy had already accelerated the journey that would end with millions of dead in Vietnam. Kennedy, more than any of his predecessors, was shifting U.S. global strategy to "radically direct [it] against the Third World," in the words of Vietnamese scholar Nguyen Khac Vien. [3] Corresponding to this shift, the United States would orient its military to be able to deal with Third World insurrection. Kennedy and his chief military adviser, General Maxwell Taylor, thus formulated and placed at the center of U.S. military strategy the "flexible response" doctrine—the ability to respond to "aggression" with whatever level of force the United States deemed necessary.

Very early on in his presidency, Kennedy determined that the United States would first test its flexible response doctrine in Vietnam against a popular national liberation struggle. Eisenhower's administration had failed to even mention Vietnam in its foreign policy briefings to the incoming Kennedy administration. But Kennedy was so attuned to developments in the Third World and to their importance to the United States that within a few days of taking office, he recognized that Vietnam's national liberation movement stood as the biggest obstacle confronting the United States' leadership over a stable world order. "This is the worst one we've got, isn't it?" Kennedy remarked following his first briefing on Vietnam.[4]

Over the next two and a half years, Vietnam's struggle, and the United States' increasingly vain attempts at containing it, would prove Kennedy's original assessment correct. In early 1962, however, the United States had quietly and confidently commenced waging what it called "special war" in Vietnam, convinced that within eighteen months it would pacify Vietnam. Special war was the first rung on the ladder of flexible response and involved social and military components. Socially, special war in Vietnam involved forcibly concentrating southern Vietnam's entire rural population into 16,000 "strategic hamlets" in order to isolate the guerrillas from the general population. Militarily, the United States was equipping Vietnamese strongman Ngo Dinh Diem's forces with the United States' most advanced weapons, and it was using a relatively small corps of U.S. advisers—8,500 U.S. troops were in Vietnam in July 1962 when the Port Huron Statement was drafted—to train Diem's army in the use of those weapons and lead them with U.S.-approved tactics. The advisers' principal function in the special war was not so much to fight as it was to defeat southern Vietnam's National Liberation Front (NLF) with Diem's proxy troops. The relatively small number of U.S. troops and their specific mission to organize Diem's troops to do the fighting minimized the number of U.S. casualties and, concomitantly, minimized the publicity attendant to their work. Moreover, the U.S. intervention—with its use of helicopters, amphibious tanks, and other advanced weapons systems—and the strategic hamlet program initially overwhelmed NLF forces and forced them onto the defensive.[5]

Slowly, however, the NLF recovered its bearings, pushed the U.S.-backed Saigon social order into a tailspin, and forced U.S. planners to reconsider their schemes. In January 1963, at the village of Ap Bac, near Saigon, NLF forces first bested the special war military tactics. In response, U.S. military and political leaders began to consider the ascent from special war toward "limited war." Limited war was the next rung up in the flexible response doctrine and was distinguished from special war by its greater reliance on U.S. troops themselves for direct fighting purposes. It would take leaders in the United States two years to actually make that decision, but in the meantime, the number of U.S. troops in Vietnam increased to 16,000 by the end of 1963 and 23,000 by the end of 1964.

As the war intensified, however, the U.S.-Diem social order continued to unravel. In 1963, Vietnamese Buddhists began a series of highly visible protests against Diem's repressive regime—including internationally televised self-immolations. More U.S. troops and more bad publicity for the U.S. client increasingly characterized the U.S. intervention. U.S. planners fixed on Diem as the source of their military and political problems, refusing to believe that the most powerful nation on the planet could fail in its quest to put down the Vietnamese rebellion. In November 1963, a U.S.-approved coup overthrew and assassinated Diem. In the two years following Diem's overthrow, there followed no less than thirteen other coups d'état, as the United States desperately sought to find a formula that would allow it to continue its adventure. In August 1964, President Johnson decisively escalated the United States' stake in Vietnam. Johnson's administration falsely claimed that Vietnamese gunboats had attacked U.S. battle cruisers without provocation, and Johnson used this as the pretext for obtaining a congressional license for expanded war—the Gulf of Tonkin Resolution. Vietnam and the U.S. backing for a series of self-evidently brutal, corrupt, and selfish regimes definitively entered the mainstream of American consciousness.

More disturbing still, news of the character of the American intervention became available to those Americans who wanted to know it. The *New York Times*, for example, reported on the strategic hamlet program's forced relocations as early as March 1962:

> In this region, 1,200 families are to be moved voluntarily or forcibly from the forests controlled by the Vietcong and resettled in new strategic villages. The abandoned villages will be burnt.
>
> Some families had been allowed to carry away beds, tables and benches before their homes were burnt. Others had nothing but the clothes on their backs. A young woman stood expressionless as she recounted how the troops had burnt the family's two tons of rice.[6]

From 1962 forward, a variety of other hints surfaced in the public media pointing at what was quickly becoming a very dirty war. Reports of routine torture, the use of toxic chemical defoliation bombings in "Operation Ranch Hand," napalm bombings, the killings of numerous innocent civilians, and other brutalities came to the public's attention, albeit in small stories buried on the inside pages of newspapers and liberal journals.[7] As early as October 1963, the *Nation*, for example, reported that U.S. Lieutenant Colonel John Paul Vann had resigned his commission in protest over the indiscriminate bombings of Vietnamese villages. U.S. advisers, Vann testified, saw the damage wreaked by these bombings, "the dead women and children and the wounded children," and understood that this death and destruction was not helping what Vann took to be the American cause.[8]

Still, in November 1964 Americans in overwhelming numbers elected incumbent Lyndon Johnson president, rejecting what they perceived to be Republican presidential candidate Barry Goldwater's aggressive foreign policy stance. Johnson's campaign openly played on the fears that Goldwater would take the nation into thermonuclear war. On Vietnam, specifically, Goldwater had the more aggressive posture, too, arguing that the United States had been fighting the war with its hands tied behind its back and that it was time to take the restraints off. Consequently, even as Johnson wrested authority from Congress to escalate the Vietnam War and initiated the United States' first "retaliatory" bombing raids against northern Vietnam, he was able to portray himself as the peace candidate. SDS, clinging to its liberal roots, and still supportive of the concept of Johnson's War on Poverty, consequently promoted the slogan, "Part of the way with LBJ."[9]

Nevertheless, less than two months after Johnson's election, SDS, at its December 1964 national conference, scheduled the first national demonstration against the war for April 1965. In the few months between December and April, events in Vietnam focused still greater national attention on the conflict. In early February 1965, NLF troops attacked an American base at Pleiku, and Johnson responded with Operation Rolling Thunder, the United States' first systematic bombing of northern Vietnam.

Consequently, in April over 20,000 people descended on Washington, D.C., to protest the war. Following picketing at the White House, the demonstrators rallied at the Washington Monument. After the crowd had heard from Staughton Lynd, I. F. Stone, Senator Ernest Gruening, Joan Baez, and others, SDS president Paul Potter closed out the rally. Potter's speech showed how far SDS had come since the Port Huron Statement in its understanding of the world and the United States' place in it. Potter began his remarks with words that echoed those of the Port Huron Statement. "Most of us," Potter reminded his listeners, "grew up thinking that the United States was a strong but humble nation, that involved itself in world affairs only reluctantly, that respected the integrity of other nations and other systems, and that engaged in wars only as a last resort." But Potter would this day go well beyond the Port Huron Statement's simple juxtaposition of rhetoric and reality, and insist to his audience that Vietnam was not a mistaken policy, was not the product of poor—or even evil—leadership, but was something that flowed logically from the values and functioning of America's social system itself.

It was the United States' brutality in Vietnam, Potter maintained, that exposed this uncomfortable truth, that "finally severed the last vestige of illusion that morality and democracy are the guiding principles of American foreign policy." President Johnson, Secretary of State Dean Rusk, Secretary of Defense Robert McNamara, or any of their chief advisers, Potter continued, would no doubt "shrink in horror" if asked to napalm a small child. Yet "their decisions have led to [the] mutilation and death of thousands and thousands of people. What kind of system is it that allows good men to make those kinds of decisions? What kind of system is it," he asked,

> that justifies the United States . . . seizing the destinies of the Vietnamese people and using them callously for its own purpose? What kind of system is it that disenfranchises people in the [American] South, leaves millions upon millions of people throughout the country impoverished and excluded from the mainstream and promise of American society, that creates faceless and terrible bureaucracies and makes those the places where people spend their lives and do their work, that consistently puts material values before human values—and still persists in calling itself free and still persists in finding itself fit to police the world?

The Vietnam War, black oppression in the South, and the alienation that SDSers themselves faced and anticipated facing in the future—these were not disparate phenomena, but a system at work. "We must name that system," Potter argued. "We must name it, describe it, analyze it, understand it and change it. For it is only when that system is changed and brought under control that there can be any hope for stopping the forces that create a war in Vietnam today or a murder in the South tomorrow or all the incalculable innumerable more subtle atrocities that are worked on people all over—all the time."[10] Some of the demonstrators responded to Potter's call for a name by shouting out the words "capitalism" and "imperialism."[11] Potter himself steadfastly refused to pick up the cries, subsequently saying that the word "capitalism" was for himself and his "generation an inadequate description of the evils of America—a hollow, dead word tied to the thirties."[12] By rejecting use of the old names, Potter made a decision of immeasurable value for SDS, a decision that corresponded with what was then the dominant ethos in SDS. To have given a name to the system at this early stage might well have short-circuited the actual process of SDS's discovering the nature of the system for itself. As SDS's subsequent development would show, all too many activists were willing to settle for preconceived notions of capitalism and imperialism, and mechanically apply those notions to the American reality, rather than deriving them from that reality.

If Potter refused to give a name to the system he was describing, he did point to two of the most important implications of his analysis for his listeners: the system's ability to insulate from its gruesome realities even those activists opposing it; and what it would take from people to make real change.

What does it mean, Potter asked, "for each of us to say we want to end the war in Vietnam?" If those there that day accepted "the full meaning of [opposing the war] . . . and the gravity of the situation," could they, asked Potter, "simply leave the march and go back to the routines of a society that acts as if it were not in the middle of a grave crisis? Maybe we, like the President, are insulated from the consequences of our own decision to end the war. Maybe we have yet really to listen to the screams of a burning child and decide that we cannot go back to whatever it is we did before today until the war is ended." Here was a crucial element in developing an understanding of the United States as an empire. On the one hand, people in the empire's center could avoid thinking about, much less feeling, the full weight of the empire's violence. On the other hand, only by facing that violence, taking it into their souls, feeling it themselves, could people begin to take responsibility for stopping it.

Stopping or changing the system, Potter continued, involved far more than petitioning Congress, signing protest letters, or supporting "dissident Congressmen." It required building a "massive social movement." By "social movement," Potter meant an effort in which masses of people were "willing to change their lives, . . . willing to challenge the system, to take the problem seriously." More, it meant

> an effort . . . powerful enough to make the country understand that our problems are not in Vietnam, or China, or Brazil, or outer space, or at the bottom of the ocean, but are here in the United States. What we must do is begin to build a democratic and humane society in which Vietnams are unthinkable, in which human life and initiative are precious.
>
> That means that we build a movement that understands Vietnam in all its horror as but a symptom of a deeper malaise, that we build a movement that makes possible the implementation of the values that would have prevented Vietnam, a movement based on the integrity of man.

Potter again connected back to the Port Huron Statement, with its emphasis on human values, the preciousness of human life, and the call to build something better. But he had also gone considerably beyond that statement and beyond a liberal critique of Vietnam. Vietnam was not an aberration, but was consistent with how the system functioned. Moreover, the origins of that problem lay not in Vietnam, but in the United States' own internal life.

Albeit incompletely, Potter also acknowledged the black movement's significance to the antiwar movement. "The reason," Potter asserted, "there are twenty thousand people here today and not a hundred or none at all is because five years ago in the South students began to build a social movement to change the system." Certainly, this was true: the civil rights movement's practical activity had created a movement with which young whites had linked up. Indeed, that movement had broken the postwar McCarthy-era quiet imposed on political life in the United States. But, as would long be characteristic of SDS, Potter did not recognize that the black movement's potential for leadership over white youth went beyond practical activity—it involved intellectual leadership as well. SNCC, for example, even in its first few years, continually placed the black struggle in America in parallel with the anticolonial struggles of the day, particularly those in Africa, and it continually contrasted America's system of segregation to its claims to be leading the "free" world.[13]

If Potter's talk only began to look at the United States as an empire, subsequent developments in Washington and in Vietnam would push SDS to construct a far more developed understanding of the United States as an empire. Indeed, between the first national anti–Vietnam War march in April 1965 and the second, at the end of November 1965, the Johnson administration internally debated and then took the definitive step to limited war. U.S. troop strength jumped from 23,000 troops at the end of 1964 to close 200,000 by the end of 1965.[14] With this massive increase of troops also came increasing reports on the war's brutal character: entire villages leveled by aerial bombardments and artillery fire; troops firing straw-roofed huts with flame-throwers and cigarette lighters; and free-fire zones in which anyone who moved was subject to annihilation. In October 1965, for example, the *Progressive* reported on the nature of the war:

> The "no sanctuary" policy that is now being followed by United States and ARVN . . .
> forces means that air support can be called in instantly to destroy any village or hamlet
> from which sniper fire is reported or which is suspected of harboring Viet Cong troops.
> This policy is complemented by another which designates certain large enemy-held
> regions as "open target areas" where an aircraft unable to dispose of its explosives on the
> planned target may drop them at will on village, rice, paddy, man or beast, wherever it
> suits the pilot's fancy. . . .
> "I could take everything but the dead kids," [explained one American official who
> visited a village shortly after an American bombing]. . . . "As a matter of fact I found only
> two persons alive—a boy of ten and his eight-year-old sister. They were sitting quietly on
> the ruins of their house, surrounded by the bodies of their mother and father and several
> other children."[15]

The image of growing numbers of dead and orphaned children did not square well with the United States' claims to world benefaction. Moreover, shortly after SDS's April antiwar demonstration, the United States sent 20,000 troops into the Dominican Republic. Ostensibly, these troops were sent to "restore order." Not so surprisingly, the order they restored was one far more favorable to the United States than was the order that the Dominican Republic would have established absent the U.S. troops. Indeed, reports from Vietnam and the invasion of the Dominican Republic compelled SDS activists to undertake a wholesale reconsideration of the United States' Cold War narrative.

More than any other individual in SDS, Carl Oglesby, elected president of SDS in June 1965, led the New Left in this reconsideration. By SDS standards, Oglesby himself was an old man, being elected SDS president at the age of thirty. And indeed, the decade that separated him from most SDSers had tempered him and given him a self-confidence and a humility that were sorely needed in the brash youth organization. Oglesby, a husband and father of three children and an aspiring playwright, first came in contact with SDS in the summer of 1964. That summer, while working as a technical writer for Bendix Aerospace Systems and studying as a part-time graduate student at the University of Michigan, Ann Arbor, Oglesby had volunteered for the congressional campaign of a local Democrat, Wes Vivian. This was the summer of the Gulf of Tonkin, and Vivian asked his staff to come up with a position on Vietnam. Oglesby offered to write the statement. Although he self-consciously sought to avoid radical analyses of the crisis, a fellow Bendix employee recommended D. F. Fleming's revisionist history, *The Cold War and Its Origins, 1917–1960*, as a source book for the Vivian position paper. Fleming's take on the Cold War thus informed Oglesby's draft, which wound up calling for U.S. withdrawal and put Vietnam in the larger context of U.S. policy in Europe and Asia. Vivan rejected the paper. Oglesby then had it printed in Ann Arbor's literary journal, where local SDSers picked it up, recruited Oglesby, and reproduced the paper as SDS's first Vietnam pamphlet. Less than a year later, as the United States continued to escalate its war in Vietnam, SDS members elected Oglesby, the organization's most cogent voice on Vietnam, as their president.[16]

Through a series of speeches and through a widely circulated essay in his 1967 book, *Containment and Change*, Oglesby criticized many of the U.S.-propagated myths of the Cold War, popularized the era's history of U.S. covert interventions, highlighted the interconnections between the U.S. government and big business interests, and gave the system a meaningful name: first, corporate liberalism and then, imperialism. But this was an imperialism that Oglesby had worked to understand, that he had arrived at, and that he helped SDSers follow, layer by layer. It was an imperialism, therefore, that was not simply a name, but had real meaning attached to it.

Speaking at the second national antiwar demonstration in Washington, D.C., in November 1965, Oglesby offered SDS's first systematic treatment of the United States as an empire and of its history in the Cold War. Oglesby began his talk by noting that since the Vietnam War was "a very bad war," antiwar activists had acquired "the habit of thinking it must be caused by very bad men." But this, Oglesby argued, only led people away from the war's truth. True, the war was brutal; the industrial and military coalition behind it was "menacing"; and the demands for silence made upon people in the United States were "ominous." Nevertheless, these frightening phenomena were "creatures, all of them, of a Government that since 1932 has considered itself to be fundamentally liberal." Truman, Eisenhower, Kennedy—they were all liberals. And leading policy makers in the Johnson administration—McGeorge Bundy, Robert McNamara, Dean Rusk, Henry Cabot Lodge, Arthur Goldberg, and Johnson himself—were "not moral monsters. They are all honorable men. They are all liberals." Consequently, Oglesby argued, to understand the war, "it seems necessary to take a closer look at this American liberalism."

Ogelsby then listed half-a-dozen seeming contradictions in U.S. policy: the United States denounced "communist tyranny," while daily trafficking in commerce with "much more vicious right-wing tyrannies." It offered pious words about Rhodesia or South Africa's racial policies, but bought their chromium and financed their governments. It sent 200,000 men to Vietnam, but was unable to send 100 voter registrars to Mississippi. "Some will make of it that I overdraw the matter," continued Oglesby. "And others will make of it that I sound mighty anti-American. To these, I say: Don't blame me for that! Blame those who mouthed my liberal values and broke my American heart." And who was it, Oglesby asked, who broke his "American heart"? In answer, Oglesby invited his listeners to accompany him on a "brief factual inventory of the latter-day Cold War."

What followed would become a standard operating text for young New Leftists, the first popular recounting of a sordid history of intrigue and U.S. self-interest.[17]

1953: The United States organized the overthrow of Iran's Mohammed Mossadegh government. Mossadegh's crime? His neutralism and "his plans to nationalize the country's oil resources to improve his people's lives. Most evil aims, most evil man. In his place we put in General [Fazlollah] Zahedi, a World War II Nazi collaborator." And the upshot of this overthrow of the Iranian government by the Central Intelligence Agency (CIA)? An increased share of Iran's oil for U.S. firms, one of which was Gulf Oil, and a subsequent vice presidency at Gulf for the CIA man who engineered the coup.[18]

1954: The United States overthrew Guatemala's Jacobo Arbenz's government. His crime? Seeking to nationalize some of the United Fruit Company's land for an agrarian reform program. A year after the overthrow, the CIA's director joined United Fruit Company's board of directors.

1960: Fidel Castro charged the United States with planning an invasion of Cuba. The U.S. government ridiculed the charge as hysterical and paranoid, but in April 1961 the invasion occurred. "Comes with it the awful realization that the United States Government had lied."

1962: The Cuban Missile Crisis and the Kennedy administration's preparations "to fight global atomic war on the curious principle that another state does not have the right to its own foreign policy."

1963: The United States toppled British Guiana's nationalist government, "ensuring that the state will remain *British* Guiana, and that any workingman who wants a wage better than fifty cents a day is a dupe of Communism."

1964: Undersecretary of State Thomas Mann announced that the United States had abandoned the Alliance for Progress principle of no aid to tyrants. Two weeks later a right-wing coup overthrew João Goulart's nationalist government in Brazil. American gunboats sat in Rio de Janeiro's harbor, and the United States quickly recognized the new government.

"Comes 1965," said Oglesby, reaching his own time. And a momentous year it was:

> The Dominican Republic. Rebellion in the streets. We scurry to the spot with twenty thousand neutral Marines and our neutral peacemaker . . . [Organization of American States ambassador] Ellsworth Bunker. . . . Most of us know that our neutral marines fought openly on the side of the junta, a fact that the Administration still denies. But how many also know that what was at stake was our new Caribbean Sugar Bowl? That this same neutral Bunker is a board member and stock owner of the National Sugar Refining Company, a firm his father founded in the good old days, and one which has a major interest in maintaining the status quo in the Dominican Republic? Or that the President's close personal friend and advisor . . . Abe Fortas, has sat for the past 19 years on the board of the Sucrest Company, which imports blackstrap molasses from the Dominican Republic? Or that [leading State Department liberal] Adolf Berle, was chairman of that same board? Or that our roving ambassador Averill Harriman's brother Roland is on the board of National Sugar? Or that our former ambassador to the Dominican Republic, Joseph Farland, is a board member of the South Puerto Rico Sugar Co., which owns two hundred and seventy-five thousand acres of rich land in the Dominican Republic and is the largest employer on the island—at about one dollar a day?
>
> Neutralists! God save the hungry people of the world from such neutralists!

Oglesby had turned the United States' Cold War mythology on its head. If Potter, six months earlier, had asserted that neither democracy nor morality guided U.S. foreign policy, Oglesby had proven the point, beyond any shadow of a doubt. Behind the government's claims to leadership over the "Free World," Oglesby revealed naked self-interest and the closest interlocking—indeed, identity—of big business leaders and interests with government planners and the U.S. government—defined "national interest."

Oglesby then brought this history home: "We do not say these men are evil. We say, rather, that good men can be divided from their compassion by the institutional system that inherits us all. Generation in and out, we are put to use. People become instruments. Generals do not hear the screams of the bombed; sugar executives do not see the misery of the cane cutters: for to do so is to be that much less the general, that much less the executive." At once, this was both a generous critique and a devastating one, the more devastating for its generosity. Generous, because Oglesby did not condemn America's leaders for willfully destroying the lives of other peoples. Devastating, because he did condemn them for being the instruments of a system that did destroy those lives; devastating, because he did condemn them for putting the position they had in that system ahead of their own humanity: they chose being generals, or being executives, over hearing the screams and cries of their victims.

Moreover, like Potter, Oglesby argued that this system insulated not only the generals from the "screams of the bombed." On the contrary, all those "born to the colossus of history, our American corporate system," were affected. One single fact, Oglesby insisted, described this "colossus," this "American corporate system" and its implications for those born to it: "With about five per cent of the world's people, we consume about half the world's goods. We take a richness that is in good part not our own, and we put it in our pockets, our garages, our split-levels, our bellies, and our futures."[19] Oglesby had made one of the New Left's most important discoveries: empire paid. Moreover, empire shaped not only the United States' external life but its internal life as well. Potter had implied as much, but Oglesby demonstrated the mechanism by which the empire insulated the lives of ordinary Americans from the poverty and pain of the empire's victims, of the majority of people on the planet. The plunder of America's empire insinuated itself down into the daily lives of millions and tens of millions of ordinary people, into the food they ate, the cars they drove, the houses they lived in.[20]

Moreover, empire shaped the United States' spiritual life, its culture, its very identity, and the willingness of ordinary people to look the other way. "On the *face* of it," Oglesby continued,

> it is a crime that so few should have so much at the expense of so many. Where is the moral imagination so abused as to call this just?

Perhaps many of us feel a bit uneasy in our sleep. We are not, after all, a cruel people. And perhaps we don't really need this super dominance that deforms others. But what can we do? The investments are made. The financial ties are established. The plants abroad are built. Our system exists. One is swept up into it. How intolerable—to be born moral, but addicted to a stolen and maybe surplus luxury. Our goodness threatens to become counterfeit before our eyes—unless we change. But change threatens us with uncertainty. . . .

Our problem then, is to justify this system and give its theft another name—to make kind and moral what is neither, to perform some alchemy with language that will make this injustice seem a most magnanimous gift.

During the colonial era, Oglesby explained, the Western powers managed to find an answer to this problem: first, the "white man's burden," and second, the gift of modernization. But the colonized were not impressed by these gifts. And so the United States came up with a new solution to the problem: anti-Communism. And anti-Communism, if it did not serve the needs of the oppressed, served U.S. needs:

This was the bind: we cannot call revolution bad, because we started that way ourselves, and because it is all too easy to see why the dispossessed should rebel. So we will call revolution Communism. And we will reserve for ourselves the right to say what Communism means. We take note of revolution's enormities, wrenching them where necessary from their historical context and often exaggerating them, and say: Behold, Communism is a bloodbath. We take note of those reactionaries who stole the revolution, and say: Behold, Communism is a betrayal of the people. We take note of the revolution's need to consolidate itself, and say: Behold Communism is a tyranny.

It has been all these things and it will be all these things again, and we will never be at a loss for those tales of atrocity that comfort us so in our self-righteousness. . . . Indeed, revolution is a *fury*. For it is letting loose of outrages pent up sometimes over centuries. But the more brutal and longer-lasting the suppression of this energy, all the more ferocious will be its explosive release.

Here was a profound insight, steeped in a real—and thoroughly unromantic—appreciation of the history of revolutions. Those who sought to discredit revolution would always have more than enough raw material for the job. But America's hatred of revolution did not derive from any love of truth or humanity. Rather, that hatred was a defense of the world's patent inequities, a defense of America's enormous wealth and power coming at the expense of the many.

Having exploded the Cold War narrative and its appeal to ordinary Americans, Oglesby then challenged his audience. If his facts were wrong, then others could correct him. But if he was right, "then you may face a crisis of conscience. Corporatism or humanism: which?" If people chose, "in the name of simple human decency and democracy," to try and change the system, if their commitment to human values was unconditional, then they needed to disabuse themselves "of the notion that statements will bring change, if only the right statements can be written, or that interviews with the mighty will bring change if only the mighty can be reached, or that marches will bring change if only we can make them massive enough, or that policy proposals will bring change if only we can make them responsible enough."

What was needed now was a real movement for social change, the same kind of movement that Potter had called for six months earlier. "We are dealing now with a colossus that does not want to be changed. It will not change itself. It will not cooperate with those who want to change it. Those allies of ours in the Government—are they *really* our allies? If they *are*, then they don't need advice, they need *constituencies*; they don't need study groups, they need a *movement*. And if they are *not*, then all the more reason for building that movement with the most relentless conviction."[21]

It was a masterful speech, at once wide-ranging and ambitious in scope, yet humble in tone. Oglesby had laid out a worldview that would serve as the basis for SDS's understanding of Vietnam and of imperialism over the next four years.

During the next several months, as he toured SDS college chapters, speaking to them and working on his book, *Containment and Change*, Oglesby refined the picture he had laid out and more explicitly named the system imperialism. In his tour of eastern college campuses, Oglesby offered a stump speech that asked what would be wrong "with a Vietnam run by Ho Chi Minh, a Cuba by Castro, a Philippines by Taruc, a South Africa by Tabata, a Peru by del La Puente or Blanco?"

> The loss of $142 billion in foreign investments and a golden future, that's what's wrong. We of course explain it differently. We are abroad in the world with our 6000 military bases to combat tyranny. Not [Spain's fascist dictator] Franco's tyranny, not [Portugal's] Salazar's, or [the Dominican Republic's] Trujillo's or [South Africa's] Verwoerdt's or [Rhodesia's] Smith's or [Formosa's] Chiang's or [South Korea's] Park's or [South Vietnam's] Ky's or [Brazil's] Castello-Branco's—only, it just so happens, those socialist tyrannies that are trying to feed, clothe, house, and cure their people, and that do not easily see how those aims coincide with the aims of the United Fruit Company.

But, argued Oglesby, we can easily conceal from ourselves our own "imperialist motives." Underdeveloped countries needed capital, and they needed markets for their products. The United States had both. It seemed only accidental, having "nothing to do with this fair-minded giving and taking," Oglesby continued, that the people of the United States "consume over half the world's abundance. Meanwhile, one and a half billion people—less easy to convince of our benevolence—are learning a bit more every day about how it happens that the more outbound cargo ships they load with their bananas, the more tin and copper they sweat to bring up from their countries' mines, the poorer and sicker and the hungrier and the less free they become."

Oglesby then proceeded to analyze the main dangers that empire posed to the United States itself, listing three such dangers: the threat of nuclear war; the inevitability of violent revolution against an empire that foreclosed any other possibility of change; and the empire's internal face. It was this last danger, Oglesby averred, that was closest to his own life. "What," he asked, "does this national capacity for computerized slaughter make of us?" In the early years, people in the United States "were all safely insulated against the realities of this Viet-Nam war." But that had changed. Now, Oglesby contended,

> no semi-literate American with a television set can . . . be unaware of the effects of
> saturation bombing. I can understand the nation that chooses danger for itself in the
> name of an idea, even a bad one. But for the people that chooses death for others in the
> name of its own dubious views of history and its unquestioning self-righteousness, there
> begins to be only lamentation or exile left. How many of us have wondered what the
> decent Germans were doing when the Stukas raked Madrid and when the punctilious
> Eichmanns carried out the orders at Auschwitz? Or where the lovers of the common man
> were when the revolutionary hangman was teaching his socialism to the Kulaks? A great
> puzzle, one that begins to lose its distance.[22]

Here again, Oglesby made a powerful moral appeal to his listeners, demanding that they not turn away from the horror; that, unblinking, they take all of it in; that they see themselves as others and as history would see them, should they avert their gaze.

In *Containment and Change*, which appeared a year later, in early 1967, Oglesby returned, still more movingly, to this theme. He asked the reader to imagine an all-American youth, an "upright young man, square-shouldered with a heart full of bravery," now proudly a Green Beret. And sent off to Vietnam, not happy there, preferring to be at home, but committed to doing the job he has been sent to do, and doing it. "You need not," cautioned Oglesby, inform this lad "that his hands are bloody." Certainly, no one "knows better than the torturer himself what torture means. No one understands bombing better than the bomber, guns than the gunner, death than he who kills." "But the blood will wash away, will it not?" asked Oglesby.

The cleansing water is victory. The sacrifice is redeemed by the rebirth for which it prepares the conquered land. But if the water is not brought, that deferred innocence in whose name the present guilt is borne vanishes from the future. And what becomes of this strange savage blood? It fuses permanently with the skin of the hands that shed it.

We ought to be able to understand a very simple thing: From now on in America it shall be with such hands that children are soothed, office memoranda signed, cocktails stirred, friends greeted, poems written, love made, the Host laid on the tongue and wreaths on graves, the nose pinched in meditation. In the forthcoming gestures of these hands—this is really very simple—we shall behold an aspect of Vietnam's revenge.[23]

"Vietnam's revenge"—the brutality the United States visited upon Vietnam could not help but come home.

Containment and Change also dug still more deeply into the driving force of U.S. empire. As was Oglesby's wont, again and again he offered his arguments in the most paradoxical or dialectical forms he could devise. For example, containment, Oglesby advised, was "most basically a response to the fact that non-Western political cultures are for the first time threatening to contain *us*, to resist or restrict that long-term expansionary onslaught of the West upon the East which is the overarching theme of modern history."[24] Oglesby traced the United States' expansion from the time of its birth, popularizing historian William Appleman Williams's work on the significance of the "Open Door" to the broader New Left. Behind the Open Door policy, Oglesby explained, lay a consistent analysis articulated over and over again for more than half a century, a consistent understanding of the problems of the U.S. economy and the solution to those problems in the markets of the world. Said Senator Albert Beveridge in 1898: "To-day, we are raising more than we can consume, making more than we can use. Therefore we must find new markets for our produce." In 1907, five years before he was elected president, Woodrow Wilson suggested the same thing: "Since trade ignores national boundaries and the manufacturer insists on having the world as a market, the flag of his nation must follow him, and the doors of the nations which are closed must be battered down." Or again, in his 1912 presidential campaign: "Our industries have expanded to such a point that they will burst their jackets if they cannot find a free outlet to the markets of the world. . . . Our domestic markets no longer suffice. We need foreign markets." In 1914, Wilson's secretary of state and former leader of the Anti-Imperialist League, William Jennings Bryan, informed a meeting of the National Council of Foreign Trade "that it was America's official policy to 'open the doors of all the weaker countries to an invasion of American capital and enterprise.'" In the 1920s, Herbert Hoover articulated the same analysis, as did New Dealers in the 1930s. And in 1944, then assistant secretary of state Dean Acheson testified before Congress that

> we cannot go through another ten years like the ten years at the end of the twenties and the beginning of the thirties without having the most far-reaching consequences upon our economic and social system. . . . You don't have a problem of production. The United States has unlimited creative energy. The important thing is markets. . . .
>
> If you wish to control the entire life of the people, you could probably fix it so that everything produced here would be consumed here, but that would completely change our Constitution, our relations to property, human liberty, our very conceptions of law. And nobody contemplates that. Therefore, you find you must look to other markets and those markets are abroad.[25]

In short, American productive capacity had developed far beyond the capacity of America's domestic market to consume and now required the whole world as its market. The only alternative to this open world market, people like Acheson believed, was unemployment, social chaos, and revolution. The quest for markets, the concerns about overproduction, the fears about revolution, all, however, hid behind the ideology of the Cold War and falling dominoes.

But while this ideology had posited world peace on the basis of free and self-determining nations, Oglesby had demonstrated that America's actual goal was something different:

> The West wants a world that is integrated and (in Max Weber's sense) rationalized in terms of the stability of resources, labor, production, distribution, and markets. As the leader of the West, America wants that integrated, rationalized world to run under the management of her own business people. Others do not. They have acquired powers of resistance in the East. Therefore there is an East-West struggle, in our time called the Cold War. [26]

The Cold War was not principally about the Soviet Union, but was itself part of a larger, ongoing struggle for and against the West's expansion and domination over the rest of the globe.

Oglesby then proceeded to give a portrait of what he called America's "Free World Empire," delving extensively into how the United States dominated the Free World by laying out a number of case histories, including a particularly illuminating study of Brazil. From the time of the Great Depression, explained Oglesby, a more or less powerful Brazilian nationalism—expressing itself through political leaders of both the populist Left and the Right—dominated Brazilian politics and violated U.S. Open Door standards. For example, one conservative president, Janio Quadros, a man who violently had suppressed leftist demonstrations, viewed Brazil's poverty as a disgrace: Brazil was the world's leader in coffee exports, with "more arable land than all of Europe," 15 percent of the world's forests, and 35 percent of the world's iron ore deposits. How could its people be poor and the entire nation be backward? Quadros asked. All of Brazil's nationalists—of the Left and of the Right—answered Quadros's question in the same manner. Only by controlling its own resources could Brazil lift itself out of poverty and underdevelopment. But to do this, Brazil would have to control foreign access to Brazil's markets and resources. In short, Brazil would have to develop its economy in violation of America's Open Door principles. The United States signaled the end to this Brazilian nationalism, as Oglesby already had reported in his November 1965 antiwar speech, when it reversed the Alliance for Progress's policy on not aiding dictators and publicly announced that it would recognize and aid rulers who had come to power by nondemocratic means. There quickly followed a military coup against João Goulart's democratically elected government; Lyndon Johnson's and "America's warmest good wishes" to the *golpistas*; $400 million in new Alliance for Progress loans; and the renewal of World Bank loans to the country after a fourteen-year World Bank redlining of Brazil. In return, the new military government reversed years of Brazilian economic nationalism; squeezed Brazil's national oil company, Petrobras, out of oil refining and sales; and generally opened Brazil's economy to the unfettered access of foreign capital. To be sure, to guarantee these "reforms," the dictatorship also eliminated all the basic freedoms assured to Brazilians. [27]

After running through similar studies of South Africa, Paraguay, Jamaica, Venezuela, Ghana, and the Dominican Republic, Oglesby then discussed the material results of this Free World empire: declining terms of trade for the Third World—a continual drop in the prices paid to the Third World for the goods that it sold to the West and a continual increase in the prices it paid for the goods it imported from the West. Loans and the West's foreign investment in the Third World operated in the same direction. In short, the Third World fell ever farther behind the West and continually subsidized the world's developed economies. [28]

How could this possibly change? queried Oglesby. Certainly, American business would not change this relationship. For American business, the "Third World is that exposed, unprotected gold mine where . . . investment dollars fare better than anywhere else. . . . Why should it want to surrender its privileged position there, all in the name of some fuzzy humanitarian ideal? Or why should it rejoice to see the emergence of local capitalists who may some day get strong enough to give it some competition?" To raise these questions was already to provide the answer. The people who would change the world were those "whose battered lives stand most in need of change."[29] As he had done earlier, Oglesby again stressed that the empire, and the conditions of life it imposed on Third World peoples, generated resistance and created revolutions.

Having run through the consequences and the necessity for America's Free World empire, Oglesby then returned to Vietnam. The United States was fighting in Vietnam not for Vietnam's sake—certainly not for freedom, and not even for Vietnam's economic potential to the United States. The United States was fighting in Vietnam for its Free World empire. Immediately, Japan's fate stood at the center of the fight. As of the early 1960s, Japan had become the United States' second largest trading partner. But Japan's natural trading partners—the sources for its foodstuffs, its fuels, and its raw materials—were China and the Pacific region as a whole. Should Japan develop an "economic interdependency" with China, ultimately Japan would take up the position of junior partner, simply by the size of the two economies. It would thus cease to play the vital role it played for the United States, and all of Asia would devolve into a regional trading block independent of America's control. The only possibility for averting this calamity would be to hold the South Pacific, South Asia, and Southeast Asia as open trading partners for Japan. Moreover, South Vietnam, as a great producer of rice, was a potential trading partner for both Japan and China. Should South Vietnam fall, this would strengthen China and make Japan's ability to resist falling into the Chinese orbit all the more unlikely. The United States' purpose, then, argued Oglesby, was "to frustrate the drawing together of this geoeconomic system by imposing political and military barricades between its elements and by holding out the alternative of other economic configurations." Of course, Eisenhower had said much the same thing in 1954, in the days immediately preceding the fall of Dien Bien Phu. Indochina's loss, Eisenhower averred, "would take away that region that Japan must have as a trading area, or it would force Japan to turn toward China and Manchuria, or toward the Communist areas in order to live. The possible consequences of the loss [of Japan] to the free world are just incalculable."[30]

But, argued Oglesby, contemporary discussion of falling dominoes only amounted to a rehash of "orthodox imperialist ideology"; closer to home, it simply continued America's "frontier" ideology, rewritten for the mid-twentieth century. Conquering the "wilderness" now was called "developing the underdeveloped," or "modernization." And "defeating the Heathen (Pagan, Barbarian, Savage)" was called defeating the "Red Menace—same as the redskin, this Red, except more ferocious, wilder, more resistant and cunning."[31]

All of this left Americans with a choice. It was not, however, the choice offered by Cold War ideology—"between freedom and tyranny." It was more pressing, more urgent, more real than that. It was the choice between continuing empire's theft or "breaking it off. If we decide to continue the theft, Vietnamese-type wars will be as typical of our worsening future as they have been of our lamentable past."[32]

In the speeches he had made around the country in 1966, Oglesby had already begun to address this choice and the possibilities that Americans had for rejecting empire. True, citizens of other empires had failed in the task that Oglesby now laid before the American people. Nevertheless, Oglesby expressed a greater hope in the American people's ability to successfully comprehend the revolutions against the United States' empire and to reject that empire. This had nothing to do with innate abilities, however; rather, it was "because America, uniquely, has a third-world nation within herself: the community of American Negroes." It was through their intimate relationship to black life and struggle that white Americans could most readily appreciate the meaning of the American empire and the rebellion against it. "White Americans," Oglesby argued,

> have an unparalleled opportunity to learn first-hand about the origins of this turbulence that vexes us in the world. We can learn that revolution comes from the casting off of slavery, and that slavery comes from masters; that it is not the rebels who produce the troubles of the world, but those troubles that produce the rebels. . . .
>
> If we want to know why a man [will subject himself to the terror and brutality to which a rebel subjects himself] . . . we must ask why Mrs. Fanny Lou Hamer still struggles for human rights, after all the churches bombed, all the children murdered, all those lynched, all the night-riders and the horrifying midnight telephone calls. Is it because she is a fool? a dupe of some far-flung conspiracy?[33]

In his November 1965 speech in Washington, D.C., Oglesby had made the same point, only more succinctly: "Can we understand," he asked, "why the Negroes of Watts rebelled? Then why do we need a devil theory to explain the rebellion of the South Vietnamese? Can we understand the oppression in Mississippi, or the anguish that our Northern ghettoes make epidemic? Then why can't we see that our proper human struggle is not with Communism or revolutionaries, but with the social desperation that drives good men to violence, both here and abroad."[34]

Oglesby was at least partially correct: black people's struggle within the United States made the anti-imperialist revolution more comprehensible to ordinary white Americans. What, apparently, he did not appreciate at the time—and what SDS continued to grapple with—was that this intimate relationship to black people was a two-edged sword. White America had constructed the very system of racial subordination—the unique form of white domination over an internal black colony—that black Americans were now rebelling against. While the black rebellion placed the terms of that domination squarely before white America, it did not do more than that. It offered ordinary white Americans the potential to reject the nation's old social contract of empire; but, given an array of factors, including the New Left's strength and clear-sightedness, white Americans might just as easily seek to renew imperialism's old social contract. In the same way that proximity to anticolonial rebellion had hardened white colonists' stands in South Africa, or Rhodesia, or Algeria, so might it harden ordinary white Americans' defense of empire.

A second shortcoming marred Oglesby's analysis of the black rebellion and of the prospects for a mass movement of white anti-imperialists. Like Potter, Oglesby saw America's black rebellion as a material fact, as an environmentally defining leadership for white Americans, but he was unable to appreciate the radical intellectual leadership that had come out of the black struggle itself. Indeed, Oglesby's *Containment and Change*, certainly the New Left's most moving and influential book, relied not at all on the voices and intelligence of the black struggle in the United States. Most strikingly in this regard, Oglesby devoted an entire chapter to "The Revolted." "The Revolted" attempted to draw a portrait of what led people to revolution, unpeeling, layer by layer, the levels of consciousness and experience attained and transcended by those becoming revolutionaries, all the while highlighting the intense humanity of those in the throes of that process. And yet even as Oglesby was writing his book in 1966 and 1967, SNCC had been going through that very process, and Stokely Carmichael was criss-crossing the nation, speaking, writing, arguing, and debating the significance of the process. SNCC's trajectory to revolution, then, was the most immediate experience that white Americans could have of this process and of appreciating the full humanity of the revolutionaries. But Oglesby failed to draw on that experience as black people themselves were articulating it. Moreover, in his travels during that year, Carmichael was defining the nature of America's empire, including black people as victims of that empire and demanding that whites take up a role in opposition to the imperialism he was defining. Oglesby ignored this intellectual leadership and all the black theoretical leadership that had come before Carmichael. That intellectual leadership, however, had long since placed the black struggle inside the larger struggle over colonialism and empire. To be sure, Oglesby's inability to appreciate and seek out that intellectual and theoretical leadership was not his individual failing. It was a failing of the entire white New Left.[35]

What did this failure mean to the New Left, and where did it come from?

First, the New Left's failure to take black theoretical leadership seriously undermined SDS's ability to understand imperialism. W. E. B. DuBois and Malcolm X, especially, provided the intellectual framework that tied the oppression of blacks in the United States to America's colonial and imperial system. Thus, DuBois was the first to describe American imperialism realistically and in its totality. DuBois connected the colonial oppression of colored peoples around the world with the oppression of blacks in the United States. In July 1900, for example, he wrote the address "To the Nations of the World" for the first Pan-African Conference. In words that he would repeat three years later in the introduction to *Souls of Black Folk*, DuBois proclaimed that the "problem of the twentieth century is the problem of the colour line." On that problem, said DuBois, hinged the question of how far race would be allowed to serve as the "basis of denying to over half the world the right of sharing to their utmost ability the opportunities and privileges of modern civilisation." Moreover, DuBois explicitly linked European colonialism and American racism. In pointed paragraphs, "To the Nations of the World" demanded that British, Germans, French, and Belgians recognize the rights of their subjected African peoples. Between the paragraphs addressing British and German colonialism, however, DuBois tilted at the United States, demanding that "the conscience of a great nation rise and rebuke all dishonest and unrighteous oppression toward the American Negro."[36] Thus, if at the turn of the twentieth century DuBois did not yet explicitly call America's oppression of black people colonialism, he clearly placed that oppression in colonialism's context.

Over the next six decades, DuBois continued to publicly link colonialism and racism. In 1915, for example, less than a year after the outbreak of the First World War, DuBois was able to define colonialism as the root of the conflict. Colonialism itself, he argued, was simply the determination of the white nations—England, France, Germany, and the United States—to govern and exploit "Chinese, East Indians, Negroes, and South Americans."[37]

In 1935, in the midst of the Great Depression, DuBois summed up this viewpoint in his masterwork, *Black Reconstruction*. Wrote DuBois:

> That dark and vast sea of human labor in China and India, the South Seas and all Africa; in the West Indies and Central America and in the United States—that great majority of mankind, on whose bent and broken backs rest today the founding stones of modern industry—shares a common destiny; it is despised and rejected by race and color; paid a wage below the level of decent living; driven, beaten, prisoned and enslaved in all but name; spawning the world's raw material and luxury—cotton, wool, coffee, tea, cocoa, palm oil, fibers, spices, rubber, silks, lumber, copper, gold, diamonds, leather—how shall we end the list and where? All these are gathered up at prices lowest of the low, manufactured, transformed, and transported at fabulous gain; and the resultant wealth

is distributed and displayed and made the basis of world power and universal dominion and armed arrogance in London and Paris, Berlin and Rome, New York and Rio de Janeiro.

... Out of the dark proletariat comes the Surplus Value filched from human beasts which in cultured lands, the Machine and harnessed Power veil and conceal. The emancipation of man is the emancipation of labor and the emancipation of labor is the freeing of that basic majority of Workers who are yellow, brown and black.

Moreover, and of inestimable potential significance to SDS, DuBois explicitly outlined the domestic consequences of empire. The great scholar insisted that ordinary whites were not simply the passive recipients of a portion of this ill-gotten wealth, but were active agents in constructing a system of imperialism and colonialism. And it was precisely their complicity in constructing imperialism that constituted their oppression:

The plight of the white working class throughout the world today is directly traceable to Negro slavery in America, on which modern commerce and industry was founded, and which persisted to threaten free labor until it was partially overthrown in 1863. The resulting color caste founded and retained by capitalism was adopted, forwarded and approved by white labor, and resulted in the subordination of colored labor to white profits the world over. Thus the majority of the world's laborers, by the insistence of white labor, became the basis of a system of industry which ruined democracy and showed its perfect fruit in World War and Depression.[38]

SDS would continue to wrestle with the meaning of imperialism at home and finally approach DuBois's clarity only in the last year and a half of the organization's life.

If the McCarthy era had successfully suppressed DuBois and made awareness of his contribution and access to his works difficult for SDSers, no such excuse could be made for SDS's apparent ignorance of Malcolm X's thinking. Malcolm's autobiography and a first collection of some of his most important speeches both appeared in 1965 and offered clear articulations of his worldview. At the center of this worldview, Malcolm put his definition of American imperialism. Malcolm distinguished black people in the United States from other colonized peoples simply by the fact that blacks were colonized within the United States. Consequently, Malcolm insisted that black people in the United States view their struggle in the larger context of the world anticolonial revolution. Indeed, to make his point more emphatically, Malcolm again and again referred to the anticolonial upsurge of the 1950s and early 1960s as "the black revolution." In April 1964, for example, Malcolm argued that the black struggle in the United States was joining with "the world-wide black revolution that has been taking place on this earth since 1945." Explained Malcolm:

> Our brothers and sisters in Asia, who were colonized by the Europeans, our brothers and sisters in Africa, who were colonized by the Europeans, and in Latin America, the peasants, who were colonized by the Europeans, have been involved in a struggle since 1945 to get the colonialists, or the colonizing powers, the Europeans, off their land, out of their country. . . .
>
> America is a colonial power. She has colonized 22 million African-Americans by depriving us of first-class citizenship, by depriving us of civil rights, actually by depriving us of human rights.[39]

Although Oglesby's analysis of America's empire was important, it lacked Malcolm's forcefulness and clarity. Oglesby had referred to blacks in the United States as a Third World nation, but his had been a glancing reference, made as a convenience for whites understanding the anti-imperialist struggle. However, if the black struggle was the means by which whites might better apprehend the notion of an American empire, then it was all the more important that Oglesby develop the understanding of a black colony in the United States. In order to do that, he needed to lean on Malcolm and other black thinkers.

Moreover, Malcolm understood more completely the consequences that flowed from the fact that whites understood imperialism through their understanding of black people. In an address Malcolm made to the July 1964 meeting of the Organization of African Unity, he squarely placed this problem before the African heads of state: "Your problems will never be fully solved until and unless ours are solved. You will never be fully respected until and unless we are also respected. You will never be recognized as free human beings until and unless we are also recognized and treated as human beings."[40] So long as whites could look upon blacks in the United States as inferiors, so long would the United States continue to be an imperialist power. Third World peoples could not escape the United States' imperial aspirations as long as whites looked at Third World peoples through the prism of white Americans' experience with blacks in the United States—this was Malcolm's message.

Six months later Malcolm reiterated the same point to an audience in Harlem, only in greater detail and emphasizing Africa's significance to the West. Indeed, Malcolm's explanation showed just how closely he followed the thinking of America's foreign policy planners. If the Congo, Malcolm speculated, were to fall out of the colonialist orbit, then it would only be a matter of time before Southern Rhodesia,

Southwest Africa, and South Africa would follow suit. But if these countries liberated themselves, "it would mean that the source of raw material, natural resources, some of the richest mineral deposits on earth, would then be taken away from the European economy." And without ready access to this vast wealth, Europe's economy would founder. Moreover, given the critical commercial relationships between the United States and Europe, if the European economy sank, "it would really wash away the American economy." Malcolm then admonished his domestic audience:

> I say this because it is necessary for you and me to understand what is at stake. You can't understand what is going on in Mississippi if you don't understand what is going on in the Congo. And you can't really be interested in what's going on in Mississippi if you're not also interested in what's going on in the Congo. They're both the same. The same interests are at stake. The same sides are drawn up, the same schemes are at work in the Congo that are at work in Mississippi. The same stake—no difference whatsoever.[41]

Malcolm had gone to the rational core of the domino theory, something that SDS would not do so clearly until almost two years later.[42]

SDS's inability to appreciate the black movement's intellectual and theoretical leadership thus undercut the New Left in two ways. First, in the hands of DuBois and Malcolm, imperialism was a totality. It shaped and was inseparable from America's domestic life—its racial ideology and its economic mainsprings—and it could be lopped off only at the expense of the entire system of private profit. To miss this black understanding of imperialism divorced SDS from analyses of imperialism that were far older and more deeply rooted than its own thinking. Second, Potter's and Ogelsby's inability to more seriously examine DuBois's and Malcolm's take on imperialism revealed an ongoing New Left failure that made achieving the New Left's highest aspirations more difficult. No matter how important were the struggles of nonwhite peoples to white people's ability to appreciate the real nature of their nation and their social system, the New Left—even its best, most brilliant, and most humble theoreticians—continued to see theory and intellectual constructions as a province of white people, continued to discount the all-important theoretical work that guided black and other anticolonial struggles. Imperialism's division of labor—reserving mental labor for whites—continued in SDS, continued in the New Left's very best leaders, even as SDS sought to comprehend and oppose imperialism.

The New Left's inability to appreciate and champion DuBois, Malcolm, and other anticolonial theoreticians seriously undermined its efforts at understanding imperialism and acting effectively against it. Nowhere was this clearer than in SDS's attempts at a class analysis of U.S. society. Indeed, SDS's earliest attempts at this might just as easily have been written in Marx's time as in the 1960s, so little did they take America's racial and imperial realities into account.

SDSers Kim Moody, Fred Eppsteiner, and Mike Flug offered an early exercise in a class analysis divorced from the American empire's social, economic, and political realities in their position paper, "Toward the Working Class." To be sure, at a time when the black movement had told white activists to organize whites, "Toward the Working Class" sought to push SDSers into white working-class organizing. Nevertheless, the three men offered arguments wholly based on abstract "truths," rather than social realities. "To begin with," they wrote, "the socialist view of the working class as a potentially revolutionary force is based upon an analysis of the social position of the working class." The working class, the three argued, was "at the heart of modern capitalism's . . . defining . . . institution, industry." With nary a blink of the eye, "Toward the Working Class" thus extracted the United States from its international position. For these SDSers, "modern capitalism" was the same capitalism that Marx had written of a century earlier. The massive integration of the Third World labor into American production—concentrating half the world's wealth in the hands of one-twentieth of its population, as Oglesby described it—had simply disappeared. Having disposed of the empire, "Toward the Working Class" could then insist that the "working class" was the indispensable element in any attempts at revolutionizing American society.

By way of example, Moody, Eppsteiner, and Flug contrasted the struggle of welfare recipients with the struggle of what they called the working class. If welfare recipients struggled for an improvement of their situation, they argued,

> in the end they have only helped about 8 million people. The point is not that welfare recipients or Negroes should not struggle, they should and must; the point is that the working class has a uniquely strategic position in American society—they are at the root of the economy. They are at the root of the same economy that causes poverty and creates welfare institutions. The working class is not the only group that must struggle to revolutionize American society, but it is a group that cannot be left out of this struggle.[43]

Of course, in mid-1966 welfare recipients and black people were struggling, fiercely, to change the very nature of American society. Unfortunately, "Toward the Working Class" was unable to recognize that this struggle was a working-class struggle. At the same time, the "working class"—and Moody, Eppsteiner, and Flug apparently were speaking of the white working class, since they classed black people in a different category—was carrying out no such struggle, no matter how stridently its role was declared as being essential to the class struggle.

If the authors of "Toward the Working Class" simply were imposing Marxist categories on American society, other SDSers more characteristically were attempting to join analyses of imperialism and class structure, albeit a tad mechanistically, by simply adding an analysis of imperialism to a class analysis. In May 1967, for example, SDSers Robert Gottlieb, Gerry Tenney, and David Gilbert produced a lengthy position paper, "Toward a Theory of Social Change in America." Unlike "Toward the Working Class," their paper offered a great deal of empirical data to help describe American society and a good deal of analysis concerning the United States' economic relationship to the Third World. "Toward a Theory" had clearly grasped that the relationship between the United States and the Third World was one of necessity: on the one hand, real development for Third World nations, hence, a real rise in the standard of living in these nations, could never occur so long as the United States exercised decisive control over the Third World economies. On the other hand, the United States' continued ability to control Third World wealth was the sine qua non of the nation's own economic stability. "Given this conflict of interest," Gottlieb, Tenney, and Gilbert argued, Third World nations could only improve the conditions for their people through revolution; since loss of control over Third World economies threatened the United States' economic stability, the United States was obliged to oppose revolution wherever it developed. This was an important understanding, but unless it could be integrated into an analysis of U.S. domestic social structure, it remained of little utility.

Moreover, "Toward a Theory" also provided a glimpse of some of the domestic consequences of America's extreme concentration of wealth. Wrote the authors:

> This richest country on earth has six tons T.N.T. equivalent deliverable nuclear explosive power for every person on earth; it can "afford" the war in Vietnam; it spends $15 billion a year on advertising and employs countless other techniques to absorb the surplus. But basic human needs are not met. If we could calculate the death and injury caused by inadequate medical care and research; air pollution and cigarettes; substandard housing and food; lack of needed safety devices, especially on automobiles; and socially produced violence, we might find that a large percentage of present deaths and injuries are socially unnecessary. Thus American capitalism, which has stabilized itself at the expense of the impoverishment of the Third World, proves even domestically to be a violent system.

Certainly, this was true. But imperialism's key characteristic, as Oglesby—and before him Malcolm and DuBois—had argued, was that however unequally it was distributed, imperialism's plunder did make its way to broad layers of America's white population.

Having failed to make this connection, "Toward a Theory" was unable to extend its analysis of imperialism into the ideological or structural character of domestic U.S. society. Race and racism, for example, played no significant part in the article's analysis, a stunning failure for an essay purporting to develop a theory of social change for the United States. Instead, the article simply retread the Marxist categories of alienation and class, adding the nuance of what the authors called "the new working class." Tenney, Gottlieb, and Gilbert offered a traditional Marxist criterion for distinguishing class: "The two *generalized* classes are those that perform the work necessary for economic growth and social development and those that control such growth and development. Class can be defined as the social relations of control or non-control over production as well as over the quality of one's life." While on a general theoretical level there was little to dispute in this definition, the authors simply assumed that questions of "control or non-control over production" were juridical in nature, with answers to be determined by stock ownership certificates or seats on a given corporate board of directors. Making control a juridical matter, however, greatly simplified the task of class analysis. Most white people in the United States did not own stock or sit on a corporate board of directors; hence, they did not control the means of production and consequently were workers. Forgotten, or unknown to the authors, were two of DuBois's key insights: that the labor of people of color the world over had been subordinated—working at wages "below the level of decent living," producing the great wealth of the world—at white labor's insistence; and that in the imperial centers—"cultured lands"—"the Machine and harnessed Power veil[ed] and conceal[ed]" that great theft of wealth. Forgotten, too, was the most immediate manifestation of white labor's insistence that the labor of people of color be subordinated to it: white labor's upholding of a segregated workforce, of segregated unions, of a racial division of labor that ebbed and flowed across job categories in accord with the state of the economy. This was clearly a form of control in which white labor placed itself in a different relationship to the overall domestic and world economies than the relationship suffered by the labor of people of color.

Having established its juridical understanding of class, "Toward a Theory" then identified "four main classes" in the United States: "a ruling class, a petty bourgeoisie, a working class (which can be broken down into three main sectors: new working class, middle sector, and traditional working class), and finally the poor or underclass." Conceivably, imperialism might have intruded upon Marxist categories in the paper's discussion of the "new working class." Instead, the paper offered its "new working class" theory as a mechanism for emphasizing the importance, indeed, the centrality to capitalist production, of people very much like the authors of "Toward a Theory." Argued the authors: modern production can do "without the traditional industrial worker," but it cannot do without the highly skilled or technical worker.

Neither can it do without the millions of teachers necessary for training this technical workforce. And these two sectors, the technical workers and those who train that workforce, make up the "new working class."[44] Perhaps the authors saw some connection between imperialism and this "new working class," but if they did see it, they failed to articulate the connection.

In point of fact, the authors were wrong in asserting that modern production could do "without the traditional industrial worker." "Toward a Theory" posited this notion not only because it gave added legitimacy to the struggles of intellectual workers, students, and teachers but also because the paper's authors correctly saw the beginnings of a tendency affecting domestic capitalist production and made that tendency into a universal of capitalist production. Even in the mid-1960s, the beginnings of runaway shops and the Rust Belt were becoming evident. But the transition to a "postindustrial" or service economy in the United States was not a universal of capitalist production, but was very specific to the creation of a new imperialist division of labor. In fact, at least since the British Empire's emergence, imperial nations had always sought to concentrate the highest forms of technology at home, while farming out the more labor-intensive technologies to the imperial peripheries. Consequently, new technologies constantly transformed the specific imperial division of labor. The fact that heavy industry was beginning to leave the United States did not signify an end to the indispensability of industrial workers. By putting that interpretation on the changing division of labor, however, Gottlieb, Tenney, and Gilbert were divorcing the United States' domestic economy from its international economy. Imperialism, in this vision, existed outside the U.S. borders; inside those borders, apparently, capitalism was developing in its pure form.

In November 1965, Oglesby had quite correctly pointed out that empire's wealth was shared at home and made part of the daily life of ordinary Americans. And yet a year and a half later "Toward a Theory" was still unable to comprehend how empire shaped domestic life in the United States. For the remaining years of their organization, SDSers would continue to grapple with this problem, struggling to comprehend imperialism's domestic face, its impact on the structure of American society, on its culture, on its ideology, and on the character of the oppression confronting ordinary white Americans.

Whatever the difficulties SDSers had with integrating an understanding of imperialism with their understanding of the United States' domestic social structure and ideology, the United States' escalating assault on Vietnam through 1966 and 1967 compelled New Leftists to go still deeper into Vietnam's meaning. The United States escalated the war on every front. At the beginning of 1966, the United States had just under 200,000 troops in Vietnam. Less than eighteen months later this number had more than doubled, to 450,000 troops, and by the end of 1967 the United States had 500,000 troops in Vietnam. In 1966, the United States tripled the number of bombing sorties against North Vietnam over the previous year. U.S. bombers dropped 136,000 tons of bombs in 1966—more than double the previous year—and 226,000 tons of bombs in 1967. In South Vietnam itself, U.S. bombing steadily escalated from 1966 through 1967, U.S. bombers dropping more than one million tons of bombs on the South during these two years.[45] Beginning in 1965, the United States intensified its Operation Ranch Hand, and began pouring the first of nineteen million gallons of the carcinogenic Agent Orange on South Vietnam's tropical rain forests, defoliating one-third of southern Vietnam in the process.[46] U.S. ground assaults during the period were also increasingly vicious. One account of the United States' major 1967 dry season military offensive, Operation Cedar Falls, for example, gives a sense of the scope and brutality of the southern campaign, despite the antiseptic language it uses:

> After B-52s saturated the area, American forces surrounded it, and helicopters dropped large numbers of specially trained combat troops into the villages. Following removal of the population, giant Rome plows with huge spikes on the front leveled the area, destroying what remained of the vegetation and leaving the guerrillas no place to hide. The region was then burned and bombed again to destroy the miles of underground tunnels dug by the insurgents.[47]

This steady and brutal escalation could not help but focus the world's attention on Vietnam and on what Vietnam said about the United States and the world. In Stockholm, Sweden, for example, the English philosopher and mathematician Bertrand Russell, together with the French existentialist philosopher and author Jean Paul Sartre, organized an International War Crimes Tribunal to examine whether the United States had violated international law in its war against Vietnam. In his "Appeal to the American Conscience," which SDS republished in mid-1966, Russell rehearsed the United States' use of poisonous chemicals, gases, napalm, and phosphorous against Vietnam. He also detailed more mundane, but no less deadly, conventional weapons, like the antipersonnel "Lazy Dog" bomb, each bomb containing 10,000 razor-sharp steel darts. Russell insisted that there was "no pretending that the war crimes are not occurring, that the gas and the chemicals do not exist, that the torture and napalm have not been used, that the Vietnamese have not been slaughtered by American soldiers and American bombs." Americans, Russell maintained, could have "no dignity without the courage to examine this evil and oppose it."

Moreover, Russell argued, who were the people who sought to impose their vision on Vietnam, and on the world? Despite the United States' "immense wealth," despite its control "over the world's oil, cobalt, tungsten, iron ore, rubber and other vital resources," despite the billions in profits that its largest corporations took at the expense of the starvation of millions across the planet, tens of millions of people still lived in poverty in the United States itself; the United States' urban areas were "covered in slums"; and the poor carried "the burden of taxation and the fighting of colonial and aggressive wars." What, then, gave the United States the right to presume that it could rule the world? Russell asked people in the United States to

> make an intellectual connection between events which occur daily around you, to try to see clearly the system which has taken control of the United States and perverted its institutional life into a grotesque arsenal for a world empire. It is the vast military machine, the great industrial combines and their intelligence agencies which are regarded by the people of three whole continents as their main enemy in life and the source of their misery and hunger.[48]

Carl Oglesby attended the International War Crimes Tribunal and reported back to SDS with still more information and analysis on what the United States was doing in Vietnam. First, the tribunal reconfirmed the barbaric nature of the United States' war in Vietnam. Oglesby reported that evidence had been presented showing that every provincial hospital and many district hospitals in northern Vietnam had been leveled by U.S. bombings. Moreover, the United States was extensively cluster-bombing Vietnam. Military experts testified at the tribunal that these cluster bombs served no military purpose whatsoever: made up of thousands of small, ball bearing–type objects, the cluster bombs were incapable of destroying or damaging any kind of military installation protected by the most primitive methods. The cluster bombs had one use: killing and maiming people.

But to what end? Oglesby insisted that the United States' choice of weapons and targets was no accident or oversight. On the contrary, Oglesby came back from Stockholm convinced that U.S. war planners understood northern Vietnam as a "complex social organism," and attacked it in a "premeditated, precise and politically structured" manner, using "detailed economic, cultural, political and sociological 'maps'" of the country. U.S. military textbooks, introduced at the tribunal, noted four "components of national structure" to attack: a nation's military, economic, political, and "psychosocial" structures. Oglesby focused his discussion on the psychosocial structure, a nation's "morale." Destroying a nation's morale, asserted one textbook, *Fundamentals of Aerospace Weapons Systems*, was a key element in overcoming an enemy. Indeed, *Fundamentals* posited the notion that the single greatest blow to a nation's morale would be the "destruction of an enemy's major cities with high-yield nuclear weapons." Short of that, however, *Fundamentals* spelled out the United States' historical experience in breaking morale:

> Some of the conventional targets for morale attacks have been water supplies, food supplies, housing areas, transportation centers, and industrial sites. The objectives of these attacks in the past have been to dispel the people's belief in the invincibility of their forces, to create unrest, to reduce the output of the labor force, to cause strikes, sabotage, riots, fear, panic, hunger, and passive resistance to the government, and to create a general feeling that the war should be terminated.

Oglesby then sought to address the concerns of those Americans who continued to "anxiously cling" to the notion that the United States would not willfully destroy "hospitals, churches, schools and people," and that if such destruction occurred, it was accidental. It was clear that, by the United States' own official military doctrine, such destruction was "possible, plausible, and indeed . . . probable."

Given United States' objectives in the war, it could be no other way, argued Oglesby. A "historical gulf" separated "master and slave, empires and colonies." Once the oppressed questioned the oppressor's moral legitimacy, the oppressor's only recourse was violence. "For America even to dream of victory in Vietnam," Oglesby concluded, "it must destroy the revolutionary society. The enemy is the revolution, the breaking of the empire, and it is in the liberated people that the revolution has its being. To say that America commits war crimes in Vietnam is merely to elaborate legalistically the simpler fact that America is fighting in Vietnam. From the decision to fight that fight, the necessity of war crimes follows irresistibly."[49] From the war's unceasing, escalating brutality, from the ever more frequent images of napalm-scarred children and burned villages and homes, Oglesby had worked backward to ascertain the war's objectives and character. Brutality unmasked empire.

Other New Leftists would more and more frequently come to this same conclusion, particularly as they came in contact with Vietnamese revolutionaries. For their part, the Vietnamese seemed to have set their hopes on communicating three essential points in their meetings with American New Leftists. The first two points centered precisely on unmasking empire. First, invariably they sought to convey an accurate sense of the military situation in Vietnam. By highlighting what seemed incomprehensible—the world's most powerful nation bogged down in, and losing a war to, a small, technologically backward people—they sought to convey a second point: the overall character of the war, the war as a contest over empire. Finally, as they reiterated time and again, the Vietnamese stressed the need for greater unity in the antiwar movement, for more visible large-scale actions, and for more public education on the nature of the war. And although they probably had not intended to, the Vietnamese also conveyed a fourth point to their North American counterparts: a different sense of self-identity, of self-worth, of humanity, very strange and desirable and revealing to the eye and the ear and the temperament of young people raised in a society that ruled the world.

Although direct contact between SDS and the Vietnamese dated at least as far back as 1965 when SDS founder Tom Hayden traveled to Hanoi with Staughton Lynd and American Communist Party leader Herbert Aptheker, it was only in 1967 that contacts became somewhat regular. Starting in July, SDSers met at least four times in nine months with representatives of South Vietnam's NLF and North Vietnam's government: first, international youth festival delegates from Vietnam and the United States got together in Moscow in July; second, a large delegation of U.S. antiwar leaders met with the Vietnamese at a weeklong gathering in September in Bratislava, Czechoslovakia, specifically called for that purpose; third, in December a small delegation of SDSers met with the Vietnamese in Cambodia; and fourth, in April 1968 antiwar activists met with Vietnamese representatives at an antiwar meeting in Stockholm.

In these four meetings, the Vietnamese apparently went out of their way to convey to the New Leftists that the United States was failing militarily in Vietnam. For example, the NLF's delegation head to Moscow's international youth festival, Ngo Quy Du, emphasized that "all the [United States'] principal military campaigns ... had been failures." According to Jeff Shero, an SDS attendee at the festival, Du named a number of the campaigns and strategies and suggested that even in America's own press, the conscientious reader could discern the failure. A successful engagement might be reported in the American press, Du argued, but then a month or two later the press would report "another successful battle under another operational name in the same territory." Apparently, despite the United States' repeated "successes," it had to do the same job over and over again.[50] Cathy Wilkerson, following her meeting with the Vietnamese in Cambodia, insisted "above all" that New Leftists had to more thoroughly understand "the details of the war in Vietnam and the situation in all of Southeast Asia" if they wanted to "understand more precisely the nature of American imperialism and the most effective means to combat it."[51]

Indeed, two weeks before the 1968 Tet Offensive, at a time when U.S. military and political leaders were still taking in America's people with their claims that the NLF was finished, Wilkerson reported back to SDS that "no one can win the war in Vietnam except the Vietnamese, and they have won the war in many ways already." Wilkerson then substantiated her assertion with one of the most detailed accounts of the war SDSers had heard. Southern Vietnam, she reported, had two seasons during the year, a dry season from October to March and a wet season for the remainder of the year. Clouds, rain, and mud hindered U.S. helicopters, bogged down armored vehicles and troops, and slowed or prevented air support during operations. And it was precisely on these technological and material advantages that Washington based its strategy. Consequently, the United States looked to the dry season as the time during which it could maximize its military advantage and carry the war to the NLF forces. Since the United States had opted for "local war" in 1965, it had organized three dry season offensives. In the first of these offensives, the dry season of 1965–66, the United States initiated offensives in all four of the military zones into which the United States divided South Vietnam. Despite massive troop deployments—U.S. troops, South Vietnamese (or Army of the Republic of Vietnam [ARVN]) troops, and the troops of U.S. allies—despite massive aerial bombardments, and despite the burning and plowing over of entire villages, this first dry season offensive failed to engage the enemy; on the contrary, the NLF consistently succeeded in engaging U.S. forces at the times and places of its own choosing. What the United States assumed would be a walkover in fact accomplished little militarily, other than frustrating the U.S. command structure and wounding and killing a growing number of American, allied, and ARVN troops. During the next dry season offensive, 1966–67, the United States attempted offensive operations in only one of the four military zones; in the other three zones, U.S. forces found themselves on the defensive, unable to mount any significant offensive. By the 1967–68 dry season, the United States was unable to mount any offensives in any of South Vietnam's military zones. In contrast, NLF forces were on the offensive in all the zones, Wilkerson reported.[52]

What did this failure mean? What did it represent? Here was the second point the Vietnamese sought to convey: the political implications of the military situation. On the one hand, the brutality of a war that the United States claimed was being fought for the benefit of Vietnam's people enlightened ever greater numbers of U.S. troops, said Wilkerson. U.S. propaganda efforts were losing their credibility, and U.S. troops were revolting against their leadership more and more frequently. On a larger scale, it was clear, Wilkerson argued, that

the United States cannot continue with its current strategy of "localized war." ... The only other direction in which they can intensify their military efforts is the development of new kinds of weapons, such as the high intensity heat bombs that are able to reach even the deepest tunnels and shelters and immediately bake all within them. In this way, with the continued defense budget increases providing for weapons, the United States could in fact completely destroy the entire country. However there are also certain restraints, such as world opinion, that could serve to curtail this sort of expansion.

On the other hand, the Vietnamese were struggling for independence, and that desire grew out of a long history. Each and every Vietnamese fighter "has himself, or among his family and friends suffered very deeply at the hands of foreign imperialists," Wilkerson affirmed; "each has experienced the deep anger which becomes determination, each has understood the vision of an independent country which sustains the struggle."[53]

In short, the United States was losing in Vietnam because the war it waged was an unjust war and because it was fighting a people who, since 1940, unrelentingly had fought and learned to fight for their rights. This was a prime lesson the Vietnamese sought to convey to New Leftists and, through them, to the larger American society.

Steve Halliwell, a Columbia SDSer who attended the Bratislava meeting, drew the same lesson from his discussions with the Vietnamese. "The incredible brutality" of America's war revealed both the failure and the underpinnings of that war. Said Halliwell:

> Since the military is faced with a society in revolt, all it can do is go out and shoot some of the people or better yet (safer) bomb them to death from planes. If women and children from 15 years of age are carrying guns, then women and children must be killed. And since the only possible "victory" for the American government would come from a winning-over of the populace, the greater and greater brutality of the military indicates how badly the American effort is failing.

Halliwell took back from Bratislava the same understanding that Oglesby had gained at the International War Crimes Tribunal and Wilkerson had learned in Cambodia: "Against a society demanding freedom and independence from an imperialist force, there is no weapon save destruction of every individual in revolt that will bring about any end other than victory for the liberation forces."

The Vietnamese, according to Halliwell, also saw that the United States' intensifying brutality was itself certain evidence of "how badly the American effort is failing." Indeed, only by winning over the population could the United States really prevent Vietnam's domino from falling; that the United States was resorting to increasingly barbaric methods indicated that it was growing ever more frustrated in its efforts.[54]

While the Vietnamese were extremely cautious in their efforts at providing guidance to New Leftists, their emphasis, as reflected in the reports that issued from virtually every meeting, leaves little doubt about what they were seeking from SDS and the antiwar movement. First, of course, they wanted SDSers to broadly disseminate the

Vietnamese perspective on the war—on its character, on the balance of forces between the two sides, and on the war's political implications. Second, the Vietnamese were knowledgeable about the state of the antiwar movement in the United States and pressed SDSers on ways of more effectively uniting the movement and creating larger, more visible demonstrations. Sue Munaker, a Chicago SDSer and early radical women's liberationist, reported back from the Stockholm conference that the "first question" raised by the Vietnamese to the U.S. delegation "revealed their concern with the fragmentation of our movement." According to Munaker, the Vietnamese specifically requested that the U.S. delegates discuss with them "the possibility of strengthening cooperation" within the U.S. antiwar movement.[55] Similarly, Cathy Wilkerson revealed that although the Vietnamese with whom she met had not made any specific recommendations to the SDS delegation, nevertheless they were "all enthusiastic about large actions which receive a lot of international publicity, such as Oct. 21 [the Pentagon demonstration] and [Oakland/Berkeley's] Stop the Draft Week."[56] This was particularly telling in that Wilkerson was part of SDS's National Office staff at the time, and the National Office had, for some time past, been less than "enthusiastic" about involving SDS in large-scale protests. At Bratislava, apparently, the Vietnamese delegation tactfully suggested a coordinated national student strike against the war. SDS, however, rejected this suggestion.[57]

Probably without intending it, the Vietnamese also conveyed something else in their meetings with those in the antiwar movement: a sense of self, a dignity, a humanity, a humility so different from the sense of self cultivated by a society that consumed half the world's wealth. Munaker, for example, maintained that her "outstanding impression" of the Vietnamese was "one of warmth, sincerity, and bravery." Although Munaker saw "camaraderie and sacrifice" as characteristic of people in the antiwar movement, her "meeting with the Vietnamese revealed to me how far we have to go. Every crisis throws us into a fervor; we've not learned to live with death, to accept its inevitability as part of our work."[58]

Halliwell went so far as to suggest that the U.S. antiwar delegation might entirely fail to convey the information and insights they had garnered at Bratislava unless they communicated "the feeling that emerged in the conference." What had been of "crucial importance" to the U.S. delegation's understanding, Halliwell averred, had been "the manner of the people from both North and South who presented that information ... for their manner is that of men and women struggling in a society in revolution." Informed, for example, that the Vietnamese saw the United States' intensified bombing campaigns, with all their attendant destruction, as a sign of U.S. weakness, as something to take heart in, members of the U.S. delegation responded with disbelief. Could real people possibly respond in this manner? Halliwell sought to understand his own incredulity. "We don't believe," Halliwell suggested, that such people are possible,

> because we don't believe in ourselves. We can't believe in their triumphs against the man's machine of war because somewhere inside us we still believe in the power of the man.... We have yet to develop in ourselves the confidence that is so evident in the Vietnamese. We realize that our society is not a stable one—there are fissures deep into the system that only deepen as the war continues and national politics grows more hypocritical and banal. And yet we have not learned how to move with confidence in that society. We believe that every room is bugged, every phone tapped, not as a principle of security, but because we believe in the power of the police, the stability and the efficiency of the powers of the state.

Because they lacked this confidence, this real belief in self, Halliwell continued, activists built up "an overburdened belief in our own sanctity." This self-righteousness acted as an obstacle to doing the real work that needed to be done in order to transform American society.

> We assume that unless other elements in the society speak our language and share our responses, they are worthless. The NLF has managed to put together an all-nation coalition on the basis of a deep sense of the movement of a whole society, not by isolating themselves in language, thought or purity of principle. There was in fact, a noticeable slackening of hostilities among different movement types at the conference when confronted with the Front's ability to weld together a whole nation.[59]

Halliwell had put his finger on two important points. First, the Vietnamese, like the black movement, exerted an extraordinarily powerful gravitational pull on the white New Left, keeping it focused on its task, keeping it from flying off in a hundred different directions. Second, Halliwell sharply named some of the specific tendencies within the New Left that led to fragmentation and that SDS would have to overcome in order to make real change: a belief in one's own purity, a belief that the true path was owned by one group on the basis of its theoretical clarity, and the concomitant belief that those people were "worthless"—or counterrevolutionary—who did not follow that true path. Halliwell identified where those tendencies came from. If SDS really believed in its own vision for social change, it would not smash those other movement factions that did not share SDS's vision. On the contrary, it would allow other factions to make their own mistakes, with the confidence that the movement as a whole would discover the same truths that SDS had discovered.

In the same fashion as meetings with the Vietnamese engendered self-reflection for SDSers, so, too, did their trips to Cuba and their experience of Cuba's revolution. Former SDS president Todd Gitlin, for example, was positively humbled by his experience in Cuba. Gitlin's report to SDS from an early 1968 trip to Cuba contained a level of cultural self-reflection rare for SDSers, particularly SDS leaders. As Halliwell had emphasized in his account of the Bratislava meeting with the Vietnamese, Gitlin insisted that Cuba's importance could only be properly conveyed if activists found some means of communicating "the powerful, transfusing, distinctive tone" of the experience, the "qualities of the ordinary life of ordinary Cubans." In the same fashion that Halliwell's meetings with the Vietnamese sparked a self-reflection in the American, so, too, did the manner of Cuba's people continually force Gitlin to examine his own assumptions, to see the ideological blinders placed on him by the culture in which he lived. While traveling across the island, for example, Gitlin spotted slogans calling for the remaking of people as "moral animals." Gitlin's instincts rebelled, he reported. "Brave rhetoric, another slogan that some part of ourselves as Americans is taught to discount. A little voice says, 'Come on, man, get serious.' But they are serious. Like many of the revolution's central processes, this seems incredible. The way to establish the credibility of the credible, before sour and bitter souls, is to make it happen." That Cubans could be serious about this, that they would work and urge each other on, not for self-gain but out of a concern for humanity, for becoming better human beings? This had to be a scam. Gitlin rightly understood that the voice that questioned this, that refused to believe in the possibility of people acting in this manner, was a profoundly cynical voice, a voice shaped by a particular culture, an American voice.[60] Seeing Cuba's revolution, seeing people living a genuinely different life, with different, humane goals, allowed Gitlin to see, if only for a moment, his own culture and his own identity more clearly—to see imperialism not as something external to America's domestic society but as something that lived and breathed deep down into the very souls of those individuals raised within its confines. In short, Gitlin had viscerally grasped the fact that American culture and identity were not natural but were constructions. Nor were these constructions advanced or developed, as Americans had been told again and again and again; they were instead quite backward and were keyed to a Hobbesian society whose operative value was the war of all against all.

But it was only with extreme difficulty that SDSers could maintain this vision. One of the obstacles confronting SDS in this task was PL's dogmatic understanding of imperialism and class. PL's youth group, the May 2nd Movement (M2M), to be sure, had been one of the first groups to seriously and militantly oppose the United States' war in Vietnam, antedating SDS's own antiwar work. This early antiwar work, with its denunciations of American imperialism, certainly lent credibility to the Maoist organization within SDS.[61] By the time that PL dissolved M2M and moved into SDS, however, PL's emphasis had shifted in two significant ways. First, by the beginning of 1967 PL was already hinting at a new element in its antiwar stance. PL had started to take the purity of its own line—and the purity of Mao's line in China—and measure struggles outside the United States on the basis of how closely they conformed to this pure line. Thus, in the December 1966 number of its theoretical journal, PL began to counterpose the possibility of a "revisionist" Vietnamese leadership to the purely revolutionary struggle of Vietnam's people.[62] In the long run, this application of the most pure revolutionary doctrine to struggles outside the United States, or to black struggles, while practicing an extraordinary tolerance for American "working-class" racism or opportunism, would clearly reveal the American underpinnings of this kind of revolutionism. But for now, all this was only a hint in PL's practice.

Second, and of more immediate import to SDS, PL, as part of its central campaign against Soviet and American Communist Party revisionism, more and more promoted the centrality—and purity—of the "working class" as the agent of social change. Indeed, PL repeatedly insisted that isolation from this working class was the student antiwar movement's greatest liability.[63] But this uncritical reference to the working class reinforced the notion that imperialism was what happened outside of the United States; that capitalism confronted workers inside the country; and that capitalism simply divided America's population into two warring camps—the ruling class and the working class. Those SDSers who were beginning to understand that imperialism shaped America's domestic social life thus had their efforts undermined by a consolidated and credible force that was increasingly shaping SDS's discourse on the question of class analysis.

By mid-1968, PL's threat to SDS's ability to consolidate a realistic understanding of imperialism, and its deep influence on SDS's process for doing that, had become apparent. First, the June 1968 SDS national convention had elected Fred Gordon, a PL member or sympathizer, as one of its three national officers, together with two non-PLers, Mike Klonsky and Bernardine Dohrn. Klonsky, SDS's newly elected national secretary, acknowledged that the National Council had been a real battleground between PL and regular SDSers. While Klonsky believed that the battle had been "fought in a subtle sort of way, with the combatants never even confronting each other," the manner in which Klonsky chose to frame the debate suggested just how influential PL already was in the organization. "The question of labor is probably in the forefront of these issues," said Klonsky. "We must develop a correct strategy for labor in America and the rest of the world of advanced capitalism.... We must begin to define and redefine capitalism through an analysis of the working class. This must include its many sectors and segments, and the changing relationships of working people to the means of production."[64] Putting it in this fashion, however, allowed PL to frame the discussion. As we have already seen, SDS National Office leaders might just as easily have framed the debate in terms of race or in terms of empire.

Moreover, PL's emphasis on a working class unaffected by U.S. imperialism reinforced the thinking of those people within SDS who did not understand imperialism's domestic significance. For example, Mike Spiegel, SDS's 1967–68 national secretary, authored an article for the 1968 *New Left Notes* national convention issue. Titled "The Growing Development of a Class Politics," Spiegel's article explicitly suggested that anti-imperialist analysis was inadequate for winning new people to the struggle for social change. "Our rhetoric," said Spiegel, "has jumped from protest to resistance, and that has had a profound effect on our conception of ourselves." That "jump," he asserted, "was made within the unique context of the Vietnam War and our need to address ourselves to that primary focus of tension in America." But building a broader movement for social change demanded that SDS now examine the "historical connection between imperialism and capitalism." Specifically, according to Spiegel, SDS needed to understand "the deeper capitalist values which result in imperialism" and which also structured America's domestic society. SDS had successfully defined and criticized imperialism and centered that critique "on the exploitation of the developing countries and the black ghettos as internal colonies." But, continued Spiegel, SDSers

> reside within the mainstream of the imperialist country. Thus, our anti-imperialist analysis is only as good as it is able to make clear to people their own oppression here in America. We must reach beyond the anti-imperialist position which only makes clearer the oppression of others to a critique of the values—and their operational structures—which are oppressing our lives. . . .
>
> In order to reach into America with a viable critique, we must begin to strike at the evils of capitalism, for it is there, not through imperialism, that most people in America experience their oppression. Not just in economic terms—maybe least of all there—but in terms of how the values of capitalism dictate the operation of all institutions.

Speigel was clearly grappling with the complexities of imperialism, but in a manner that ultimately negated the meaning of imperialism to America's domestic society. He understood that a set of values, assumptions—really, an ideology—was common to America's domestic and international stance. But he continued to interpret imperialism as what happened to other people and capitalism as what happened to "mainstream"—really, white—Americans. In making this separation, Spiegel was negating the real relationship that whites had to imperialism and interpreting the position of whites in pure terms again: black and Third World peoples were victims of imperialism, and whites were victims of capitalism. On the basis of each group's victimhood, they could unite against their common oppressor. Spiegel had simply reformulated in terms of capitalism and imperialism the common-victimhood line that Noel Ignatin had already convincingly challenged as it had been applied to uniting whites with blacks. "No organization," Spiegel argued in defense of this view, "ever succeeded in building a strong movement for social change out of guilt—by building the consciousness of a movement on the motivation that one is in fact a member of the class of the oppressors."[65]

The uncomfortable truth that Spiegel and most SDSers were having difficulty facing was that, as members of the imperialist center, whites of all classes had helped to construct the empire, and benefited from it, that is, they were part of the oppressor class. To be sure, poor whites, working-class whites, and middle-class whites were all junior partners in the American imperial endeavor. But if these classes of whites were going to oppose empire, they would have to recognize that what they got from privilege, what they got from empire, was more costly than they imagined, was precisely the source of their own pain, their own "plight." Moreover, that growing numbers of young white people were coming to oppose the brutal treatment they saw meted out to nonwhite peoples, and were beginning to see behind that treatment an imperialist system, suggested that this recognition was possible.

The April and May 1968 struggle at Columbia University provided more clear evidence that young whites could oppose what they saw as imperialism and self-consciously reject the privileged role that imperialism offered them. Shortly after the Columbia rebellion, Mark Rudd, one of the main SDS leaders at the Morningside campus, suggested just such a broad reading of the experience. In one of his first analyses of the struggle, Rudd insisted that Columbia had confirmed an old SDS "dictum that you organize people around 'the issues that affect their lives.'" But people had usually raised that slogan in the same manner that Spiegel had raised it: the issues that affected people's lives were those issues that seemed closest to them. Columbia's experience had borne the slogan out in a different sense, however. It was not the fight over "dorm rules, curriculum, faculty tenure," and so on that really motivated people to understand and fight the system, although all these issues directly affected and oppressed students. Rather, Rudd argued, what really concerned students, the issues that really affected their lives, were Columbia's "racist expansion policies and its support for the war against Vietnam." For four years, Rudd explained, Columbia's SDS chapter had been raising the realities of Columbia's real estate ownership over and expansion into the surrounding black community of Harlem; of its displacing poor black tenants in order to house white middle-class and well-to-do students and faculty; and of its constructing new campus facilities to serve the overwhelmingly white Columbia University community. It had also been raising the war-making functioning of Columbia's participation in the academic—Defense Department partnership, the Institute for Defense Analysis (IDA). In return for counterinsurgency research and analysis, IDA had been pouring millions of dollars into faculty and graduate student research projects on campus. More and more, Rudd reported, students "began to be upset when exposed to the facts of the University's policies. En masse, students chose Harlem and Vietnam over the ivied halls of Columbia. More to the point, they decided they did not want to be students in a school that perpetuated itself by stealing land and developing anti-guerrilla weapons systems."[66] Columbia, in short, had been about rejecting the privileges of empire and race, or, more accurately, understanding that those privileges came at a high price. People in Harlem and people in Vietnam certainly paid the price for that privilege, but so, too, did Columbia's students. SDS had continually reminded the campus community over a number of years that the good housing and superior academic facilities they enjoyed at Columbia came at the expense of other people. Over time, thousands of Columbia students came to recognize that when they accepted those material benefits, they became accomplices after the fact and compromised their own dignity as human beings. When Columbia's students attacked the privileges of their own institution, they spoke of being liberated themselves. Indeed, for the people of a society that denied human solidarity as its guiding principle, the opportunity to express solidarity had become the most pressing issue affecting people's lives.

But Columbia had arisen in a rare set of historical circumstances. The Vietnam War had reached its height only three months earlier, with the Tet Offensive. And three weeks earlier, Martin Luther King Jr.'s assassination and the subsequent mass urban uprisings had highlighted how oppressive American society was to black people, on the one hand, and the strength of black resistance to that oppression, on the other. Whether young white people could consolidate their understandings of imperialism in the absence of these direct stimuli, or whether they would find new means of reinscribing their position in an empire, remained to be seen.

Chapter Three

The New Left and Feminism,
1965–1969

If by mid-1968 SDS had not yet risen to the black movement's challenge, had not grasped how "white" it was, still less did it recognize how "male" was its worldview, its strategy, tactics, values, and identity. Indeed, if the era's unprecedented black social movement could not compel SDSers to throw off their white racial blinders, the feminist critique of SDS—arising largely from women in SDS itself and not from a movement of the size or scope of the black movement—stood even less of a chance of deeply affecting the New Left's self-understandings. Moreover, while young white women activists struggled to define the nature of gender in American society and in the New Left, their efforts unfolded in the context of the same defining black social struggle that was challenging the New Left. This black social motion gave language to white women and allowed them to describe their oppression. But it also challenged them in the same ways that it challenged the New Left. Radical women struggled to comprehend gender's social construction in American society; but while they did so, their grasp of racial identity as a social construction always remained tenuous, at best. More concretely, only by way of exception did radical white women understand that the gender oppression they faced was a particular form of gender oppression, and not the universal embodiment of that oppression. Far more often, radical white women followed the path already trod by the New Left, seeing their whiteness as a natural attribute, and claiming for themselves a leading role in the struggle for social change based upon that unexamined whiteness. From 1965 to 1969, radical women decisively broke with the New Left by defining and attacking its male supremacy; at the same time, their critique of male supremacy was a white critique. In this sense, although radical white women did break with the New Left, the path they followed ran parallel to the New Left's path.

For its part, the New Left used radical women as a foil against which it measured the purity of its own racial politics, that is, it legitimated its own racial stance by charging radical women with "racism." Moreover, and this is the main point, the New Left systematically refused to deal seriously with its own male supremacy, isolated and alienated even the radical women closest to itself, and, ultimately, defended its white male perspectives and values. In defending its male supremacy by falsely casting itself as pure in its antiracism, however, the New Left strengthened the feminist tendency that sought to forego all struggle save that which it defined as "women's" struggles. If antiracist politics meant male supremacy—the daily affronts and indignities of a subordinate status in the movement—radical feminists reasoned, they would pass on antiracism.

Historians of the New Left and the feminist movement generally attribute the emergence of a radical women's movement to the work of white women, largely southern, in the southern civil rights struggle of the early and mid-1960s.[1] Even from this earliest time, however, radical feminism's contradictions were apparent. On the one hand, radical white women correctly began to perceive sex roles, gender, as a social construction, and not an immutable reality of nature. On the other hand, from the start, white female radicals, like their radical white male counterparts, had great difficulty maintaining a consistent hold of race as a social construction.

Proportionately, white female New Leftists played a far greater role in the southern civil rights battles than did male New Leftists. In this civil rights activism, young white women garnered a deeper sense of racism's impact and meaning and of the black community's strengths and mores than did most male New Leftists. Again and again, women who worked in the early civil rights movement expressed the sense that they had crossed over the great divide of race and saw the world and white people as black people saw that world. For example, Sue Thrasher, who worked in the early SNCC and went on to help found the SSOC, testified that it had been at a Nashville civil rights meeting that she first "heard black people speak for themselves." It was, she explained, the "first time I got any real inkling about the costs and the pain of segregation."[2] Similarly, SNCC activist Teresa Del Pozzo's work in the civil rights movement allowed her for the first time to glimpse the black community's intense and "bitter distrust of and disdain for the white world" and its "unity of vision about how" the United States "had long operated at the expense of blacks."[3]

Young white women activists glimpsed something beyond racism's virulence. They also glimpsed the vitality and strength of the black community. Most particularly, they saw black women playing far different roles in the black community than the roles that white women played in white American society.[4] Joyce Ladner and Doris Ladner were typical of the strong black women that white female civil rights activists met in the early 1960s. At a 1988 SNCC reunion, Joyce Ladner, who began her civil rights work as a high school student in Mississippi in 1959, described the kind of upbringing she had had as a black woman, so different from the culture in which young white women had been raised. In a telling incident, Ladner recalled going with her older sister, Doris, to the grocery store to buy doughnuts. As the white clerk, an older man, reached over to give the twelve-year-old Doris the doughnuts the girls had bought, he deliberately touched her breasts. Doris grabbed the dough-nut bag and slapped the clerk across his head. The Ladner sisters then ran home and told their mother what had happened. "You should have killed him," the mother responded. Explained Ladner:

> Mother never heard of Harriet Tubman, Sojourner Truth; Mother was one of eleven children; Mother went through third grade. But Mother also inherited the tradition that a Sojourner Truth or a Harriet Tubman set before her. I'm not speaking autobiographically so much as I am trying to strike a responsive chord for a generation of young black women from the South who came into SNCC. Our mothers and fathers taught us that we are "as good as anyone." Never allow anyone to call you out of your name. Never allow anyone to abuse you or to misuse you. Always defend yourself.[5]

Out of such a history, tradition, and culture came powerful women, women like the sharecropper Fannie Lou Hamer, who would lead the Mississippi Freedom Democratic Party delegation to the 1964 Democratic National Convention; or Diane Nash, the Nashville student leader who in 1961 would insist that the Freedom Rides continue when CORE, under attack by southern whites and pressured by the Kennedy administration, called a halt to them; or Gloria Richardson, the unques-tioned leader of the civil rights struggle in Cambridge, Maryland; or Ella Baker, who, in her midfifties, would see the tremendous potential generated by the 1960 student sit-in wave and help found SNCC as an organization that really belonged to young people.

As Sara Evans argues, young white women, particularly young southern white women, "were constantly inspired by the examples of black women who shattered [white] cultural images of appropriate 'female' behavior." "For the first time," white civil rights activist Dorothy Dawson Burlage told Evans, "I had role models I could respect."[6] Jo Freeman, one of radical feminism's pioneer advocates, echoed Dawson Burlage. Working with the SCLC in half-a-dozen southern communities in the

mid-1960s, Freeman recalled seeing in black women and the black community's attitude toward those women something entirely new to her:

> Black women seemed different from white women. They seemed stronger. More
> important, that strength was accepted, not denigrated [by the black community]. They
> occupied more social space than white women, played more roles, were a bigger presence
> in their communities. None fit the "clinging vine" stereotype popular then—or seemed
> to want to. . . . In effect, the black women I saw and worked with provided a different
> model of what it meant to be a woman in our society, and the black community a
> different attitude.[7]

These black female role models stood in sharp contrast to the political, social, physical, and intellectual passivity white society demanded of white women. Moreover,
when white women actually involved themselves in the civil rights struggle, they
decisively broke with white social expectations of women, including the young wom-
en's own expectations. Civil rights involvement gave women a new breadth of experience: white women came to see their own power and contrast that power to women's
socially ascribed attributes. Out of this contradiction, these young white women, in
Evans's words, forged "a new sense of self, a new definition of femininity apart from
the one they had inherited."[8]

But the flowering of this new sense of self, this new sense of what it meant to
be a woman, itself occurred within another context: SNCC's evolution toward black
nationalism. Although SNCC began its life with a traditional liberal civil rights
belief in integration, numerically it had always been a black-dominated organization. From the start, although staff members could be white, most SNCC workers
believed that white SNCC activists should be organizing white communities. Only
when this mission proved too difficult for the young whites did SNCC accede to
white staff organizing in black communities.[9] Mississippi Freedom Summer and
the influx of almost 1,000 young whites into Mississippi freedom projects, however,
brought to a head the struggle over the role of whites in the movement.

Jane Stembridge, daughter of a white Southern Baptist minister and SNCC's
first paid staff member, described the problem clearly: no matter how sensitive
whites were to black needs, the presence of white organizers placed a "cap on the
development of local leadership to some extent." Although—or perhaps, because—
Stembridge had been involved in SNCC from the very beginning, had been its first
executive director, and had put out the first edition of SNCC's publication, the
Student Voice, she drew from 1964's Freedom Summer the same lesson that black
SNCC workers drew: "You can't bring in white kids to develop Negro leadership. It's

an impossibility. . . . And it was after the summer project that I learned that I could not help develop Negro leadership because I was white. There was no other reason."[10] Stembridge, of course, was not speaking of being white in a biological sense. Rather, she was acknowledging that too much history existed between blacks and whites for individuals to bridge the gap, no matter how well intentioned people were. On the one side of this gap lay a deep distrust founded in long and bitter experience; on the other, a profound ignorance, and, far too often, arrogance, based on unexamined structural inequalities and assumptions of superiority.

Moreover, the Mississippi Summer Project and its Mississippi Freedom Democratic Party challenge brought to a head a wide variety of other questions for SNCC: on the broadest level, SNCC's very success had taken the organization to the limits of its original vision. With the Mississippi Freedom Democratic Party and the Summer Project, SNCC again brought the plight of southern blacks and the violence and duplicity of whites into an international spotlight. More than this, however, SNCC's actions exposed the federal government's and the Democratic Party's moral bankruptcy. In Mississippi and in the Mississippi Freedom Democratic Party's challenge at the Democratic Party's National Convention in Atlantic City in 1964, SNCC had tested the liberal vision of civil rights reform and had found that vision wanting. To move forward, SNCC would have to rethink its strategy and its relationship to liberalism and to reform generally.[11]

Thus, when SNCC activists gathered in November 1964 at a retreat in Waveland, Mississippi, their agenda involved the most basic issues of the organization's existence. At Waveland, white SNCC activists Casey Hayden and Mary King wrote and mimeographed the 1,000-word "Position Paper: Women in the Movement." New Left and feminist historians generally agree that this paper was a historic first manifesto of a new, radical women's consciousness.[12] And it was that. Nevertheless, when Hayden and King, fearing ridicule, anonymously slipped their paper into the pile of Waveland position papers, they necessarily inserted themselves into the broader debate over SNCC's future, above and beyond their paper's explicit content.

Few whites had played as significant a role in the civil rights movement as had Hayden and King. Born and raised in Texas, Hayden entered the University of Texas, Austin as a junior in 1957. Even before the 1960 student sit-in movement against segregation, Hayden was a leading Austin activist, urging young whites to become part of the civil rights struggle. At a debate at the August 1960 congress of the National Student Association (NSA), then the largest U.S. student organization, Hayden played a decisive role in pushing the NSA to go on record for the sit-ins. Said Hayden in a widely reproduced speech from the congress: "I cannot say to a person who suffers injustice, 'Wait.' Perhaps you can. I can't. And having decided that I cannot urge caution, I must stand with him. If I had known that not a single lunch counter would open as a result of my action, I could not have done differently than I did." Hayden concluded her talk by recounting the story of Ralph Waldo Emerson's visit to Henry David Thoreau when Thoreau was jailed for his opposition to the Mexican War and slavery. "What are you doing in there?" Emerson asked Thoreau. "Thoreau looked at him and replied, 'Ralph Waldo, what are *you* doing out *there*?'" "What are you doing out there?" Hayden asked the NSA congress. Recalling Hayden's speech nearly forty years later, Connie Curry, another early white civil rights activist, avers that she could still "hear again the thunder of the standing ovation and see all the eyes filled with tears." "There is no question," Curry insists, "that this was a personal turning point for many of the white delegates and probably a decisive moment in the history of the NSA's civil rights activism."[13] By the time of the Waveland conference, Hayden had coordinated a number of Young Women's Christian Association (YWCA) interracial programs in the South; had played a leading role in SNCC's work around the Freedom Rides; was the northern coordinator for Friends of SNCC; was one of the first white women to work in SNCC's Mississippi organizing project; and had played a leading role in the Mississippi Summer Project and the Mississippi Freedom Democratic Party.[14]

Mary King also began her civil rights activism early on. During 1962 and 1963, she served in Atlanta as part of an integrated YWCA team organizing to improve racial understanding in the South. With her YWCA office located in Atlanta and Ella Baker as one of her chief advisers, King came into close contact with SNCC staff and in 1963 joined the staff as an assistant to the organization's press secretary, Julian Bond. From that vantage point, King worked closely supporting SNCC's projects throughout the South, most notably the Mississippi Summer Project and the Mississippi Freedom Democratic Party.

Here, then, were two white women who clearly had committed themselves to civil rights work, had taken real risks, and had played defining roles in the work they did. Their paper necessarily reflected both the wealth of their experience and the contradictions then unfolding in SNCC.

Their paper began with a list of eleven particulars—incidents demonstrating an assumed male dominance in SNCC: only men were appointed to SNCC's constitutional revision committee; only men were in the Mississippi Summer Project leadership group; women regularly took minutes and did the typing, regardless of their experience; even women in leadership positions were expected to defer to men. The document then laid out its argument, taking what the authors had learned about white supremacy, paternalism, and racism and transferring those lessons bodily to questions of gender and male supremacy. "The average white person," King and Hayden argued,

> finds it difficult to understand why the Negro resents being called "boy," or being thought of as "musical" and "athletic," because the average white person doesn't realize that he assumes he is superior. So too the average SNCC worker finds it difficult to discuss the woman problem because of the assumptions of male superiority. Assumptions of male superiority are as widespread and deep rooted and every much as crippling to the woman as the assumptions of white supremacy are to the Negro.

In SNCC, King and Hayden charged, "women who are competent, qualified, and experienced, are automatically assigned to the 'female' kinds of jobs such as typing, desk work, telephone work, filing, library work, cooking, and the assistant kind of administrative work but rarely the 'executive' kind." King and Hayden then explained that they were presenting their paper anonymously because they feared the kind of reaction they would get if the authors were known: "Nothing so final as being fired or outright exclusion, but the kinds of things which are killing to the insides— insinuations, ridicule, over-exaggerated compensations." Still, presenting the paper, they argued, was important in order that SNCC activists understand "that many women in the movement are not 'happy and contented' with their status" and "that much talent and experience are being wasted by this movement when women are not given jobs commensurate with their abilities."

"Women in the Movement" discounted the possibility of any immediate change in women's situation. In a reference to the pop sociology of the day, Hayden and King speculated that perhaps black men, only "recently broken away from a matriarchal framework," were not yet ready for the kind of serious discussion necessary to break down sex roles in the movement. Many women, too, seemed as "unaware and insensitive" to their plight as men were—in the same way that many blacks seemed to ignore the reality of their oppression in American society. What could come out of raising the issue, the authors queried. Perhaps, after the laughter had died down, King and Hayden concluded, more women would "begin to recognize day-to-day discriminations. And maybe sometime in the future the whole of women in this movement will become so alert as to force the rest of the movement to stop the discrimination and start the slow process of changing values and ideas so that all of us gradually come to understand that this is no more a man's world than it is a white world."[15]

It was a daring and prophetic intervention. On the one hand, the paper did recognize, for the first time in the 1960s, that white women's roles within the movements for social change did not seem so radically different from their roles in traditional white society. In so doing, "Women in the Movement" presaged and laid some of the groundwork for radical feminism's subsequent development. And the paper did meet with some of the ridicule that its authors feared. Indeed, Hayden and King's paper is most widely known for the response that it elicited from SNCC's Stokely Carmichael. "What's the position of women in SNCC? The position of women in SNCC is prone," laughed Carmichael on the evening SNCC discussed the paper. (King and others generously recount this story, making much of Carmichael's sense of humor. King places the story in the context of the Mississippi Summer Project in which many young white northern women found themselves in the prone position. Thus, Carmichael's original statement was meant as a humorous statement of fact. Moreover, Carmichael made his remark in a postmeeting gathering with King, Hayden, and a crew of SNCC regulars drinking wine together. Apparently, no one took offense at Carmichael's remark at the time.)[16]

On the other hand, "Women in the Movement" undoubtedly reflects its authors' whiteness. In the first place, the paper speaks only of women in general; it does not mention white women or black women. Nor does it mention sexual relationships, and certainly not the most volatile and controversial variant of that relationship within SNCC—interracial sexual relations. Yet by the time that Hayden and King offered their paper, interracial sex and the consequent tensions between—and therefore, definitions of—women as white and women as black had become quite pronounced. With its influx of hundreds of young white women, the Mississippi Summer Project had guaranteed that. Hayden and King, then, chose to sidestep this question, although it had already deeply affected all women in SNCC.

More telling still, although some SNCC activists initially believed that an outspoken black woman and a central figure in the Atlanta SNCC office, Ruby Doris Smith Robinson, had authored the paper, "Women in the Movement" received almost no support from black women, Smith Robinson included. In a widely reproduced 1977 letter, Cynthia Washington explained why SNCC's black women did not support Hayden and King's paper: "During the fall of 1964," Washington recalled,

> I had a conversation with Casey Hayden about the role of women in SNCC. She complained that all the women got to do was type, that their role was limited to office work no matter where they were. What she said didn't make any particular sense to me because, at the time, I had my own project in Bolivar County, Miss[issippi]. A number of other black women also directed their own projects. What Casey and other white women seemed to want was an opportunity to prove they could do something other than office work. I assumed that if they could do something else, they'd probably be doing that.[17]

Paula Giddings, a historian of the movement, insists that with women like Washington, Nash, Smith Robinson, Donna Richards, Muriel Tillinghast, and others playing central roles, black female influence in SNCC was "actually increasing" at the same time that white female influence was waning.[18] Evans reports that Jean Wiley, another black female SNCC activist, insisted that "if white women had a problem in SNCC, it was not just a male/woman problem . . . it was also a black woman/white woman problem. It was a race problem rather than a woman's problem."[19]

In short, when Hayden and King argued that SNCC was wasting the talent of its members by assigning work on the basis of gender, rather than on the basis of ability and experience, they were ignoring the experience of black women. They had made their experience as white women stand in for all women. White women, Hayden and King foremost among them, had played critical roles in SNCC's earliest years, bringing their talents to bear in fostering SNCC's growth. But SNCC's growth, and the growth of the black social movement from which it sprang and to which it gave leadership, demanded new roles for black people and white people. Hayden and King were losing their old roles in the organization principally because they were white, and not simply because they were women. In short, "Women in the Movement" was at least as much a protest against SNCC's advancing black nationalism as it was a protest over gender roles assigned white women.

Ruby Doris Smith Robinson's attitude about SNCC's struggles over gender and race gives further evidence of this side of the Hayden and King paper. Smith Robinson joined SNCC in the organization's first year of life, when she was eighteen years old, and quickly won a reputation for her fierce determination in the freedom struggle. Indeed, Smith Robinson was undoubtedly one of the strong black women role models for young white SNCC women. One white SNCC woman contended that SNCC men who had the courage to go up against "ten Southern sheriffs" trembled if they had to go up against Smith Robinson. A black female SNCC activist told Smith Robinson's biographer, Cynthia Griggs Fleming, that SNCC men feared Smith Robinson. "A lot of guys would come out of [Smith Robinson's office], like, whipped . . . having dealt with her." On one occasion, when some hapless male SNCC worker repeated Carmichael's "prone" comment within earshot of Smith Robinson's office, Smith Robinson came charging out of her office and slapped the man she thought had made the comment.[20] Smith Robinson, in short, had no tolerance for the thought that women should stay in any predefined place relative to men.

Nevertheless, Smith Robinson did not seem to have had much sympathy toward Hayden and King, and for the allegations that white women made concerning sexual discrimination in SNCC. Recollections of Smith Robinson's stand on the Hayden and King paper are contradictory. Smith Robinson succumbed to cancer in the fall of 1967 and thus cannot give her own account of the matter. In Mary King's memoir, King remembers that "the majority of black women in SNCC," including Smith Robinson, "repudiated" the paper "when it first appeared." In contrast, Hayden suggests that Smith Robinson "was actually sympathetic to some of" Hayden and King's views.[21] King's impression, however, is corroborated by black women in SNCC. Several remember that Smith Robinson had limited patience for the kinds of complaints that Hayden and King raised in their paper. Bobbi Yancy, for example, insisted that Smith Robinson believed that SNCC's white women were "too vocal and too eager" and that "she remarked on it openly and often." Doris Ladner stated that Smith Robinson thought that white women "had a different agenda and that they had to be kept on the course as to what the agenda of the blacks was." Doris's sister, Joyce, similarly insisted that

the impression Ruby conveyed was that . . . white women were always at kind of an uneasy peace around her. She didn't mistreat them, but they sure didn't pull that shit, I mean bullshit on her. She was the last person they would run to with some complaint about, "Oh we're poor, oppressed white women here. . . . " She'd been in jail and was from a poor background herself. So it was hard for her to have sympathy for a girl from Sarah Lawrence who felt put upon.[22]

One year after their Waveland paper, and after both Hayden and King left SNCC, the two women drafted another, longer paper, "A Kind of Memo." King says quite explicitly that "healing a rift that was developing between black and white women" stood as one of the memo's central goals. Historian of radical feminism Sara Evans argues even more pointedly that "the memo was addressed principally to black women . . . in the hope that 'perhaps we can start to talk with each other more openly than in the past.'" Such intentions notwithstanding, "A Kind of Memo," like "Women in the Movement," refers to women in general, and not to black women or white women, with only a single exception: the memo announces, but does not analyze, "problems with relationships between white women and black women."[23]

In describing "A Kind of Memo," King more explicitly places the document in the context of SNCC's larger struggles. Although she does not denounce black nationalism per se, it is clearly a part of her critique:

Our second document was in part a call for a return to the fundamental values of the sit-ins and the early vision of SNCC, according to which any community should be free to define its own political agenda, spark its own local movement, and raise up its own leaders. . . . When I told Sara Evans that I had felt "relatively powerless" as a member of the SNCC staff, I was referring to a general feeling that I was losing ground within the movement with regard to the principles and beliefs of the early SNCC years that I valued.[24]

SNCC's vision in 1964 and 1965 still included community organizing and developing local leadership. Principally, by the time of Waveland, what had changed was the role of whites. King mourned for the earlier SNCC, for that period when her skills were needed and valued. Evans more correctly sees through this and argues that "A Kind of Memo" "was a parting attempt to halt the metamorphosis in the civil-rights movement from nonviolence to nationalism, from beloved community to Black Power."[25] This was precisely the reason that not a single black woman responded to the memo, despite its authors' stated hopes and intentions.[26]

Certainly, gender roles existed in the black community and in SNCC. But the particular oppression that black women faced was different than the particular oppression that white women faced. Black women could only win their liberation as part of the struggle for the black community's liberation. That liberation, in turn, was the direction SNCC was heading toward as it evolved its black nationalist consciousness. When Hayden and King attempted to "halt" SNCC's "metamorphosis" to black nationalism, they were not simply misunderstanding black women's different "historic trajectory," as Evans argues. Rather, they were putting themselves in opposition to that trajectory. This is why black women repudiated or did not respond to Hayden and King's papers. In rejecting Hayden and King's analysis, these black women did not reject the struggle for gender equality, something that they firmly believed in and attempted to practice in their lives. Rather, they rejected an attack on black nationalism couched in the language of gender.[27]

While "A Kind of Memo" failed to "halt" SNCC's evolution toward black nationalism, it did expand its critique of gender roles in the movement out beyond SNCC. In so doing, for the first time it challenged SDS's "male" culture and found a receptive audience among young SDS women, long held in check by that maleness.

Like "Women in the Movement," "A Kind of Memo" placed women's position in society in parallel with black people's position and noted that even people who are "very hip to the implications of the racial caste system . . . don't seem to be able to see the sexual-caste system." When such people were confronted with evidence of that system, they responded in much the same way as "a white segregationist confronted with integration." "A Kind of Memo" centered, however, upon the actual character of this "sexual-caste system":

The caste-system perspective dictates the roles assigned to women in the movement, and certainly even more to women outside the movement. Within the movement, questions arise in situations ranging from relationships of women organizers to men in the community, to who cleans the freedom house, to who holds leadership positions, to who does secretarial work, and to who acts as spokesman for groups. Other problems arise between women with varying degrees of awareness of themselves as being as capable as men, but held back from full participation.[28]

One month after Hayden and King mailed out their critique, SDS women at SDS's National Council meeting demanded and held a workshop, "Women in the Movement," and formed the organization's first women's caucus to deal with the issue of sex roles in SDS. Although the caucus issued an extremely mild resolution, "On roles in sds," a number of incidents associated with the workshop spoke volumes concerning the organization's male character.

Initially, both men and women attended the workshop. As the men became increasingly defensive and insisted that neither they themselves nor the organization had any "sexual-caste" problem, one group of women broke off from the mixed grouping in order to work without male interference. This left a mixed-section meeting, and, eventually, a third, separate and disaffected group of men, seemingly speechless, "for the first time in the conference." Moreover, some men demanded that they be allowed to attend the all-woman meeting—this, in the name of SDS's shibboleth of "participatory democracy." Evans reports that one black male SNCC organizer challenged these men and spoke out for the women's right to meet separately. Within the women's caucus itself, two black women "were the only ones with the courage to tell the men to leave."[29]

The mixed group, on the other hand, had its own characteristic problem. Todd Gitlin recounts that this group was meeting on the veranda outside the student union—it was late December 1965 in Champaign-Urbana, Illinois. As the workshop wore into the evening arguing over "whether women were essentially passive," Barbara Haber, wife of SDS founder Al Haber, noted how cold it was becoming and urged the group to move to a warmer spot. She repeated her suggestion two or three times. Each time the group discussion continued, as though she had said nothing. Sitting next to Barbara, Al Haber "nudged" his wife "and said, 'Watch this.' He repeated the same proposal in the same tone of voice. Everyone moved."[30]

SDS vice president Paul Booth's report on the conference also characteristically reflected the organization's attitudes toward women. Although the Women in the Movement workshop resolution explicitly mandated the National Council to "encourage wide distribution and discussion of the [workshop's] statement," Booth failed to mention either the workshop or the resolution in his report. Apparently, SDS's "real" business was more important than the insights and concerns women expressed about the organization's sexual division of labor.[31]

And so it was and would be throughout SDS's life. Feminist historians of the subject almost universally agree that SDS was far more "male" than was SNCC. SNCC was an organization of organizers, and organizing relied far more heavily upon those traits U.S. society defined as "female" than did the intellectual SDS. Good SNCC organizers needed to be good listeners; they needed to empathize with the people they were organizing, share their hopes and fears, validate their concerns. Particularly given SNCC's organizing philosophy—that of raising leadership indigenous to the communities in which SNCC worked—arrogance or disregard for a community's beliefs was antithetical to SNCC practice. Not so with SDS. Young white men, situated in the nation's best universities, among the brightest of their generation, founded SDS. They were school newspaper editors, leaders of their student governments, and active in local politics. In years to come, young men with such training would be cast as the nation's leaders, defining problems and policies on the national level in much the same way they were being trained in their daily lives at Michigan or Harvard or Berkeley. Consequently, these young men were "bred" not only in "at least [the] modest comfort" that the organization's Port Huron Statement acknowledged, but with the expectation and the belief that their voices counted and would be heard. As young white men, this was their patrimony. It was no wonder, then, that from the beginning, SDS put a premium upon verbal or theoretical prowess as the best measure of leadership. And if contriving grand schemes of power was the male prerogative in SDS, then just as inexorably, looking after life's messy, trivial details, being the helpmate to these white male leaders, would be the role assigned women.[32]

By the time SDSers read Hayden and King's memo at the December 1965 National Council, SDS claimed 10,000 members—four times the number claimed just one year earlier. The intervening year had been a momentous one: Johnson's administration, elected on a peace platform in November 1964, had by February 1965 begun its public escalation of the Vietnam War; Malcolm X fell to assassins during the same month; SDS organized the first major antiwar demonstration in April 1965 in Washington, D.C.; and in August 1965 Watts announced unmistakably that the nation's racial problems, far from ending with civil rights legislation, had entered a new, far more volatile phase. Thus, a new urgency gripped young people on the nation's campuses. That urgency, building over the next several years as both Vietnam and the racial crisis continued to escalate, highlighted the contrast between SDS's stated goals—a revamped, moral, egalitarian politics based on human needs and human relations—and its actual male-dominated and -oriented practice.

Older women in the movement were the first to notice the contradiction. These women had worked in the civil rights movement and in the early SDS and had the experience to lead in this time of growing crisis. Nevertheless, they found themselves pushed aside by the wave of new male SDS recruits: younger men, men without significant movement experience, but with ample experience in being white males and in assuming women's deference to their leadership as men. To be sure, within SDS it was an old insult, but women now suffered it at the hands of men younger and less experienced than they were, making the insult all the more galling.

Naomi Weisstein was one woman who would not be pushed aside so easily. In 1963, Weisstein earned her doctorate in psychology from Harvard University, graduating first in her class. Nevertheless, her advisers assured her that her future in the field was limited. "How can a little girl like you teach a great big class of men?" her chairman asked her. Denied use of Harvard's advanced perceptual evaluation equipment, she moved to New Haven, Connecticut, and worked at Yale, joining the New Haven CORE chapter. The following year she moved to Chicago with her husband, radical historian Jesse Lemisch, and worked with Chicago SNCC. Subsequently, she became leader of the antiwar movement at Loyola, where she had obtained a teaching position. Together with Heather Booth, active in the civil rights movement since 1960 and wife of former SDS vice president Paul Booth, Weisstein organized the first women's studies classes in the country in the summer of 1967. Nevertheless, like most of the New Left women, Weisstein found that her accomplishments, her struggle, and her years as an activist meant little when it came to speaking for the movement in public. Only one woman, she recalled, had been able to speak coherently at a 1966 University of Chicago demonstration. "I tried [to speak]," Weisstein recalled. "I got up on a chair and announced that we were organizing classes in the administration building, but no one would listen. I shouted for awhile and then I said, 'Fuck' and I got off the chair."[33]

Another slightly older woman, Beverly Jones, active in the civil rights movement in Gainesville, Florida, summarized women's experience trying to make themselves heard in SDS:

> You are allowed to participate and to speak, only the men stop listening when you do. How many times have you seen a woman enter the discussion only to have it resume at the exact point from which she made her departure, as though she had never said anything at all? How many times have you seen men get up and actually walk out of a room when a woman speaks, or begin to whisper to each other as she starts?
>
> In that kind of hostile, unresponsive atmosphere it is difficult for anyone to speak in an organized, stringent manner. Insulted by that atmosphere, a woman becomes angry. In order to say what she wanted to say and not launch an attack upon the manners of her audience, she musters the energy to control her temper, and finally she wonders why

she is bothering at all, since no one is listening. Under the pressure of all this extraneous stimulation, she speaks haltingly, and if she gets to the point at all, hits it "obliquely."[34]

Most male SDSers could not even conceive that women might have something significant to say about the problems of the day, or so it seemed.

Kathy McAfee, a longtime activist and worker with SDS's Radical Education Project (REP), together with Myrna Wood, also highlighted women's inability to be heard in SDS. In the same manner as other movement women were beginning to do at the time, however, McAfee and Wood explicitly tied women's inability to make themselves heard to social constructions of gender in American society. "Most full-time women organizers," McAfee and Wood argued,

> work in an atmosphere dominated by aggressive "guerrilla" street fighters and organizers (who usually have a silent female appendage), of charismatic theoreticians (whose ability to lay out an analysis is not hampered by the casual stroking of their girl's hair while everyone listens raptly), of decision making meetings in which the strong voices of men in "ideological struggle" are only rarely punctuated by the voice of one of the girls more skilled in debate, and of movement offices in which the women are still the most reliable workers (after all, the men are busy speaking and organizing).

Characteristics that people needed to succeed in the atmosphere of this movement, "like the ability to argue loud and fast and aggressively and to excel in the 'I'm more revolutionary than you' style of debate," McAfee and Wood continued, "are traits which our society consistently cultivates in men and discourages in women from childhood. But these traits are neither inherently male nor universally human, rather they are particularly appropriate to a brutally competitive, capitalist society."[35]

Indeed, the male leaders' disdain for women in the movement extended even into personal conversations. One male SDS national leader, for example, reportedly "hummed" to himself whenever female activists tried to speak with him.[36] But of course if male leaders were not that interested in what women had to say, they were certainly interested in maintaining women as a workforce and as a source of sexual pleasure. Indeed, from very early on, even before the "sexual revolution" of the mid and late 1960s, SDS leaders began to use the power of their criticism of American society as a means of securing sexual advantage over women hungry for meaning in their lives. Casey Hayden, for example, reports that her marriage with SDS founder Tom Hayden broke up when the latter, cutting "a charismatic swath ... through the world of student politics," took up with a woman on the East Coast "and started spending weekends there."[37] By the late 1960s, one Seattle woman activist reported that male SDS leaders, each cutting his own "charismatic swath" across the country, would "breeze in and out of Seattle, cavalierly [making] passes at every SDS woman."[38] This was representative conduct, characteristic not just of Seattle but of the hundreds of cities and campuses in which SDS had a presence.

In 1969, Marge Piercy, poet, author, and activist, described the "dreary" sex lives led by movement women. Piercy found that sexual relations for these women fell into one of two patterns: the more conventional had the women exactly mirroring the roles of a traditional marriage, or, perhaps more precisely, that kind of a marriage in which the wife puts the husband through graduate school.[39] The second pattern was that of "the liberated woman." This woman, Piercy maintained, "can expect to get laid maybe once every two months, after a party or at councils or conferences, or when some visiting fireman comes through and wants to be put up." Such "firemen" Piercy placed into two categories: "those who make it clear that what they are doing is fucking, and those who provide a flurry of apparently personal interest, which fades mighty quick." "The first category," Piercy continued, "are on far fewer hate lists than the second. There are men in the Movement who have left women feeling conned and somehow used, emotionally robbed, in every city in the country. Rarely have I heard any man in the Movement judge any other man for that kind of emotional exploitation, and never so it could hurt him. The use of women as props for a sagging ego is accepted socially." Such emotional and sexual conquests, Piercy concluded, "can even be called organizing."[40]

By mid-1969, Weisstein, together with two other SDS veterans, Evelyn Goldfield and Sue Munaker, were able to summarize succinctly women's position in the movement. If that position was not entirely "prone," it was very nearly so. The three women argued that women's place in the movement was "no less foul, no less repressive, no less unliberated, than it had been" outside the movement. The three women insisted:

> We were still the movement secretaries and the shit-workers; we served the food, prepared the mailings and made the best posters; we were the earth mothers and the sex-objects for the movement men. We were the free movement "chicks"—free to screw any man who demanded it, or if we chose not to—free to be called hung-up, middle class and up-tight. We were free to keep quiet at meetings—or if we chose not to, we were free to speak in men's terms. If a woman dared conceive an idea that was not in the current, limited, ideological system, she was ignored or ridiculed. The work done by women organizers (the status role for movement activists) was often considered of secondary importance in the overall effort. We found ourselves unable to influence the direction and scope of projects. We were dependent on the male elite for direction and recognition. We were free, finally, to marry and raise liberated babies and clean liberated

diapers and prepare liberated dinners for our ass-hunting husbands, or "guys we were living with."[41]

Literally hundreds of underground newspapers—the radical media of the 1960s—reflected and promoted this view of women's role in the movement. As one contemporary account put it, women served as "revolutionary cheese-cake" in the underground press.[42] Even the most serious movement publications, New York's "radical newsweekly" the *Guardian*, for example, were not above publishing blatantly male-supremacist articles and graphics. For example, the *Guardian* ran a notorious cartoon circulated by the movement's Liberation News Service. The cartoon had two characters, both naked: a muscular looking long-haired man who was labeled "the movement"; and an overweight, middle-aged, and terrified-looking woman labeled "the establishment." The male character stood in a menacing position, holding the woman's bra, as though he had just stripped her of it. Readers were left to imagine what "the movement" had in store for this "establishment."[43] Still, the *Guardian* was relatively reserved in its use of overtly titillating or male-supremacist material. Its preferred means of dealing with women paralleled the majority SDS position: it most often simply ignored women.

Not so with the vast majority of the hundreds of underground papers in the United States. New York City's the *Rat* was probably fairly representative of how most underground papers used women. Jeff Shero, an alumnus of the University of Texas, Austin's SDS chapter and SDS vice president in 1965, founded the *Rat* and was its editor. With Shero's movement pedigree, the paper stood on the more political side of the underground press spectrum. Nevertheless, the *Rat* did not shy from liberally sprinkling its issues with photos and drawings of nude women, crude sexual puns, and discussions of pornography. As did much of the underground press, the *Rat* also found a principal part of its income from sex advertising. In one particularly provocative incident, Shero defended this income in an editorial he titled, after one of these sex ads, "Wanna See My Pussy."[44] When movement women were mentioned at all in the *Rat*'s columns, they were invariably "chicks," and the paper explicitly set aside clerical jobs for "chicks."[45] In early January 1969, *Rat* editors offered their readers a portrait of what, for them, was probably the ideal movement woman:

> By day she is at SF [San Francisco] State in a visored crash helmet battlin' the cops. At night she sheds everything and dances nude on Broadway before 200 faceless cop-outs.
> Would you call her a topless revolutionary—or just Vicki Drake?
> Vicki is a [*sic*] innocent faced, blond chick who is the main attraction at Tipsy's on San Francisco's boob avenue. She first busted into the news when she ran for student body president at Stanford last spring.[46]

Drake's story received wide syndication throughout the nation's underground press. It ran with a photo of Drake, in professional work outfit, of course.

SDS's ERAP projects were perhaps the only places in SDS where white movement women could play leading roles. Because SDS self-consciously modeled ERAP on SNCC organizing projects, at least on the surface, ERAP placed its priorities on organizing. Thus, "female" organizing skills—the kind of skills that made SNCC a more conducive environment for white women than campus SDS—came to the fore in the urban ERAP projects. Consequently, women found a strong foothold for developing their skills and leadership in ERAP.[47] Evans identifies two ERAP projects (out of the approximately dozen projects going on at ERAP's height), the Cleveland and Boston projects, as practically being led by women and oriented toward organizing women in the community, particularly welfare recipients.

But even in these urban organizing projects, male SDSers continued to define ERAP on a national scale and had the preponderant voice in directing most of the local projects. Perhaps the most critical element in defining a project was its target community. Who was going to be organized? Young white unemployed males, or their wives, sisters, and mothers? Most male ERAPers had an unexamined answer to this question, that is, they simply assumed that their target community consisted of the "unemployed"—meaning young men—and did not raise the question at all. When women in ERAP nevertheless sought to organize women, their male ERAP counterparts would ask them questions such as whether they really believed "that teen-age girls had anything to do with the revolution."[48] JOIN (Chicago's ERAP project) leader Rennie Davis articulated what were probably the underlying ERAP understandings of organizing and the organized. Said Davis in 1965:

> There was an informal gang structure on the corner where we began our office. It was possible to get to know them by going out of your way and I went out of my way the first week—I was virtually drunk all week—the fellows drink all day on that corner. My feeling is that they are *the* potential revolutionary force in Uptown Chicago, if there can be said to be such a force. They are the force that is least afraid of the police, do have some sense of justice—and are willing to act on that sense. . . . [When] you're OK with the guys . . . you can talk about how poor people get screwed, and how people who back each other up can stop that from happening. . . . Complications are very great. One is that to work with them really requires that you live their way . . . that you run, and fight and drink and do the things they do, and still have the capacity to direct it towards something. It means you have to have some sort of separation from the other community people you are trying to organize; welfare people and older people, because those older people consider the kids Hillbilly punks [my emphasis].[49]

By late 1968, after several years of ferment and agitation over the role of women in the movement, not much had changed in the Chicago project. Chicago JOIN leader Mike James was touring the country trying to drum up support for urban organizing projects. In Seattle, a stronghold for women's liberation work within SDS, James spoke in front of a packed house. According to a female activist, Barbara Winslow, James explained "in an affected SDS accent (their fantasy of a Southern, white, male [stupid] worker) how to relate to white workers."

> At one point he said, "and then sometimes we all get together and ball some chick." Silence. There wasn't even a gasp in the room. Jill Severn, a member of Radical Women, stood up and in a clear voice wanted to know "what did that do to the chick's consciousness?" Again, silence. James did not know how to answer the question and began to backtrack. He finally admitted that they never really ever gangbanged women; they just said they did to appear tough.[50]

Being "tough," then, continued as the preferred organizing model for young white intellectual men from the best universities in the country—and would continue to be the organizing model, with only slight nuance, for Weatherman a year later. But being tough was a highly competitive venture, and competition did not work well as an organizing strategy. ERAP organizer Vivian Leburg Rothstein told Sara Evans that the male ERAP organizers competed with "any male leadership from the community." In consequence, the only men that the ERAP projects "could attract were quite incompetent men who were willing to be bossed around."[51]

Despite SDS's male-oriented environment, young white women worked enthusiastically in the New Left. They did so not because of the Port Huron Statement's abstract propositions of equality. Nor did they work, at the beginning, because they believed that the New Left could serve as an instrument through which they could attain their own equality. Indeed, in the early 1960s few women consciously recognized any significant problems with the way U.S. society constructed gender, that is, most young white women saw their roles in society and in the movement as "natural." Rather, hundreds, then thousands, and then tens of thousands of young women worked in SDS and in the New Left because the multiple crises of the period—the tremendous struggle of black people and the growing war in Vietnam—demanded that they play an active part in transforming what appeared to them as transparently inequitable and unjust social relations. In attempting to address the period's social crises, women necessarily had to rethink the passive identities and roles they had inherited. Yet the movement atmosphere in which they worked continually affronted their dignity and devalued their efforts. From 1965 on, young white women slowly began to define the nature of their oppression and confront that oppression, first of all within the movement in which they worked.

It would be nearly two years before women again raised the issue of their place in SDS at a national conference. In 1966 and 1967, the Vietnam War escalated significantly; black activists formally enunciated the Black Power doctrine in mid-1966; and black urban rebellions continued to spread during this period. White women increasingly felt the urgency to participate directly in the antiwar and burgeoning antidraft movements and to relate in some fashion to the pitched battles occurring in the nation's urban centers. In the short term, this sense of urgency seems to have pushed to the side women's concerns over their treatment in the movement.[52] Still, women continued to feel the pinch of working in a male-supremacist environment. In the antidraft movement, especially, the subordinate role of women became all the more pronounced: men were the ones resisting and the ones facing penalties for that resistance. At best, in this configuration of the antidraft movement, women could only play a supporting role—type, file, run the mimeo machine, make sandwiches. And, of course, they had one other role: as a popular slogan of the time had it, "Girls say 'yes' to guys who say 'no.'"

By time of the June 1967 SDS national convention, women had had enough. The convention's women's liberation workshop drafted an analytic and programmatic statement that went beyond Hayden and King's "A Kind of Memo" and the watered-down SDS December 1965 conference resolution that the Hayden and King memo spawned. The June 1967 "liberation of women" resolution opened its analysis by arguing that the world was divided into three camps: capitalist, socialist, and Third World. The Third World's role, the resolution argued, was revolutionary, and "an integral part of their fight is the necessity of their own independence." While Hayden and King had put the struggle of women in parallel with the struggle of black people and argued that women's oppression was analogous to black oppression, "liberation of women" boldly declared that "women are in a colonial relationship to men and we recognize ourselves as part of the Third World. . . . Women, because of their colonial relationship to men, have to fight for their own independence. This fight for our own independence will lead to the growth and development of the revolutionary movement in this country. Only the independent woman can be truly effective in the larger revolutionary struggle." In its programmatic section, "liberation of women" called for "all programs which will free women from their traditional roles" so that women could participate "with all of our resources and energies in meaningful and creative activity." Since the "family unit" stood at the root of women's oppression and men's paternalism, the resolution called for "new forms" of child rearing, including creating communal child care centers staffed by men and women; birth control and abortion rights for women; and equal sharing of housework. Perhaps most striking, "liberation of women" demanded that "our brothers recognize that they must deal with their own problems of male chauvinism"; that SDS leaders self-consciously cultivate female leadership; and that the entire organization take up the study of women's oppression in order to formulate a more concrete program for liberation.

Despite its specific targeting of male chauvinism, "liberation of women" sought to appeal to men in a way that would be inconceivable two years later: "We seek the liberation of all human beings. The struggle for liberation of women must be part of the larger fight for human freedom. We recognize the difficulty our brothers will have in dealing with male chauvinism and we will assume our full responsibility in helping to resolve the contradictions. freedom now! we love you!"[53] To no avail. Men were not buying. Women were not colonized. That was taking things too far. When the women who drafted the resolution announced that the analysis was not subject to debate, the convention "erupted," according to Evans. "Men were yelling, arguing, cursing, objecting all over the floor" and "creating a 'constant hubbub' of noise interspersed with derisive hoots and catcalls."[54] The women's workshop ultimately withdrew the analytic section, and the convention voted and approved only the programmatic section.[55]

In fact, the resolution probably represented the divided consciousness of women at the time: on the one hand, the bald announcement that women were colonized had practical implications that were not reflected in the resolution's practical program. If white women were in fact colonized, then organizational independence from the colonizer—men—would be the proper solution to the problem and the solution adopted by colonial peoples the world over. Sara Evans and Alice Echols both suggest that men recognized this practical implication and responded as negatively to the proposal as they did because of that recognition.[56] On the other hand, the mild practical program reflected a different analysis. Women were oppressed, but the oppressor was more ambiguous than men. It was the family unit. Men, to be sure, adopted an air of superiority—male chauvinism—but this seemed to be primarily a question of male ignorance, and men could be educated out of this ignorance. Indeed, women could appeal to men: men's freedom, too, was compromised by the family and the oppression of women. At least one pair of feminist critics would call this program and its underlying analysis Uncle Tomming (from "Uncle Tom," the bowing and scraping protypical "Good Negro" of the day): a select group of young white women were looking to parley the disaffection of a large group of women into personal power for themselves within male SDS's highest councils. It would be difficult to picture the colonized pledging aid to the colonizer and insisting to the oppressor that "we love you!"[57]

The internal contradictions of "liberation of women," the divided consciousness of its authors, also represented the forerunner of a split between radical white women: what would come to be known as the division between the "politicos" and the "radical feminists." That division turned on the meaning of the word "independent." Whatever "liberation of women" argued concerning women's colonial status, the resolution also gave "independence" a distinct meaning. Women were to achieve their independence in order to be "truly effective in the larger revolutionary struggle." "Independence" meant independence within the New Left. But a consistent elaboration of the "woman as colonized" analysis necessarily arrived at a different interpretation of the meaning of independence. In an anticolonial struggle, independence is the goal of the revolutionary struggle; it is the revolution and not simply a means for consummating revolution. Those who saw women's liberation as a means for fighting a "larger revolutionary struggle" came to be known as the "politicos." They sought equality in the New Left in order to make the revolution. Those who saw women's liberation as an end in itself, indeed, as the most fundamental and most radical struggle, as the revolution, came to be known as the "radical feminists." Radical feminists did not seek independence within the New Left; rather, they sought independence from the New Left.[58]

One further contradiction characterized "liberation of women." This was the same contradiction that had characterized the original Hayden and King papers: "liberation of women" did not distinguish between white women and black women, or more generally, women of color. Like the two Hayden and King papers, it substituted the word "women" for the people in whose name it was really speaking, white women. In other words, it made the particular experience of white women the universal measure of women's experience and oppression. In so doing, "liberation of women" clearly showed its New Left roots. By the summer of 1967, the New Left had repeatedly played the same card: it had made the black struggle a particular part of the more universal struggle led by white radicals. If white women had commenced an assault upon the New Left's male supremacy, at least as of mid-1967, they continued to follow in the New Left's footsteps in assuming the universal significance of the struggle they were waging.

Whatever the resolution's contradictions, however, SDS treated the matter dismissively. *New Left Notes*, for example, offered two not-so-subtle comments on the entire question of women's liberation. When *New Left Notes* published the convention's "liberation of women" resolution, it included both the programmatic and analytic sections and noted that the convention approved only the former portion of the resolution. The paper did not mention any of the convention floor antics that accompanied the resolution's discussion. *New Left Notes* separated the programmatic and analytic sections with a graphic of a frivolous-looking young women holding up a poster saying: "We want our Rights & We want them NOW!" The poster was signed "WLF," presumably Women's Liberation Front. The young woman in the graphic had large eyelashes and earrings and wore a polka-dotted waist-high miniskirt with matching bloomers and black stockings. If most men at the convention responded angrily to the women's resolution, *New Left Notes* would take the more considered response—and treat the matter as a joke.

On the cover of its issue reporting on the convention, *New Left Notes*' editors put a somewhat different spin on the discussion, a spin that would become increasingly characteristic over the next several years: in the upper left corner of the front page, they placed a photograph of a smiling woman holding a rifle. *New Left Notes* captioned this photo: "THE NEW AMERICAN WOMAN."[59] This was a women's liberation—or "revolutionary cheese-cake"—that most men could relate to.

Implementation of the resolution's mandates presented a still more significant measure of SDS's response to the women's liberation workshop than did *New Left Notes*' coverage of the debate. Although the resolution called for a broad educational campaign around women's liberation in the organization and specifically mandated the organization to "develop an analysis of the exploitation of women" and to present that analysis at SDS's December national conference, little actual work appears to have been done in accord with the resolution's demands.

If SDS was standing pat, however, more and more women were in motion, demanding an end to the limitations that society and the movement had imposed upon them. Within a few weeks of the gavel's closing SDS's national convention, urban rebellions erupted in Newark, Detroit, and dozens of smaller cities. The social crises of the 1960s were reaching their peaks. As the New Left strove in the wake of these urban rebellions to move "from protest to resistance," so, too, women acted with greater urgency and began to present their struggle in ever more dramatic terms.

The NCNP at the end of 1967's long hot summer would be the next battleground upon which radical women would raise the women's liberation banner. While the thousands of attendees at the NCNP were busy wrangling over black caucus demands that the conference cede effective conference leadership to the black activists, a minimum of thirty and as many as seventy women met in closed caucus for several consecutive days. The radical women worked out a resolution on women's liberation, including demands for equal pay for equal work and abortion rights, to present to the plenary. It was not terribly radical by standards that would hold even six months later, but it nevertheless raised the issue of women's place in society as a distinct focus of activity. However, when caucus representatives brought their resolution to the Resolutions Committee, they were told that Women's Strike for Peace had already submitted a resolution on women and that the NCNP would only entertain one women's resolution. But the Women's Strike for Peace resolution was not about women per se. It was about women's opposition to the Vietnam War. Jo Freeman, who had worked with the Southern Christian Leadership Conference in half-a-dozen southern cities and was one of the caucus leaders, angrily left the Resolutions Committee meeting vowing to force a floor fight by submitting the caucus resolution as a minority report. Freeman, fresh out of the committee meeting, ran into a twenty-two-year-old caucus member and recent graduate of Chicago's Art Institute, Shulamith Firestone. She told Firestone what had happened. Firestone, even more outraged by the incident than Freeman, agreed to work with Freeman and draft a minority report. The two women talked and wrote through the night, and with each passing hour the report became "more radical." In its final form, Freeman and Firestone's report trumped the black caucus demand for 50 percent voting power at the NCNP, the two women insisting that women have a 51 percent voting power at the conference, in accord with women's actual numbers in the population at large. That morning, they mimeoed 2,000 copies of their resolution, sought to round up support for a discussion, and, they thought, got the meeting's chair, William Pepper, to agree to a plenary reading and discussion of the resolution. When the time for the discussion came, however, Pepper railroaded the Women's Strike for Peace resolution through—"All in favor, all opposed, motion passed.... Next resolution." Freeman, Firestone, and a number of other women stormed the platform. Pepper, a national leader of the antiwar movement, "literally patted" Firestone on the head. "Cool down, little girl," he reportedly told Firestone. "We have more important things to do here than talk about women's problems."[60]

It may not have seemed like a terribly significant remark or incident to Pepper, but it set off a chain reaction among radical women. In Chicago, site of the NCNP conference, radical women were outraged at the NCNP's conduct. They began meeting on a regular basis to discuss the plight of women in society and in the movement—the first women's liberation group in the United States. Within six months they were publishing the country's first radical women's newspaper: *voice of the women's liberation movement*, which popularized the term "women's liberation" and sent news of the movement out across the country. Radical women were soon meeting independently in a dozen U.S. cities—most notably, in addition to Boston, New York, and Chicago, in Washington, D.C., Berkeley, Madison, Seattle, Detroit, and Gainesville, Florida.[61] SDS's National Office estimated that by mid-1968, thirty-five women's groups had sprung into being.[62] Moreover, by mid-1968 *voice of women's liberation* was joined by *Notes from the First Year*, out of New York, and *No More Fun and Games*, out of Boston.

The proliferation of women's groups and publications across the country also intensified the divisions between the radical feminists and politicos. Although women initially came together under the single banner of women's liberation, as the number of women considering themselves women's liberationists multiplied, so, too, did the analytic differences between women sharpen. In Chicago, for example, site of the national SDS office and one of the strongest regional SDS apparatuses, the majority of the women's liberationists had personal connections to male SDS leaders, and conceived of their mission as reshaping a New Left that would be inclusive of women's leadership. Jo Freeman, who developed a radical feminist perspective, however, increasingly found herself isolated in the Chicago group. In New York, the two sides, developing initially within a group called New York Radical Women (NYRW), were more evenly matched. Firestone, who had moved to New York shortly after helping found the Chicago women's group, moved toward a radical feminist position; but Pam Parker Allen, who together with Firestone had cofounded NYRW, stood on the politico side of the divide. Eventually, divisions within women's organizations would evolve into divisions between women's organizations.

By mid-1968, less than a year after the founding of the first women's liberation groups, those divisions would become pronounced enough that both those inside and outside of the women's movement could begin to recognize the differences. Indeed, in June 1968 three written pieces appeared in which the differences could not have been more marked: on the politico side, Marilyn Salzman Webb, a longtime SDS activist and wife of a national SDS leader, penned an article for *New Left Notes*, "Women: We Have a Common Enemy." On the other side, two manifestos of radical feminism also appeared. NYRW published the pamphlet *Notes from the First Year*, a collection of articles articulating various components of radical feminist thought. Perhaps more striking, two activists from Gainesville, Florida, published a lengthy pamphlet titled *Towards a Female Liberation Movement*.

Salzman Webb's article tried to hold together the contradictory parts of SDS's June 1967 resolution—women were colonized, but men weren't the enemy. It was already clear, however, that Salzman Webb was shaping her thinking in relation to the radical feminists—who had developed the colonial analysis without its conciliatory attitude toward men. She began by discussing a January women's action against the war held in Washington, D.C. Calling themselves the Jeanette Rankin Brigade, named after the only congressperson to have voted against the U.S. declarations of war in the First and Second World Wars, 3,000 women descended on the Capitol in order to petition members of Congress against the war. The overwhelming majority of the brigade were older women associated with the action's main sponsor, Women's Strike for Peace. But a core of radical women also participated, and these women, Salzman Webb reported, used the opportunity to meet and discuss the issue of women as radicals that had been roiling SDS and the New Left over the previous year. "We saw ourselves colonized in the same way as Fanon has described the Algerians," she explained "and our enemy was not men, but rather an oppressive system that pits group against group, denying each self-control and self-confidence." She cited some of the specific issues that the radical women discussed: the sexual division of labor in the movement itself, and the role of advertising and the media in defining women as consumers and commodities in society. Salzman Webb then came to the heart of her position, the politico position. "We are not at all anti-men," she claimed, "but see men as much victimized by this social system as we are." Men, just as much as women, she argued, had their roles shaped and defined by the "unfettered free-enterprise system" and by the exploitation they suffered as consumers. Consequently, "in building a women's movement, we clearly see that we have to be active with other, co-ed . . . movement organizations and actions." As the June 1967 "liberation of women" resolution had affirmed women's love for men, so Salzman Webb, a year later, felt compelled to reiterate that affirmation, even more strongly than the earlier statement: "We have developed our own kind of feminity [sic] and enjoy being women who love men and do not see them as the enemy. We are not the cold, gray-suited women of the Twenties, nor the 'masculinized' ones of the present. Staid suits have been replaced by the colorful dress of a turned-on generation of women who are asserting themselves as females as well as intellectual politicos."

Salzman Webb concluded her article with the major SDS argument against the radical feminists—the example of Vietnamese women. According to Salzman Webb, the Vietnamese themselves insisted that women's rights in the Vietnamese struggle "could not but identify itself with the common struggle for national liberation. . . . The Vietnamese woman has literally won her equality with a weapon in her hand and through the sheer strength of her arms." Her answer to those women who were already insisting that women jettison the New Left and go it alone for women's liberation was simple: Vietnamese women had won whatever equality they had in Vietnam by participating in the common struggle, not ignoring it. Since Salzman Webb had already defined sexual roles as a form of oppression that assailed men also, the common struggle was indeed a "common struggle for liberation."

Aside from the problem of trying to hold together the women are colonized/men are not the enemy analysis, Salzman Webb's article had two other major contradictions. First, as with most of the women's liberation literature and resolutions that had appeared to this point, Salzman Webb had made the particular case of white women stand for the case of women in general. For example, she pointed her finger at the "consumer economy," with its manipulative portrait of women, as women's principal oppressor. "In order to appeal to men and be sexy we now must buy mini-skirts and wear curly hair," Salzman Webb complained. Even by 1968, these were not problems, or not major ones, for the majority of black women.[63]

Second, Salzman Webb's report on the Jeanette Rankin Brigade action was not quite accurate. Radical women had indeed met in Washington during the action, but a core of these women, led by members of NYRW, had actually denounced the action and organized an action of their own to appeal to radical women at the event. In fact, Salzman Webb's report was very much a response to this, one of the first significant actions taken by the radical feminists. That her account glossed over this may have been SDS's way of trying to contain the spread of an unwanted rival for the allegiance of radical and potentially radical women.

The radical feminists published their account of the Jeanette Rankin Brigade event, in *Notes from the First Year*, at virtually the same moment as Salzman Webb's account appeared. In the radical feminist account, Shulamith Firestone argued that the Jeanette Rankin Brigade action was "actually playing upon the traditional female role in the classic manner." Women were seeking to petition Congress as "tearful and passive" "wives, mothers and mourners." In short, women were appealing to Congress as symbols of weakness, and this, according to Firestone, was an inappropriate basis for women organizing "AS WOMEN."

Firestone's group, in counterpoint to the brigade, invited women to attend their action at Arlington National Cemetery—the "Burial of Traditional Womanhood." *Notes* also ran the polemical "funeral oration" for "traditional womanhood" that one member of NYRW, Kathie Amatniek, delivered at Arlington. Amatniek began by asking why, at a time when the U.S. government was slaughtering hundreds of thousands of people, should women concern themselves with something so seemingly irrelevant as "traditional womanhood"? Should radical women not be devoting all their energy to stopping the slaughter? Women who asked that kind of question, Amatniek answered, were not understanding the significance of women's oppression in the United States. Women, insisted Amatniek, "really do have a problem as women in America." She continued: "Their problem is social, not merely personal . . . and . . . their problem is so closely related and interlocked with the other problems in our country, the very problem of war itself . . . that we cannot hope to move toward a better world or even a truly democratic society at home until we begin to solve our own problems."[64] As early as January 1968, then, radical feminists were beginning to define the oppression of women as a central element in a complex of oppressions that led up to and included the war itself.

In the same month as *Notes from the First Year* appeared, two women from Gainesville, Florida, who had been active in the civil rights struggles in that town issued a still more challenging document, *Towards a Female Liberation Movement*, soon known throughout the women's movement as "the Florida paper." In thirty-two single-spaced pages, Beverly Jones and Judith Brown sharply critiqued the New Left as a "male power structure." They argued that SDS women who sought reform within the New Left were actually Uncle Toms, that female radicals failed to appreciate "the desperate condition" of women in general, that "people don't get radicalized ... fighting other people's battles," and that women, both for "their own salvation and for the good of the movement, ... must form their own group and work primarily for female liberation."

According to Brown and Jones, SDS was an old-boys network, and maintaining a secondary role for women in SDS was a necessary part of the organization's structure. In fact, the Florida paper argued that "almost all men are involved in" upholding what the authors termed "the male mystique." This male mystique actually served as the basis for leadership in SDS. While men would commonly whisper among themselves and even walk out of meetings when women spoke, men of widely varying degrees of talent and understanding were accorded a uniform respect simply because they were men. In the same way that whites "derived ego-support" from the fact of their whiteness, men derived that same ego support because they were men. No matter how inept the man, no matter where he stood in relation to other men, he could still rest assured that he was above women. Even the most talented and self-confident men, those men who personally might not be threatened by the existence and leadership potential of intelligent women, nonetheless were bound by a "male mystique." If a male leader accorded full respect to women in SDS and thereby disclosed "the basic superiority ... of some of the women to some of the men" in the group, he would be breaking the "covenant," and other men would not follow his leadership.

SDS women who insisted on equality within SDS therefore were rejecting "an identification with their sex" and were using "the language of female liberation ... to advance themselves in the male power structure of the movement." Brown and Jones, both of whom had worked with the developing Black Power movement in Florida, then brought the Black Power critique of reformist blacks into their critique of SDS women. The June 1967 SDS "liberation of women" resolution, they noted,

> reeks of the bourgeois black who can't quite identify with the lame and mutilated casualties of the racist system; ... who takes it upon himself to explain problems he doesn't understand to a power structure that could care less; who wants to fight for blacks but not very hard and only as a member of the city council or perhaps one of its lesser boards. ... The trouble with using the language of black or female liberation for *this* purpose—essentially demanding a nigger on every committee—is two-fold. In the first place it is immoral—a Tom betrayal of a whole people. In the second place it won't work.

Behind this "Uncle Tomming," Brown and Jones saw young SDS women's lack of connection with the realities of life for women in the United States. On the one hand, SDS women were in a unique place in their lives, a place in which they faced far less discrimination than they would face at any other time. On the other hand, very few SDS women were married, and still fewer had children. It was this reality— the reality of marriage in U.S. society—that defined the lives of women. SDS women could still believe in great affairs and perfect marriages. But women outside of university settings experienced something very different than the romantic illusions entertained by SDS women. The Florida paper insisted that "a relationship between a man and a woman is no more or less personal a relationship than is the relationship between a woman and her maid, a master and his slave, a teacher and his student." Whatever individual qualities might exist in a given relationship, they were far "overshadowed by the class nature of the relationship." Indeed, Brown and Jones argued,

> There is something horribly repugnant in the picture of women performing the same menial chores all day, having almost interchangeable conversations with their children, engaging in standard television arguments with their husbands, and then in the late hours of the night, each agonizing over what is considered her personal lot, her personal relationship, her personal problem. If women lack self-confidence, there seems no limit to their egotism. And unmarried women cannot in all honesty say their lives are in much greater measure distinct from each other's. We are a class, we are oppressed as a class, and we each respond within the limits allowed us as members of that oppressed class. Purposely divided from each other, each of us is ruled by one or more men for the benefit of all men. There is no personal escape, no personal salvation, no personal solution.

It was a powerful, ringing indictment. Brown and Jones eloquently demonstrated that what most women imagined to be personal failings—either their own or their husbands'—were in reality social and political problems. And if the problem confronting women was a collective problem, it demanded a collective solution. Yet with all their militance and outrage and cutting logic, Brown and Jones were not so very far from Betty Friedan's 1963 critique of the "feminine mystique" and "the problem with no name." As Friedan had done with her *Feminine Mystique*, Brown and Jones placed the stultifying life of woman as homemaker at the center of their argument. If they shared with Friedan this central critique, they also shared Friedan's class and racial standpoint. The "lame and mutilated casualties" of this system of sexual hierarchy, the women who suffered in this "desperate condition," were white middle-class women; but Brown and Jones, like Friedan (and Salzman Webb), simply called these victims "women."

With this as the center of women's problems, Brown and Jones argued that women needed to fight "their own battles" and "work primarily for female liberation." Women, the authors argued, had for too long fought to help other people and, in so fighting, had failed to come to grips with their own oppression. They then made their essential argument by analogy:

> No one thinks that poor whites can learn about their own lives by befriending black people, however laudable that action may be. No one even thinks that poor whites can help black people much, assuming some might want to, until they first recognize their own oppression and oppressors. Intuitively we grasp the fact that until poor whites understand who their enemies are and combine to fight them they can not understand what it is going to take to secure their freedom or anyone else's. And no one seriously doubts that if and when the light dawns upon them collectively, it will be, in the first instance, their battle they will fight.[65]

Unfortunately, this notion of "fighting one's own battles" was not merely the Florida paper's particular take on developing a radical feminist movement. In fact, "fighting one's own battles" as white women's primary work was only the logical elaboration of the "women as colonized" argument. In *Notes from the First Year*, Shulamith Firestone had made the same argument from a historical perspective: the women's rights movement in the United States, and in the various socialist nations of the world, had failed in the past because women were only too willing to act in the interests of "more important" struggles or in the interests of "the Revolution." The lesson from this? "Put your own interests first," Firestone argued, "then proceed to make alliances with other oppressed groups. Demand a piece of that revolutionary pie before you put your life on the line."[66]

What did this mean, concretely, this demand to put one's own interests first? Elizabeth Martinez, a former SNCC staff member and one of the few Chicanas to work with the early feminist movement, recounted her experience at an NYRW meeting on the night of April 4, 1968. Martin Luther King Jr. had been shot on that day. "But at our women's meeting," Martinez recalled, "no one said we should talk about it before our usual business.... It was a night to realize that if the struggle against sexism did not see itself as profoundly entwined with the fight against racism, I was gone."[67] NYRW lost one of its few nonwhite women on that night. King's death was not a "women's issue," or at least not a white woman's issue. This was what putting one's own interests first, fighting one's own battles first, came down to.

In fact, it was a poor argument. When Brown and Jones argued that "no one even thinks that poor whites can help black people much, assuming some might want to, until they first recognize their own oppression and oppressors," they implicitly separated the oppression that poor whites faced from the fact that poor whites were white. But as early as 1963, James Baldwin had already shown, quite clearly, that the condition and plight of white people were inextricably intertwined with those of black people. "The price of the liberation of the white people," argued Baldwin, "is the liberation of the blacks—the total liberation, in the cities, in the towns, before the law, and in the mind." Still earlier, W. E. B. DuBois had insisted upon the same thing. The "plight of the white working class," DuBois maintained, was "directly traceable" to black slavery in the United States, and to white labor's determination to "adopt, forward and approve" capitalism's "subordination of colored labor to white profits the world over."[68] In short, poor whites, in being racist, were complicit in their own oppression. Rejecting racism and aligning themselves with blacks were prerequisite in order for poor whites to fight "their own battles." Indeed, they could not fight their own battles without aligning themselves with blacks and rejecting the alliance that racism had forged between themselves and their bosses. But this was true not only for poor whites, but for all whites, male and female. White people had constructed their identities historically in relation to a black "other." They could only deconstruct that identity by coming to terms with that other.[69] Brown and Jones, and Firestone, had narrowed the definition of a group's "own battle." Society defined poor whites not only as poor, but as white; society defined white women not only as women, but as white. Therefore, white women could not fight their "own battle" simply over their identity as women, but also had to fight over their identity as white.

Moreover, the inordinately large number of white women who entered the black southern freedom movement did so not simply out of liberal do-gooderism—fighting other people's battles—as Brown and Jones suggested. Rather, their participation likely reflected an intuitive understanding of the intertwined nature of the freedom struggles involved. And it was more than that: if the battle for black freedom had reawakened white women's aspirations for freedom, then that suggested that winning black freedom might also be the concomitant to winning female liberation. From a practical standpoint, if the black freedom struggle created a cadre of white women who, in the light of that struggle, were beginning to understand their own oppression, then extending participation in that struggle would bring more white woman into touch with an understanding of the oppression they faced as white women. In short, fighting against racism was not someone else's battle, but was a central component of the battle for white women's liberation.

Towards a Female Liberation Movement took on one more important question: it answered Salzman Webb's Vietnamese women argument. Brown and Jones correctly claimed that this Third World analogy was "inappropriate" for women in the United

States. The conditions of Vietnamese women, they insisted, were not the conditions facing women in this country. At the same time, Brown and Jones themselves failed to appreciate the significance of Vietnamese women's struggles and, by extension, the struggles of black women and Third World women. Argued Brown and Jones:

> What we have got to recognize is that women living in Viet Nam face very different circumstances than our own. Their children, and they themselves, are being murdered daily, and a third of the population goes about missing a limb. Under constant military attack, it is necessary to defer designing new institutions in order to preserve life itself; Vietnamese women have no choice.... Marilyn [Salzman Webb] tells us that Vietnamese women found out that the only way they can get equality is to participate in the national political struggle. The strict analogy between Viet Nam and the United States is more realistically phrased: American women would get a lot more equality if they gave militant support to our *national* struggle: to colonize, to murder, to enslave.[70]

While Brown and Jones were quite correct in critiquing the Third World analogy for women's conduct, they themselves used that analogy to express white women's oppression: we are colonized, our oppression is analogous to black oppression. Moreover, they explained Vietnamese women's conduct by saying that the Vietnamese had no choice—there was a war going on, and Vietnamese women had to "defer" creating new gender institutions "in order to preserve life itself." But this was wrong. If no war had been going on, if Vietnam was as it had been in the decades of "peaceful" French colonial rule, would Vietnamese women have taken a different course? Would they have carried on an independent struggle as women? In fact, even with the war, Vietnamese women had not deferred their struggle as women. On the contrary, as with black women, the path to Vietnamese women's liberation had to run through the struggle against colonialism. Vietnamese women could not be free so long as Vietnam suffered under colonial rule. Anticolonial struggle was the prerequisite for Vietnamese women's liberation.[71]

Two months after the Florida paper and *Notes from the First Year* appeared, some twenty women representing both women's liberation movement tendencies debated this very issue—the relationship between white women's liberation and the struggles of women of color, especially black women's struggles—at a Sandy Springs, Maryland, women's liberation retreat called by Marilyn Salzman Webb. The debate specifically centered on whether black women would be invited to a projected national conference on women's liberation. Although the meeting transcript does not identify individual speakers or groups represented, the lines of the debate were fairly clear, and the genuine anguish felt over the questions was evident.

Radical feminists argued that to invite militant black women, like Black Panther leader Kathleen Cleaver, would be to "muddy the issue" of female liberation. Explained one radical feminist: "You're opening a can of worms.... They [black women] are going to want to discuss different things, have different concerns. We're going to get so involved with them that we are not going to talk about female liberation." Radical feminists thus sought to avoid tangling up what they saw as the clear-cut issue of women's subordination with black women's views of their relation to the liberation struggle. Explained another radical feminist: "Anything that gets us fucked up into anything [outside of what we think women's liberation is] should not be brought to this conference." Someone else commented that "black militant women rule the day.... They hold the cards on oppression.... I don't want to go to a conference to hear a black militant women [sic] tell me she is more oppressed and what am I going to do about it."[72]

In contrast, the politicos seem to have been far more aware of the need to incorporate—from the start—a black female perspective into something that sought to call itself a women's liberation movement. When, for example, one of the participants confessed that she had "problems dealing with black people" and suggested that the fear of working with black women came out of fear of not knowing what white women's relationship to black people was, a radical feminist responded, "That's another problem." But one of the politicos shot back: "That's not another problem if we are talking about building a women's liberation movement in this country. It's very much our problem and it's our problem because we are racists." One woman worried that the movement would "expand and expand and expand and may be essentially all white." "If that happens," another politico echoed, "our ideology will be wrong." This position, however, was a distinct minority position at Sandy Springs.[73]

Long before Sandy Springs, some women were already identifying race as a critical test for the nascent women's movement. Most notably, in January 1968, less than two months after she had cofounded the first women's group in New York City, Pam Parker Allen was able to discern that women in her group were using analogies between racial and sexual oppressions in self-serving ways. Allen, whose understandings of race had been shaped by her experiences as one of a handful of white transfer students at Spelman College and by her subsequent activity in the Mississippi Summer Project, early on read to her women's group her "Memo to My White Sisters in Our Struggle to Realize Our Full Humanity." In "Memo," Allen questioned white women's motives in drawing "numerous analogies" to the black struggle. "I question our motives precisely because we are white and middle-class," suggested Allen. "What a relief it is to discover that we too are oppressed, if not exactly like, in similar ways to black men. We need no longer feel as guilty. White men can now take all the blame for an oppressive, racist society. We too have been 'used,' humiliated, scorned.

We too are part of the oppressed." Allen also noted that her women's group tended to see the black struggle itself not in terms of black women, but in terms of the male-dominated black movement. But it was far more important, Allen argued, that white women attempt to understand what they had in common with poor black women, and poor women the world over, than it was to simply affirm their legitimacy by placing their oppression in parallel with the oppression suffered by black people. Indeed, white women's success in finding their "own humanity," Allen maintained, depended upon their making this link. Explained Allen:

> We have something in common with poor women all over the world—our sex, but unless we affirm our identification with them and assert their right to a decent life over all other values (including our personal advancement) we will continue to be a part of the oppressor class improving our own positions at the expense of our fellow women throughout the world. . . . A significant women's liberation movement cannot develop among middle-class women unless the questions of racism and class bias are dealt with. For these are the factors which separate us from other women and which make us oppressors at the same time as we are being denied our full humanity.[74]

The position that had made little headway at Sandy Springs, and the understanding that Allen had been pointing to, was that imperialism and colonialism had done more than colonize men and women of color; imperialism and colonialism had created white men and white women, in terms both of material and social privilege and culture. In the United States, specifically, slavery and the oppression of black people, more than anything else, had created white men and white women. Indeed, slavery and racism had created the white woman in all her most essential characteristics: as the model of beauty, as socially isolated and dependent upon men for protection, and as passive politically, intellectually, and sexually. These were the characteristics that white women were rebelling against. Yet so long as imperialism and racism existed, they would continue to re-create white men and white women; so long as American society oppressed black people, it would continually create and re-create its model of white womanhood. Hence, white women could not be free so long as they were white women. In this sense, the struggle for white women's liberation also ran through the anti-imperialist and antiracist struggle.

Of course, how white women related their struggle for liberation to anti-imperialism and antiracism depended upon a variety of factors, not the least of which was how the struggle unfolded between the women's liberation movement's tendencies and the attitude taken toward women's liberation by the main white New Left organization styling itself anti-imperialist and antiracist.[75]

Differences in goals and theories aside, both women's liberation movement factions sought to organize a much larger base of women into the movement. How they attempted that organizing was itself characteristic of the differences between the groups. Both used consciousness-raising as an organizing strategy, although the radical feminists seem to have relied more heavily on consciousness-raising than did the politicos. Both groups also attempted to generate concrete actions that would highlight women's oppression, although on this level the politicos, at least initially, seem to have dominated.

Consciousness-raising came to be the predominant organizing tack that the radical feminists followed. Especially as developed by NYRW's Kathie Amatniek, consciousness-raising consisted of a small group of women getting together and examining a particular question. For example, women would go around the room and discuss whether they would prefer a girl baby or boy baby, or their experiences with abortion, or the nature of the relationships they had with their boyfriends or husbands. The value of the consciousness-raising was that it took what each woman regarded as a personal experience, or failing, and showed the commonality of that experience in the lives of many women. As NYRW member Carol Hanisch described it, women began to discover that "personal problems are political problems."[76]

Radical feminists championed this approach to organizing and insisted on its truly radical content. Ellen Willis, another NYRW member, answered a critic of consciousness-raising and radical feminism by insisting that "the first requirement of thinking is to look at a problem without preconceptions." "For an oppressed group," Willis argued, "the first step in a serious analysis is to think about one's personal experience. Why do I feel oppressed? (No glib quoting from some book about why I am supposed to feel oppressed, but what in my daily experience makes me feel oppressed?) What unpleasant experiences have I shared with other women? With both men and women? Who, specifically, is hurting me? . . . How? Then I look for an underlying pattern that fits the facts."[77]

Consciousness-raising marked a big step forward for the movement. Indeed, it was a remarkable and powerful experience: to sit with a small group of women and discover that what each individual held as her deepest private fears and insecurities were collectively held fears. But if all these individual fears were held in common, then they must have originated in some common external experience or source. In short, consciousness-raising identified the structural nature of white women's oppression—it politicized that oppression and exposed the family unit as a principal source of that oppression.

Unfortunately, as practiced by the early women's liberation movement, consciousness-raising also contained an unexamined racial content. This racial content concealed sexual oppression's fullest structural portrait and distorted the relationship that white women's oppression had to other forms of oppression. Shirley Geok-lin Lim's experience illustrates this. Geok-lin Lim, a young Malaysian woman who arrived in Boston in the midst of the "feminist revolution" in 1969, recalled that she was never invited to a consciousness-raising group, despite the fact that she knew fellow graduate students who regularly attended meetings. Now a professor of English and women's studies at the University of California, Santa Barbara, Geok-lin Lim evaluates her experience with the early women's liberation movement and argues that the family position, class, and cultural backgrounds of women of color, immigrant women, and blue-collar women did not "permit them the time to participate" in the consciousness-raising groups, nor were such women comfortable discussing "the intimate details of their lives" with the young white women whose backgrounds were so different from their own. Consciousness-raising group members, argues Geok-lin Lim, "were unaware that what they saw as universal ideas and cultural experiences were thoroughly alien to masses of other women. Class and race norms"—and not the universality of "womanhood"—actually "fused the unity" of these groups.[78]

Ultimately, consciousness-raising's unexamined racial content reinforced the radical feminist propensity to place what white women termed "women's oppression" at the center of all oppression, or as the oppression that had to be dealt with first, at least by white women. In short, helped along by the unexamined whiteness of the consciousness-raising experience, radical feminism catapulted from the point of first recognizing women's oppression in 1965 to that of determining in 1968 that that oppression, as experienced by white women, was the main struggle confronting white women.

If consciousness-raising constituted the principal means of internally developing a women's liberation perspective for white women, bold actions constituted the means for attracting national attention for the fledgling movement. NYRW's "Burial of Traditional Womanhood" action, at the Jeanette Rankin Brigade protest, marked the first attempt by radical women to speak to a larger audience. To a certain extent the "Burial" worked—women who felt the pinch of working in a male-dominated New Left but who had not yet heard of the growing protest against that male domination discovered the women's liberation perspective.[79] Moreover, the "Burial" also caught some limited, if mocking, media attention. In its February 1968 edition, the nation's most widely read left-liberal journal, *Ramparts*, issued a particularly notorious report on "women's power" that alluded to the radical "mini-skirt caucus" that had acted at the Rankin Brigade protest. Still, mainstream America remained largely oblivious to women's liberation until the September 1968 Miss America protest at Atlantic City, New Jersey.

The Miss America protest evolved directly out of the conflict between the radical feminists and the politicos at Sandy Springs. The politicos repeatedly charged the radical feminists with self-indulgence "for sitting around doing consciousness-raising" rather than acting in a time of war and ghetto upheaval. In the wake of that criticism, several New York radical feminists first raised the idea for the Atlantic City protest. Once they brought it to NYRW, however, a NYRW politico, Robin Morgan, seized upon it and took the primary hand in its organization.[80]

Certainly, the protest itself focused on the beauty pageant's oppression of women: "the Pageant contestants epitomize the roles we are all forced to play as women," protest organizers explained. It was, they continued, very much like "the 4-H county fair, where the nervous animals are judged for teeth, fleece . . . and where the best 'specimen' gets the blue ribbon." Miss America, they insisted "represents what women are supposed to be: unoffensive, bland, apolitical." But Morgan and the core of radical women organizers also made every effort to connect women's oppression with racism and the Vietnam War. Protesters pointed out that in the nearly half century of Miss America contests, black, Puerto Rican, Mexican, Native American ("the real Miss America"), Alaskan, or Hawaiian women had never been finalists in the contest. It was, the protesters claimed, "Racism with Roses." Moreover, Miss America was a "Military Death Mascot." Her job—indeed the "highlight of her reign"—included her efforts at pep-talking "our husbands, fathers, sons and boyfriends into dying and killing [in Vietnam] with a better spirit."[81]

Protest organizers also used the action as a platform for attacking the New Left's male supremacy. In an article written just after the protest, Morgan warned that the Atlantic City protest was only a beginning for women's liberation. "Women are angry now," Morgan intoned. And this anger came out of a broader base of women than middle-class white women:

Women are sick of dying on kitchen tables from abortions. Welfare women are sick of living under the threat of losing their kids unless they deny their own sexuality. Black women have had it with pronouncements such as Stokeley's [sic]: "The only position for women in SNCC is prone." Poor women are sick of being even more oppressed than their husbands, who can beat them up in order to regain lost "manhood." College women are sick of prison-dorm rules. Even "Establishment" women are sick of job-discrimination and being patronized for doing equal work at less pay than men. And Movement women are sick and goddamned mad at playing home-fires to their revolutionaries, at being lays but never comrades, at being called frivolous to demand their own rights as human beings "when more serious revolutionary problems are at stake."

In Morgan, who had been a child television actress, a published poet, an early anti-war activist, and an early member of the Yippies, the politicos found one of their most angry and articulate voices. If her experience in the New Left pushed her to try to appreciate oppression outside of the oppression of young white women, her experience in NYRW, with its ongoing debate between radical feminists and politicos, pushed her to articulate a radical feminist epistemology and a real hatred for the New Left's male-supremacist hypocrisy:

> Your own gut issue is the key to your commitment. Empathy for others never causes radical change; only an awareness of your own oppression accomplishes this. Men will not be free until women are free. Malcolm said it. Algeria, Cuba, China, North Vietnam—they're all learning it. But don't let's wait to admire women as people until we carry machine guns the same as men. We'll all do that when the time comes, and it's coming. What about NOW, unglamorous now? Look at how you live, brothers. Look at how you are being made into oppressors to further oppress us. The Revolution begins at home.[82]

To be sure, Morgan's position had its share of weaknesses, particularly in attempting to subsume the struggles of Third World women under the banner of women's struggle in general, and in adopting the radical feminist narrowing of the meaning of one's "own oppression." At the same time, however, Morgan was struggling to integrate an understanding of women's oppression with other oppressions and doing that in a way that uncompromisingly called white men to task for their male supremacy.

Shortly after the Atlantic City action, Morgan, together with other like-minded radical women in New York and in the politico strongholds of Chicago and Washington, D.C., founded the Women's International Terrorist Conspiracy from Hell (WITCH), with each city having its own separate "coven." Unlike the radical feminists, who as early as the Rankin Brigade protest objected to organizing antiwar protests "AS WOMEN," WITCH self-consciously sought to establish women's leading roles in tackling the problems of empire and race. WITCH, for example, initiated a series of actions in which members "hexed" Wall Street, big banks, corporations, and university-based domestic counterinsurgency programs. Of course, while WITCH attacked these symbols and agents of "corporate imperialism," it sought to raise the awareness of women's oppression and give women a new space from which they could operate as full political people. Marilyn Salzman Webb extolled the group, insisting that it gave "women a new, aggressive, revolutionary identity," and that it provided "new tactics" that allowed "publicity and discussion of major power institutions in America's economy and their cultural shaping of women." WITCH also insisted that New Left men get their house in order. In a minihistory of the new organization, for example, Morgan emphasized that it was bad enough that women were second-class citizens in society at large; this second-class citizenship was still more galling in a movement supposedly aimed at human equality. How hypocritical was it, she insisted, "to hear some young male 'revolutionary' . . . order his 'chick' to make supper or wash his socks or to shut up—he's talking now." Morgan demanded that "this infiltration of old sick sexual stereotypes has got to go now, before any new alternative society . . . gets hopelessly contaminated by it."[83]

Here, then, was a possible synthesis: in WITCH, women had carried forward the best of the New Left's analysis of empire and race. The New Left could work with this kind of women's movement, could participate in constructing a still larger coalition against the empire, but it could do so only on the condition that it take seriously women's demands, that it take on the movement's male supremacy. If the past was any measure, SDS would have a hard time of it.

Once again, at SDS's June 1968 national convention—the same month in which *Notes* and the Florida paper appeared—women raised the issue of the organization's male supremacy, albeit in a somewhat unorthodox fashion. In the midst of a plenary section, seven women marched down the aisles to the speakers' platform. Four were dressed as movement leaders and carried signs identifying them—Karl Theory, Max Praxis, Stu Alliance, and Ben Bullshit. Three other women—labeled Girlfriend, Chick, and Joe Chapter—trailed after them, unable to keep up with them. When the seven reached the speakers' platform, the lights in the auditorium went out, and women seated throughout the hall began the ululating cry of Algerian women, made famous in the recently released film, *Battle of Algiers*. When the ululating stopped, three women grabbed the floor microphones and began an antiphonal reading charging SDS with elitism, male chauvinism, and arrogance. SDSers, women and men, did not receive the performance very well. Their catcalls and hooting drowned out the reading.[84]

If this women's action was itself unsuccessful in provoking a serious discussion of the organization's male orientation, the growing importance and strength of the women's movement found reflection from another direction—Bernardine Dohrn's election as SDS's interorganizational secretary, the first woman elected as one of SDS's top three national officers. Dohrn, a recent law school graduate and an officer of the National Lawyers Guild, first reached a national SDS audience in a March 1968 *New Left Notes* article she coauthored with Naomi Jaffee.[85] Pushed on, perhaps, by Jaffee, a NYRW member, New York regional office SDSer, and future member of WITCH, Dohrn would make her strongest explicit statement against the movement's male supremacy in the article. Titled "The Look Is You," Dorhn and Jaffee's piece sought to analyze the material basis for women's oppression in U.S. society, and linked that oppression to the "dynamics of imperialism." It also sought to understand white women's place—again, without specifically naming white women—in its contradictory aspects, as both "the beneficiaries and the victims of the productivity made possible by advanced technology." But its condemnation of male supremacy, although strong, was also characteristic of how Dohrn would approach the entire problem of women's secondary place in the New Left. "The Look Is You" failed to make any explicit demands for change on the part of men. On the contrary, although Dohrn and Jaffe's article began by recognizing that women were "unfree within the Movement," it placed the burden of change on women themselves: women must stop "internalizing the view that men define reality and women are defined in terms of men." Dohrn and Jaffee continued:

> We are coming together not in a defensive posture to rage at our exploited status vis à vis
> men, but rather in the process of developing our own autonomy, to expose the nature of
> American society in which all people are reified (manipulated as objects)....
>
> Our strategy will focus on the unique quality of our exploitation as women,
> primarily in our vanguard economic role as consumers. Women Power is the power
> to destroy a destructive system by refusing to play the part(s) assigned to us by it—by
> refusing to accept its definition of us as passive consumers, and by actively subverting the
> institutions which create and enforce that definition.

Nine months earlier, "liberation of women" had condemned male chauvinism. No need for that now; women would attain their freedom in the movement by refusing to play the part of women.[86] This was Dohrn's message, and the philosophy that SDS apparently embraced when it elected her its interorganizational secretary.[87]

Whatever SDS did by this point, however, could not stop the burgeoning women's liberation movement. The Atlantic City action, the WITCH hexings, and the continued growth of women's groups, both inside and outside of SDS, throughout the summer and fall of 1968 demonstrated that fact beyond any doubt. On the contrary, the growth of this autonomous women's movement placed the question of women's subordinate status in SDS in ever greater relief. If, in the past, national SDS could avoid looking squarely at the question, or ridiculed those who raised it, or mouthed token phrases on the subject, these were luxuries that were no longer open to it. Henceforth, and for the remaining life of the organization, SDS would have to put something on the table for women's liberation if it was going to maintain its credibility as a revolutionary organization and if it was going to prevent SDS women from defecting to the women's movement.

Thus, in preparation for the December 1968 SDS National Council meeting, Noel Ignatin, the same man who had played such an important part in reshaping SDS's understandings of race and privilege, drew up a resolution on the "revolutionary struggle for women's liberation." Unlike Ignatin's work on race, however, this resolution was anything but groundbreaking. On the contrary, it abstractly depicted women's condition in capitalist society, buttressing its arguments with Marxist terminology. From the failure of the richest, most technologically developed society in the world to "provide equality for half its citizens," Ignatin drew two "inescapable conclusions" : first, "women who desire equality must become revolutionaries," a convenient conclusion for SDS, and second, "all revolutionary organizations and all individuals, both male and female, who desire revolution must fight for the equality of women." Ignatin's resolution then articulated a concrete program for challenging universities' channeling and treatment of women and concluded by offering up some guidelines for the campaign: women should organize women; men should organize men; and the entire campaign should be used to promote women's leadership within SDS. He then offered a particularly obscure formulation, which nevertheless said a great deal about SDS: "The campaign should be seen as the backdrop and the mirror against which to examine SDS and correct any tendencies within it to keep women in a subordinate position."[88] In short, Ignatin's resolution only palely reflected radical women's demands and concerns. The resolution focused the battle against male supremacy externally and made no effort to define its face within the organization. Indeed, the campaign would only reveal any male-supremacist "tendencies" if they existed.

By this time, however, women in SDS were far too active on the issue to let Ignatin's resolution stand as he had written it. At the National Council meeting, a core of women SDSers sat down with Ignatin and redrafted the proposal. In its final form, the revised resolution, "Advance of women's struggle," retained Ignatin's practical campaign against the way schools tracked, treated, and employed women. But "Advance" also substantially strengthened Ignatin's original analysis. Most notably, it distinguished, although somewhat abstractly, between the conditions facing black women and those facing white women: "black working class women are the most oppressed group in the society." If "Advance" did not say much beyond this simple rendering, still it was an important acknowledgment for the women's movement. Then, "Advance" attempted to define the "material basis" for women's oppression in U.S. society. First, the resolution argued, women served as a "reserve army of labor" to bring down wages for all workers. Second, women "perform free services . . . providing the necessities of life for the working class man at the lowest possible costs." Finally, women's oppression helped "obscure the class nature of . . . society." Male workers focused their "justified anger" stemming from their condition not at their bosses, but at those beneath them. "Again the analogy with racism is relevant," claimed the resolution's authors:

> White workers carry out racist oppression of black workers in the shops. While racism may serve to perpetuate the relative privilege of white workers, this is in no way to say that white workers ultimately profit by dominating black workers, or that men ultimately profit by dominating women, but rather to say that women (or black workers) suffer their immediate oppression at the hands of men (or white workers) who maintain a dominant position for themselves, and as supremacists, try to perpetuate that position of dominance.

The resolution's convoluted writing perhaps reflected SDS's efforts at walking a thin line. Against Old Left, PL-type arguments (and together with radical feminist analysis), the resolution insisted that white workers and men, believing in their superiority ("as supremacists"), did seek to maintain their domination. White workers and men were not the helpless victims of ruling-class subterfuge; rather, they were active agents of racial and sexual oppression. Against the radical feminists, however, "Advance" argued that whites and men had relative privilege; but it wasn't of ultimate significance. White workers and men were the immediate instruments of racial and sexual oppression, but implicitly the basis of that oppression was to be sought not in the immediate short-term interests of male workers, but in the systemic ruling-class interests. In short, unlike the radical feminists, "Advance" insisted that whites and men had a basis for being able to change.

Whatever its analytic or literary shortcomings, "Advance" did transcend the contradictions of the June 1967 "liberation of women" resolution. But the most substantial change that "Advance" made over Ignatin's original resolution involved male supremacy in the New Left itself: "Male supremacy in the movement mirrors male supremacy in capitalist society. The fact that male supremacy persists in the movement today raises the issue that, although no people's liberation can happen without a socialist revolution in this country, a socialist revolution could take place which maintains the secondary position of women in society. Therefore, the liberation of women must become a conscious part of our struggle for people's liberation." Concretely, the resolution insisted that "for women to become full political people in SDS" and for SDS to play a role in challenging women's oppression, "male supremacy must be eliminated within the organization itself." This was the strongest statement that SDS had made concerning its own organizational male supremacy. But like Ignatin's original resolution, "Advance" neither defined what male supremacy looked like nor prescribed any concrete means for dealing with the problem. Indeed, "Advance" left the door open to challenging male supremacy without challenging men: male supremacy could be defined wholly as women's passivity. Overcoming male supremacy, then, would involve only women ceasing to act like women, which was Dohrn's line.

Less than a month after the National Council passed the "Advance" resolution, male supremacy's intractability within the New Left made itself felt in the most dramatic fashion. The Mobe had called for a counterinaugural demonstration in Washington, D.C., to protest Richard Nixon's January 1969 presidential inauguration. From the start, Mobe leaders played reluctant host to the women liberationists. Although they agreed to a women's movement presentation at the counterinaugural rally, they did not publicize the radical women's participation. But if this oversight was typical of the New Left at the time, the fact that women's liberation movement people nevertheless secured a public role in the event reflected the movement's growing strength. As the event approached, radical feminists and politicos wrangled to define the nature of the women's participation in the event and finally agreed upon two statements: one by politico Marilyn Salzman Webb, and one by radical feminist Shulamith Firestone. Each side thought that the other side's position endangered the movement. Radical feminists worried that Salzman Webb's statement would be "too conciliatory" toward men, while the politicos worried that Firestone's would be "too antagonistic toward Movement men."[89]

Whatever their worries prior to the event, the program itself provided a convincing demonstration of how far the New Left stood from women's liberation. As soon as the moderate, conciliatory voice of women's liberation, Salzman Webb, began to assert the importance of women's equality, a tumult began in the crowd. Men began to shout, "Take it off!" and "Take her off the stage and fuck her!" By 1969, movement functions of this scale always had movement security people detailed in the crowd, and especially in front of the stage, in order to deal with provocateurs and right-wing counterdemonstrators. But this time movement security made no effort to quash the "pandemonium" breaking out. Nor did Mobe emcee, David Dellinger, the respected pacifist, make any effort to quiet the hecklers. On the contrary, Dellinger attempted to hustle the women off stage.

If this crowd, composed solely of people who had come to Washington to protest Nixon's inauguration and the Vietnam War's continuation, was in any way representative of the New Left's rank-and-file membership, it highlighted the absolute necessity for SDS to make a concerted effort at challenging men in the movement around their male-supremacist attitudes. The near-riot that occurred had exposed as inadequate any tack that failed to challenge movement men, or that relied only on insisting that women not act like women. Marilyn Salzman Webb, to the most limited degree, had not acted like a traditional woman.

When Salzman Webb returned to her Washington home on the evening of the event—and while she, Firestone, and others debated the event's significance—she received an anonymous phone call warning her against any future speeches like the one she had given at the counterinaugural. SDS, the caller told her, had "*the line*" on women's liberation, and she would have "the shit" beaten out of her if she crossed that line again. Although the caller was obviously trying to disguise her voice, at the time Salzman Webb believed that the caller was Cathy Wilkerson, a leading SDSer close to the national office and a member of Salzman Webb's Washington, D.C.-based women's group. Subsequently, Wilkerson denied that she had made the call and insisted that the call was a U.S. government counterintelligence operation. Nevertheless, in 1969 Salzman Webb believed Wilkerson had made the call, and that belief was sustained by the reality that SDS did have a line on the women's movement, a line that was antagonistic to that movement's development.[90]

Less than two months after the counterinaugural, national SDS publicly reiterated its commitment to "the line" on women's liberation, that is, to the line that placed the burden of change upon women for upending SDS's male supremacy. On March 8, 1969, SDS issued a special four-page "International Women's Day" edition of *New Left Notes*. Although this special edition was the first, and only, edition of the paper devoted to the women's movement, it was notable for its complete failure to attack male supremacy. Instead, this International Women's Day issue served only to reemphasize SDS's disdain for the women's movement, all the while proclaiming its fidelity to the principle of women's liberation.

The issue itself consisted of four articles, a poem, a fact sheet, and front page composed of two graphics and a photo. One of the graphics was borrowed from the Black Panther Party newspaper's talented artist Emory Douglass. Depicted was an African-garbed woman, a child slung upon her back, a rifle in one hand, and a "Black Studies" book in the other. The second graphic was a typical Chinese cultural revolution graphic: a martial arts–stanced woman, wind-whipped scarf about her neck, eyes determinedly set to the future, both arms upraised with rifles in each hand. The final photo on the page consisted of what appeared to be a woman resisting the police.

Two of the four articles dealt with Third World women. The first, titled "Women's Liberation in Revolutionary China," was an extract from the recently published *Fanshen*, by William Hinton. The second article was titled simply, "Arab Women Fight." Hinton's article described the process through which Chinese women attained rights in the course of China's revolution against Chiang Kai Shek's Nationalist government. Male peasants would deny their wives and daughters the right to attend revolutionary meetings and beat them when they disobeyed. Finally, the women's association would visit and, if necessary, trounce an errant husband. Certainly, this went beyond anything SDS contemplated, although radical feminists had been advocating similar steps. Nevertheless, the article emphasized something else, more in line with SDS's approach:

> Without the successful transformation of society, without the completion of land reform, without a victorious defense of the Liberated Areas against the probing attacks of the Nationalist armies, it was impossible to talk of liberation for women. Many women realized this as if by intuition, and they made the Women's Association an instrument for mobilizing the power of women behind the revolution in all its aspects.... [If the demand for women's equality] alarmed the men, the all-out support which the women gave to over-all revolutionary goals disarmed them and won from them a grudging admiration. In their hearts they had to admit that they could not win without the help of "half of China."

Here was the path to women's liberation advocated by SDS: fight in the common struggle and win men's admiration and finally their understanding of the significance of women's equality. In "Arab Women Fight," however, all notion was lost of fighting against male supremacy. It was "the requirements of total war, resistance to the occupier, [that] are again transforming traditional [sexual] relationships."

The issue's poem, "The Mud of Vietnam," was contributed by former black SNCC worker and regular *Guardian* columnist Julius Lester. Lester was one of the few male voices to have championed women's liberation as revolutionary and as a responsibility for men to take up. Nevertheless, his poem probably represented male SDSers' romanticization of Vietnam and fantasies of the "revolutionary woman." In it, Lester lyrically described Vietnamese women working in rice paddies, repairing bombed-out dikes, and planting rice, each venue refrained with the words "woman-thigh high/woman-thigh deep" in Vietnam's mud. He concluded:

I would like
to make love
woman-thigh high
woman-thigh deep
in
the
mud
of
Vietnam.

Two other articles rounded out the issue. "Women's Struggles in U.S. History," by Marilyn Katz, probably came closest to actually reflecting the consciousness of the existing women's liberation movement. But it did that only by indirectly challenging men and, once again, putting the accent on women's initiative. In discussing the struggles of female antebellum abolitionists, for example, Katz noted: "On the one hand, [the female antebellum abolitionists] . . . constantly fought the notion that women were inferior to men, and on the other hand they stressed the fact that women had to have political and social freedom in order to fight against slavery and all the increased exploitation that was manifesting itself as capitalism developed. Without the right to speak and organize, they would be by their inactivity supporting the continuation of slavery." In other words, what gave legitimacy to women's claims was that without recognizing women's rights, the evil of slavery would go unchallenged. It was, at best, unclear in this argument whether women's rights were a legitimate demand in and of themselves.

But pride of place in the issue went to SDS interorganizational secretary Bernardine Dohrn's article, "Toward a Revolutionary Women's Movement." Unlike the other articles in this special *New Left Notes*, Dohrn's article was about the contemporary domestic political scene. This was SDS's line on women's liberation.

Dohrn began by announcing that women's liberationists were split into two camps: the politicos and what Dohrn scornfully called the "professional women." Dohrn defined the politicos as "full time movement organizers," women who understood the nature of women's oppression, who raised the question of women's oppression as part of their overall work, and "who discount[ed] the revolutionary potential of a women's movement." By "professional women," Dohrn did not mean female lawyers, doctors, teachers, and the like, although certainly this was an implication in her choice of terms. By "professional women," Dohrn meant those women who were "women" by profession, who prioritized developing a women's liberation movement, "and who are generally cynical about the movement, any ideology, and SDS."

Dohrn then repeated the politico charge that the radical feminists and their consciousness-raising were self-indulgent—"personal liberation" and "therapy" she called it, evasions of real practice. And then some heavy language for SDSers: "Most of the women's groups are bourgeois, unconscious or unconcerned with class struggle and the exploitation of working class women, and chauvinists concerning the oppression of black and brown women." Dohrn had made a telling criticism of the radical feminists, but she used the criticism as a bludgeon to knock down her opponents and not as a means for elucidating what the actual relationship was between white and black women, and the oppression that each group of women faced. Moreover, SDS's own record of chauvinism and class bias, even as it struggled over these matters, left much to be desired. By hurling the charge of racial chauvinism against the radical feminists in this manner, Dohrn was creating a white "other" against which SDS could measure its own revolutionary appreciation of race.

And then some more heavy language: "the tendency represented by the separatists, the men-haters, the fanatical feminists share many of the reactionary dangers of cultural nationalism." Again, by likening the radical feminists to cultural nationalists, Dohrn was reaffirming SDS's position on race, setting itself up in parallel with the Black Panthers as a revolutionary vanguard, and using the Panthers' analysis as a tool for affirming SDS's own legitimacy. The Panthers had labeled cultural nationalism reactionary in the black movement. Cultural nationalists—as represented at the time by the Los Angeles–based black nationalist Ron Karenga and black poet LeRoi Jones—emphasized the need for black people to return to African culture and minimized the import of black political struggle. By placing radical feminists in parallel with the black cultural nationalists, Dohrn was suggesting that the radical feminists were not concerned with political struggle, but were only concerned with themselves as women. But this was not true. In March 1969, what feminist historian Alice Echols calls "cultural feminism" was a tendency in radical feminism, a tendency that would come to dominate the movement by the mid-1970s. Like cultural nationalism, cultural feminism would focus upon building women's institutions and women's culture, discounting the import of political struggle and structural change. But in 1969, none of the most important radical feminist theorists—Firestone, Brown and Jones, or the women in Boston's radical feminist Cell 16—had renounced political struggle or the necessity of revolutionary change. On the contrary, however they approached the question, the leading radical feminist theorists were attempting to situate their struggle as women in a larger context of revolutionary struggle.

No matter. Dohrn continued her attack: in being concerned only with "women," the radical feminists were leading "to a middle class single issue movement—and this at a time when the black liberation movement is polarizing the country, when national wars of liberation are waging the most advanced assaults on U.S. Imperialism, when the growth of the movement is at a critical stage." Earlier in her article, Dohrn had acknowledged that the radical feminists had correctly uncovered the historical tendency to submerge women's struggle "in favor of 'more important issues.'" But now Dohrn was doing precisely that. She continued: "Instead of integrating (not submerging) the struggles of women into the broader revolutionary movement, these women are flailing at their own middle class images. To focus only on sexual exploitation and the tyranny of consumption does not develop a mass understanding of the causes of oppression, and it does not accurately point at the enemy." Dohrn was demanding that the struggle against women's oppression be integrated into "the broader revolutionary movement." But this was a demand that SDS, which considered itself revolutionary, needed to take up, in the first place by trying to understand the nature of women's oppression. Moreover, the radical feminists did not limit their analysis of women's oppression to "sexual exploitation and the tyranny of consumption." On the contrary, they had developed some sophisticated analyses of the family and its significance for maintaining capitalism and empire. Nor were the radical feminists "flailing at their middle class images." All the radical feminists—and many of the politicos outside of SDS—were criticizing SDS for its rampant male supremacy. They were saying that they could not work in SDS's male-supremacist environment, that that environment itself robbed women of their dignity and thwarted the stated goals of the movement, the movement's "broader revolutionary" aims.

While Dohrn avoided directly addressing this criticism of SDS, she did make a glancing reference to the movement's male supremacy. Dohrn insisted that women be organized "around the totality of their oppression," linking given struggles in which women were involved with other struggles in society. By this, Dohrn was arguing that women should be organized against the oppression of class, race, capitalism, imperialism, as well as sex. With this as its organizational framework, Dohrn promised that the movement would succeed in "organizing masses of radical women." And with this growing base of radical women, Dohrn continued, "we will be in a much stronger position to destroy male supremacy within the movement, and to build the basis for future society." To radical feminists—and many politicos—this must have sounded very much like the old argument that other, more important issues needed to take precedence over women's issues, that the struggle against male supremacy needed to wait for a better day.[91]

Many years before this, the Italian Communist Party leader Antonio Gramsci had insisted that in polemics, one must be fair with one's opponents—that is, unless one's object was to create a desert around oneself. Being fair with one's opponents meant clearly and faithfully articulating their ideas and their analysis, critiquing those ideas and analysis at their strongest points and not mainly or simply at the point of obvious mistakes. The object of polemics, in this view, was to raise the level of discussion, to help one's followers, and opponents, understand the issues in a clearer light. Dohrn, and SDS more generally, wholly failed to live up to Gramsci's demand. On the contrary, even women's liberation movement politicos like Salzman Webb had collaborated in closeting the radical feminist analysis and in labeling its proponents "man-haters" and the like. New Left Notes had never published a radical feminist analysis, nor did SDS, which offered an extensive pamphlet line to its members, ever reprint leading pieces produced by the burgeoning women's movement. The National Office, flouting the charge given it by June 1967's "liberation of women" resolution, did not organize studies on the question, and most of the more than 300 SDS chapters were woefully ignorant of the developing literature on women's liberation. Even the major national New Left publication, the *Guardian*, only ran one or two brief articles and a few letters reflecting the radical feminist viewpoint prior to mid-1969. Dohrn's attack on radical feminism, then, was not a serious criticism. Rather, Dohrn was attempting to create a desert around SDS, to prejudice and secure SDS's base, especially its female base, from falling into the radical feminist camp, or from being swayed by its criticism of SDS's male supremacy. And it was more than this. Dohrn and, more generally, SDS and the New Left were not simply suppressing the radical feminist view; they were defending the movement's male supremacy.

If SDS leaders honestly had wanted to answer the radical feminist critique, if they really believed that the radical feminist argument on the centrality of sexual oppression was wrong, they could have answered these arguments effectively. They need only have launched a serious effort to uproot SDS's male supremacy. No answer would have disarmed more effectively radical feminism; no answer would have championed more clearly the principles that SDS claimed to uphold; no answer could have built more effectively a movement that really acted in solidarity with the struggles SDS professed to see as important.

Conversely, SDS's defense of male supremacy strengthened radical feminism and weakened antiracist politics in two significant ways. First, SDS had far more institutional weight than did the women's liberation movement. It had a national structure connected by a national newspaper, regional and national organizers, and regional and national conferences; it also stood at the center of a still larger movement with hundreds of local underground newspapers. Consequently, when SDS claimed the ground of antiracist politics and used that ground in order to defend its male supremacy, its institutional weight made it exceedingly difficult for women—inside or outside of SDS—to disentangle antiracist politics from male supremacy. More and more white women thus opted for jettisoning any politics that did not directly address their perceived oppression. Second, by attacking women's liberation as racist, SDS was seeking to prevent its own base of women supporters and members from defecting to the women's liberation movement. In carrying out a heavy-handed campaign of labeling women's liberation as racist, SDS sought to hold within the New Left those women with the longest antiracist experience. This meant that after its first year or year and a half, the women's liberation movement recruited new activists from among women with minimal or no prior movement experience. In short, SDS sought to prevent from working with women's liberation precisely those women who could most successfully integrate white women's struggles with antiracist and anti-imperialist analysis. It thereby strengthened radical feminism's propensity to place white women's concerns at the center of its agenda, to the exclusion of other issues.[92]

Aside from its defense of male supremacy, Dohrn's article had one further significance: it presaged the Weatherman paper, which would appear publicly in two months. "Toward a Revolutionary Women's Movement" anticipated Weatherman's use of the black movement and the Vietnamese struggle as bludgeons, as answers to any criticism raised against SDS or the line taken by the SDS national office.

Chapter Four

The New Left Starts
to Disintegrate

Even as late as mid-1968, SDS was unable to break with its historic ambivalence toward the black freedom movement. Eldridge Cleaver's repeated appeals to SDS to secure Carl Oglesby's participation as Cleaver's vice presidential candidate, and SDS's repeated dismissal of these appeals, here stands as the prime evidence. A number of factors went into SDS's ability to reject Cleaver's overtures. First, from the moment the Black Panther Party was founded, police subjected the Panthers to a campaign of harassment, arrest, and killings. This campaign weakened the Panthers' ability to lend guidance to the New Left. The Panthers not only had to defend themselves, but they needed the New Left's help in the process. Various stripes of New Leftists, liberals, and Old Leftists sought to manipulate this need in order to avoid a principled relationship with the Panthers. Second, and perhaps of greater importance, SDS itself was growing rapidly. Between April and November 1968, SDS had more than doubled its numbers, from 35,000 to over 80,000 members. This vast increase in membership brought with it a tremendous unevenness in SDS's political development. More significant, however, SDS's leadership came to see this huge membership—the largest Left organization in the nation since the 1930s—as a base for its own power and ego gratification. How easy it was to see SDS's growth as the product of its leaders' wisdom; how easy it was to forget the tremendous black social motion that had called SDS itself into being and had precipitated its growth again and again; how tempting it was for its leaders to see themselves as the new Lenins, leading an army of revolutionaries into battle.[1]

Moreover, within SDS itself, the Maoist PL was playing an ever more active role, reinforcing Old Left visions of white vanguards leading the world revolution. From its start in the early 1960s, PL conceived of itself as the American revolution's vanguard. Originally, the party had formed a youth organization, M2M, from which it sought to recruit new members. But less than two years after M2M's formation, PL dissolved the group in favor of working within SDS. As one historian put it, PL was more certain of recruiting out of the extant mass organization SDS than it was out of a minuscule M2M.[2] And, as a self-proclaimed vanguard, PL had a greater interest in SDS than simply recruiting from its ranks. Above all, PL needed to give proper guidance to SDS. As SDS grew into a formidable national organization, guiding SDS became all the more important. Moreover, given the black social movement's power and the leadership that that movement created for itself, defining for SDS a "correct" understanding of race, that is, an understanding that subordinated race to class in the Old Left fashion, came to have a paramount significance. Indeed, a self-acting and self-defining black movement challenged the very basis for PL's existence.

By the time of SDS's December 1968 Ann Arbor National Council meeting, PL had attracted a sufficient base within SDS ranks to make a real play for leadership over the organization. It would attempt to seize the initiative precisely on the issue through which it was most in danger of being overwhelmed by social realities—the issue of race. Thus, PL brought a large contingent of its supporters to Ann Arbor in order to fight, and narrowly win, the organization's centerpiece proposal, "Fight Racism; Build a Worker-Student Alliance; Smash Imperialism."

Of course, "Fight Racism" put forward the traditional Old Left understanding of race: race was subordinate to class. But the resolution's real heart lay in PL's new discovery that all nationalism, including black nationalism, was reactionary. In a section titled "Defeat Nationalism," PL argued:

> Nationalism has replaced pacifism as the main ideological weapon of the ruling class within the Black Liberation Movement. Nationalism is used to divert Third World people from struggle on a class basis and from making alliances with white workers and students. Because of the special super-exploitation of black people, their struggle is national in form and working class in content. Thus, at SF State there was a separate TWLF [Third World Liberation Front]. Usually a nationalist feeling is the initial conscious impetus towards struggle among black people. But the material basis of this struggle is class oppression. Consciousness of this oppression must become the predominant ideology for these struggles to win.[3]

PL had staked out its position in the struggle for SDS leadership. On the basis of political line, its main opponent was not any faction in SDS so much as it was revolutionary black nationalism: the Black Panther Party and the movement that had developed with SNCC's call for Black Power. In PL's view, the Panthers were not simply mistaken but actually represented the enemy within the revolutionary camp. By calling for Black Power, black nationalists diverted black people from their real enemy—the capitalist ruling class—and pushed them away from alliances with their real allies—the white working class.

The fact that PL could secure passage for its "Fight Racism" proposal indicated its growing strength within the organization. This strength was deceiving, however. In reality, PL had the loyalty of only a small fraction of the roughly 80,000 SDS members. But PL was a disciplined cadre organization. Its internal discipline allowed it to mobilize its closest adherents and turn them out for SDS's national conferences in greater proportion than their actual numbers in SDS. This was the key element in PL's national SDS strength.

PL's strength threatened SDS in two ways. First, despite its hyperrevolutionary rhetoric, PL was a profoundly conservative organization. Its stance toward black nationalism gave a seemingly revolutionary cover to people who felt threatened by the black movement's militancy and rhetoric. Young white people frightened by black assertiveness could reassure themselves that they still had a clearer vision of society and social change than did young blacks. Bolstered by PL, they could, along with the rest of liberal society, confidently proclaim that race was really not so important. PL's position on Vietnam had the same "white" content. While other elements in SDS were struggling to stand in solidarity with the Vietnamese struggle—that is, side with the Vietnamese against the United States' war of aggression—PL criticized the Vietnamese for accepting aid from the revisionist Soviet Union. As the United States was busy bombing Vietnam "back to the Stone Age" and killing two to three million Vietnamese, PL denounced what it termed "the Washington-Moscow-Hanoi Axis." While opposing the war, PL made it possible for young white people to continue to avoid committing themselves to anything larger than their own narrow, racialized vision. Moreover, PL complemented this political conservatism with a cultural conservatism: short hair, no dope, clean clothes, so as to appeal successfully to the "working class." Thus, PL's largely white cadre could continue to believe in their superior vision.

Second, and more important, SDS's growth depended upon its ability to remain open to the developing struggles of the black movement. From SDS's inception, the black movement had consistently set the tone for SDS politics, strategy, and tactics. SDS had certainly fought over the meaning of the black movement and often sought to define that movement's developments in ways that safely accorded with SDS's self-conceptions. But it had never so systematically discounted the movement as PL discounted it. If SDS adopted PL's stance toward the black movement, it would cut itself off from precisely the kind of social motion that had built SDS. Indeed, condemning the black movement would have transformed SDS into a sect, into a group that maintained its analysis in opposition to the real social struggles of the day.

Given this growing threat, mainstream SDSers scrambled to develop a coherent vision that would both counter PL's growing strength and remain open to the black movement as it was really developing. RYM politics in SDS developed out of these dual concerns.

RYM came from three distinct geographic regions of SDS activity: the Chicago National Office and Chicago regional SDSers led by Bernardine Dohrn, SDS national secretary Mike Klonsky, and Chicago SDSers Walter "Slim" Coleman, Noel Ignatin, and Howie Machtinger; the Jesse James Gang in the Midwest region, centered around Bill Ayers, Jim Mellen, and Terry Robbins; and the Columbia and New York regional SDS's action faction people, centered around Mark Rudd, John Jacobs (JJ), and other Columbia leaders. In general, the Chicago people had the most theoretical bent, looking to reshape Marxism in light of the upsurge of the black liberation movement. Coleman and Ignatin, in particular, were searching for a real understanding of the interrelation between racial and class dynamics in American society. Ignatin, who came out of an Old Left background and, at twenty-eight years of age, was older than most SDSers, had gone farthest in recasting Marxist theory to accord with America's racial realities.

In contrast, the James Gang arose in opposition to the theoretically inclined Ann Arbor SDS chapter leadership. Though Mellen had a history with the Left that dated back at least as far as PL's M2M and had a strong theoretical grounding, the James Gang SDSers were the most adamant actionists in the RYM coalition. Indeed, even their choice of name reflected the James Gang's "in your face" proclivities, although it is likely that the James Gang actionists would have chosen a different name had they known the history of the real James Gang. Nevertheless, Ayers and Robbins found PL's "base-building" strategy particularly irksome. Because PL insisted upon the industrial proletariat's centrality, it opposed any actions that might "alienate" SDS from this supposed constituency. But action—action that placed its leaders in the center of the storm—was precisely what the James Gang thrived upon.

In this initial period of RYM's formation, the James Gang actionists gave the least attention to the black movement. Ayers had become fully involved in SDS only within the previous year, inspired by the Columbia rebellion and the action he had seen at the Democratic National Convention demonstrations in Chicago in the summer of 1968.[4] By the fall of 1968, he and Robbins were traveling the Midwest SDS circuit, looking to reorient SDS politics in the direction of a far greater militancy. In language characteristic of the enthusiasm they brought to their task, Ayers and Robbins proclaimed: "There's a whole new set on campus. SDS is coming out of isolation; it's growing, maturing, developing—and not by watering down radical rhetoric, analysis, or practice; but by being and saying exactly who we are, and by offering to students real alternatives to the plastic jive-ass society the Man wants to put them in." If Ayers and Robbins pulled on black language to sustain their argument, they in no way saw the integral power of the movement from which that language sprang. On the contrary, the importance they ascribed to their mission left the content of militant politics aside. In Ayers and Robbins's assessment, the "base-builders" sorely underestimated the alienation that young people felt, and the consequent receptivity that those young people would have for militant politics. "Aggressive confrontation politics," the duo argued, would "begin to provide people" with options for life outside the confines of American society. Thus, the kinds of struggles that Ayers and Robbins were leading in midwestern chapters centered on "the most important issue facing the Movement today: that of the use of confrontation and aggressive politics in building revolutionary consciousness." And what was the role of the black movement for the James Gang? "We're saying to people that youth is the revolution," Ayers and Robbins argued, "that politics is about life, struggle, survival. . . . We're saying that there ain't no place to be today but in the Movement. . . . And we're saying to kids all over the place that if you're tired of the Vietnamese eating napalm for breakfast, if you're tired of the blacks eating gas for dinner, and YOU'RE tired of eating plastic for lunch, then give it a name: Call it SDS, and join us."[5] Thus, James Gang politics operated at least in part off a paternalistic notion of the black struggle, to the extent that it mentioned that struggle at all. Action and youth took precedence for the James Gang, along with the desire to put themselves at the head of a mass of angry white youths.

Finally, Columbia's action faction seems to have stood somewhere between the Chicago national office grouping and the James Gang, on the whole leaning toward the actionists, and, in the person of Jacobs, giving action factionists a powerful anti-imperialist theoretical framework. Moreover, as we've seen, the Columbia action faction had itself taken shape in the very shadow of Harlem. Consequently, like the Chicago RYM center, Jacobs and Rudd both accorded a tremendous significance to the black movement.

By December 1968, as PL's challenge became more and more pronounced, the three RYM streams came together behind the first RYM proposal. Submitted by SDS national secretary Mike Klonsky, the proposal offered the first systematic response to PL's challenge and, shortcomings notwithstanding, defended the black movement as it was actually developing. Klonsky began the piece by establishing his bona fides with "revolutionary Marxism" and by undermining PL's monopoly of "class" language. According to Klonsky, SDS was facing "its most crucial ideological decision, that of determining its direction with regards to the working class." Unlike

PL, however, which subordinated everything to a narrowly defined class struggle, the RYM proposal offered a vision of class struggle that defined anti-imperialist struggles, including the struggle of black people in the United States, as being the truest "expression of the working class at its most conscious level."

Having established a broader notion of the working class to which it would address itself, RYM also defined a "transitional strategy" to get from where it was—a white student organization—to where it wanted to be—an organization of the white working class. Reaching white working-class youth would be the key that transformed SDS. Moreover, this was not an arbitrary strategy. White working-class youth, RYM argued, faced particularly sharp contradictions: they had not been socialized to the same extent as older workers; the government made youth fight in Vietnam; young workers did not yet have secure jobs; nor did they have the kind of commitments to stability that older workers possessed. In short, white working-class youth were more open to revolutionary politics than were older workers. Consequently, RYM argued that the path to organizing the working class lay through organizing working-class youth.

Moreover, Klonsky insisted that "building a class-conscious youth movement means fighting racism. SDS must see this fight as a primary task." In fact, white racism—"white supremacy"—tied "white people to the state by splitting them from the most aggressive class struggle." Racism therefore was a "central contradiction in American society." In order to fight it, SDS had to recognize and ally with the struggle that blacks were waging for liberation in America. That struggle, Klonsky continued, was both "an anticolonial struggle against racism and the racist imperialist power structure" and a central part of the class struggle within the United States.[6]

The RYM proposal, then, which passed at the December 1968 National Council meeting by a narrow margin, clearly defended black nationalism. But since the National Council had also passed PL's "Fight Racism" proposal, with its opposition to black nationalism, SDS was now on record as both attacking and supporting the black nationalist movement at one and the same time. Once again, however, the reality and the power of the black movement, and the attacks upon it, intruded upon SDS's debates, pushed SDS forward, and unified the RYM tendency to a still greater extent.

First, in the fall of 1968 black students seized the agenda for campus-based activism. Beginning at San Francisco State (SF State) in November 1968, black students led a veritable wave of rebellions across the nation's campuses. On November 6, following SF State's suspension of professor George Murray, who was also the Panthers' minister of education, the campus Black Student Union (BSU) called for a strike. In addition to demanding Murray's reinstatement, BSU demanded an autonomous black studies department and open admissions policies for black students from the city's high schools. SF State's Third World Liberation Front (TWLF), composed of

Asian and Latino students, quickly endorsed the demands, joined a coalition with BSU and added demands for establishing Third World studies programs.[7] Ironically, PL dominated SF State's SDS chapter, and several of the TWLF leaders were PL members. Initially, PL supported the strike and falsely presented itself to SDS as leading the action of what would become the longest running, and one of the bloodiest, campus confrontations of the decade. Indeed, PL gained credibility in SDS by virtue of its proximity to the SF State struggle. But politics ultimately outed PL. Following its December "Smash Racism" proposal victory, PL reversed itself on the strike and denounced the strike demands as nationalist and therefore reactionary and racist.[8]

The media intensively covered the SF State struggle, particularly after the appointment of hard-liner S. I. Hayakawa to the school's presidency. Hayakawa repeatedly sanctioned police attacks on the protesters, and images of police with three-foot riot batons bloodying students flooded the media, spreading word of the struggle across the country. Black and other Third World students rapidly followed the example of SF State students. Black students at state and community colleges in the Los Angeles area, for example, shut down their schools in January 1969: San Fernando Valley State College (SFVSC) students won black and brown studies departments; Southwestern Junior College students and East Los Angeles College students shut their schools down over the same demands; between 4,000 and 6,000 students and community members demonstrated at Los Angeles Valley College demanding police off their campus and expressing solidarity with the SFVSC demands. In small black colleges and community colleges across the nation, the story was the same. Administrators closed Wiley College in Marshall, Texas, "indefinitely" and had the Texas Rangers sweep and clear the campus in the wake of student struggles. At Mississippi Valley State College in Ita Bena, administrators suspended 200 students in struggles over the same demands. At Stillman College in Tuscaloosa, Alabama, 150 students occupied the administration building, demanding the firing of racist teachers. Black and Third World students at Swarthmore and Brandeis occupied campus facilities raising the same type of demands. Similar struggles occurred at Duke; City College of New York; the University of Illinois, Champaign-Urbana; the University of California, Berkeley; Roosevelt University; the University of California, Santa Barbara; Williams College; Brooklyn College; Eastern Michigan University, Ypsilanti; the University of North Carolina, Chapel Hill; and the University of Houston. Black high school students also mobilized against racist teaching practices and inferior facilities across the country: in Los Angeles, 10,000 black students took part in confrontations in support of their demands; in Orlando, Florida, 3,000 black students boycotted classes in support of their demands. These struggles culminated in the armed seizure of a building by black students at Cornell University.[9]

To be sure, antiwar, antirecruiting, and antiwar-research demonstrations continued during this time on campuses across the nation. But in their militancy and in their breadth, the black and Third World student struggles through the winter and spring of 1969 clearly set the terms for campus activism. Even black nationalism's opponents were compelled to acknowledge this fact. SDS's Southern California Regional Council, for example, admitted that SDS had to sort out its relationship to "black and brown movements on campus." Citing what it called "San Francisco State Fever," the council noted that these black and brown movements had "to an increasing degree ... taken the initiative in, and the leadership of campus struggles." SDS's primary error in relating to these struggles, the council complained, involved uncritically accepting black leadership.[10]

But the New Left's uncritical acceptance of black leadership was not the problem that black student leaders perceived in this period. One of the SF State BSU leaders, Nesbit Crutchfield, for example, criticized white radicals for their inability to accept black leadership. Even though white leftists considered themselves "the vanguard" of the New Left, many of them, said Crutchfield, were still "racists." "They found it very difficult, very, very difficult," Crutchfield explained, "to take directions and orders from a third world group." First, argued Crutchfield, "I think they found it difficult because it's never been done before." Second,

> they found it difficult because in the past they had been accustomed to telling other people what to do and telling other people how good what they were doing for them was for them; and for the first time they found themselves doing something for not only the third world people, but for themselves, and getting the direction from those third world people. And for white people no matter how radical they are this is very difficult. We are beginning to realize more clearly every day, that no matter how radical you are, being white in this society you are bombarded with so much racism that you can't help it if a little bit rubs off.[11]

RYM people, while supporting black nationalism in theory, saw problems in RYM's response to the black-led struggles as well. Mike Klonsky noted that the many black struggles, "all blowing up, one after another, left many newly developing chapters in a frenzy" and politically unprepared. "While the contradictions were sharpening each day for the small percentage of black students on the college campuses," Klonsky complained, "the white students were, as usual, thinking white."[12] Thus, the black and Third World student struggles pushed all of RYM's tendencies to fortify their theoretical understandings of race, and strengthened their resolve to support the black nationalist struggle.

Simultaneously, U.S. and local government attacks upon the Panthers intensified. In November 1968, San Francisco police raided the local party headquarters. In
January 1969, members of a Los Angeles black cultural nationalist group, instigated
by COINTELPRO forces, assassinated two local Panther leaders. Los Angeles police
followed up the assassination by arresting the entire Los Angeles Panther leadership.[13]
Less than three months later, New York police arrested the entire New York City
Panther leadership—the "Panther 21"—charging them with a massive conspiracy to
carry out a bombing campaign in New York.[14] This conspiracy bust foreshadowed an
entire wave of conspiracy busts across the nation: authorities arrested Panthers in virtually every city in which the party operated.

In the wake of the massive black and Third World student uprisings, and the
intensifying government campaign against the Panthers, RYM people sought to
shore up their theoretical analysis of race and their practical support for the Panthers.
In preparation for the Austin National Council meeting in March, RYM people put
forward four proposals: a James Gang proposal for an SDS summertime white community organizing project that would counter a PL summer "work-in" organizing
proposal; and three resolutions from Chicago's RYM people: one for a May Day
action, one for a program giving specific guidance in light of the black student struggles, and, most important from a theoretical perspective, another resolution supporting the Panthers and formally repudiating PL's "Smash Racism" resolution.

The James Gang proposal, "Hot Town: Summer in the City, or, I Ain't Gonna
Work on Maggie's Farm No More," coauthored by Bill Ayers and Jim Mellen, showed
Mellen's more theoretical hand at work. More important still, it showed the radical
influence that the black and Third World student struggles and the repression against
the Panthers had made on the James Gang actionists. In lines that directly attacked
PL's Old Leftism and would later find fuller development in the Weatherman
proposal, Ayers and Mellen argued that the "sharpest struggle against the ruling
class" was that struggle "waged by the oppressed nations against U.S. imperialism."
Contrary to PL's understanding of a class struggle that centered on the internal
workings of the United States, Mellen and Ayers insisted that "all our actions must
flow from our identity as part of an international struggle against U.S. imperialism."
Moreover, "Hot Town" argued for recognition of the "vanguard character of the
black liberation struggle." To the James Gang RYM people, this meant recognizing
the black movement's importance to the New Left. In a rare acknowledgment from
SDSers, Ayers and Mellen explicitly recognized that

the black liberation struggle has been instrumental in winning much of the white
movement to a clearer understanding of imperialism, class oppression within the United

States, the reactionary nature of pacifism [*sic*], the need for armed struggle as the only road to revolution, and other essential truths which were not predominant within our movement in the past. It must be clear that setbacks to the vanguard are tremendous setbacks to the people's movement as a whole.

Above all, however, "Hot Town" was a practical program aimed at setting up a prototype organizing project in Detroit over the summer. The project's main objective would be to attempt to win white youth in Detroit neighborhoods to "a consciousness of solidarity with the black movement and of their own class position in imperialist America."[15] Thus, the actionist James Gang, pushed by PL's attack on black nationalism as well as by the state's attacks on the Panthers, and by the Panthers' growing strength and the huge upsurge of black student struggle, articulated one of SDS's clearest statements of support for the black movement. Indeed, "Hot Town" had set as its goal just what Carmichael had asked of the white radical movement almost three years earlier. Nevertheless, it remained to be seen just how SDS would implement "Hot Town."

Two of Chicago's RYM proposals were not so concrete as the James Gang proposal, but nevertheless contained some important theoretical insights. The May Day resolution reiterated the argument that white workers had a white skin privilege that tied them to national chauvinism and racism; that black worker struggles—such as black worker-led wildcat strikes in the auto industry—were breaking down that chauvinism in white workers; and that, in general, as the U.S. empire came under increasing attack, so the material basis for chauvinism would be undermined.[16] RYM's "The Schools Must Serve the People" proposal came directly out of RYM leadership's desire to avoid the "frenzy" and confusion it saw as chapters sought to orient themselves in relation to the burgeoning black and brown student struggles. Slim Coleman, author of the proposal, explicitly argued that "the key fight today is against white supremacy" and that that fight had been "raised primarily by the black liberation movement." The proposal's practical portions reiterated black and brown student demands for black studies programs, open admissions, and an end to tracking, and stressed the import of white radicals backing these demands.[17]

But the most important—and curious—of the RYM proposals was the proposal to support the Panthers, "The Black Panther Party: Toward the Liberation of the Colony." As with the "Hot Town" proposal, "Toward the Liberation of the Colony" began by affirming that "the sharpest struggles in the world today" were the struggles of the oppressed "against imperialism and for national liberation." Within the United States, "the sharpest struggle is that of the black colony for its liberation." Complementing this support for the black nationalists, the resolution explicitly repudiated PL's "all nationalism is reactionary" line and December's "Fight Racism" resolution. But then RYM went beyond anything it had argued in the past and asserted that the Panthers constituted the vanguard of the black liberation movement in the United States. As the vanguard, with its "correct and uncompromising leadership," the Panthers had brought down on themselves "the most vicious repression" from the government. With the number of Panthers killed, jailed, or forced into exile mounting daily, Chicago's RYM people argued that it would be a "mockery" for SDS to do less than offer total support in defense of the Panthers. Moreover, support for the Panthers included the necessity for SDS to take on the strongest possible struggle against white supremacy, both outside and inside the movement.

Significantly, while the resolution praised the Panthers' entire ten-point program as "essentially correct," it insisted that "an especially important part of the Panther program is the Black People's Army—a military force to be used not only in the defense of the black community but also for its liberation."[18] Here was the old male ERAP predilection for being "tough" manifesting itself in how SDS chose to support the Panthers. It was an unfortunate, if typical, SDS determination. The Panthers themselves, coming under increasing attack, were understanding that their organizational and even personal survival depended upon their ability to base themselves strongly in the black community. SDS's emphasis upon the Panthers' military program occurred just as the Panthers themselves chose to de-emphasize that program and strengthen their community-organizing programs.

Given SDS's emphasis on Panther militancy, manifest earlier in its rejection of the Panther electoral program, one older SDS member wondered pointedly whether "we really mean to follow them, or just let them get mowed down?"[19] It was a good question, and one that would have increasing weight over the next several months.

One other major contradiction marked SDS's Panther resolution: SDS had not simply affirmed support for the Panther program in the face of concerted government attacks and in opposition to PL's "all nationalism is reactionary" line. Rather, SDS had declared, quite unequivocally, that the Panthers were the vanguard of the black revolution. Six months earlier, however, SDS had rejected an electoral alliance with the Panthers on the grounds, in part, that that alliance would involve an unwarranted intervention in the internal affairs of the black liberation movement. Whether that particular concern was accurate or not, designating the Panthers as the vanguard of the black struggle very clearly intervened in the black movement's internal process.

Former black SNCC worker and *Guardian* columnist Julius Lester took SDS to task precisely for this intervention. Lester acknowledged that the Panthers were under serious government attack and insisted that it was wholly within SDS's province to completely support the Panthers against this attack. However, with its assertion that the Panthers were the vanguard of the black liberation movement, SDS had gone beyond simply defending the beleaguered group. With the rise of Black Power, Lester argued, blacks had asserted that black people would "define for themselves" the course and trajectory of their struggle. SDS, by declaring that the Panthers were the vanguard of the black struggle, had intruded on the internal business of the black movement and had shown its white supremacist features in the process. SDS's real business, Lester contended, was organizing whites. In that business, SDS had fallen far short of defining the parameters of a "revolutionary ideology, program and strategy." Yet SDS presumed to determine for the black community "categorically who the black vanguard is, what the correct ideology is, what the correct military strategy is and the what the correct program is." SDS was in no position to know what was correct for the black community's struggle; at the same time, if it presumed to determine that the Panther program was correct, it needed to discuss why the programs of other black organizations—SNCC included—were incorrect. To have done so, of course, would have made it still more clear that SDS was intervening in a debate within the black community.[20] Moreover, Lester averred, white radical infatuation with the Panthers seemed to stem from what the former SNCC activist termed the "'Oh I wish I were black' syndrome." And this syndrome itself, Lester argued, was "merely whites once again side-stepping the difficult work of organizing in the white community."[21]

Even at Austin, at the very high tide of the black liberation movement, SDSers found it very difficult to break with their traditional white views on race. Declaring that the Panthers were the vanguard of the black revolution was perhaps the sharpest manifestation of this white thinking. SDS had, over the life of the organization, continually played catch up with the understandings generated by the black movement. But it had continually tried to deny that it was playing catch up by defining the black movement's work as particular work, or by taking advanced black social thought, rewriting it into white language, and forgetting its origins. Determining that the Panther organization was the black revolutionary vanguard only updated SDS's "welcoming" of the turn to Black Power. SDS was attempting to put itself back in the driver's seat.

One other major contradiction marked RYM's efforts in the winter and early spring of 1969: its continued inability to deal with the organization's male supremacy. SDS had issued its "International Women's Day" edition of New Left Notes less than a month before Austin. This attack on the women's movement had corrupted SDS's antiracist politics by using those politics to deflect women's criticisms of the New Left's male supremacy. Thus, RYM had entered on a dangerous path. RYM was using its more advanced understandings of race not only to combat racism but also to defend its own male supremacy. This contradiction would continue to play itself out over the next several months.

At the Austin National Council, the RYM proposals all passed, and RYM forces succeeded in repudiating PL's line on black nationalism. But the real showdown loomed at SDS's annual national convention, slated for June in Chicago. If PL could mobilize for the June convention sufficient to win the national officers' elections, it could more than exact revenge for the Austin defeat.

Moreover, while RYM partisans had been victorious at Austin, RYM's position was still riven with the contradictions of whiteness and maleness. Its analysis of race had advanced, but it had not decisively broken with a white perspective. RYM would mobilize again for the June convention, both politically and practically. Its opponent, however, was not only PL but also the kind of thinking that held it to the past, to the notion of white centrality in the struggle for social change. But while RYM's SDSers were aware of the threat posed by PL, they were considerably less well prepared to take on their own internal weaknesses.

Of course, RYM was more than simply a coalition of three regional groupings. From the start, RYM had included people who genuinely were working to understand the tremendous struggle unfolding before their eyes so that they might better contribute to it. It also included those who more simply sought to throw themselves into the thick of the action, as leaders of course. To be sure, all RYM people probably held within themselves varying proportions of both elements, and those proportions were themselves constantly changing in accord with the general ebb and flow of the black movement. By the late spring of 1969, what had been regional groupings had coalesced into two groupings based on emphasis. The numerically dominant group, RYM I, Weatherman, represented the actionist approach, with Ayers, Rudd, Jacobs, and Dohrn leading the group. RYM II, led by Klonsky, Coleman, Ignatin, and the San Francisco Bay Area's Bob Avakian, grounded itself in a more traditional take on Marxism than did RYM I. Nevertheless, the split itself, and the actual positions taken by both RYM I and RYM II, reflected the strengthening of "white ideology" in SDS as the black movement rapidly weakened.

Even before RYM's split, however, one New Leftist, Clayton Van Lydegraf, discerned the political tendencies in RYM and their connection to RYM's white-centered thinking. It was probably in order to take on PL that RYM's leaders first turned to Van Lydegraf. An older white leftist—indeed, at least a quarter of a century older than most SDSers—Van Lydegraf had been a Communist Party USA member and had split from the party to help found what would become PL. When PL more and more explicitly repudiated revolutionary nationalist struggles, Van Lydegraf broke with PL. As a former PL leader, Van Lydegraf would be a handy ally against the Old Left group. Still, if RYM was calling on Van Lydegraf for his aid in taking on PL, Van Lydegraf, a serious student of Marxism, had his own agenda and hoped to sway RYM. Like Ignatin, Van Lydegraf had given deep thought to the problem of white supremacy, and on this count he would challenge not only PL but RYM as well.

Following the Austin National Council, *New Left Notes* ran an insightful piece by Van Lydegraf based on a pamphlet he had published some months earlier, *The Movement and the Workers*. The article, "About Privilege," was a polemical piece that quickly dismissed PL, neatly packaging its line as "the false claim that anti-imperialist struggle and anticolonial war are 'reactionary nationalism.'" Van Lydegraf's real target in the polemic, however, was RYM itself and its continuing efforts to place white activists in the center of the struggle at the very moment those activists were most passionately asserting their fealty to "black and Third World leadership." Moreover, Van Lydegraf discerned and confronted the two ways in which RYM people were managing to reassert their centrality to social struggle: the tendency to transform privilege into the totality of white working-class life; and the tendency to liquidate privilege and transform it into something wholly psychological. In a matter of months, these two RYM tendencies would split into Weatherman and RYM II.

Van Lydegraf focused the bulk of "About Privilege" on depicting imperialism's structural relations and the significance of white skin privilege to empire and to the white working class. RYM had adopted the concept of white skin privilege as part of its struggle with PL. But less than three months after RYM's founding, that part of RYM that would become RYM II was already interpreting white skin privileges as being "insignificant." "Well," said Van Lydegraf, "the hell they are":

> In fact, white workers (the male first, but also the female and the young to an important degree) possess immediate selfish advantage automatically accorded to white persons. This advantage exists as an indispensable prop of the super-exploitation and colonial oppression practiced by imperialism at home and abroad; all economic activity of the United States rests upon this foundation and proceeds both directly and indirectly at the expense of oppressed peoples....
>
> These facts are clear as daylight to blacks and to most of the world. Only among whites in imperialist nations ... is there muddled talk about "privilege" which comes from heaven, but not at the expense of the oppressed.

On the other hand, Van Lydegraf argued, it was as much an abdication of RYM's responsibility to see privilege as entirely defining the character of the white working class as it was to see it as having no meaning. Here Van Lydegraf was targeting the nascent Weatherman tendency. White privilege tied white workers to imperialism, true, but it also separated them from their own interests as workers. White workers' lives, consciousness, and politics were defined by the struggle between these two contradictory elements: white workers' privilege as against their place as workers. Consequently, argued Van Lydegraf, "this contradiction exists and must be fought out—not falsified by presenting the worker as either a pure fighting man free from any taint of opportunism or to the contrary as nothing but a complete and utterly hopeless sell-out." By making privilege all or nothing, both of the nascent RYM groups were liquidating their responsibility to make social change, to organize white workers.

Back of this failure lay the structures and associated ideologies of race and empire. Racism and imperialism were not external evils, Van Lydegraf insisted, but existed in the lives and brains and souls of ordinary white people, SDS "revolutionaries" included. As was his wont, Van Lydegraf argued this with all the drama and color he could muster:

> We live as constituent parts of a social system which has been mass-producing all kinds of filth and garbage for generations....
>
> It is not surprising that even as we discover that revolution is the only basic solution, we also find that we are still carriers of the festerous and lingering stench which permeates everything connected with imperialism and slavemaking.
>
> A few quick showers do not wash away contamination ground in by years spent as willing or unwilling flunkies to the rulers of a monster system. The movement is beginning to understand this. It is organizing programs to fight against white supremacy and to support black liberation....
>
> Nevertheless, it is not easy to break clean away from the old patterns....
>
> Serious revolutionaries, and there are beginning to be serious ones who are white, have to scrub away at the old system stink. The exploiters and oppressors have been using our minds as an outhouse for ages. We need to analyze this and work out the contradictions to know what we have to do.[22]

Less than six weeks after *New Left Notes* published "About Privilege," the first returns appeared against Van Lydegraf's analysis at SDS's final national convention.

RYM I people prepared a lengthy political statement titled "You Don't Need a Weatherman to Know Which Way the Wind Blows" for the national convention. While Weatherman, as the paper and the group came to be known, did not definitively categorize white workers as sellouts, the statement's tone and emphases laid the groundwork for that categorization. The paper reiterated much of what the earlier RYM proposals had argued, but in still sharper language and greater detail. It began by arguing that since the United States was the center of world capitalism and imperialism, revolutionaries needed to assess all struggles from the standpoint of whether those struggles aided or opposed U.S. imperialism. The United States' relative affluence, Weatherman argued, was "directly dependent upon the labor and natural resources of the Vietnamese, the Angolans, the Bolivians and the rest of the peoples of the Third World." Given that fact, "any conception of 'socialist revolution' simply in terms of the working people of the United States ... is a conception of a fight for a particular privileged interest."

Here was an important elucidation of the "Hot Town" proposal's assertion that struggle in the United States needed to be assessed by its relation to world anti-imperialist struggles. This also accorded closely with the black struggles' historical assessment that lower-class white struggles had been struggles for privilege.

Following the lead of the Panthers and of SNCC, Weatherman also argued that blacks within the United States constituted an internal colony and that their struggle was every bit as much a fight against imperialism as were the struggles of other peoples outside of the United States. Indeed, the black struggle within the United States "reflect[s] the interests of the oppressed people of the world from within the borders of the United States; they are part of the Third World and part of the international revolutionary vanguard." What made the black struggle within the United States especially significant, Weatherman argued, was the fact that it could not succeed without taking down the whole of U.S. imperialism.

Even in the sharp form that Weatherman laid out its argument, most of what it said was not new. Carmichael had said as much in 1966 when he rejected his "piece of the American pie," and the Panthers had been saying the same things for some time. Even in the early 1960s, Malcolm X had offered the same arguments, minus the Marxist-type language. Perhaps it was significant, or perhaps it was simply an oversight, but Weatherman failed to explicitly acknowledge this intellectual debt.[23]

Weatherman then proceeded to argue for the old RYM strategy—organizing working-class youth was a transition to organizing the larger white working class. But, the paper cautioned, simply because RYM had not yet reached "a certain percentage of the working class" did not mean that it was not a working-class movement. On the contrary:

We are already that if we put forward internationalist proletarian politics. We also don't have to wait to become a revolutionary force. We must be a self-conscious revolutionary force from the beginning, not be a movement which takes issues to some mystical group—"THE PEOPLE"—who will make the revolution. We must be a revolutionary movement of people understanding the necessity to reach more people, all working people, as we make the revolution.

Having established themselves as a revolutionary movement, Weatherman continued by laying out a "Hot Town" community-organizing perspective. More than "Hot Town," however, Weatherman laid out its philosophical approach to organizing—a real actionist, James Gang approach:

"Relating to motion": the struggle activity, the action, of the movement demonstrates our existence and strength to people in a material way. Seeing it happen, people give it more weight in their thinking. For the participants, involvement in struggle is the best education about the movement, the enemy and the class struggle. . . . We must build a movement oriented toward power. Revolution is a power struggle, and we must develop that understanding among people from the beginning.

What did this mean in practice? As an example, Weatherman argued that rather than making a demand that the schools "should serve the people"—taking a swipe at Coleman's Austin National Council resolution—RYM should be calling instead for shutting the schools down. Why? "Kids are ready for the full scope of militant struggle, and already demonstrate a consciousness of imperialism, such that struggles for a people-serving school would not raise the level of their struggle to its highest possible point."[24] RYM did not need to take on the hard work of winning people to an understanding of imperialism and racism. Young whites already understood that. What these young people needed was not an explanation of the problem, but a demonstration of the solution—action. (Hence, "you don't need a weatherman to know which way the wind blows.") Two months later, Weatherman leader Bill Ayers would expand on this vision in his address to a Weatherman National Action conference. Explained Ayers:

When [Weatherman activists] . . . in Detroit go into a drive-in, and talk to those kids about the war and about the international struggle, and talk to those people about racism and male supremacy and pigs, they're not just talking on an intellectual level and saying see, here's what's happening, this is why you're fucked up, because those kids know that already. We don't have to say to people what's wrong, we have to say to people what do you do about it, and what you do about it is you fight, you fight back, and you join together with your brothers and sisters, and you kick ass, that's what you do about it.

Thus, Weatherman did not need to grapple with the contradictory nature of white experience—white privilege versus white class. Simply by acting, by setting an example, Weatherman would cut open that knot.[25]

In short, Weatherman answered the question of how it would make revolution in two opposing ways. On the one hand, Weatherman designated the international struggle against imperialism as the vanguard of the socialist revolution. Within the United States itself, Weatherman assigned the vanguard status to the black struggle, as representative of the world anticolonial struggle. On the other hand, Weatherman posited no necessary practical connection to that vanguard. On the contrary, Weatherman derived an authority for itself simply by recognizing the international character of the struggle. "We ... don't have to wait to become a revolutionary force" or a working-class movement. "We are already that if we put forward internationalist proletarian politics." Like other SDSers in the past, Weatherman managed to salvage a vanguard role for itself—it could yet play a defining role in the social drama of its time. And this defining role, might, if the need arose, extend to Weatherman defining the nature, tactics, and ideology of the black struggle itself.

In the face of the actionists having consolidated a RYM proposal, the core of the Chicago RYM people responded with RYM II. Unlike Weatherman, RYM II was a far more traditional Marxist reading of revolution, especially with its emphasis on the "industrial proletariat." Nevertheless, RYM II also began with a reiteration of the RYM position: "the principal contradiction in the world is that between U.S. imperialism and the oppressed nations." The working class in the United States, if it were to assume the role of carrying the struggle against U.S. imperialism to the end, would have to "link up its struggles with those of the oppressed peoples." To establish that link, however, would require that white workers take up "as their own slogan the right to self-determination for the nations oppressed by U.S. imperialism."

What was most curious about the RYM II proposal, however, was what it said about the black struggle. SNCC and the Panthers had both defined the conditions of blacks in the United States as being colonial in nature. But neither SNCC nor the Panthers had defined the parameters of that colony. Implicitly, the Panthers' ten-point program suggested that all blacks were members of the colony. Point ten, for example, demanded that all blacks be permitted to vote in a plebiscite on the status of an independent black nation within the United States. Practically, the Panthers called for black community control of the institutions that affected the black community. But if the two most significant black nationalist organizations of the latter 1960s had not defined the black colony, that was no reason for white New Leftists not to. RYM II went back to the deliberations of the Communist International (Comintern) in 1928 and discovered in those arcane debates that a black nation existed in the Black Belt region of the South. White workers, RYM II insisted, had to support the self-determination of this Black Belt nation.[26]

If RYM II did not hesitate before defining the nature of the black colony, at least it acknowledged that SDS would have to organize white workers against white skin privilege in order to win support for black self-determination, something Weatherman failed to do. Moreover, RYM II also at least paid lip service to the extant black liberation movement: it would also seek to organize white workers to support all democratic rights for blacks, including the right to community control of the institutions affecting the black community.

With the caveat of a black nation, RYM II returned to the more traditional Marxist industrial proletariat as the ultimate grave digger of capitalism. "We will never be able to destroy U.S. imperialism," RYM II argued, "unless the proletariat—white, brown, and black—is brought solidly into the anti-imperialist movement.... Imperialism is not in the interests of the mass of the working class."[27] Implicitly, RYM II was insisting that blacks could only attain their liberation first, as proletarians, and second, as part of a united proletariat, white workers included. Moreover, the notion that "imperialism is not in the interests of the mass of the working class" seemed to indicate, ever so cautiously, a backing away from the notion of white skin privilege. As Van Lydegraf had indicated, the interests of the mass of the white working class were both tied to imperialism and opposed to it.

In defining the exact parameters of the black colony it would support, and in insisting on the need for black workers to ally with white workers as a means of attaining their liberation, RYM II ran up against Carmichael's argument from three years earlier—that the oppressor, which included white workers, could not be allowed to define the struggle of the oppressed. RYM's temerity also stood far distant from the white radical attitudes in the summer of 1967—the "high tide of black liberation"—when black representatives at the NCNP demanded and were ceded 50 percent of the convention's votes.

Both Weatherman and RYM II represented retreats from positions taken at the Austin National Council; or, perhaps more realistically, RYM I and RYM II reflected how shallow were the positions taken at Austin. Weatherman reflected a strengthening of the actionist James Gang tendency that had, to some extent, been submerged in the "Hot Town" proposal. In retreating to a Comintern position dating to 1928, RYM II had definitely slipped back to an older Marxist analysis. Moreover, both the Weatherman and RYM II papers represented a strengthening of the most backward elements of the Panthers-as-vanguard proposal. In the face of escalating government repression against the black movement, then, both RYM factions had taken steps to reassert more strongly their own white-centered definitions of the nature of the struggle.

Two other significant struggles occurred at the June 1969 National Conference in Chicago: the struggle over SDS's attitude to the still-growing women's liberation movement, and PL's expulsion from SDS. The two issues were joined dramatically on the second day of the five-day conference. SDSers had gone to Chicago knowing that the struggle with PL would take center stage. To bolster their position in that struggle, RYM leaders engineered a show of solidarity for the second day of the convention in which representatives of the Young Lords, a Puerto Rican nationalist group, and the Black Panthers would address the assembly.[28] It would be a powerful blow to PL and its "all nationalism is reactionary line." Yet despite the hatred many SDSers felt for PL, prior to the National Council, few New Leftists conceived of booting PL from the organization. The Panthers, however, were fully aware of PL's animosity toward black nationalism. Hence, the Panthers were unrestrained in their contempt for PL. Chaka Walls, a Chicago Panther, mounted the rostrum and, in an obvious critique of PL, denounced those "armchair Marxists" who condemned all nationalism as reactionary. But then Walls seemed to veer from his subject and raised the issue of women's role in the movement.[29]

Gender politics in the black movement had developed apace since the Hayden and King SNCC paper in 1964, largely to the detriment of black women's roles. Because of its community-organizing philosophy, SNCC in the early and mid-1960s had emphasized culturally ascribed female characteristics—the ability to empathize with people and to draw out their concerns, interests, and leadership skills. Black women thus played significant and leading roles in the organization.[30] However, as Black Power roiled across the country and as urban ghettos spontaneously rose up in rebellion, Black Power's self-conscious leaders could not keep pace with the spread of the movement. SNCC, the Panthers, and other black nationalist formations, perceiving the need to quickly and effectively address the ghetto rebellions, to some extent shunted aside community-organizing efforts in favor of militant tactics and rhetoric—male characteristics. Women's roles were accordingly degraded. This discounting of women's roles joined with preexisting popular white sociological prescriptions on the need for black men to assert their manhood and with preexisting black nationalist notions that emphasized the same need. The Nation of Islam, for example, segregated its functions by sex and, as Malcolm X described it, inculcated its adherents with a deep distrust for women. But while Malcolm came to recognize how wrong this training had been, black nationalism as a whole did not follow his example.[31] On the contrary, groups like Ron Karenga's Los Angeles-based US counseled women that it was their revolutionary duty to subordinate themselves to men, to be men's helpmates, and to bear them African revolutionary children.[32]

Although the Panthers self-consciously set themselves in opposition to US's cultural nationalism, the older black nationalist attitude toward women remained part of the political and cultural environment in which the Panthers operated. Still more important, the Panthers' early emphasis on "the gun" necessarily created a male-gendered perspective. Nevertheless, under the leadership of Panther founders Bobby Seale and Huey Newton, the Black Panther Party said little about the role of women in the movement. After Newton's imprisonment, however, Eldridge Cleaver's leadership came to the fore, and Cleaver brought with him a considerable amount of sexual baggage. A brilliant writer, Cleaver had been imprisoned for raping a white woman. While in prison, he discovered Malcolm X and black nationalism and their associated attitudes toward women. Out of prison and in the Panthers, Cleaver brought these negative attitudes toward women out in the open. While the Nation of Islam and US had couched their male supremacy in tones of respect for women—"the African Queen"—Cleaver was up front. Women indeed had a role in the revolution: "pussy power." They could give pussy to revolutionary men and deny it to counterrevolutionaries.

The meaning of "pussy power" became evident to Los Angeles Panther Elaine Brown when she was called to the Panthers' national headquarters in Oakland in April 1969 and introduced to the national leadership. As Panther women cooked and cleaned dishes in the kitchen, Brown met with a claque of Panther men in the living room. Panther chairman Bobby Seale called in a fifteen-year-old girl and introduced her to Brown. "Tell the Sister here," Seale instructed the girl, "what a Brother has to do to get some from you." "First of all," she replied,

> "a Brother's got to be righteous. He's got to be a Panther. He's got to be able to recite the ten-point platform and program, and be ready to off the pig and die for the People.... Can't no motherfucker get no pussy from me unless he can get down with the party.... A Sister has to learn to shoot as well as to cook, and be ready to back up the Brothers.... A Sister has to give up the pussy when the Brother is on his job and hold it back when he's not.' Cause Sisters got pussy power." Male Panthers appreciatively hooted and howled their approval of the girl's rap.[33]

It is not too hard to imagine how a woman like Ruby Doris Smith Robinson or any of the SNCC women would have reacted to this display, or for that matter how Stokely Carmichael or any of SNCC's male veterans would have reacted. Carmichael may indeed originally have intended his "prone" comment as a joke, but Cleaver had transformed it into a policy. Black women would fight that policy, but by the late 1960s it had clearly gained the upper hand in the black nationalist movement.[34]

It was this policy that Panther spokesman Chaka Walls veered into as he denounced PL's line as racist. Quite possibly because Walls saw PL's "armchair Marxism" as unmanly—these armchair Marxists hadn't even "shot rubber bands"— he connected his denunciation of PL with women's liberation. And discussing women's liberation could only mean reiterating Cleaver's line on "pussy power." When he could not continue for the chants of "fight male chauvinism," a second Panther, Jewel Cook, took the stage and again denounced PL, this time by name. Moreover, Cook insisted that if PL did not change its stance on nationalism, the Panthers would consider the organization "counterrevolutionary traitors" and accordingly judge SDS "by the company it keeps." It was the strongest call yet for kicking PL out. But Cook also determined to call for "pussy power" and topped that call with Carmichael's "the position for you sisters ... is *prone!*" "Pandemonium" erupted. PL adherents seized on the comment to discredit the anti-PL line and the Panthers, while simultaneously appearing as the champion of women: "Fight male chauvinism! Fight male chauvinism!"[35]

Of course, PL hated and opposed the actual women's movement as much as the rest of SDS did. PL saw the struggle for women's rights in much the same terms as it viewed the struggle for black rights. Women in American society faced no special oppression, they were simply "superexploited" as workers. Male chauvinism was an attitude that backed up this superexploitation but could be fought by convincing men that it held back the "class struggle." Similarly, to attain their liberation, women needed to organize in their principal role—as workers—for the overthrow of capitalism and class rule. Existing women's liberation groups, according to PL, organized "women to discuss their personal problems about their boy friends."[36]

For all its opposition to PL, Weatherman did not have such a terribly different attitude toward the women's movement. In its "You Don't Need a Weatherman" paper, Weatherman acknowledged that it did not have an answer to the question of how "we organize women against racism and imperialism without submerging the principled revolutionary question of women's liberation." Weatherman did, however, "recognize the real reactionary danger of women's groups that are not self-consciously revolutionary and anti-imperialist." And while Weatherman did speak of the necessity to "smash male supremacy," it again offered no picture of how male supremacy manifested itself in men. Instead, Weatherman reiterated Dohrn's old line: "Women will never be able to undertake a full revolutionary role unless they break out of their woman's role."[37]

More concretely, Weatherman stressed James Gang actionism as its organizing model. James Gang actionism, applied to white urban communities in Detroit or Cleveland, meant a return to the old ERAP emphasis on being "tough"; it meant organizing street gangs, hanging out in bars and pool halls, getting people to "fight the pigs."[38] In short, Weatherman offered a real "male" organizing program. Even female Weatherman supporters recognized the contradiction. "We can't organize street gangs," said one female Weatherman. A New York WITCH and future Weatherman, Naomi Jaffee, insightfully noted that Weatherman sought to create a "women's auxiliary" to the real RYM: "RYM says, that if street gangs are important to work with, then women organizers should organize street-gang members' wives."

At the same time, if members of Weatherman were divided about the adequacy of the organization's street-gang approach to organizing, they were united on a general approach to organizing women: it would be wrong to organize women directly against male supremacy. "We must organize women around the primary contradictions— anti-imperialism, antiracist issues," argued another female Weatherman. "In these struggles women's particular oppression will have to come out."[39] Those in Weatherman might hate PL, but on the matter of women's liberation, they had only changed PL's demand that women focus upon the "class struggle" to the demand that they focus on anti-imperialism and antiracism.

RYM II leaders scattered several paragraphs on male supremacy throughout their lengthy founding document. Although the RYM IIers made a more concerted effort to analyze the basis of male supremacy, nevertheless, like Weatherman, RYM II confined itself to abstractions when it came to really defining male supremacy's face in the movement: "We must wage a vigorous attack on male supremacy both inside and outside the movement.... Within the movement, the fight must be waged by purging the movement of male chauvinist attitudes and encouraging the leadership of women."

But what were these "male chauvinist attitudes"? Were they confined to overt put-downs of women, that is, calling women "chicks," expecting women to bring the coffee or do the secretarial work? Or were they deeper, going to the very content of movement work: Who will the movement organize—street gangs, "industrial workers," welfare recipients, the unemployed? Each answer had a gendered content. On what terms would the movement define its organizing—the Marxist "class struggle" or solidarity with the Third World? Again, each answer had a gendered content. "Male chauvinist attitudes" thus transcended the specific attitude that a man might hold about a woman. RYM II, however, left ambiguous the meaning of male chauvinism in the movement.

Defining male supremacy outside the movement was a bit easier. Unlike Weatherman, RYM II urged support for women's struggles against male supremacy, concretely advocating for "day care centers, equal employment, humane abortion laws, and access to higher education."[40]

After PL's expulsion, RYM II also drafted a proposed SDS set of unity principles, the second principle reiterating RYM II's practical program on women's liberation and condemning male supremacy in slightly sharper language than the RYM II statement itself. "We are dedicated to fighting male supremacy, to destroying the physical and spiritual oppression of women by men, and the achievement of full equality for women in every sphere of life," the proposal declared.[41] Although this proposal also failed to concretely delineate how male supremacy manifested itself in SDS, the combined RYM forces nevertheless rejected it. Weatherman supporters, according to one source, "objected to 'struggling for equality with men' and argued that no change in the status of women could occur until socialism was achieved."[42] Once again, Weatherman's defense of male supremacy in the movement was sounding very much like PL's defense.

Nevertheless, the fact that both Weatherman and RYM II felt compelled to address the issue of male supremacy in the movement, indeed, to insist that male supremacy be "smash[ed]" or "destroy[ed]," suggests two things. First, it showed the women's liberation movement's growing strength. Three months earlier, when SDS issued its "International Women's Day" edition of *New Left Notes*, SDS did not feel the need to speak in such dramatic language. Indeed, SDS scarcely had acknowledged male supremacy in the movement. Second, SDS's use of terms like "smash" and "destroy" reflected the organization's male mindset. If women condemned SDS for its male environment, SDS would go those women one better and vow to "smash" that environment.

Despite the brouhaha over "pussy power," SDSers, following Dohrn's singular leadership here, succeeded in reading PL out of SDS, or, more realistically, in splitting with PL. On one level, SDS was certainly warranted in expelling the conservative PL. PL had a consolidated line that opposed the actual struggles that black people were waging, both on the campuses and in the communities, and SDSers were quite correct in separating themselves from PL. Indeed, SDS could not have continued to develop while constantly engaged in an internal battle against this Old Left formation. The danger in PL's expulsion, however, was simply this: having dramatically rid itself of a racist force, SDS, unchecked by the strength of the black movement, could foist off onto PL all its own white supremacy. In other words, PL could serve as the white supremacist "other" to SDS's purity and antiwhite supremacism. This, of course, was the trick SDS had already played against the disagreeable women's liberationists.

The black movement's rapid weakening at the hands of the U.S. government made the likelihood all the greater that SDS would misinterpret the significance of its parting company with PL. Indeed, government repression against the Panthers and other black nationalists entered high gear in the fall of 1968 and escalated throughout 1969. Already in September 1968, the *New York Times* reported that FBI director J. Edgar Hoover considered the Panthers to be "the greatest threat to the internal security of the country."[43] Hoover and his COINTELPRO consequently intensified their targeting of the Panthers. In 1969, police raids and COINTELPRO-fostered activities took the lives of at least eleven Black Panther members.[44] From April to December, police raided Panther offices in most of the major cities in which the party had chapters: New York, San Francisco, Chicago, Salt Lake City, Indianapolis, Denver, San Diego, Sacramento, and Los Angeles. Media scare tactics accompanied all the major busts. In September alone, police arrested Panthers in forty-six distinct incidents.[45]

This massive repression had a contradictory impact on SDS. On the one hand, it definitely pushed the New Left to defend the Panthers and to understand the significance of the attack being waged upon them. But the repression decisively weakened the Panthers and undermined their ability to work in their own communities. Consequently, it also undermined the Panthers' and, more generally, revolutionary black nationalism's ability to guide the New Left, to remind the New Left of the real base of social struggle in contemporary America. In the past, the black movement had had the ability to check SDS's vanguardist tendencies, that is, to bring SDS back down to earth. Whether expressed organizationally through SNCC or the Panthers, or simply through massive social struggles, as in the summer of 1967, or the riots after King's assassination, the black movement had the gravitational pull to continually orient SDS's understandings of the nature of the society and of New Left activists' own identities as young white people. Now, however, the government's assault on the Panthers was dissipating the black movement's gravity and creating the conditions wherein SDS could spin off into its own white vanguardist fantasies.

SDS's phenomenal growth—the organization more than doubled in size from April to November 1968—added further fuel to these fantasies and made the black movement's job of checking the New Left all the more difficult. If in 1966, with 15,000 members, SDS could conceive of itself as "the most creative force on the Left"—how would its leaders conceive of themselves with 80,000 or 100,000 members? Moreover, if even the high tides of black struggle could elicit self-criticism and a degree of humility from SDS only by way of exception, what effect would the dismemberment of the largest black nationalist organization have upon SDS?

One white Panther supporter summarized what she saw as the impact of the repression against the Panthers on white New Leftists:

A lot of movement people have resigned themselves to being witnesses of the destruction of the Black Panther Party. We chant "off the pig," but don't mean it. We affirm support for the BPP, but give none in practice. Some would like to provide support, but don't know how. Others, find all sorts of excuses for not supporting the Panthers, "they're taking a bad line," etc. Some are even honest enough to use the rats-leaving-a-sinking-ship metaphor. The Panthers have many fair weather ideological friends.[46]

The government's repression, SDS's growth, and PL's expulsion all came together in July 1969 at the Panthers' conference to build a United Front Against Fascism (UFAF). Seeking to cope with the government's mounting repression, the Panthers called on all their potential allies to unite behind a single program of political self-defense. Specifically, the Panthers sought to create "committees against fascism" across the country and initiate a nationwide petition campaign for "community control of the police" to be carried out in both black and white communities. The petition demanded black community control of the police in black communities and white community control of the police in white communities. The Panthers hoped to create hundreds of committees involving thousands of people and in so doing create a buffer between themselves and the repression stalking them.[47]

In effect, the Panthers once again were asking SDS to take the notion of black self-determination into racist white communities—giving practical substance to Carmichael's 1966 demand on the New Left. Since 80 percent of the 3,000 people who showed up at the UFAF conference were white, this was not a wholly unrealistic strategy.

SDS's response to the UFAF program took a characteristic form. National Interim Committee members—Rudd, Jones, Ayers, Machtinger, and Phoebe Hirsch from Weatherman, and Avakian, Ignatin, and Klonsky from RYM II—issued a statement explaining their decision. They began their statement in typical RYM-speak: "SDS participation in the UFAF conference was based on our complete support of the black liberation struggle and of the leadership of that struggle, especially the Black Panther Party. At a time when the black and brown peoples and the Panthers and other organizations are facing increasingly brutal fascist attacks by the ruling class and their agents, the police, all revolutionaries must defend those who are leading the anti-imperialist struggle." This sounded terrifically revolutionary and loyal: "our complete support" of the "leadership" of the black liberation movement and of the anti-imperialist movement as well. Having established their fealty to the black revolution's leadership (which no longer, apparently, was the Black Panther Party by itself, as it had been three months earlier at Austin), SDS's tone began to shift. Explained NIC members in the very next sentences: "Strategically, this defense, this attack on fascism is accomplished by continuing to build the anti-imperialist movement; our part of the task is to involve the white working class in the struggle against imperialism. This can only be done by winning whites to support and fight on the side of black and brown people within this country, and on the side of all oppressed and colonized peoples abroad." SDS then lectured the Panthers on the significance of combating white supremacy and class politics. Unless SDS attacked white supremacy, it could not build a real working-class solidarity, a "revolutionary internationalist consciousness," but would instead only continue chauvinism and racism. SDS wholly supported community control of the police in black and brown communities. But white community control of the police deflected the issues of fascism, racism, and self-determination by creating a "parity" between communities that, because of white supremacy, were not equal. Moreover, class divided white communities, and SDS stood only for the working class. Finally, the two RYM factions also worried about the use of the legal tactic of petitioning. While not raising "principled opposition" to legal forms of struggle, SDS patiently explained to the Panthers the significance of using militant tactics: "We should understand that at this time smashing the illusion of reform through voting and other capitalist channels is a priority in the building of a revolutionary anti-imperialist movement. The level of struggle is being raised and should continue to be raised among white youth. This is a necessity in building the 'fighting force' which will eventually defeat imperialism."[48]

What did this all mean concretely? RYM's "complete support of the black liberation struggle and of the leadership of that struggle, especially the Black Panther Party" meant that RYM rejected the UFAF proposal, and this at the very moment that the government's repression against the Panthers had reached its peak.

Here was the denouement of an era. From 1966 to 1969, the black movement had forced SDS to define and redefine its understandings of the world, pushing SDS "from protest to resistance," and from resistance to revolution. It had repeatedly urged SDS to take on racism in the white community. Despite continual resistance to that charge—stronger at times of black movement quiescence and weaker at times of black movement strength—SDS, in a variety of RYM proposals, slowly came to define its role in just such terms. But now the Panthers, whom SDS three months earlier had designated the vanguard of the revolution, had posed the question to SDS point blank: Will you support us on the terms that we are asking for your support? And SDS—both remaining factions—answered in unqualified fashion: "No. What you have asked of us does not accord with our conception of ourselves as revolutionaries."

Some white radicals understood that the problem with the UFAF was not the Panthers, or their UFAF program, but the inability to do the real work of organizing whites against racism. Columbia SDS's Lew Cole, for example, understood that the Panthers saw UFAF as creating a "first real attempt to reach the white working-class in a mass way, and begin to organize it into a consciously antiracist force within society." If, in fact, the Panthers had erroneously structured this attempt at organizing white workers against racism in "lowest common denominator" terms—black community control in black communities/white community control in white communities—"the fault lay not with the Panthers but with SDS, which had done nothing to demonstrate that whites could be organized on any other basis." White leftists, Cole maintained, "could argue against the politics of the petition only *abstractly*, and had few examples to point to of whites going on the offensive and beginning to combat racism and win white support of and alliance with the Black Liberation Movement."

Cole also saw SDS's rejection of the UFAF program as a window into the deeper political problems of both RYM groups. RYM politics, argued Cole, justified RYM's support for black liberation on one ground only: that black people were going to make the revolution. But, said Cole, this "challenges nobody's racism at all. It, once again, relegates the anticolonial struggle to a purely 'black' thing: one of *their* issues.... But the anticolonial struggle isn't simply *their* issue; it's ours, too."[49]

But Cole was the exception. Boston's underground paper, the *Old Mole*, reported the more typical white Left response: "Many of the delegates left the conference confused and disappointed. The radical movement feared that the Panthers UF [United Front] tactic was attempting to enlist liberal support at the expense of revolutionary militancy."[50] Weatherman supporter Susan Stern was one of these disappointed delegates. The Panthers, Stern complained, seemed to be "stepping back from armed struggle and militancy" at the very moment Weatherman members were "gearing to become urban guerrillas." When the Panthers, following SDS's rejection of the UFAF, denounced Weathermen as adventurists and refused to work with any SDS faction, Weathermen were shocked. "It was hard to follow a vanguard who despised you," Stern concluded.[51] She neatly summarized the united RYM's position: RYM would willingly follow a black vanguard whose requests coincided with RYM's inclinations. But if that vanguard requested something that RYM rejected, this was clearly a problem for the vanguard, and not for RYM. And the Panthers, and the black nationalist movement it represented, reeling from government attacks, no longer had the strength to call RYM I and RYM II to task for this desertion.

For their part, the Panthers understood that SDS had taken a significant step backward with their rejection of the UFAF. Panther chief of staff David Hilliard, speaking a few weeks later, condemned SDS's decision as coming from "national chauvinism." Hilliard also recognized the clear implications of SDS's refusal. "We're sick and tired of those motherfuckers ... trying to dictate to us how we should run our struggle, who to align with." Panther chairman Bobby Seale emphasized Hilliard's point: "We want to make it clear to all the S.D.S.'s ... that we have a mind of our own . . . and that we make our own decisions and we support who we want to support."[52]

Weatherman, secure in the understandings of imperialism and white supremacy it had achieved over the last year, rapidly spun to a position of white and male exceptionalism over the next several months. RYM II, on the other hand, having successfully defined the existence of a black nation that neither the Panthers nor SNCC had asked for, quickly began to splinter into a host of tiny vanguard parties.

Four projects defined Weatherman's descent into white and male exceptionalism: its summer urban organizing projects; its development of a "women's militia"; its July 1969 meeting with the Vietnamese in Cuba; and its organizing for the "Days of Rage" national antiwar action in Chicago in October.

Weatherman's summer organizing in Detroit became a model that Weatherman held up to SDS nationally. Ayers and Mellen originally had promoted the Detroit project in their "Hot Town" proposal. "Hot Town" had come as close to echoing Carmichael's demand that white radicals organize white communities against racism as anything that SDS had or would ever put forward. But "Hot Town" had been written three months earlier. By the early summer, organizing whites in Detroit against racism did not mean patiently attempting to understand how white working-class youth understood race, and moving those young people on the basis of their own antiracist humanity; nor did it mean attempting to garner white youth's concrete support for any of Detroit's black liberation groups. On the contrary, Weatherman saw its job as putting white youth's racism "up against the wall." Weatherman would out-macho white working-class youth, and by out-machoing them, win them to antiracist politics.

Two actions, in particular, became famous and reflected Weatherman's mode of organizing: the Metro Beach riot and the McComb Community College action. The Metro Beach action closely followed the line of the Weatherman proposal: by militantly touting the Vietcong, Weatherman would create a strong presence for the international revolution in Detroit's white working-class communities. Thus, one sultry July 1969 afternoon, a Weatherman squadron marched across Detroit's white working-class Metro Beach distributing literature for the Chicago national action and carrying a Vietcong flag. Setting up camp under the flag, they engaged in heated arguments with the crowd that assembled around them. Finally, a group of working-class youth attacked the Weathermen and, according to New Left Notes, the Weathermen fought these youth to a "standstill." Still carrying the flag, Weathermen then marched off the beach. While people's reactions varied widely, Weatherman proudly claimed that it had confronted "kids on the beach . . . with the fact that we were taking sides with the Vietnamese and the blacks." This, after all, was the job Weatherman had designated for itself: not organizing youth, but confronting them.

A Weatherman flyer handed out at the time in Detroit gave a sense of Weatherman's approach to white (male) youth. Indeed, this may have been the flyer handed out at Metro Beach. Titled "Break on Through to the Other Side," after the title of a tune by the Doors, the flyer, in its entirety, read:

BREAK ON THROUGH TO THE OTHER SIDE.

Cats are being fucked over *everywhere*. Like, what is there to do? You can go to school, but we know their schools are just jails. They've even got pigs there to make sure we don't make any "trouble" for the jail wardens. And what happens when you finally flunk out or graduate? Man, the army takes you and sends you over to get shot up in Vietnam. And why are we there? They say to protect freedom—but mostly the freedom of those rich dudes in Grosse Point and Birmingham to run our lives. And if you make it out of the army alive, you get stuck in some bullshit job—maybe in a factory or something. It doesn't make any difference where you work cause it's all jive shit. It's not that we can't do hard work, but what the hell do we care if Chrysler or GM meets its damn quotas. We'll still be paying $3,000 for a car that's made to break down in 2 years. We're still getting only $3.44 an hour while "owners" get millions. And what do we do after our work? Hang out—on Woodward maybe or at a park somewhere. Be we can't get too many people together cause then the pigs come and break it up and bust everybody. Then you have to go to some damn courtroom where you know what's going to happen to you before it even starts.

And all this isn't just happening around Denby or Redford. It's *everywhere*. Man, things are fucked up all over the place. But we can't just sit here. We got to get our shit together. Got to fight back!

And we aren't the only ones doing it either. The blacks have been fighting the Man for 400 years. And look at those Vietnamese. They're fighting everyday to stop the United States rulers from fucking them over. And dig it, man, that little country is *winning*. But those dudes running GM and Standard Oil and U.S. Steel aren't just messing with cats in Vietnam. They're doing it in all the other countries in Asia, Africa, and Latin America too. That ain't bullshit either. The Vietnamese are leading the wars of all those people. And in the United States here the blacks are *leading* the fight against the ruling class and the pigs. That means that if we're gonna fight the pigs, we have to follow their leadership. It doesn't mean we're fighting just for the black man's freedom. We're doing it for our own freedom, man, and the black people are leading the fight for *everyone's* freedom.

All these things are happening right now. Just look at today's News. And dig it. More people are getting themselves together. More pigs are being hired to break us up.

And just dig what's happening in Chicago. A lot of the gangs stopped fighting each other and got together to stop the Man. The Black Panthers, the Young Lords (a Spanish gang), the Young Patriots (a southern white gang) and SDS are all fighting side by side.

We're working with SDS and we're tired of all the shit in this world. And the time is right for fighting in the streets!

The thing is this: *the Man can't fight everywhere*. He can't even beat the Vietnamese. And when other Vietnams start, man, he's just gonna fall apart. SDS is recruiting an army right now, man, a people's army, under black leadership, that's gonna fight against the pigs and *win*!!![53]

While Weatherman was busy berating RYM II for its failure to stress white skin privilege, Weatherman's propaganda to white working-class youth contained no mention of white skin privilege. Indeed, Weatherman's rap was remarkably similar to Mike James's 1966 Chicago ERAP spiel: your life is bad, and you've got to fight back to change it. Blacks and Vietnamese have gotten themselves together and are fighting against the same people you are fighting against. We should ally with them, or follow their leadership, because they've been successful, and they are going to win. In short, Weatherman was calling for white youth to join the struggle solely because the struggle was going to "win!!!"—not because the black or Vietnamese struggle was just, not because white privilege was unjust or was actually part of white oppression.

This position was extremely condescending. The Old Left believed that the political, spiritual, and moral consequences of white racism, empire, and male domination on white workers were too complex for white workers to comprehend. Old Left formations sought to capture white allegiance by appealing to white "material interest"—wages, or hours, or benefits. White workers would, in short, improve their material conditions if they allied with black workers, or women, against the bosses. Weatherman had transcended this simple "economism," as it was called, only to bring it to a higher level. Neither wages nor hours would lure white workers out of the embrace of racism and male domination and empire, it was being on the side that would "win."

Second, Weatherman certainly advocated following black leadership. But what did following this "black leadership" concretely mean? Did it mean supporting the Panthers? Did it mean supporting the various black liberation groups in Detroit or organizing Detroit's segregated white communities against racism? No. White working-class youth could follow black leadership by "fighting the pigs"—under Weatherman's direction, of course. Weatherman, in short, had invented its own black leadership and was asking white youth to follow that black leadership.

Moreover, Weatherman's "Hot Town" propaganda reinforced the women's auxiliary concept of organizing, "man." What happens when you finally flunk out or graduate from the high school/jail? Why, the "man" ships you off to Vietnam or puts you on an assembly line. Already at the June National Conference, even the female Weathermen recognized and rejected this auxiliary role for women.

Perhaps it was out of this contradiction, this perceived auxiliary role for women, that the McComb Community College action evolved, together with Weatherman's answer to the women's liberation movement. At McComb, nine female Weathermen invaded a class of forty to fifty students taking a sociology final. One of the Weatherwomen began a rap on "how American imperialism fucks over the people the world" and on imperialism's oppression of the black colony, as the other Weatherwomen barricaded the classroom. Then they confronted the white students themselves "with their dual position in capitalist society"—as oppressors and oppressed. When the teacher attempted to leave the room to call the police, the nine women, who had been training in karate, stopped him. Unfortunately, at the outset of the action, one of the students had gotten out of the classroom and had called the police. The police arrested the nine women as they exited the classroom.[54]

Whatever the consequences, here was the women's liberation model that Weatherman had been casting about for. The Motor City Nine, as they dubbed themselves, had done two things: they had rejected the weak woman stereotype and, in an all-women's action, had managed to "confront" young whites in the same way that male Weathermen confronted them. In other words, female Weathermen were not a women's auxiliary because they could fight and confront white youth just like their male counterparts. Like the model of Vietnamese women that Dohrn had promoted months earlier, Weatherman had developed a mode of action for women that did not focus on women's oppression, but focused on racism and imperialism, the "common struggle."

The McComb action, Weatherman claimed, had wholly borne out the Weatherman analysis: "We've become fighters this summer. . . . Our words have content because they are backed up by a growing base of power. Opening a new front here at home can only be achieved by striking blows at the enemy and building a movement that understands that to aid the Vietnamese and blacks we must develop a white fighting force that FIGHTS!"[55] Weatherwomen had done no previous work at the school, and *New Left Notes* failed to mention whether any of the students in the class that had been disrupted went on to join Weatherman. What was of moment, apparently, was not Weatherman's ability to raise the consciousness and win the participation of new masses of people, but instead was simply Weatherman's own willingness to "fight."

Outside of Detroit, one other Weatherman summer action, modeling itself after the McComb action, gained quick fame or notoriety in SDS circles: the Pittsburgh "jailbreak" action. Indeed, if any single action reflected Weatherman's politics in its purist form, it was the Pittsburgh action. After briefly rallying in front of Pittsburgh's predominantly white working-class South Hills High School on the first day of school, seventy-five Weatherwomen, carrying Vietcong flags, marched around the school and then through its halls, war-whooping and shouting "jailbreak." The women then rallied again outside the school and explained their presence. According to an account of the action, one of the Weatherwomen, standing atop a parked car, explained that "the school was programming the women for housework and the men to be cannon fodder in Vietnam. She warned that the pigs who were about to show up were the same pigs who murder blacks in the ghettos, who beat up blacks protesting their exclusion from Pittsburgh's highly racist construction unions, and, in fact, the same pigs who occupied South Hills High the previous year." She also specifically emphasized Weatherman's understanding of the role of women in the world and in the struggle for social change. Half the world's population, women had been told that it was "unladylike to fight, that their only role [was] ... to appeal to men by being passive and 'feminine.' Women are fed up. They are beginning to think that if Vietnamese women can take up arms against the U.S. monster and win, they, too, can win by aiding that struggle from within." That was why the Weatherwomen had come to Pittsburgh, rather than picket "outside a Revlon factory or some other operation that directly works on turning women into their boyfriends' rag dolls."

Some of the high school students attacked the women and attempted to seize one of their Vietcong flags. The Weatherwomen successfully fought these students off and forced them to retreat. Police on the scene then attacked the Weatherwomen. Following a "ferocious" battle in which the Weatherwomen managed to free those women whom the police had seized, the women fled the high school. Police arrested twenty-six of them at roadblocks they had established around the school.

While there was much that was remarkable about the action, two things stood out: first, as at McComb, Weatherman had not attempted to organize at the school prior to the action; the group had built no base, had no contacts or history with the people it was attempting to "organize." Second, although Weatherman vowed to return and set up a Pittsburgh organizing project to follow up the action, their actual efforts amounted to very little. In short, Weatherman had made some headlines, offered some public polemical sallies aimed at the women's movement and at the non-Weatherman SDS, gotten a bunch of its people arrested, but avoided the real problems of organizing.

Most striking, perhaps, was that while Weatherman attacked Pittsburgh's racist craft unions and its racist police, some significant portion of the predominantly white working-class high school's students undoubtedly were the sons and daughters of police or union members. Weatherman had "confronted" these students under the theory that when the students saw an alternative—people who sided (verbally) with black people, and women who did not act like women—they would join the revolution. And if they did not . . . well, that question could wait for a few more weeks, for Weatherman's Chicago National Action.[56]

Weatherman's summer projects in Columbus, Ohio; New York; Chicago; and other cities all closely mirrored the "Hot Town" and Pittsburgh models and molded the core of the "white fighting force that FIGHTS!" Weatherman justified all of this, of course, in the name of aiding black people and aiding the Vietnamese.

But just as Weatherman's "Hot Town" organizing model refused the principal task that SNCC and the Panthers had asked of SDS's white radicals, so, too, did these young whites reject the Vietnamese vision for antiwar work. In the meetings between the Vietnamese and U.S. antiwar activists that had occurred over the previous year, the Vietnamese repeatedly made it clear that principally they sought more education on the nature of the war and on how the war laid bare the mainsprings of U.S. society, and more unity among the antiwar activists focused on generating larger and ever more visible actions against the war.

Weatherman, however, was developing an opposing view of its antiwar work. The contradiction between its vision and the Vietnamese vision also came to a head in the summer of 1969 following a Havana meeting between the Vietnamese and U.S. antiwar activists. Unlike the earlier joint meetings, however, the Havana meeting, called at the behest of South Vietnam's newly formed Provisional Revolutionary Government (PRG), involved not the broad range of antiwar activists, but only what one young activist termed "the hard core of the new left, mostly SDS."[57] Despite this difference, it appears that the Vietnamese sought the same kind of things from this hard core that they had sought in the earlier meetings: education and unity.[58]

As with all the earlier meetings, the Vietnamese in Havana emphasized the military situation: the demoralization of U.S. troops and their increasing use of drugs; the U.S. command's increasing inability to carry out offensive operations; and the roots of demoralization and military failure in the United States' imperialist ends. But the Vietnamese also deemed it necessary to provide some more explicit guidance on overall U.S. antiwar strategy. On the first day of the conference, for example, the head of the Vietnamese delegation, Nguyen Van Trong, urged the New Leftists to consider the Vietnamese experience during the 1946–54 war against French colonialism. In notes that she took at the conference, Bernardine Dohrn recorded

Van Trong's observations. Apparently, the Vietnamese believed that it had been essential to make the French people "understand true nature of war—imperialism always tries to beautify its wars; ... organizers must go deep into the masses; many diff forms of organizations; if we put forward a slogan which is too high for people, will not have broadest possibility of unity; must carefully study the situation." Of course, these were the tasks that the Vietnamese had been encouraging U.S. antiwar activists to take up. Van Trong and the other Vietnamese delegates then reinforced their perspective on developing the U.S. antiwar movement by addressing a series of questions to the U.S. delegates: Did the American people know about and understand Nixon's "De-Americanization" strategy in Vietnam? Did they know about and understand the PRG's ten-point peace program, or of the existence and significance of the PRG? What did the "ruling circles" think of the PRG's peace program and the formation and significance of the PRG? What about American women, especially those with sons and husbands in Vietnam: what were they doing and thinking? What was the capacity of the U.S. government to continue the draft?

In subsequent days, the Vietnamese would reiterate these questions and add others of a similar nature to the list: How many organizations opposed the war? What kind of coordination existed between these organizations? What kind of women's organizations existed, and what was their relationship to the antiwar movement? Why did different social strata entertain different attitudes toward the war? What relationship existed between the mass antiwar movement and conflicts and contradictions within the ruling classes? What about American GIs? How can they be worked with?[59] For the most part, SDS had never systematically explored these kinds of questions, much less acted on the basis of answers to these questions. But this was precisely what the Vietnamese were asking the SDS activists to do, to "carefully study the situation."[60]

Former SDS vice president and RYM II partisan Carl Davidson brought back from Havana an important sense of what the Vietnamese were saying. On the one hand, the Vietnamese delegation affirmed that they had defeated the United States in Vietnam, Davidson observed; on the other hand, the PRG believed that the antiwar movement in the United States could be playing a crucial role in bringing the U.S. troops home and bringing an early end to the war, but was not doing that. It seemed to the Vietnamese that antiwar sentiment in the United States was at an all-time high. Yet they were puzzled as to why massive antiwar mobilizations had declined since the spring of 1967. Of course, the liberal and radical antiwar activists had different perspectives. But why, the Vietnamese wanted to know, could they not unite around the demand for immediate withdrawal? According to Davidson, then, "the message was clear: Now, more than ever, Vietnam must be a central issue taken to the American people. Hundreds of thousands, even millions must be moved to understand and act in solidarity with the Vietnamese people."[61] The Vietnamese were asking the antiwar movement's radical wing to take responsibility for deepening the understanding of the tens of millions of white Americans who, only after the Tet Offensive in 1968, began to question the war, began to realize that their government was lying to them, and for the millions more who opposed the war but saw it as an unfortunate mistake, as "Johnson's war" or "Nixon's war" rather than as an imperialist war. They were also asking that these millions not be shunted aside as backward by the movement's left wing; that instead, they be educated and mobilized, first in opposition to the war, and then in solidarity with the Vietnamese struggle. It was a tremendous task, but not so different from the one that the Panthers and SNCC had asked of SDS.

If this message was reasonably clear to Davidson, it was not so clear to the dozen or so Weatherman cadre attending the Havana meeting, or rather, these people quickly lost sight of the lessons they had learned in Havana once they returned to the United States. Bernardine Dohrn recalled that the return trip on a Cuban freighter to St. John's, Canada, was marked by a tremendous degree of unity by all factions on board. Years later, Dohrn would acknowledge that "there's no question but the influence on all of us as Weathermen at the time ... was that we had to do mass organizing work, that we had to reach out to new sectors, that the task at hand could include militancy but that it also had to include much more of a push for unity, and much more of a push for a focus on the war."[62] Two Weatherman leaders, Bill Ayers and John Jacobs (JJ), met the returning Weatherman cadre when they arrived at St. John's. Convening a meeting in the ship's mess hall, Ayers and JJ quickly brought the cadre back into line. As Bo Burlingham described it, the Weatherman cadre came out of the meeting spouting a very different line than the one they had developed in Havana with the Vietnamese: "They started talking about all this 'bring the war home' stuff and they started talking about these people going out on the beaches and planting NLF flags; and they started talking about this slogan from Ohio, 'beat the people,' and I thought they were totally out of their minds."[63] Subsequently, Weatherman offered its new sense of the Havana conference in a special *New Left Notes* "Vietnam Supplement." The supplement dutifully reprinted the PRG's ten-point peace platform—the Vietnamese had, after all, specifically indicated their desire that activists promote the program in the United States. The supplement's real content, however, centered on an unsigned account of the Havana meeting, "Bring the War Home." Weatherman began its account by disparaging the results of earlier Vietnamese and U.S. antiwar activist conferences. "The people [meaning Weatherman's cadre] who met with the Vietcong in Cuba," insisted Weatherman, "tried to bring back more than 'a feeling I can't express in words' (the only result of so many trips in the past)."[64] Of course, this "feeling I can't express in words"—a universal theme in the Moscow, Stockholm, and Bratislava reports and in the reports from the smaller trips to Southeast Asia—centered on the U.S. activists' personal, subjective response to the Vietnamese: the great, deep humanity and humility of the Vietnamese; their care, concern, and respect for one another; their quiet, thoughtful determination, so different from the competitive, loud, arrogant, Hobbesian world of North Americans. No, Weatherman was beyond these "sentimental journeys or Caribbean romance."[65] Weatherman had gleaned the real reason why the Vietnamese had called the Havana meeting—to "kick ass":

> We understood that the reason the Vietnamese called the meeting was to get us moving against the war again. The Vietcong were giving us a kick in the ass at a time when they've defeated the U.S. militarily, but when the Nixon administration is trying to cling to its bases, bombing South Vietnam and bullshitting in Paris more and more intensively. Kicking us in the ass when the revolutionary movement in the United States could be making its internationalism real by getting the United States out of Vietnam, once and for all. Kicking us in the ass because for the first time we're really strong enough TO END THE WAR, and we've hardly mentioned it for a year. Kicking us in the ass so we could start kicking ass inside the monster.
>
> Kick ass is the main message we brought back from the meeting. Some people are saying that now we should be fighting to end the war; kicking ass is for later. Building a revolutionary movement is for later. Bullshit. Fighting to end the war, to bring it home, is the same as building a revolutionary movement. It involves the same things: reaching out to more oppressed sectors of youth, militant struggles with a clear internationalist focus, building cadre into a real fighting force. That's what we need to do to organize white people to help smash imperialism. That's also what we need to do to end the war.[66]

"Kicking ass"—here was the white and male vision in command. Weatherman had completely rejected the Vietnamese vision—and this, in the name of supporting Vietnam. The Vietnamese had encouraged "the broadest possibility of unity" and had specifically encouraged the radical antiwar movement to "carefully study" the situation and deepen the American public's understanding of the war and of its meaning in American society. Weatherman had determined that making the revolution and smashing imperialism—"kicking ass"—provided for the broadest possible unity.

To be sure, the task before radicals in the antiwar movement was extraordinarily difficult. Radicals needed to secure the broadest possible unity of antiwar sentiment, while at the same time not sacrificing their ability to take masses of people beyond

182 | The New Left Starts to Disintegrate

a liberal understanding of the war. But Weatherman rejected this role. As it had done with race, the group liquidated the real social and political contradictions that defined the radical position by simply insisting that the revolution was now. If masses of people did not follow, that was not Weatherman's fault or responsibility, but the determination of those masses to stay with the counterrevolution.

Secured by the interpretation they placed on their meetings with the Vietnamese in Cuba, and pursuing the "Hot Town" model of organizing in half-a-dozen cities, Weatherman organizers forecast a massive national action in Chicago in October. "The National Action is building fast," trumpeted Dohrn, Terry Robbins, and Kathy Boudin. In cities all across the country, "people are digging on the action—and digging on SDS." SDS's experience in organizing for the action was confirming the truth of Weatherman politics: "putting forward our politics in an aggressive way was the ONLY way to organize the masses of people in this country."[67]

But despite the glowing forecasts, hints of trouble appeared. First, the young radicals themselves admitted that both the Chicago Panther chapter and the Chicago chapter of the Young Lords had "raised strong reservations about the action." Chicago's Panthers feared that Weatherman's action would breeze through Chicago, leaving behind an increased police presence in the black community. Indeed, Chicago Panther leader Fred Hampton denounced Weatherman's action as "adventuristic" and "Custeristic," and he repeatedly criticized and physically confronted Weatherman leaders. But this did not faze the young white radicals. Resorting to an argument that they had used when they rejected the Panther request for Carl Oglesby's vice presidential candidacy, Weatherman insisted that while the black and brown movements did not need the kind of action that Weatherman was projecting, whites, "riddled by timidity" and lacking experience in the struggle, did.[68]

Second, RYM II broke off its work for the national action and focused instead on building its own separate national action. In announcing his resignation from the national action staff, RYM II's Mike Klonsky complained that the movement would not succeed "without the working class as its main component." Weatherman was running this action, Klonsky argued, as if it did not care whether it would win the working class to anti-imperialism. Indeed, Weatherman's handling of the national action stemmed from its analysis that "the working class benefits from imperialism because they share in the profit stolen by the imperialists."[69] Thus, RYM II, while correctly critiquing Weatherman's tactics, continued to distance itself from the significance of white skin privilege.

Still, Weatherman's leaders were supremely confident of their course. Susan Stern, working in a Seattle Weatherman project, recalled that all of Weatherman's "big wheels"—Dohrn, Rudd, JJ—"had promised us ... that at least 25,000 people were coming to the Days of Rage." They had assured the Seattle and other Weatherman collectives that Detroit's white youth were coming in a chartered train and that at least 10,000 youth would be coming from the Chicago area alone.[70] The Chicago action would start with a nighttime march and rally on Wednesday, October 8—the second anniversary of Che Guevara's death—and conclude with a "mass march" on Saturday, October 11. In between, on Thursday, October 9, Weatherman women's militia would march to Chicago's induction center and carry out a militant action there; and on Friday, October 10, Weatherman would conduct a "jailbreak" at some unnamed Chicago high school during the day and have a countercultural celebration, a "wargasm," on Friday night.

Weatherman kicked off its Days of Rage two days early, dynamiting a monument to Chicago policemen at Haymarket Square on Monday. However uplifting this surprise attack may have been for the Weatherman cadre, it must have been dispiriting for at least a few of them when they arrived at Lincoln Park on the night of the October 8. Instead of the promised 25,000 white youth ready to tear up "pig city," between 700 and 800 people gathered. Half of these people were simply spectators. Still, it was an unprecedented action. A round of inspirational speeches addressed Weatherman disappointments and fears. Seattle Weatherwoman Susan Stern recalled the basic theme of the speeches: the need for courage, the realization that "we were the only white people in the country who realized what it . . . took to make the revolution," and that "we were the revolutionary vanguard in America." Somewhat sardonically, Stern summarized the Weatherman's leadership rap: "only five hundred people in this country were good, strong, and brilliant enough to come to Chicago." After an hour of Weatherman speeches, Stern, together with several hundred others, was ready for action, although several years later she herself did not understand why she and the others went ahead with the action. "Maybe," she thought, "it was mass hypnosis. Maybe it was just that the notion of us being the only non-racists, and the only americong in the country appealed to our egos, and spurred on our revolutionary lust."[71]

Following the speeches, at a prearranged signal, less than half the crowd—estimates ranged from 250 to 350 people—moved out of Lincoln Park at a trot, surprising Chicago's police. On reaching Chicago's upper-class Gold Coast district, not far from the park, Weatherman let loose its first volley of bricks and stones. The Days of Rage had arrived: bank windows, department store windows, apartment windows, car windows shattered. Police managed to form a skirmish line several blocks beyond the first trashings. Swinging pipes and chains, Weatherman's front line slammed into the startled police. But Weatherman's secondary leadership failed to follow this lead and headed down side streets, continuing trashing windows. Police cars sped into the ranks of now-dispersing demonstrators; isolated police fired pistols or shotguns at the Weathermen. When the action was over, sixty minutes after it began, police had arrested seventy-five Weathermen, shot and wounded seven of them, and suffered twenty-one injuries themselves. A Chicago Newsreel collective member, arrested with a group of thirteen Weathermen, testified to the severity of the treatment they had received at the hands of the police: "Most of the people were beaten up pretty badly. Bodies were just mangled, people were bleeding out of their mouths and their noses and their heads. Clearly it was not an action by the police to subdue them and arrest them, it was vengeance." Illinois governor Richard Ogilvie responded to the first night of rage by calling out 2,600 National Guardsmen to contain the handful of Weathermen.[72]

Early the following morning, seventy helmeted and club-carrying Weatherwomen gathered in Grant Park to march on Chicago's induction center. Hundreds of police surrounded the women. Weatherman leader Bernardine Dohrn addressed this women's militia, preparing to send them off to battle and sharply distinguishing them from the burgeoning women's liberation movement: "We are born in 1969 in America behind enemy lines. People are determined to fight here. We are here to tell the people that this is not a women's movement of self-indulgence. This is not a movement to make us feel good. We are here to teach the people the lesson of what it means to be a 'good German.' There are people fighting every minute of every day here in America. We are going to be part of that fight." The women then jogged toward the first line of police. A dozen Weatherwomen fell upon the police and after a brief battle were subdued and arrested. Police forced the remaining women to remove their helmets and to surrender their pipes and clubs before they allowed them to disperse.[73]

That evening, Weatherman's leadership, the Weather Bureau, initiated a "criticism/self-criticism" session to properly orient the Weatherman cadre to the disappointment and fears engendered by Chicago's events. Beyond that, of course, the Chicago turnout seemingly had dealt a serious blow to the theory behind Weatherman's summer's organizing efforts. Aggressive, confrontational politics that underlined Weatherman's seriousness had not won masses of white working-class youth to the revolution. Indeed, Weatherman politics had not organized anyone. Could the theory that guided those politics have been wrong?

After extensive discussion, the Weather Bureau identified a number of "advanced Weather errors," including a dogmatic and sectarian spirit and a blind obedience to leadership. But Weatherman's experience led to deeper evaluations, too, evaluations that transcended how Weathermen individually and collectively carried out the Weatherman line. The consensus, one participant recalled, was that because of white skin privilege, "most people in America would never fight on the side of revolution." Said one of the Weatherman leaders: most white Americans "are going to be fighting on the side of the pigs if they ever fight at all." Only from the ranks of the counterculture's "alienated youth" could Weatherman find any white youth who might commit themselves to revolution in solidarity with black and Third World leadership.[74]

It was from this slim hope of attracting "alienated youth" that Weatherman determined to continue with the action it had slated for Saturday. It was a risky proposition: Wednesday's action had had the element of surprise going for it. Yet to not go ahead with the action would reinforce the notion that when the going got tough—when the National Guard arrived—the "hippies punked out and went back to their campuses." Hence, between 300 and 400 Weathermen, in combat boots, helmets, and padded clothing, and with taped wrists, gathered on Saturday morning for the final Days of Rage action. Before the action began, while Weathermen were still gathering at the rally site, police moved in and arrested some of the Weatherman leaders. Once again, after some inspiring speeches from the remaining Weatherman leadership and with arms linked, the Weathermen moved out at a trot. Police lined both sides of the march route, and as the march passed, the police fell in behind the Weathermen. After trotting with arms linked for several blocks, "everything seemed to shatter," one radical journalist reported. "The screams and shouts and the clubs came out and the pipes and the bricks." After another series of brawls, police carted off 110 more Weathermen.[75]

All told, the Days of Rage cost Weatherman 290 arrests, with bail bond set at over $1 million. On the other side, Weatherman managed to send fifty-seven police to the hospital, in addition to the city's corporation counsel, Richard Elrod. In his enthusiasm for pursuing Weathermen, Elrod had attempted a diving tackle of Weatherman Brian Flanagan—and Elrod had broken his neck when he smacked into a wall. Elrod, a friend of Chicago mayor Richard Daley, was temporarily paralyzed. Weatherman also caused $1 million in damages to a "ruling class neighborhood." The several hundred Weathermen also claimed to have preoccupied for several days the "same amount of imperialist pig power that a VC [Vietcong] regiment would attract." Moreover, some of the police who were occupied with Weatherman had been withdrawn from the city's black communities. This was what Weatherman termed "material support" to the Vietnamese and to the black liberation movement.[76]

But, of course, this was not the kind of support that either the black movement or the Vietnamese had been seeking. The black movement had asked SDS to win white Americans to an antiracist solidarity. "The 'Weathermen' should have spent their time organizing the White working and lumpen class instead of 'prematurely' engaging in combat with the trigger-happy pigs," reiterated Illinois Panther lieutenant Eugene Charles following the Days of Rage.[77] And the Vietnamese had asked for something similar. In its organizing for Chicago, Weatherman had claimed that it was answering these calls; that it was seeking, by its militancy, to win whites to the black and Vietnamese struggles. When white "kids" did not respond to Weatherman's tactics, however, when they did not rise to the challenge of "fighting pigs," the fault lay with these young white people, and not with Weatherman. Weatherman, in short, had renounced the job of building an antiracist and antiwar solidarity in the name of how backward white Americans were.

It was an extraordinarily seductive position to take. Simply by affirming the leadership of the oppressed nations and the black colony, Weatherman had secured itself—at least verbally—against the historic shortcomings of white radical leadership.[78] If Weatherman could legitimate its own leadership against the Panthers, it certainly would be no problem to secure that leadership against masses of young white people, or rather, against the failure of those young white people to respond to Weatherman's leadership. It did not matter that of the tens of thousands of "kids" that Weatherman projected as coming to the National Action, less than 600 hard-core SDSers actually showed up. Weatherman had become the exceptional white people in the world, those few whites who really understood and acted on the reality of U.S. imperialism and racism. The failure of other whites to take up the Weatherman line and practice only confirmed Weatherman's identity as a group of exceptional white people.

In being exceptional whites, however, Weatherman had only reinscribed its own whiteness in the world. The black movement had repeatedly asked white radicals to find the means to organize greater numbers of whites to an antiracist solidarity. Weatherman had found just one more excuse for rejecting that leadership and charge.

Rudd, Jones, and Ayers—all Weathermen—had been elected SDS's national officers at the June national convention. But if following the Weatherman line was the way to be revolutionary, and if the bulk of the SDS membership rejected that leadership, what purpose would there be in having an organization of tens of thousands of reactionaries and racists? There would be none. Tom Hayden recalls that it was in the period of the Days of Rage that a Weatherman friend approached him and proudly proclaimed, "Well, we offed the pig." By this, Hayden's friend had meant that Weatherman "had closed down the SDS national office."[79] Weatherman's leadership had helped to scuttle SDS, the largest radical student organization in American history and the largest and most powerful white Left organization of its day.

And RYM II? Like the Weather Bureau, RYM II's leaders had far more grandiose visions for themselves than could be satisfied within SDS. As with Weatherman, rejecting Panther leadership and the leadership that had come from SNCC was central to RYM II's stance toward SDS. With deeper roots in traditional Marxism than Weatherman leaders, RYM II leaders would find their vanguard role in salvaging the position of America's black and white united proletarian class. Thus, while RYM II proclaimed the vanguard role of the oppressed nations against imperialism and acknowledged black liberation's vanguard role in the United States—this, after all, was what had distinguished RYM from PL—it also engineered a vanguard role for the industrial proletariat in the United States.

In its first position paper, RYM II balanced the two vanguards—black liberation and the industrial proletariat—by defining the parameters of a Black Belt nation in the South. White workers, RYM II insisted, had to support the self-determination of this Black Belt nation.[80] Temporarily, this resolved the problem of contending vanguards. Black nationalists would lead the struggle for the Black Belt nation. In the rest of the country, the united industrial proletariat would lead the revolution and would support Black Belt self-determination and black democratic rights outside the South. But, of course, the Panthers, whom RYM II partisans had designated the vanguard of the black struggle just two months prior to their discovery of this Black Belt nation, had not asked for such a nation, and had not defined the parameters of a black nation. Neither, for that matter, had SNCC, the other leading black nationalist organization with whom SDSers worked. On the contrary, both the Panthers and SNCC insisted on the vanguard character of the black struggle—not only in black communities but throughout the United States.[81] SNCC's Stokely Carmichael, years earlier, had argued that black people would define the terms of their own liberation and that it was inappropriate for the oppressor to tell the oppressed how that liberation would be achieved. RYM II, like Weatherman, knew differently.

With the destruction of the Panthers and the deterioration of the black struggle, RYM II more and more stressed the role of the industrial proletariat. And if organizing the workers, even in the transitional youth movement strategy, was central, what good was there in a national student organization, the bulk of whose membership did not understand or appreciate the nuances of the class struggle? RYM II would thus not step forward to salvage SDS. Moreover, in the absence of the kind of check on white radical leadership provided by the black movement, RYM II splintered into a number of Marxist, Marxist-Leninist, and Marxist-Leninist-Maoist vanguard parties and "preparty formations." While these parties—most notably the October League (OL) and Revolutionary Union (RU)—disagreed on the finer points of many issues, they agreed on one thing: subordinating the black struggle to the class struggle.

Four days after Weatherman closed its Days of Rage in Chicago, two million people participated in what at the time was the largest single day of protests against the war, the October 15 Moratorium. The antiwar movement's liberal wing—the young people who had diligently worked on the Gene McCarthy, Robert Kennedy, and George McGovern antiwar presidential candidacies of the previous year—had called the Moratorium and had defined its politics.[82] SDS, the largest and most radical wing of the antiwar movement, the organization that had called the first national demonstration against the war, had no significant national influence in the Moratorium's direction.

Chapter Five

Reasserting the Centrality
of White Radicals

One month after the massive October 15, 1969, Moratorium against the war in Vietnam, still larger demonstrations against the war rumbled across the United States. In San Francisco, over 100,000 people marched through the city to Golden Gate Park on November 15. On the same day in Washington, D.C., more than 250,000 people—some said it was as high as 750,000—marched across the nation's capital to protest the war. Smaller marches, involving hundreds or thousands of people each, occurred in dozens of other communities across the country. With the Republican Richard Nixon as president, larger numbers of Democratic Party senators and representatives for the first time found it possible—and to retain their constituencies, necessary—to speak out against the war and to address the large antiwar crowds. Similarly, segments of the nation's press began to give greater play to the antiwar movement and began to editorialize against the war. As one underground newspaper described it, "Suddenly, all sorts of people were against the war: senators, clean-cut students, Wall Street Brokers."[1] Antiwar sentiment and activities were cresting in the country.

With this antiwar movement's expansion, however, with its increased respectability and the legitimacy conferred upon it by leading liberals, came an ascendance of liberal analysis of the war: the war, these liberals broadcast, was a "colossal mistake."[2] Pushed roughly aside were the notions that SDS, through its hard-won experience, had accumulated: Vietnam was not a mistake. It continued an entire history of interventions against Third World peoples, a history rooted in the fact of American empire.

As in the previous month's mammoth mobilizations, SDS—or, rather its increasing number of factions—played virtually no role in planning the November mobilization and so could do little to offer anti-imperialist understandings to the hundreds of thousands of fresh antiwar forces—not that they had not been given the opportunity to be part of the planning process, however. Unlike October's Moratorium events, which had been organized by the liberal youth forces of 1968's Democratic Party antiwar presidential campaigns, forces closer to the New Left organized the November events: American Communist Party stalwarts, longtime pacifists led by David Dellinger, a smattering of former SDSers, and a variety of Trotskyist factions dominated by the Socialist Workers Party.[3] In July 1969, this coalition formed the New Mobilization Committee to End the War in Vietnam (the New Mobe), and started planning the November actions. Dellinger, at the time a codefendant with SDS founders Tom Hayden and Rennie Davis in the notorious Chicago Conspiracy case, invited SDS's national officers to attend the New Mobe's founding meeting. Weathermen Mark Rudd and Kathy Boudin attended the conference but apparently said very little. At a subsequent New Mobe meeting, however, Rudd argued for the New Mobe's participation in Weatherman's October Days of Rage. Although the New Mobe was already on record as advocating mass mobilizations for "immediate withdrawal" of U.S. troops from Vietnam—a central part of what the Vietnamese had been asking for—Rudd wanted more. "What was needed, he declared, was an 'anti-imperialist movement' in the United States acting as the American arm of the National Liberation Front of South Vietnam.... It was not enough, declared Rudd, to demand immediate U.S. withdrawal from Vietnam. Instead, the movement must 'Bring the war home.'" Rudd, in short, was insisting that the New Mobe call people out into the street for revolution—to "kick ass." Moreover, Rudd made it clear that the Chicago action would be conducted under Weatherman's leadership. The New Mobe kindly rejected Rudd's proposal.[4]

The New Left's isolation from the mass of newly emerging antiwar forces manifested itself in particularly striking fashion in the November 15 San Francisco mobilization. Although the *New York Times* acknowledged that the protest was the "Largest Ever Staged in the West," the *Times* conspicuously headlined its article, "More Than 100,000 on Coast Demonstrate in Moderate Vein." For the *Times*, the "strongest indication that the moderates were in control came at the rally when David Hilliard, chief of staff of the militant Black Panther party, was booed. Mr. Hilliard attacked what he called 'the capitalistic, fascistic American society.'" Cries of "peace, peace, peace" forced Hilliard to cut short his condemnation of the society and of Nixon, in particular. San Francisco's mayor, Joseph Alioto, not known for his antiwar fervor, later commented that Hilliard's speech had "marred OUR demonstration."[5] Here was the responsibility that both the Panthers, and the black movement more generally, and the Vietnamese had laid before white activists: to transform the consciousness of these newly mobilized antiwar people and to help them understand the relation

between the war they protested in Vietnam and the militant struggle they were boo-
ing in San Francisco.

November's Washington mobilization went off largely as planned, with two
major events. Prior to Saturday's mass mobilization, 45,000 marchers, each carrying
a placard bearing the name of a dead U.S. soldier, marched single file from Arlington
National Cemetery to the White House. There they deposited their placards in cof-
fins. This "March Against Death"—nearly 1,000 marchers stepping off each hour for
two straight days—was almost twice as large as SDS's first national antiwar rally four
and a half years earlier.[6] On Saturday, over a quarter of a million demonstrators—
"a solid moving carpet of humanity," the *New York Times* called it—marched down
Pennsylvania Avenue, skirting the White House, and then down Fifteenth Street,
completely filling the grassy Washington Monument mall. It was the largest demonstration in the nation's history. People who had been to both the 1963 civil rights
March on Washington and the November 15th march agreed that the antiwar march
was far the larger.[7]

Radicals at the march—all SDS's main factions, including Weatherman,
RYM II, and the latest addition to the splintering SDS, New York's "Mad Dogs"
(RYM I and a half), together with the Yippies—made headlines twice during the
Washington mobilization, although New Mobe leaders consciously sought to mini-
mize their impact.[8] They need hardly have worried: SDS's factions were doing a fine
job of keeping themselves isolated without any external help.

On Friday, November 14, while the March Against Death was still going,
2,000 radicals calling themselves the Revolutionary Contingent in Support of the
Vietnamese People attempted to march on the U.S.-backed South Vietnamese
embassy. Police using tear gas quickly managed to rout the contingent, which then
scattered and went on a window-breaking tear through the area. Demonstrators
broke fifty to sixty windows, damaged forty to fifty police cars, and burned one
police motor scooter.[9] How this concretely supported the Vietnamese people, SDS's
factions did not say.

On the following day, as the New Mobe's rally at the Washington Monument
wound down, a Yippie-led contingent of 6,000 people marched from the grassy mall
to the Justice Department. Replete with Vietcong flags, red flags, black flags, and
banners taut in the brisk, November air, the contingent surrounded the building and
began pelting it with rocks, bottles, and smoke bombs. In unison with nearby demonstrators' chants, a few dozen demonstrators began pounding on the building's huge
metal doors. A series of dull explosions rent the air as police began to fire "canister
after canister" of CS tear gas at the demonstrators. Attorney General John Mitchell,
surveying the battle from a Justice Department balcony, likened it to a scene from the

Russian Revolution and ordered all windows in the building sealed to protect department employees from the wafting clouds of tear gas. Once again, demonstrators dispersed into small groups and charged through the streets, breaking more downtown business windows.[10]

After it was all over, after the largest single demonstration in U.S. history, Weatherman modestly offered its appraisal of the event in its new "mass" newspaper, *Fire*: "The most important tension in the march on Washington last week wasn't over the war," announced Weatherman. "Washington was really all about the question of violence." Weatherman then ripped into the Mobe's March Against Death: "So," said Weatherman, "45,000 kids walked five miles single file, not rapping for 36 hours. Each one dropped the name of a dead GI into a coffin. All between two rows of pigs. That was the parade of death." But neither Weatherman nor "a couple thousand kids" could "dig" this scene: "We were the people our parents warned us about. We moved through the streets in groups, marching, dancing, running, chanting, singing, downing jugs of wine. Running together with the people we knew well and trusted a lot. We carried VC flags and used the flagpoles as weapons. Trashing windows and pig cars. Setting fires at street corners." In the wake of Chicago and Weatherman's decision to appeal to the alienated white youth culture, Weatherman had embarked upon a "life trip": sex, drugs, and violent revolution. And the message that Weatherman sought to convey to this running, dancing, singing, wine-swilling youth was: "THE VIETNAM WAR ISN'T THE ISSUE ANY MORE. Mainly because the war is over. The Vietnamese people have won a military victory over the most powerful empire in the history of the world.... The only thing left is for Nixon to find the American ruling class a diplomatic way of admitting defeat."[11] Weatherman could not have put its opposition to the Vietnamese perspective on building an antiwar movement more bluntly. The Vietnamese, under whose flags Weatherman trashed Washington department store windows, had asked for the broadest mobilizations under the slogan of immediate withdrawal and had repeatedly sent public statements of praise to the antiwar movement for its moratoriums and mobilizations. Moreover, the Vietnamese had repeatedly insisted that while the United States had been militarily defeated, the antiwar movement still had an essential role to play: through its actions, it could hasten the United States' withdrawal from Vietnam and put an end to the carnage wreaked by a defeated empire.

Shortly after November 15, Weatherman produced a cartoon strip for *Fire* in which it again offered its "mass" perspective on the demonstration. The first of the images showed Nixon, New York governor Nelson Rockefeller, and Defense Secretary Melvin Laird happily viewing and flashing V signs to those demonstrators who had come to Washington for the traditional peaceful march. The second frame showed the

Revolutionary Contingent and explained that these folks had come to Washington "digging and loving every second of being part of the winning peoples war.... The Viet Cong, Cubans and Koreans have shown us the only way to beat pig Amerika— violence and armed struggle." Then followed several frames describing the Vietnamese embassy action—again, the Revolutionary Contingent eagerly anticipating trashing the Vietnamese and other "pig" embassies. Several frames followed on the Justice Department action. The final frame was captioned in the upper right corner: "later we did all those things the pig says are bad." The frame showed a crowd of people having sex, smoking dope, and playing guitars. In the bottom right corner, a young man, head on the stomach of another person and with a woman lying on his own stomach, offered a commentary on the experience: "I may be white, but I sure am tripping."[12]

It would be three full years before the United States completely withdrew from Vietnam. Antiwar movement activity would peak in May 1970 and rapidly decline thereafter. During these years, 11,000 more American soldiers would die, as would countless hundreds of thousands of Vietnamese. But for Weatherman, "THE VIETNAM WAR ISN'T THE ISSUE ANY MORE."

The contest between radical feminists and politicos over the women's liberation movement's relation to the New Left and the overall struggle for social change reached a definitive conclusion as SDS dissolved into its vanguard factions. Two interrelated issues drove the contest: first, what was the place of women's oppression, as white women were defining that oppression, relative to battles against racism and empire? Second, where would the predominantly white women's liberation movement stand in relation to the New Left: As the women's front for the New Left? As the New Left's autonomous ally? Or as the opponent to yet another old boys' network, a part of the patriarchal power structure, the New Left? To be sure, SDS's factions and the attitude they took toward women's liberation, and toward their own male supremacy, would play a large role in resolving both conflicts.

RYM's white male leaders were in no position to offer an honest contribution to the debate over male supremacy. Setting themselves loose from the constraints imposed by the black movement and by the Vietnamese, RYM's leaders were spinning out theories of revolution, theories that placed themselves at the center of revolutionary struggle. Women's liberation threatened to undermine women's loyalty to the New Left, however, and thus threatened to pull the rug out from under all these white male fantasies. RYM's leaders therefore threw themselves into the task of reconstructing women's liberation and redefining women's oppression to accord with their new theories of revolution. The result of all this theorizing? White men would assume the vanguard role over the women's struggle as well. Weatherman was the most out front of SDS's factions in its claims to be leading the struggle for women's liberation, although it was only more extreme in its actions, and not in its claims.

By the early summer of 1969, Weatherman had already pioneered its all-women anti-imperialist actions in Detroit. But Weatherman needed an internal face and a theoretical backing to its women's liberation model, and it began to develop these at a September 1969 Weatherman conference in Cleveland. Weatherman had called the conference to prepare cadre for the Chicago National Action. On the second day of the meeting, however, Weatherman women broke off and met separately. It was here that the Weatherwomen decided on their Pittsburgh jailbreak action. More important still, the Weatherwomen also worked out the means of defining their leadership within Weatherman's white-male-defined "tough" politics. In one public account of the caucus, "A Weatherwoman" revealed that the women spent long hours discussing "how male chauvinism holds women back as revolutionaries." Male chauvinism, the women maintained, was "the way men see women as sex objects who can't either think very well or fight." Moreover, women too often viewed themselves in this male chauvinist fashion, which prevented them "from assuming any real kind of role in the revolution because most of us felt there was very little we could do."

Here was SDS's old line on women: women had to cease acting like women to break male chauvinism. But "Weatherwoman" took this line one step farther and offered a practical means for helping women in this task: Weatherman would "break up monogamous relationships." By doing this, Weatherwomen believed that they would break the "cycle" of negative male images of women reinforcing women's negative image of themselves. Following Cleveland and Pittsburgh, "Weatherwoman" suggested that "our monogamous relationships broke up because we simply didn't need them any more." "We began," she stated,

not to have to identify ourselves through men and could become total human beings. Women began digging one another; jealousy and competition were not necessary anymore because our point of existence was the revolution; and the old way of life became intolerable to us. . . .

Relationships were built around these struggles and not on bourgeois conceptions of love. No more crying because we were being fucked over by men. We were forced to fight it out with them when they tried to make us feel stupid.

We do not view ourselves as sex objects but as part of the revolution. Sex isn't something to happen isolated from daily work. Destroying the one man/one woman relationship was perhaps the most liberating thing that happened to us.

Becoming liberated from male self-conceptions allowed women to take on leading roles in the Weatherman collectives. But this leadership was a different kind of leadership—"Something strange and new in a revolutionary organization." It was, "Weatherwoman" claimed, a noncompetitive leadership, a leadership that "attempted to build people and not play the whole ego trip."[13]

Some activists' actual experience in the Weather collectives suggested something else again, however. Mark Naison, a former Columbia graduate student SDSer, less than fondly recalled his experience in a Brooklyn, New York, Weatherman collective. When he joined Weatherman, Naison had been involved with a black woman for a number of years. Over the course of his relationship, he had received considerable flak for the then far more daring interracial relationship. Indeed, his comrades in Columbia SDS had been among the few people supportive of the relation. Now, however, Naison's Weatherman comrades—some of them the same people who formerly had supported Naison's relationship—insisted that he break up with the woman, not because it was an interracial relationship, but because it was a monogamous one, and Weatherman insisted that Naison's total commitment be to "the collective." After having endured a number of criticism sessions devoted to the topic, Naison decided that he would leave the collective the next time the issue was raised.

Fate intervened before Naison had to deal with the monogamy issue again, however. He and ten other male Weathermen were practicing martial arts in Brooklyn's Prospect Park when some local white working-class youth approached them, complaining that a nearby diner had refused them service because they looked like "hippies." The Weathermen knew the youth from previous organizing efforts and jumped at the opportunity to stand up for them and prove how tough the Weathermen were. The Weathermen rushed to the diner, sat down, and demanded service. They, too, were told to leave, but they persisted in demanding service until two New York policemen entered. The officers ordered the eleven Weathermen to leave, and when they refused, the police attempted to arrest them. A brawl ensued, and the Weathermen disarmed the police. Several squad cars arrived, and police arrested all the Weathermen, charging them with felonious assault.

With felony charges pending against him, Naison was not eager to risk further arrests. But this was exactly what his Weatherman collective had in mind for the large, former Columbia tennis star. Naison's collective was planning a jailbreak action at a Queens, New York, high school and had chosen Naison to "overpower" the school's gym teacher. Naison resisted this new Weatherman injunction. Subsequently, "five women in the collective undertook to change my mind," Naison recalled.

They flattered me, telling me how my comrades admired my strength, fitness, and ability to fight; and when I resisted, they shifted to contempt. My machismo was a facade, they said, a ruse to extract sexual favors from women rather than a sign of real courage and commitment. Like most men, I was more bluster than substance. Most of the women were half my size, yet they were willing to risk their lives for the revolution. I was a coward and a blowhard, a weak-minded intellectual trapped inside a powerful body. Like most white men, I was a pathetic creature. Stripped of the privileges of race and gender, I became too weak to function. In the first serious challenge to my comfortable life, I had proven myself unfit for the revolution.

In keeping with what "Weatherwoman" called "building" people, the session went on for five hours, and Naison "grew increasingly upset." He recalled that he withdrew into a "fetal position, began crying and whimpering but would not give in to their pressure. The women in the room had somehow transformed themselves from gentle, considerate idealists into iron-willed revolutionaries, but I had no desire to imitate them. I wanted out of this group, wanted to be freed from these pressures to strip myself bare and remake my life." Finally, when Naison admitted to the women that he was the weak, pathetic creature that they painted him as, they let him alone, and he left Weatherman.[14] But such scenes were repeated again and again in the dozen or so Weatherman collectives spread out across the country.

It was difficult to discern how this leadership model was significantly different than the male leadership model that "Weatherwoman" had denounced, with the single exception that, at least in Naison's case, women were the actors who staged Naison's purge. Looking back many years later, Naison believed that what was really at issue in Weatherman was not monogamy, not women's leadership, and not opposition to male supremacy, but "control"—discipline—to the predominantly male Weatherman leadership.[15]

Susan Stern's experience in a Seattle Weatherman collective underlined Naison's contention. In Seattle, following the Days of Rage, two members of the local Weatherman leadership collective, with ongoing encouragement from Weatherman's national leadership collective, the Weather Bureau, set about destroying the monogamous relationships of several Seattle Weathermen. But since much of Weatherman's practical leadership in Seattle came from some of the people being targeted—Stern, who was involved with a non-Weatherman, and a Weatherman couple, Beverly and Jay—the local leadership's attempts made little headway. Weather Bureau leader Mark Rudd then arrived in Seattle to help straighten the collective out.

In Rudd's first meeting with the group, he focused his criticism on the monogamous Beverly and Jay, accusing Jay of being "pussy-whipped," among other things.

Beverly, according to Stern, was the only member of the collective to call Rudd on this male chauvinism. But as the collective meeting wore on, and as Rudd successfully encouraged the other collective members to vent their anger at the pair, Beverly's resistance crumbled, and her spirit broke. In the subsequent session, Rudd turned the criticism on Stern. Although collective members acknowledged that Stern was the most energetic and successful high school organizer in the collective, Rudd charged that she was not working for the revolution, but was instead working for her own ego gratification, her own self-aggrandizement. On and on, hour after hour, the collective, with Rudd's encouragement and approval, attacked Stern's alleged egocentrism. When the session ended, Rudd took the Weather Bureau's designated Seattle collective leader, Carol, to bed. Stern, shell-shocked, fell asleep upstairs but was awakened several hours later when she heard Georgia, the other woman sleeping in Stern's room, cry out "No, please, no." Rudd, having finished his organizing downstairs, was now attempting to get into bed with Georgia. He answered Georgia's cry by insisting that she, Georgia, together with Carol, "had to assume command of the collective," and that she "had to strengthen herself to fight the reactionary tendencies within the collective." Georgia continued to resist Rudd, confessing to him that she loved one of the other Seattle Weathermen. Rudd replied: "You have to put the demands of your collective above your love. Nothing comes before the collective."[16]

Weather Bureau theoretician John Jacobs (JJ) followed up on Rudd's visit several weeks later, continuing the criticisms that Rudd had begun. Stern observed that JJ sexually pursued the same women that Rudd had pursued, although JJ unsuccessfully sought to sleep with the still monogamous Beverly, apparently attempting to accomplish through a sexual liaison what Rudd had been unable to accomplish through intimidation alone. As Stern wryly noted to JJ, there was more than one way "to skin a cat."[17]

Weatherman's smashing monogamy was looking suspiciously like a new form of male domination—and not all that new. Women's movement activists critiqued Weatherman's continuing male domination, under its new and changing guises. Radical feminists, the women's liberation sector that called for a complete break with the New Left, certainly were not surprised by—or all that interested in— Weatherman's smash monogamy campaign. Smashing monogamy was simply the latest means of maintaining male supremacy in the New Left. Leading women's liberation politicos, however—those women's liberationists most closely allied to the New Left—also came to see Weatherman's campaign in this same light.

Bread and Roses, Boston's insightful political women's liberation group, for example, saw Weatherman's campaign to smash monogamy not as liberation for women—or men—but instead possibly as "a relief to the men—freeing them from emotional involvement and responsibility." Behind the campaign lay SDS's old line on women's liberation: politically, Weatherman, like SDS, placed its priority on getting women to fight imperialism and support black liberation. Fighting "male chauvinism" was important only "when it occurs within those struggles." Weatherman thus "delegitimized" women's oppression and measured women in terms of how well they fought in the struggles that Weatherman's male leadership sanctioned. Weatherwomen became "heroine[s]" in the organization when they were "tougher, better fighter[s] than the men." Women's oppression, in and of itself, was "less important or compelling than the oppression of blacks or Vietnamese." Moreover, Weatherman's campaign against monogamy reduced a "complex oppression" based in the nuclear family to the single aspect of monogamy. "Such emphasis," Bread and Roses argued, "does not deal collectively with the daily pressures—like children— that most women face." This guaranteed "that only a small elite of young women without families could ever participate in Weatherman struggles."[18]

More important still, women's liberation politicos came to see Weatherman's actions as only an extreme of New Left practice as a whole. Like Weatherman, the other RYM factions and subfactions were all pushing tokenism instead of substance in the struggle against the movement's male supremacy. The New Left's failure—and pretense—in dealing with its male supremacy pushed the politicos toward the radical feminist position on an independent women's liberation movement. Politicos, who six months earlier had been advocating working as part of the New Left, found themselves alienated by Weatherman and, increasingly, by the entire New Left.

Longtime movement activist and author Marge Piercy gave a name to the kind of "organizing" practiced by Rudd and JJ: "fucking a staff into existence." However, Piercy's November 1969 *Leviathan* critique was not of Weatherman per se, but of New Left institutions in general. Indeed, as her critique made clear, Weatherman's mode of deflecting the struggle against male supremacy simply put the veneer of women's leadership onto practices that the New Left had been developing for years. This practice, this organizational structure, Piercy insisted, was a "microcosm" of the larger society's structures and relations of power. In name, these institutions existed to elucidate the nature of the society and create the means for allowing larger numbers of people to participate in the process of social transformation. In reality, however, Piercy argued that movement groups—chapters, projects, whole factions—existed to achieve and enhance the prestige of a host of what she called "machers"—male movement leaders. Each of these machers dutifully sought to shuffle and reshuffle the existing movement's labor pool in order to secure his own movement fiefdom. Prestige and power in these institutions concentrated at the top, while "the shitwork," Piercy contended, was "concentrated at the bottom." And "the largely unpaid, largely female labor force that does the daily work" stood as the basis of the movement's very existence.[19]

New Left organizations and institutions, recognizing women's indispensable role in the movement and the women's liberation movement's threat to the continuation of that role, offered token leadership positions to women—in return for these women accepting the theoretical definitions of women's oppression developed by white male movement leaders. While RYM II's efforts at co-opting the women's movement were less dramatic than Weatherman's efforts, they were no less "male."

RYM II women staged a brief rebellion in the fall of 1969, but quickly relented behind the good behavior promises of RYM II's male leadership.[20] At bottom, however, the die already had been cast against RYM II's women. RYM II's male leaders included some of the New Left's most studied Marxist activists. But as Piercy noted, white males long had been adept at manipulating the "rhetorical counters" that characterized Marxism-Leninism, or any other jargon.[21] If RYM II's white machers could manipulate these rhetorical counters to oppose the most important social movement of the 1960s, and recast that black movement in a manner most comfortable to these young white radicals, white women could hardly expect that their concerns would be honestly reflected by the machers.

At its birth, RYM II articulated an abstract critique of male supremacy in the New Left, condemning it, but refusing to name its concrete manifestations. Within an extraordinarily short space of time, one of RYM II's founding components, the San Francisco Bay Area's RU, already had abandoned even this timid formulation. In the same summer that RYM II emerged, RU issued its first ideological broadside, *The Red Papers*. Here, under the ideological leadership of SDS NIC member Bob Avakian, was a stern, serious look at revolution in the United States. *The Red Papers'* cover adorned itself with portraits of Marx, Engels, Lenin, Stalin, and Mao. In its thirty-two pages, *The Red Papers* devoted almost an entire page to "male supremacy, women's liberation, and U.S. monopoly capitalism." Here *The Red Papers* defined male supremacy as male control of the means of production and "male domination over women in the monogamous family." Concomitant with this material domination, male supremacy promoted an ideology that saw women as "creatures of nature, passive and inferior to men, and men as decisive, self-fulfilling makers of history." While both men and women generally accepted these definitions, "Marxist-Leninists" needed to ask themselves which classes "benefited" from male supremacy and which classes were hurt by it. Marxism-Leninism—or at any rate, this strain of Marxism-Leninism—dictated one answer: "Male supremacy does not benefit working men." On the contrary, by preventing working-class unity, by enabling the "realization of surplus value," and by promoting the myth that men held real power in the family structure, male supremacy "only benefits the ruling class." *The Red Papers* concluded its discussion of women's liberation with a flourish:

> The struggle for women's liberation represents a major and integral part of the overall movement for the defeat of U.S. monopoly capitalism and its replacement by a socialist America. Within the revolutionary movement, the women's liberation struggle will be led by working women. These women will play a major role in the defeat of the enemy and the building of a society in which men and women will participate equally in all spheres of social existence with no sexually predetermined roles.[22]

In short, *The Red Papers* managed to discuss women's liberation without once referring to the existing women's liberation movement, to the analysis that the women's movement was itself developing, or to the fact that by addressing women in the New Left, the women's movement was forcing the New Left to address the issue of male supremacy. For RU, women's liberation derived not from the actual struggle of women, but from the minds of vanguard Marxist thinkers. Moreover, unlike the RYM II women's liberation discussion that had come out of SDS's June National Convention, *The Red Papers* failed to explicitly condemn male chauvinism or male supremacy in the movement itself.

Such theoretical disdain for the women's liberation movement had to play itself out practically. Roxanne Dunbar-Ortiz, a founding member of Boston's radical feminist group, Cell 16, experienced RU's practical antipathy to the women's movement—and to women—firsthand. Dunbar-Ortiz had moved quickly to radical feminism in the women's movement's early days, but her commitment to anti-imperialist struggles drew her toward the politico position. On a summer 1970 Venceremos Brigade trip to Cuba, Dunbar-Ortiz had worked with RU members, and on her return she met with Avakian to discuss the nature of her relationship to RU. Two other men were in the kitchen where the pair met, although they were not introduced to Dunbar-Ortiz. They simply stood, arms folded, and laughed when prompted to do so by Avakian. All three, Dunbar-Ortiz, recalled, "wore identical light blue work shirts, faded Levis, lace-up boots, and dark blue Mao caps with Mao buttons on them." Speaking in an affected "working-class" accent, Avakian chided Dunbar-Ortiz from the moment she entered the room. "So you think," Avakian began, that the collective that he headed was "made up of male chauvinist pigs. You want to be a little more specific in your analysis?" Dunbar-Ortiz refused the bait and insisted that she had not come to discuss male chauvinism, but rather the status of her membership in the organization. Avakian, however, would not be mollified and demanded that Dunbar-Ortiz explain "this male chauvinism complaint of yours." Dunbar-Ortiz replied that she had not "even used the term" since she had been in the Bay Area. "But we want to know," Avakian replied. "'See, we're here listening, awaiting criticism.' He spread his arms like Jesus on the cross. The other two men laughed."[23] Dunbar-Ortiz walked out. Other politicos, confronted again and again by such behavior, did the same.

Politicos Kathy McAfee and Marcia Salo, for example, admitted that radical feminists had "raised disquieting questions" concerning New Left tokenism and the politicos' roles within the New Left. However, what had been "really decisive" in forcing the politicos to recognize the validity of the feminist critique had been the New Left's ongoing intransigence, its "male-supremacist structure." "The contradiction is glaring," argued McAfee and Salo; "in the name of building a new society, we have been playing out every oppressive role of capitalist society." Sometimes, the women asserted, this recognition came with a seemingly "trivial" incident and offered an illustration: "A man at a Mad Dog meeting was describing the 'good leadership role' the group had played in a building takeover in support of the Young Lords. 'I finally began to feel,' he concluded, 'that Mad Dogs was a collective.' A woman who had been in the building was shaken. 'Mad Dogs! You mean the *men* in the Dogs who consulted each other, did all the talking, and completely forgot I was even a member!'"[24]

What was behind this "glaring contradiction," this inability to see or take seriously women in the New Left? Almost two years earlier, pioneering radical feminists Judith Brown and Beverly Jones had warned New Left women that male chauvinism was an essential part of male identity. The New Left's continued ability to blithely overlook women in the movement inexorably drove politicos to the same conclusion. McAfee and Salo later stated: "We had underestimated the power of the 'simple' ego threat. We had been thinking of male chauvinism as a bad habit, but it turned out be a basic male identity. The men saw themselves not just as people, but as *men*, and being a man meant having power over others." So men held tenaciously to this "old system of power relationships," offering "lip-service," at best, to women's concerns. Through their actual experience in the New Left, McAfee and Salo, together with many of their politico comrades, were forced to conclude that "women's liberation has not affected the politics of men in any fundamental way.... Although they have gradually come to realize that male chauvinism has to be dealt with ... they still assume women will do all the struggle. They look at women's liberation as an aid to fighting the real enemies—racism and imperialism—rather than as a revolutionary struggle, as part of the politics we *must* put into practice and bring to people."[25]

No one articulated the politico anger and disaffection with the New Left more sharply than did Robin Morgan. A founder of the politico WITCH, Morgan had never minced words, warning male New Leftists that they had best get their house in order. By warning male New Leftists, however, Morgan had left the door open to the possibility that male radicals might change and that women's liberationists could continue to work with them. But in a powerful piece titled "Goodbye to All That," Morgan went beyond warning New Left males and definitively set them on the other side, as upholders of the old oppressive order. In this, she reflected the sentiments of a significant segment of the women's movement: the white male New Left had been tested and had been found wanting.

"Let's run it on down," Morgan began. "White males," she insisted, were the ones "most responsible for the destruction of human life and environment on the planet today." Who, she asked, was "controlling the supposed revolution to change all that? White males (yes, yes, even with their pasty fingers back in black and brown pies again)." The astute Morgan had grasped something that the white New Left was studiously ignoring and denying: even as it proclaimed its fealty to black revolution, white people were once again attempting to dictate the terms of their support for the black revolution, and even the very nature of that revolution.

Morgan then proceeded to indict, point by point, the male supremacy of virtually all sectors of the New Left: the pacifists, PL and the other Old Left formations, Weatherman, RYM II, the Chicago Conspiracy defendants, the countercultural Left, the Yippies, and the White Panthers. Morgan was particularly cutting in her rhythmic reproach to Weatherman. "Goodbye," said Morgan, to Weatherman and its campaign against monogamy; to Weatherman, "with its Stanley Kowalski image and theory of free sexuality but practice of sex on demand for males."

"Left Out!"—not Right On—to Weather Sisters who, and they know better—they know, reject their own radical feminism for the last desperate grab at male approval that we all know so well, for claiming that the *machismo* style and the gratuitous violence is their own style by "free choice" and for believing that this is the way for a woman to make her revolution . . . all the while, oh my sister, not meeting my eyes because Weathermen chose [killer cult leader Charles] Manson as their—and your— Hero. (Honest, at least . . . since Manson is only the logical extreme of the normal American male's fantasy (whether he is Dick Nixon or Mark Rudd): master of a harem, women to do all the shitwork, from raising babies and cooking and hustling to killing people on order.) Goodbye to all that shit that sets women apart from women; shit that covers the face of any Weatherwoman which is the face of any Manson slave which is the face of [Ted Kennedy's recently drowned companion] Mary Jo Kopechne which is the face of [black welfare rights activist] Beulah Saunders which is the face of me which is the face of [First Lady] Pat Nixon which is the face of [fugitive bombing suspect] Pat Swinton.

President Richard Nixon and Weatherman leader Mark Rudd were on one side against Nixon's wife, with fugitive bomber Pat Swinton and black welfare activist Beulah Saunders on the other side. Morgan had gone over to the radical feminist position not only in condemning the New Left as part of the patriarchal power structure but also in asserting the primacy of sexual oppression over both class and racial oppressions. She continued:

> *In the dark we are all the same*—and you had better believe it: we're in the dark, baby. (Remember the old joke: Know what they call a black man with a Ph.D.? A nigger. Variation: Know what they call a Weatherwoman? A heavy cunt. Know what they call a Hip Revolutionary Woman? A groovy cunt. Know what they call a radical militant feminist? A crazy cunt. Amerika is a land of free choice—take your pick of titles. Left Out, my sister—don't you see? Goodbye to the illusion of strength when you run hand in hand with your oppressors; goodbye to the dream that being in the leadership collective will get you anything but gonorrhea.[26]

Indeed, in those dark cold days of the winter of 1970, gonorrhea was spreading as rapidly through the Weatherman collectives as was the tokenism of a male-defined women's leadership throughout the New Left.[27]

Perhaps it was the hypocrisy, more than anything, that drove women like Morgan away from the New Left; the pretense and lip service given women's leadership against the reality that white males were defining the New Left's trajectory and the role of women in the New Left. Explained Morgan:

> There is something every woman wears around her neck on a thin chain of fear—an amulet of madness. For each of us, there exists somewhere a moment of insult so intense that she will reach up and rip the amulet off, even if the chain tears at the flesh of her neck. And the last protection from seeing the truth will be gone. Do you think, tugging furtively every day at the chain and going nicely insane as I am, that I can be concerned with the puerile squabbles of a counterfeit Left that laughs at my pain? Do you think such a concern is noticeable when set alongside the suffering of more than half the human species for the past 5,000 years—due to a whim of the other half? No, no, no, goodbye to all that. . . .
>
> Goodbye, goodbye forever, counterfeit Left, counterleft, male-dominated cracked-glass-mirror reflection of the Amerikan Nightmare. Women are the real Left. We are rising, powerful in our unclean bodies; bright glowing mad in our inferior brains; wild hair flying, wild eyes staring, wild voices keening; undaunted by blood we who hemorrhage every twenty-eight days; laughing at our own beauty we who have lost our

sense of humor; mourning for all each precious one of us might have been in this one living time-place had she not been born a woman; stuffing fingers into our mouths to stop the screams of fear and hate and pity for men we have loved and love still, tears in our eyes and bitterness in our mouths for children we couldn't have, or couldn't *not* have, or didn't want, or didn't want *yet*, or wanted and had in this place and this time of sorrow. We are rising with a fury older and potentially greater than any force in history, and this time we will be free or no one will survive. Power to all the people or to none. All the way down, this time.[28]

But as James Baldwin once put it, "Every goodbye ain't gone." Morgan's good-bye to the New Left, powerful and insightful as it was, held on to a part of the New Left, even as she rejected working with the New Left. She bade farewell to the New Left's organizational embodiments, and to its continued male-supremacist ideology and practice, even as she uncritically accepted the New Left's claims about itself. Weatherman, RYM II, and the various Old Left and pacifist stripes Morgan condemned so forcefully justified not dealing with their male supremacy in the name of battling some "greater" oppression—racism, imperialism, class oppression. Morgan, instead of seeing that the New Left, in fact, was as little challenging its own racism as it was challenging its own male supremacy, accepted these claims. The upshot of accepting these claims was to draw this conclusion: if battling racial or class or imperial oppressions stood as an obstacle to battling women's oppression, this affirmed that women's oppression transcended these other oppressions. As a transcendent oppression, women's oppression was primary and would have to be taken on before taking on racism, imperialism, and class oppression. Hence, Morgan placed Pat Nixon in parallel with Pat Swinton and with herself. Hence, in her essay's valediction, Morgan offered a series of slogans, the first of which was "Free Kathleen Cleaver!" In short, Morgan's whiteness, the presumption that her vision was the clearest, continued to link her with the New Left, her "good-bye," notwithstanding.

A poem that circulated in parts of the women's movement at the time directly addressed the line that Morgan and a large number of politicos were adopting. Titled "A Black Woman Speaks . . . of White Womanhood, of White Supremacy, of Peace," the poem spoke to white women:

What will you do?
Will you fight with me?
White supremacy is your enemy and mine.
So be careful when you talk with me.
Remind me not of slavery, I know it well

but rather tell me of your own.
Remember, you have never known me.
You've been busy seeing me
as white supremacist would have me be,
and I will be myself.
Free![29]

To be sure, Kathleen Cleaver was oppressed as a woman; but it was a different kind of oppression than the oppression faced by Morgan. Like Ruby Doris Smith Robinson and the SNCC women who rejected Casey Hayden and Mary King speaking for them and who saw black liberation as the necessary concomitant to black women's liberation, so Kathleen Cleaver would have rejected Morgan's claims to a transcendent women's oppression. Speaking many years later, Cleaver argued that "Blacks are oppressed in their communal, collective existence. . . . If you're dominated as a community, then how in the world are you going to liberate yourself if you're not struggling in a communal sense. . . . Fannie Lou Hamer and Jacqueline Kennedy [are] . . . not in the same category. They [are] . . . not subjected to the same type of gender discrimination. . . . That's so obvious, it's not even worth discussing."[30]

Repression and the war's stark horror always had been elements driving the New Left. Now, in the late fall of 1969, two key events rocked white activists anew: the My Lai massacre revelation and the assassination of Chicago Panther leader Fred Hampton. In the wake of the New Left's determination—and especially Weatherman's determination—to ignore the Vietnamese and the Panthers, these events helped set the tone for the New Left's further dismemberment.

On November 17, 1969, two days following the largest demonstrations in U.S. history, the *New York Times* published its first full account of My Lai, "Vietnamese Say G.I.'s Slew 567 in Town." On November 19, the *Cleveland Plain Dealer* published the first photos of the massacre taken by a former army combat photographer, Ronald Haeberle. Haeberle had struck a deal with *Life* magazine, however, that temporarily prevented the shocking photos from going out beyond Cleveland. Press interviews with a number of the GIs involved at My Lai nevertheless substantiated the allegations. On November 24, the scope of what had happened reached its widest audience when CBS TV broadcast a Mike Wallace interview with Paul Meadlo, a GI at My Lai.

Meadlo recalled that at the beginning of the operation, his squad had rounded up between forty and fifty Vietnamese and placed them in the center of the village. Meadlo's lieutenant, William Calley, then came over and said, "You know what to do with them, don't you?" Meadlo assumed that Calley meant that he should watch the Vietnamese, but Calley returned fifteen minutes later and "said how come you ain't killed them yet? . . . So he stepped back about 10, 15 feet and he started shooting them. And he told me to start shooting. So I started shooting. I poured four clips into the group." Wallace asked the young GI how many Vietnamese in the group he, Meadlo, had himself killed.

> Meadlo: Well, I fired them on automatic, so you can't—you just spray the area on them and so you can't know how many you killed 'cause they were going fast. So I might have killed ten or fifteen of them.
> Wallace: Men, women and children?
> Meadlo: Men, women and children.
> Wallace: And babies?
> Meadlo: And babies.

In answer to another of Wallace's questions, Meadlo estimated that his company killed nearly 400 Vietnamese civilians on that day.[31]

Life followed this up with the edition that hit newsstands on December 1. Here, in Haeberle's graphic color photographs, together with his lengthy account of the action, were the realities that the Vietnamese had been urging on New Leftists: the war's unbelievable brutality and the inescapable fact that the United States had as its enemy all of Vietnam's people.[32] Haeberle recounted, for example, seeing "a little boy walking toward us in a daze. He'd been shot in the arm and leg. He wasn't crying or making any noise." The photographer "knelt down to photograph the boy." A GI also knelt down close by Haeberle: "The GI fired three shots into the child. The first shot knocked him back, the second shot lifted him into the air. The third shot put him down and body fluids came out. The GI simply got up and walked away." Haeberle had been accompanied at My Lai by a GI publicist, Jay Roberts. Roberts recalled that "there was this big pile of bodies. This really tiny little kid—he only had a shirt on, nothing else—he came over to the pile and held the hand of one of the dead. One of the GIs behind me dropped into a kneeling position, 30 meters from this kid, and killed him with a single shot."

Haeberle and Roberts also saw the beginnings of the rape of a thirteen-year-old girl, her mother desperately attempting to protect the child. When the GIs involved saw Haeberle photographing the scene, which included several adults and four or five other children huddled together, Roberts reported that "they left off and turned away as if everything was normal."

Then a soldier asked, "Well, what'll we do with 'em?"

"Kill 'em," another answered.

"I heard an M60 go off . . . a light machine gun, and when we turned back around, all of them and the kids with them were dead."

Perhaps more disturbing, Haeberle and Roberts left My Lai at midday to follow another combat company. They were near the company's captain when he received radio reports relayed from My Lai claiming that GIs had killed 125 Vietcong there. The captain, who knew nothing of the incident, laughed, "Yeah, probably all women and children!"[33]

Three days after *Life's* account of My Lai appeared, police took the life of Chicago Black Panther leader Fred Hampton and fellow Chicago Panther Mark Clark. By the time he was killed in the predawn raid, the twenty-one-year-old Hampton had already established his reputation as a tough, charismatic, and deeply humane leader. Hampton had founded the Chicago Panther chapter in 1968 and quickly elevated its visibility by organizing a Breakfast for Children program and a free health clinic. He was also the moving force in founding Chicago's "Rainbow Coalition"—a progressive united front organization that included the politicized Puerto Rican gang, the Young Lords, and the politicized white Appalachian gang, the Young Patriots. Hampton also worked to politicize Chicago's largest black gang, the Black P. Stone Nation.[34] In short, Hampton fit to a tee J. Edgar Hoover's COINTELPRO profile of a dangerous black nationalist.

Prior to December 4, Chicago police had made repeated efforts to derail Hampton and the Chicago Black Panther Party. At the time of his death, Hampton was free on appeal bond from a two-to-five-year sentence he had received for allegedly stealing $71 in ice cream that had been given away to black community youth. Normally, sentencing for a crime of this nature would have involved a one-year minimum sentence. After his release on bond, Chicago police continued to pile charges on Hampton. A *Guardian* reporter estimated that "at the time of his death he had at least a dozen cases against him pending in the courts." Moreover, the FBI and the Chicago police repeatedly mounted major operations against the Chicago Panthers, raiding their office on a variety of trumped-up charges on June 4, July 31, and October 4, 1969. During these raids, the assorted police forces destroyed files, office equipment, and Panther newspapers and literature; stole Panther funds; and set fire to the office. Chicago police also arrested numerous Panthers on a wide variety of charges.[35]

Finally, in the predawn hours of December 4, a team of Chicago police, aided by a detailed diagram of Hampton's apartment drawn up by an FBI informer in the Panthers, entered the apartment with guns blazing. The police arsenal included a submachine gun, several shotguns, and the usual complement of police revolvers. Police killed Mark Clark at the apartment's entrance, wounded four other Panthers in the apartment, and shot Fred Hampton dead as he lay on his bed. Police initially claimed that the deaths and injuries had occurred in a gun battle initiated by the Panthers. But as soon as the police left, the Panthers opened the apartment to public display. Over the next several days, thousands of people passed through the apartment and saw with their own eyes Hampton's bloodstained mattress and the numerous bullet holes that covered the apartment's walls. Contrary to the police claims, all the bullets were fired inward toward the apartment and toward Hampton's bedroom. The president of Chicago's Afro-American Patrolman's League, Renault Robinson, quickly denounced the official version of the raid, insisting that the "physical evidence" at the scene bore out the Panther version of the murders. Local black alderman A. A. Raynor termed Hampton's death an "assassination" that was part of a "systematic extermination" of the Panther leadership. Chicago's chapter of the National Association for the Advancement of Colored People (NAACP) called the murders a "modern day lynching," and Southern Christian Leadership Conference leader Ralph Abernathy insisted that "the black community is the target, and the Black Panther Party is the bullseye [sic]. . . . The nation that conquered Nazi Germany is following the same brutal course as Nazi Germany."[36]

There was a horror here that transcended the horror of the My Lai pictures and testimony and the horror of Fred Hampton's death. It was a horror that struck young white activists with particular intensity. On the one hand, the country that had raised them with the notion that it was the fount of freedom and righteousness stood before them irrevocably exposed: it was a brutal killer of children. They had been lied to. On the other hand, that same country had also raised these young white people to believe that they had a particular relation to power, that they could transform their dreams into realities in ways that others could not. To a limited extent, this belief had a real foundation to it. Only the tale that had been told to white youth had the most important part left out of it. Young whites could transform their dreams into realities, but only so long as those dreams presupposed or acquiesced to the subjugation of nonwhite peoples. Now, in the face of an interminable war in Asia and the killings of young black activists in America, young white people would hold on more firmly to this belief in their own power, would embrace that belief, not seeing—or wanting to see—the limitations their country had put on this privileged power. They had been betrayed, they had been lied to; now, by might and main, they would set things aright.

In contrast, the Vietnamese had been fighting almost continually for close to thirty years—against Japan, France, and now the United States. What happened at My Lai had been horrible; but it did not strike the Vietnamese as surprising or unbelievable. Indeed, they understood that what had happened at My Lai was inevitable, given an enemy whose aim was to subjugate their country. Thus, the Vietnamese response to My Lai—or rather their response to the totality of the American invasion—was a measured response that appreciated the realities of power. Vietnam's people did not have the illusion that simply because they wished for something, it would occur. On the contrary, only by "carefully studying the situation," by assessing the balance of forces between the sides, by examining and playing upon the contradictions within the oppressor's camp, and by working steadfastly to build the unity of one's own camp could the Vietnamese make the progress they had made in the war. It was this approach that the Vietnamese unsuccessfully had attempted to impress upon their North American allies.

Neither did Fred Hampton or black people generally share the illusions that young white activists held. Indeed, Hampton's popularity in the New Left stemmed, in part, from the courage and confidence with which he faced the seeming inevitability of his own death and the deaths of those around him. In the last public speech he gave prior to his assassination, Hampton had put it bluntly: "This system is out to kill us and we know it. Some say we are not ready to take on this monster. We say that we do not want to, but that is not the question any longer. The monster has taken us on and we have to deal with reality."[37] Two months after Hampton's death, a young white activist, Karen Wald, interviewed James Baldwin and solicited his reaction to the murders of Hampton and Clark. Baldwin calmly informed Wald that the killings were "only the latest examples" of the U.S. government's activities. But were not these assassinations "so much more obvious?" Wald asked. Baldwin shot back:

> It's amazing to me how difficult it is for people to see what they don't want to see. Black people see, but how many parents of white children see it, that's another question. The difference between my experience and that of white America, even the very best of white America, is that they have difficulty believing that the country can act this way. And that is not my problem at all. I've always known it could, and it always has been my experience and I'm no longer young.[38]

For many young white activists, My Lai and Fred Hampton's assassination were revelations. Most SDSers knew what their country was capable of before; but My Lai, spread out in *Life* in full color photos, and Fred Hampton's death, "so much more obvious," because SDSers knew Hampton, or knew of him and admired him, made visceral understandings that hitherto had been intellectual. These were disillusioning days, days filled with thoughts of death and despair—despair at the enormity of crimes that they never before had seen so clearly, and despair at the enormity of confronting a monster. Having now seen the bloody reality, they clung more desperately to their other white-bred illusion: that they, above all other people, could set it right. Whether through bold, courageous, dangerous action or through clear-sighted Marxist-Leninist-Maoist analysis, the former SDSers could play a meaningful, leading role in reconstructing the world on just principles.

Many years later, Weatherman leader Bill Ayers would recall the tone of the times for New Leftists: "We felt, personally and specifically, the full weight of the catastrophe unfolding before us. . . . The dreadful and inescapable fact was that it was up to us to rescue everyone. We imagined that the survival of humanity depended on the kids alone. . . . We could think of no basis on which to defend inaction, and so our watchword was simple: Action! Action! Action! We were kids in combat, with little to lose."[39] But, of course, there was a lot to lose, not the least of which was SDS, which young white people had painstakingly built for just such a period as this one; not the least of which was the ability, in conjunction with revolutionary black nationalists at home and successful national liberation movements abroad, to transform the consciousness of millions of young white Americans, to transform that consciousness in ways wholly new to the history of the United States.[40]

SDS's last National Council meeting, renamed by Weatherman the National War Council, opened on a cold, late December 1969 evening in a black community dance hall in Flint, Michigan, and finalized Weatherman's determination to be the catalyst for world revolution. As they entered the dance hall, attendees were greeted by large posters of Che, Fidel, Ho Chi Minh, Mao, Lenin, and Eldridge Cleaver. Alternating red and black posters of the recently slain Fred Hampton covered an entire wall of the ballroom. A large cardboard machine gun was suspended from the ceiling and pointed menacingly at enemies of the people: Richard Nixon; Chicago mayor Richard Daley; the prominent New Left newspaper the *Guardian*, which had denounced Weatherman; and, to those not in the know, inexplicably, an actress, Sharon Tate, recently the victim of a gruesome murder carried out by followers of cult leader Charles Manson.

The council, also dubbed a "wargasm" by Weatherman, was to have been a final attempt at reaching out to the youth counterculture. Weatherman had invited the White Panthers, Yippies, and Motherfuckers, all on the New Left's countercultural wing, to see if they might forge a common front. But unlike SDS's prior council meetings and conventions, Weatherman offered no resolutions, and very little discussion or debate occurred in the plenary sessions. Indeed, the plenaries consisted of speeches by Weather Bureau leaders, followed for the most part by an amen chorus of "Right on!" from Weatherman's loyal cadre. Weatherman leaders were simply taking their post-Chicago politics—at the center of which stood the impossibility of organizing sold-out white workers—and adding a veneer of sex, drugs, and rock and roll in the hopes that they could entice the countercultural Left to reinforce Weatherman's ranks.

Bureau leader Bernardine Dohrn opened the War Council with its first plenary speech. Dohrn was self-critical of the organization post-Chicago. "Since October 11," she averred, "we've been wimpy on armed struggle. . . . We didn't fight around Bobby Seale when he was shackled at the Conspiracy Trial. We should have torn the courtroom apart. We didn't smash them when Mobe peace creeps hissed David Hilliard on Moratorium Day in San Francisco. We didn't burn Chicago down when Fred was killed."[41] Weather Bureau leader Mark Rudd also focused a part of his plenary talk on Hampton. Pacing in front of the assembled Weathermen cadre, Rudd vowed that "we are going to meet and map plans to avenge the deaths of Fred Hampton and Mark Clark." Years later, Rudd would recall that "'AVENGE FRED HAMPTON' became our battle cry and the obsession of the War Council."[42] Similarly, an anonymous "Weatherwoman," writing in *Rat* just after the War Council, claimed that "the heaviest thing that we realized at the Weatherman War Council was that our allowing the murder of Fred and other Blacks to go on unavenged was to take a defeat from the pigs and to continue in the racist role that Amerika has defined for us."[43]

Such determination to avenge Fred Hampton's death notwithstanding, neither Dohrn nor Rudd made any mention of Hampton's ongoing opposition to the path Weatherman had been taking, or of his insistence that the white radicals should be organizing white workers to support black liberation. When he was alive, Weatherman ignored Hampton's leadership, ignored Hampton's views on what would best protect both him and the black liberation movement from police assaults and murders. When he was dead, however, Weatherman could put Hampton forward as the perfect symbol for continuing the very line that the young Panther had opposed in life.[44]

Dohrn continued her opening talk by sketching out Weatherman's approach to revolution anecdotally. She informed the council that she had recently been on an airplane with a number of other Weatherman leaders. According to Dohrn, they had gone "up and down the aisle 'borrowing' food from people's plates." "They didn't know we were Weathermen," explained Dohrn, "they just knew we were crazy. That's what we're about, being crazy motherfuckers and scaring the shit out of honky America."

From here it was only a short step to what would become the most notorious pronouncement to come out of the council: Weatherman's designation of killer cult leader Charles Manson as revolutionary hero.[45] Manson had been charged at the beginning of December with sending out a little band of his followers to a Hollywood home where they had, on his orders, murdered the occupants. Among those murdered was the actress Sharon Tate, at the time eight months pregnant. Dohrn was elated over the murders. The murderers had even scrawled the word "PIG" in a victim's blood on the front door. As the speculation went at the time of the cult's arrest, Manson apparently wanted to ignite a race war in the United States—hence, the use of the term "pig," identifiable as coming out of the black movement. When enough blacks and whites had killed each other in this race war, Manson and his followers, who had moved to the desert to steer clear of the conflict, would step forward and gain control. Moreover, Manson was reputed to have had a hypnotic-like control over his followers, and lent the cult's women out in order to help recruit male followers.

Perhaps Manson's extraordinary racism and sexism escaped or were unknown to Dohrn and her Weather Bureau comrades—or, perhaps more plausibly, as Robin Morgan had suggested concerning Manson's male supremacy, Manson's vision and practice closely mirrored Weatherman's own white and male supremacy. Dohrn: "Dig it, first they killed those pigs, then they ate dinner in the same room with them, then they even shoved a fork into a victim's stomach! Wild!"[46] Weathermen cadre saluted each other with the sign of the "fork" for the remainder of the convention.

Many people criticized Weatherman at the time for adopting Manson. Some Weathermen—Susan Stern, for example—saw the "Mansonite trip" as not corresponding with the "quality of the rest of Weatherman politics."[47] Most critics, however, just saw Dohrn's use of Manson as bizarre, which accorded with the general notion that Weatherman was bizarre. There was no need for any further explanation. Morgan was perhaps the only contemporary critic who saw through to the actual affinity—women on demand—that existed between Manson's male-supremacist politics and Weatherman's smash monogamy politics. Apparently, however, no one at the time linked Manson's playing with "race war" with Weatherman's desire to do the same.

Plenary speeches by Weather Bureau leaders were interspersed with smaller, regional meetings. The goal of these meetings, apparently, was to "build people," that is, to mold people into better followers. *Rat*'s reporter at the council meeting described the process: "When doubts come up you got 30 other people to smash them for you. . . . Sure doubts are repressed by this . . . your brothers and sisters tar them over, beat them down, dismiss them . . . but uncertainty always goes inward to be covered by a shell of frenzy-hatred which prevents you from dropping out or giving up."[48] At the heart of this frenzy, however, was to be support for the politics of chaos and race war in the "mother-country."

At the time of the Chicago National Action, Weatherman had given up on the overwhelming mass of white working people in the United States. That Weatherman's efforts had not been rewarded with a turnout of tough white working-class youth proved to Weatherman that whites had made their decision: they were going with their privilege, with their racism, and with the counterrevolution. Non-Weathermen at the War Council recognized this defining element of Weatherman strategy. Said the Liberation News Service reporter at the council, for example: "Weatherman continues to promote the notion that white working people in America are inherently counter-revolutionary, impossible to organize, or just plain evil—'honky bastards,' as many Weathermen put it." Still, Weatherman's analysis suggested that the U.S. empire was overextended, that it was suffering hammer blows in every corner of the globe, and that the black movement at home—Watts, Detroit, Newark—stood on the verge of real people's war against America. Moreover, America's intransigent holding on to Vietnam suggested that the United States might only leave Vietnam when the U.S. empire itself faced imminent collapse. If Weatherman did not act now to hasten the collapse, how many more My Lai massacres might occur? But how could Weatherman hasten that collapse, given that the organization's base—white people—would stay with the coun-terrevolution? Weatherman could contribute to revolution by creating chaos in the mother country and supporting the onset of race war. Liberation News Service summed up the organization's strategy: "The Weatherman position boiled down to inevitable race war in America, with very few 'honkies'—except perhaps the 400 people in the room and the few street kids or gang members who might run with them surviving the holocaust."[49] The revolution, in short, would unfold in the United States as race war. Weatherman determined that its responsibility was to help blacks make this revolution.

Somewhere in the course of the National War Council, the Weather Bureau realized that its attempt at forging an alliance with the countercultural white New Left had failed. The bureau retreated into a private meeting and emerged a day later with the new line, which was really only the logical conclusion to the politics that it had been leading since it rejected the Panthers' UFAF. As Susan Stern summarized that line, "To hold back now would be to fail the Vietnamese, the blacks, and the revolution."[50] Or as Weatherman put it in a little pamphlet it issued at the time:

Armed struggle starts when someone starts it. International revolutionary war is reality, and to debate about the "correct time and conditions" to begin the fight, or about a phase of work necessary to prepare people for the revolution, is reactionary. . . .

The experience of our movement until the emergence of Weatherman was one of grabbing every chance not to move, not to struggle, not to jeopardize ourselves or our positions as professional "radicals." That opportunism has contributed to the continued oppression of people in the colonies and here in the United States: the expansion of the empire, and the increased militarism and fascism in this country which we now face in the struggle.[51]

In February 1970, a dozen Weatherman cadre were called to a secret meeting in Cleveland, in which Weatherman leaders Mark Rudd and Linda Evans expanded on the line coming out of Flint. FBI informant Larry Grathwohl was present and reported that Rudd and Evans criticized the cadre "for being passive and specifically they were saying that because we had been passive the black struggle, the struggle in Vietnam, the struggle in Korea and China, all over the world, had been hampered because we had not shown the members of these various revolutionary groups that we were committed to our revolution, and that criticism, line of criticism went on for the entire first meeting, which lasted about 6 hours." In a second meeting, Grathwohl reported, "Mark informed us that the so-called national organization of Weathermen was to be disbanded and that we would be divided into cells which would set as our goal strategic sabotage against all symbols of authority. This way we would be able to push the black militants, the Vietnamese, the Koreans, the Chinese, the Al Fatah, and so on."[52] This was the line coming out of Flint, put in broad, practical terms. An anonymous New York Weatherman, recalled the thinking of the time: "We wanted to encourage the Vietnamese. We wanted another Tet. We thought that the Tet Offensive was this huge turning point of the whole history of Indochina, and we thought that we might be able to help push for another one."[53] In other words, Weatherman, having forsaken the tasks placed on white radicals both by the Panthers and the Vietnamese, having given up on organizing white workers, now saw as its base the international struggle against American imperialism. Weatherman would initiate armed struggle now with the intent of "encouraging" national liberation revolutions abroad and the black liberation movement at home.

Weatherman's National War Council had resolved one problem—what can a small number of white revolutionaries do in the absence of a white revolutionary base? Following the War Council, another, perhaps knottier problem presented itself to Weatherman. Black people, who were going to smash "the imperialist motherfucker" by themselves, needed an organized leadership for the task. Unfortunately, for some Weathermen, the Panthers were not up to the mark. On the contrary, the Panthers were continuing to try to organize their base, and they continued to denounce Weatherman for its adventurism. Fred Hampton, for example, had to the moment of his death steadfastly resisted the notion of being driven underground, saying that his role was to organize the masses of people.[54] The Panthers, evidently, did not appreciate the meaning of being a revolutionary vanguard.

Internally, some Weatherman members began to build their case against the Panthers: the Panthers had been smashed by government repression; they were leaning on the revisionist Communist Party for support; and they themselves had become revisionist. The editor of one of the most important New Left newspapers remembered that in his contact with Weatherman at the time, "there was this utter contempt for the Panthers." From Weatherman's perspective, "the Panthers' day had passed, Breakfast for Children had passed." Columbia SDSer Lew Cole remembered that Weatherman "was way off the Panthers.... For them, the idea of the blacks was always 'armed vanguard, armed vanguard,' and nothing else." Weatherman leader Bill Ayers would also acknowledge, in an interview with historian Jeremy Varon, that he saw the Panthers' " 'serve the people' programs as 'gun-toting liberalism.' "[55]

Many years later, a Bay Area activist recalled having had this line on the black struggle and Weatherman's responsibility run down to him when Weatherman attempted to recruit him following his return from a 1970 trip to Cuba. A Weatherwoman in a "short mini-skirt and knee-high boots," he remembered, insisted that "we were living in historic times; the antiwar movement was intensifying. Unfortunately, because of the recent police attacks against the black community (particularly against Fred Hampton and the Chicago Panther office) the black community was suffering from great demoralization. What could we do about this?" In answer to her own question, the Weatherwoman "suggested this scenario": Weatherman cadre, posing as black revolutionaries, would attack a prominent oppressor of black people. The potential recruit recalled that he was stunned when he heard this. "Shaken from the lethargy induced from the long meeting I began to ask some questions": "Wouldn't this action, I asked, only bring down more heat on a beleaguered black community? On the contrary, was the reply: the black community, suffering from demoralization, would be revived by this action, especially because it would appear to have been done by 'their own.' "[56]

Four former Weatherman activists who left the organization during this period publicly described and denounced these same politics at the time: "Since black and third world revolutionary groups such as the Black Panther Party, the League of Revolutionary Black Workers and the Young Lords Organization disagreed with" Weatherman's call for black armed struggle and race war against the United States right now, "Weatherman labeled them 'revisionist.' Weatherman then argued that whites would 'fight on the side of blacks' only if there was 'non-revisionist' black leadership. Therefore, it was necessary for white revolutionaries to carry out actions in black communities in order to develop new black leadership which believed in race war, armed struggle now, and other Weatherman positions. This was the height of their [Weatherman's] racism."[57] In short, at least one faction of Weatherman had determined that it would carry out militant, armed actions whose authorship was racially ambiguous or even deliberately designed to appear as black. By so doing, this faction of Weatherman believed that it would inspire the emergence of a new black revolutionary vanguard, committed to the kind of armed struggle Weatherman deemed essential for the revolution.

To be sure, following the Days of Rage, Weatherman did receive some reassurance in its quest for a new black vanguard. Shortly after the Chicago Panthers' criticism of Weatherman appeared in the *Black Panther* newspaper, Eldridge Cleaver, now in exile, responded in an article titled "On Weatherman." In clear reference to Weatherman's Chicago action, Cleaver affirmed that he preferred "a paralyzed pig to well-criticized pig." Moreover, Cleaver insisted that while a "dead pig" was "desirable," "a paralyzed pig is preferable to a mobile pig. And a determined revolutionary doesn't require an authorization from a Central Committee before offing a pig. As a matter of fact, when the need arises a true revolutionary will off the Central Committee."[58] Cleaver's reassurance to Weatherman thus presaged, indeed, threatened, the coming split in the Black Panther Party itself. Moreover, Cleaver's article first appeared not in the *Black Panther* but in a white radical underground paper, the *Berkeley Tribe*. Only subsequently did the *Black Panther* publish "On Weatherman." Perhaps the Panthers also understood Cleaver's implicit threat.

But whether Cleaver and a faction of the Panthers supported Weatherman or not, the fact remains that prior to Cleaver's statement, Weatherman had already repeatedly dismissed the Black Panther Party's leadership. The Panthers had spoken organizationally in a clear voice: organize your own communities on behalf of black self-determination. SDS and the people who would later become Weatherman leaders rejected that charge, most recently by rejecting the UFAF. Moreover, Cleaver voiced his support for Weatherman after the Days of Rage. Weatherman made its decision to proceed with the October demonstration, then, at a point at which both the national Black Panther Party and the local Panther chapter under Hampton spoke with a single voice. In organizing the Days of Rage under the banner of solidarity with the black liberation movement, while concretely opposing the most important black nationalist organization in the United States, Weatherman was casting about for a new black revolutionary vanguard, a vanguard that did not exist in the black community, a vanguard that conformed to Weatherman's notion of what a black vanguard should be doing. Weatherman, in short, had assumed the traditional stance of white intellectual superiority.[59]

If from 1967 to mid-1969 parts of SDS acknowledged the leading role of the black movement in guiding the white movement, by 1970 Weatherman believed that it had transcended the black movement and was looking to school the black movement in the meaning of revolutionary politics. Carmichael's admonition to white activists that they stay out of the black community and that they organize whites against racism had been forgotten, or rather set aside as not applying to these white people.

In New York City, a small Weatherman cell operating out of a town house in Greenwich Village and consisting of eleven people, with Weather Bureau leader Terry Robbins at the top, followed by four lieutenants and six cadre, began to implement this line. In the early morning hours of February 21, 1970—the fifth anniversary of Malcolm X's assassination—the Weatherman cell firebombed New York judge John Murtagh's home. Murtagh was the judge presiding over the trial of the New York Panther Twenty-one. On the same night, the cell apparently also firebombed a navy recruiting station in Brooklyn, a police patrol car in Greenwich Village, and the International Law Library at Columbia University.[60] The "Townhouse Weathermen" sent no communiqués explaining or taking credit for any of these actions. Although New York newspapers gave the bombings front-page coverage, the cell's leadership was not happy with the action—it had not done sufficient "material damage." The cell began planning an antipersonnel bombing—with more powerful dynamite bombs—at a noncommissioned officers' dance at nearby Fort Dix, New Jersey.[61]

Terry Robbins was the moving force behind the Greenwich Village cell and its plans. Indeed, if individual personalities occasionally can come to embody the politics of an organization, Robbins fully embodied Weatherman's politics. Robbins had been a key organizer at Kent State, arguing there for militant politics. With Bill Ayers, Robbins had been at the head of the Midwest regional grouping that had helped form Weatherman. He had been one of the main organizers and proponents of Weatherman's Days of Rage. When Weathermen cadre and leaders expressed concerns about the Days of Rage, that the thousands projected as showing up might not really make it to Chicago, that perhaps the strategy was flawed, it was Robbins who shot them down. "How could you be so weak?" he scolded Rudd when Rudd raised doubts about Weatherman's direction. The scorn he expressed for those he perceived as weak extended to his personal relationships: he apparently physically abused his nonmonogamous girlfriend on several occasions. Weather Bureau members, according to Rudd, "either denied it was happening or knew about it and thought it wasn't important."[62] And this, too, embodied Weatherman's politics—both Robbins's abuse of women and the willingness of other Weathermen leaders, male and female, to look the other way.

In the weeks following the cell's decision to carry out the Fort Dix bombing, the tensions in Robbins's cell had become, in Rudd's words, "unbearable": "Whenever anyone had expressed a doubt about the planned Fort Dix bombing, Terry, Diana [Oughton] or any one of the several other leaders would turn around with an attack: 'You're just accepting your white-skin privilege,' or 'Don't you think white people

are pigs?'"[63] On March 6, 1970, as the cell was constructing its dynamite antipersonnel bombs for the Fort Dix bombing, one of the Weathermen—either Oughton
or Robbins—accidentally crossed a wire and detonated a cache of dynamite. The
Greenwich Village town house in which they were working was completely destroyed.
Three Weatherman—Terry Robbins, Diana Oughton, and Ted Gold—died in the
explosion, and the entire Weatherman organization hastened itself underground.

Nine months later, Weatherman issued a policy statement titled "New
Morning—Changing Weather," in which the organization gave its explanation for
the town house explosion. "New Morning" correctly insisted that the explosion
stemmed from larger reasons than simply "technical inexperience." Weatherman
argued that "because" the New York collective had begun

> to define armed struggle as the only legitimate form of revolutionary action, they did not
> believe that there was any revolutionary motion among white youth. It seemed like black
> and third world people were going up against Amerikan imperialism alone. . . .
> This tendency to consider only bombings or picking up the gun as revolutionary,
> with the glorification of the heavier the better, we've called the military error.[64]

In fact, Weatherman had glossed over the real error. The "military error" was only the
symbol of a much larger problem—the politics that drove the military error, that concentrated and set loose a handful of radicals on West Eleventh Street in Greenwich
Village. What were they doing there? What were their aims? Weatherman had chosen to criticize the means. But the important criticism was of Weatherman's ends.

Robbins's cell was in the town house because Weatherman had given up on the
project of transforming the consciousness of ordinary white working people in the
United States, of helping those people understand that the privileges they obtained
for their white skin came at too high a price: too high for others and too high for
themselves. This was the project that the both the Panthers and SNCC had urged
on SDS. Vietnam's revolutionaries had asked SDS for the same thing. But the SDS-
Weatherman cadre had grander, more glorious visions for themselves and of themselves: Weathermen were the only nonracist whites, the only whites who really
understood the course of revolution in the United States and in the world. They were
the exceptional white folks. As such, they were in the town house with the goal and
the belief that their actions would inspire a black revolution in the United States and
a world revolution against the United States. This was the vision that drove them to
the town house, that drove them to a frenzy of activity, of fighting police, of giving
up relationships, of orgies, of untreated sicknesses, of brutal criticism/self-criticism
sessions, of twenty-hour days.

Here was the error: their position required a great humility, a willingness to really listen to and respect what "the other" had to say, even when—especially when—what imperialism's nonwhite victims had to say contradicted their own vision. Their error, their failing, was that they could not do this. They could not be the humble foot soldiers of a revolution, but had to take the privileged position that was their birthright as young white people—and this in the name of combating that very privilege.

When Weatherman emphasized military means, they were at the same time emphatically rejecting the real insight offered by black and Vietnamese activists to white New Leftists. Weatherman was reasserting white arrogance and presumption. No matter what others told them concerning the nature of social change, these young white activists knew better. It was the frenzy to reassert their own centrality in the world that exploded for Weatherman on March 6, 1970, in Greenwich Village.

To be sure, it was a tragedy. The people in the town house cell hated their whiteness, hated it for the knowledge of what that whiteness meant to other people. But in hating their whiteness, they blinded themselves to what that whiteness had done to them. And it was here, in this blindness, that the tragedy lay.

At the end of November 1969, 300 RYM II activists met in Atlanta to found what they projected as a successor organization to SDS, the RYM. It was at this meeting that RYM II women made their strongest stand. Indeed, the women met in separate caucus, formulated the new organization's program and principles, and then made it a prerequisite that men accept that program before they could join. On many levels, the program represented the best of what SDS had understood over the previous years: it called for a united front against the war and made the battle against white and male supremacy, with practical programs, central to its overall program. Moreover, while RYM II's white women declared that "all women were oppressed by all men," Carl Davidson reported that the women also insisted that "the principal oppression of black and brown women was their oppression as black or brown people." "Thus," Davidson reported, "before there could be unity among all women—black, brown and white—in the struggle against male supremacy, white women had to establish as a first principle of unity the struggle against white supremacy and the repudiation of the white-skin privilege."[65] This was among the clearest articulations of the relation between white women, black women, and the struggle against white and male supremacy; unlike much of what was at the time coming out of the white women's movement, it accorded with the thinking of the majority of black women activists. Thus, from the standpoint of sound principles, real potential existed for the organization's development.

RYM II's men, however, sought to sabotage the organization. While they unanimously accepted the women's program and terms, Davidson reported that they did so reluctantly: "many of the men sat in silence in most of the sessions."[66] Writing several years later, SDS historian Kirkpatrick Sale insisted that the RYM IIers had gone "out of their way to give the new organization an unwieldy structure and an ineffective set of officers" and thus "condemned RYM to inefficiency, invisibility, and eventually disintegration." According to Sale, the RYM IIers saddled the organization with this structure in order to prevent the emergence of another "elite" or "NO [National Office] collective."[67] But RYM II leaders, the male ones in any case, had themselves been part of the "NO collective" and SDS's elite. It is far more likely that what these men feared was not the emergence of a new elite, but their own inability to be that elite; to control any longer a mass movement, now especially threatened from below in the form of the women's liberation movement.

The mass movement, in short, no longer was an adequate form for expressing white male leadership. Anything that hinted at real democracy, real ownership over a movement by its participants, invariably would threaten white and male control. Cadre organization and top-down command, with "revolutionary theory"—as formulated by this or that Marxist-Leninist—driving it, would be the new means for assuring the old control, the old role of the macher (the male strongman). A June 1971 FBI report confirmed that the new RYM had been dead as early as the summer of 1970, six months following its founding. Indeed, RYM had never even had a national office.[68]

In its founding document, RYM II had carved out a place for itself in the revolutionary leadership by defining a Black Belt nation in the South. Black revolutionaries would have undivided sway in this struggle, while the real and more important work of taking down the American capitalist empire would be left to that trusty old grave digger, the United States' black and white industrial proletariat. RYM II, however, like the original RYM, was actually a coalition of forces, divided by emphasis and understandings of the black struggle and the international struggle. Bob Avakian and the Bay Area Revolutionary Union (BARU and later RU) on the West Coast represented one strong tendency in RYM II. Chicago's National Office and regional SDS had two tendencies: Mike Klonsky and the people around him constituted the stronger Chicago tendency, while Noel Ignatin and the people around him played an important ideological role, but were weak in numbers. The RYM II document was a compromise among these different political forces, with Ignatin's tendency holding RYM II to some understanding of white skin privilege and the black struggle's independent significance. As soon as RYM II divided into its constituent parts, the retreat would begin from even the compromise understandings that held the RYM II document to some semblance of America's social realities.

Although RU's *Red Papers* appeared at about the same time as the RYM II document, *The Red Papers* nevertheless represented the future of where most of RYM II was headed, particularly as the black movement came under increasing attack. *The Red Papers* consisted of three articles, two of them theoretical and the third a summary of the BARU's practical working-class organizing experience. For the most part, the theoretical articles might have been written in the nineteenth century or, insofar as they referred to Lenin, in the 1920s, so abstracted were they from the realities of the U.S. empire in the mid-twentieth century. Nevertheless, when forced to deal with American imperial and racial realities, *The Red Papers* retreated from those understandings that had made their way into the RYM and RYM II papers.

RU began its manifesto in typical RYM fashion by emphasizing the importance of national liberation struggles and their challenge to empire. But then RU moved quickly to the process of finishing off that empire. The success of the national liberation movements, RU argued, was limiting the ability of the U.S. monopoly ruling class to "resolve its contradictions with the U.S. working class." This, according to RU, defined the "primary revolutionary duty of the people of the U.S.": "to build a militant united front against U.S. imperialism. The main force and leader of the united front must be the working class." Indeed, RU rhetorically insisted that "the U.S. working class, black and white, with its allies from other classes, together constituting a vast majority of the people and led by a Marxist-Leninist revolutionary party, will smash the existing state apparatus."

The Red Papers also paid particular attention to the "role of black people as a leading force in revolutionary struggles." Blacks in the United States had a dual character: at once they were "an imported colonial people," carrying out a struggle for national liberation like the many national liberation struggles external to the United States; at the same time, they were a key element of the working-class movement, indeed, "at the forefront of the working class movement in the United States. Ultimately they will be joined by the white working class to deal the death blow to monopoly capitalism." No evidence was provided or deemed necessary.

While *The Red Papers* made a limited effort to describe the particular place of black people in the struggle, it made no such effort to understand the place of the white working class. The closest it came was to acknowledge that "racist ideology" was "very strong in the white working class and prevents its advance." But *The Red Papers* failed to present any structural understanding of the white working class—of its particularities as the working class of an imperial power and as a class that had constructed its place in American society in direct opposition to the place of the black and minority working classes. RU had wholly retreated from RYM II's already limited understandings of white skin privilege. Indeed, *The Red Papers* did not even mention this uncomfortable reality.

RU overlooked white skin privilege for two reasons. First, doing so allowed RU to portray white workers as uncorrupted by race and empire, and therefore capable of playing a role in the anticapitalist struggle equal to that of black and other Third World workers. Second, overlooking white skin privilege offered RU leaders the same equal, independent, leading role in the social struggle. Here was the real key to RU's politics.

In "Theses on Building a Revolutionary Party in the United States," RU laid out its ultimate retreat from America's social reality. No revolutionary parties in the United States had a base in the white working class, RU leaders admitted. Neither did most of the predominantly white groups that called themselves Marxist-Leninist have a base in "the Black people's movement." "On the other hand," RU's leaders insisted,

> it is clear that among Black people, there are groups actively studying Marxism-Leninism and applying the scientific experience of revolution to the liberation of their people. And it is precisely from these groups that the greatest present advances, both in practice and theory, are coming. We believe that a major section of the leadership of a Marxist-Leninist party in the U.S. will come from these groups. The Marxist-Leninist Party is the general staff of the working class struggle. There is *one enemy*, monopoly capitalism, and to defeat it we need, and will achieve, a unified general staff.[69]

RU leaders were generously offering a place to black revolutionaries in the leadership of a future Marxist-Leninist party. That such a place was not theirs to have or to offer seems never to have crossed their minds. While it differed from Weatherman on a multitude of issues, RU agreed with Weatherman on one vital point: the vanguard would have to be recast in ways that were more amenable to these young white radicals.

The path followed by RU would be followed by other RYM II factions. While these factions did not seem to have the energy to sustain the mass organization that RYM II's women had advanced analytically, they wasted no time in establishing their own vanguard, "preparty" collectives. Already by the end of 1969, Klonsky, working in Los Angeles, formed the OL collective. In Atlanta, other former RYM II people founded the Georgia Communist League, which in 1972 merged with Klonsky's group.[70] Unlike RU, OL continued to hold to the Black Belt South thesis, but as the black struggle continued to deteriorate, OL put forward ever more stridently the vanguard role of the united working class.

As early as January 1970, Phil Hutchings, a former SNCC chair, had already discerned this overall white New Left surrender to white framings of the problem of social change. "What is particularly irritating," noted Hutchings,

> is the often unspoken and unconscious air of superiority of white leftists that blacks should become part of their movement and its activities from antiwar demonstrations, women's liberation to scholarly journals because the primacy of their activity—like all organized white activity in this society—is taken for granted. . . .

Whites in the movement, and very especially white males have been brought up and educated on the assumption that all problems can be solved (by them). Going to the better universities they have been trained to be part of the ruling elite. Once they become "radicals" they put these elite skills and training to the use of the revolution without ever realizing how manipulatory and basic to the old system much of that past training is.[71]

Perhaps the only part of RYM II that escaped the general collapse to this "unspoken and unconscious air" of white superiority was the faction associated with Noel Ignatin. In early 1970, Ignatin and other like-minded former RYM IIers formed the Sojourner Truth Organization (STO). STO, unlike either RU or OL, continued to hold to the importance of white skin privilege and apparently maintained a modest vision for itself. At least in its early years, STO did not project itself as a new vanguard, but insisted instead that the initiative for a revolutionary party would necessarily come out of the black and brown communities.[72] But standing alone amid SDS's wreckage, and doubtless deeply influenced by the general collapse, STO could not salvage the mass organization.

On April 30, 1970, President Richard Nixon publicly announced his extension of the Vietnam War into Cambodia. Students and antiwar activists immediately began mobilizing their bases in protest of the war's extension. In New Haven, Connecticut, participants in a previously called demonstration to protest the frame-up of Black Panther leader Bobby Seale immediately issued a call for a nationwide student strike focused on three demands: first, that the U.S. government cease its "systematic oppression of political dissidents, and release all political prisoners"; second, that the government cease its aggression in Southeast Asia and "unilaterally and immediately withdraw all forces from" that part of the world; and third, that universities immediately "end their complicity with the United States war machine" and cease their "defense research, ROTC, counterinsurgency research, and all other such programs."[73]

At Kent State University in Ohio, at midday on May 1, students rallied on campus demanding an end to the war and open admissions for black students. That evening, approximately 600 students poured out of bars in the downtown area and trashed windows in downtown stores. On the following evening, Saturday night, students rallied on the university commons in defiance of a university curfew. Marching across the campus and through the dorm areas, the rally gathered 4,000 students, who marched to the ROTC building. Students tossed stones and road flares at the building, which, according to one report, "burst into flames." When campus fire trucks reached the scene, students cut the water hoses, and the building was left largely in ruins by the end of the evening. Following the burning of the ROTC building, Ohio governor James Rhodes called in the National Guard. Sunday was largely peaceful, although campus police arrested sixty people that evening for curfew violations. On Monday at noon, about 800 students rallied again, under the watch of the National Guard. At a few minutes past noon, National Guardsmen would shoot thirteen of these students, killing four of them, and precipitate a vast wave of antiwar actions.[74]

Within three days, an ad hoc "National Strike Headquarters," operating out of Brandeis University, reported that between 350 and 400 schools were shut down or were on strike. California governor Ronald Reagan, who prior to the May events had boasted that he would keep his state university system open "at the point of a bayonet if necessary," ordered the temporary closing of the entire University of California and State University of California systems, encompassing 325,000 students. All the schools in Boston's massive university complex were on strike; the eighteen Pennsylvania State University campuses were closed indefinitely. In Madison, Wisconsin, 3,000 students fought local and state police for several days running; in Austin, Texas, state police used tear gas to rout students from the state capitol building; in Buffalo and Syracuse, New York, thousands of students fought battles with police on and off campuses. On May 7, students attempted firebombings of ROTC facilities at the University of Nevada, Reno; the University of Ohio; the University of San Francisco; Colorado College; the University of Virginia, Charlottesville; Case Western Reserve in Cleveland; the University of California, Davis; and the State University of New York, Buffalo. At Buffalo, police firing birdshot and buckshot wounded a dozen demonstrators. In addition, on the same day, activists firebombed a local armory in Mankato, Minnesota, and school administration buildings and facilities in Tuscaloosa, Alabama; Valparaiso, Indiana; Marietta, Ohio; Carbondale, Illinois; and Middlebury, Vermont. By May 8, Brandeis strike headquarters was reporting that between 550 and 600 schools were either shut down or on strike. On the ninth, between 100,000 and 150,000 people descended on Washington, D.C., in a protest announced seven days earlier. At Eastern Michigan University at Ypsilanti, police wounded five students with birdshot.[75]

Moderates and liberals against the war also added their voices to the protest: Ivy League newspaper editors collectively drafted an antiwar editorial that ran in all the Ivy League student newspapers and was picked up by colleges all over the country. New York University president James Hester drafted a statement to Nixon on the afternoon of the Kent State shootings. Thirty-four university presidents signed the statement: "We implore you to consider the incalculable dangers of an unprecedented alienation of America's youth and to take immediate action to demonstrate unequivocally your determination to end the war quickly."[76]

It was the greatest wave of antiwar protests and student protests in the nation's history. By any measure it was immense: the number of students participating; the number of schools closed and the number of students affected by school closures; the number of students killed and wounded; the number of National Guardsmen called out and the number of places they were called out to; the number of ROTC buildings and university administration buildings firebombed, destroyed, or occupied by students; the number of pitched battles between protesters and police.[77]

Mark Rudd, isolated from his Weathermen comrades following the town house tragedy, sat alone on a Philadelphia park bench and reflected for a brief moment: "Just months before, my friends and I had closed down the SDS national office, which could have served to coordinate the national strike and also push our anti-imperialist politics. Terry, Diana, and Ted, all excellent organizers, were now dead, and the rest of us were unable to function in this mass movement. I didn't even dare walk the few blocks to the University of Pennsylvania demonstrations for fear of being arrested by police or federal agents."[78] Indeed, if ever there had been a time when SDS could have played an important role, this was that time. With a national structure in place, with hundreds of chapters stretched out across the country, with extensive stocks of literature explaining the war, here was the moment that SDS had prepared for. And, as with the October moratorium and the November mobilization, hundreds of thousands of new people had been drawn into the protests—people whose understandings of the basis of the war were limited; people who only dimly comprehended the relationship between the war in Asia and the struggle of black people at home. But both RYM factions deemed this role of elevating the consciousness of students beneath them. Both RYM factions had set their sights on the higher goals of leading international revolutionary movements.

One week after the killings at Kent State, the relationship between the antiwar movement and the domestic struggle of black people once again came to the fore. On May 11, a sixteen-year-old black youth died while in police custody in Augusta, Georgia. Police initially announced that the teenager had fallen from his cot. A 900-person protest quickly assembled; marched on Augusta's municipal building; tore down the building's state flag, replete with its Confederate insignia; and continued to march through Augusta's downtown. Police, dressed in riot gear, confronted the marchers, who proceeded to break into small groups. Police fired on the crowds, killing six men—all apparently shot in the back—and wounding as many as sixty others. The police had given no warning shots, and no weapons were discovered on the dead bodies. Georgia governor Lester Maddox flew into the town the next day and blamed a "communist conspiracy" and the Black Panther Party for the violence. Maddox ordered the National Guard to "shoot to kill" any other potential troublemakers.[79]

Three days later, in Jackson, Mississippi, Jackson's police chief, facing a tense but peaceful crowd of black students at Jackson State University, clicked on his bullhorn: "Ladies and gentlemen—we have something to tell you." State highway patrolmen then turned what the *New York Times* termed a "heavy, concentrated barrage of gunfire, lasting seven to 10 seconds," upon the unarmed crowd of 200 black students. A subsequent *Times* report suggested that gunfire lasted as long as thirty seconds. Reporters counted more than 140 bullet holes in the women's dormitory in front of which the students had gathered. Two black students were killed, and at least a dozen more were wounded. The police fired no warning shots, nor did they give any orders to disperse. One student maintained that he heard a highway patrolman radio in a report after the killings: "You better send some ambulances, we killed some niggers."[80]

In the wake of the killings, the Mississippi United Front, a coalition of thirty civil rights and antipoverty groups known for their commitment to moderation and nonviolence, called for a statewide boycott of white businesses and the formation of an armed self-defense league. Dr. Aaron Shirley, a leader of the front and a prominent physician in Jacksonville, declared: "We are determined that from now on when we suspect that law enforcement officers are hell-bent on killing some black folks, they'll be doing it at some risk to their own lives. . . . We know it's a hell of a position to take, but we've seen too many of our people killed and nothing done." The *Times* termed the call for armed self-defense coming from "moderates" a "startling development."[81]

White students, already in rebellion by the time the killings occurred in Augusta and Jackson, nevertheless had a hard time incorporating the tragedies into their own program. "Yes," wrote black activist and author Julius Lester, "white radicals did link the killings at Kent State, Augusta and Jackson State, but I can't help but feel that if the killings of the blacks had not come in such proximity to the ones at Kent, whites would have ignored them. As it were, they were given lip-service."[82] Similarly, the *Guardian* reported that anger at the murders of black students at Jackson State "was largely absent among whites in comparison to the outpouring of anger over the murder of four whites at Kent."[83]

May 1970: never over the previous decade had there been a moment at which the consciousness of tens, and quite possibly hundreds, of thousands of young white people could so readily have been affected by white radicals. But the largest radical student organization of the decade, SDS, was dead, and the radicals who had led the organization had renounced the job that black radicals and Vietnamese revolutionaries had urged on them.

Conclusion

The Price of the Liberation

"Man," said a Negro musician to me once, talking about Norman [Mailer], "the only trouble with that cat is that he's white." . . . What my friend meant was that to become a Negro man, let alone a Negro artist, one had to make oneself up as one went along. This had to be done in the not-at-all-metaphorical teeth of the world's determination to destroy you. The world had prepared no place for you, and if the world had its way, no place would ever exist. Now, this is true for everyone, but, in the case of a Negro, this truth is absolutely naked: if he deludes himself about it, he will die. This is not the way this truth presents itself to white men, who believe the world is theirs and who, albeit unconsciously, expect the world to help them in the achievement of their identity. But the world does not do this—for anyone; the world is not interested in anyone's identity.

—James Baldwin, "The Black Boy Looks at the White Boy," 1961

History, as nearly no one seems to know, is not merely something to be read. And it does not refer merely, or even principally, to the past. On the contrary, the great force of history comes from the fact that we carry it within us, are unconsciously controlled by it in many ways, and history is literally *present* in all we do. It could scarcely be otherwise, since it is to history that we owe our frames of reference, our identities, and our aspirations. And it is with great pain and terror that one begins to realize this.

—James Baldwin, "The White Man's Guilt," 1965

SDS failed. The white New Left failed.

America's fundamental social, cultural, political, and economic structures were not destroyed and replaced with something better, the goal the New Left ultimately set for itself. Those structures were altered, and, assuredly, the movements of the 1960s had something to do with that. But the passage of time has revealed just how little they were altered.

Yes, we no longer have a rigid legal system of segregation anywhere in the United States. Yes, the nation now occasionally allows a person of color to sit at the American banquet table—the more so if that person espouses opposition to affirmative action or loyalty to America's civilizing mission in the world. But anyone who travels through the nation's great cities, and cares to look, is well aware that the United States is a profoundly segregated society, and increasingly so. Moreover, the national discourse—and its legislative discourse—follows in the train of this increasing segregation: poverty and slums, it is argued, reflect poor people's lack of personal responsibility. To be sure, in this discourse poverty has its implicit—and sometimes explicit—racial content.

And yes, this is not the 1950s for women either. But anyone who turns on the television set, or stands in a supermarket check-out line, and pauses for a moment, is well aware that the countless images of what it means to be a girl or a boy, or a man or a woman, are extraordinarily frightening. And anyone who teaches a class full of twenty-year-old male and female students is well aware of the impact these images have.

America's history of military, economic, and political interventions into the affairs of other people since the close of the Vietnam War underlines the failure of the New Left.

And so the failure of the 1960s is significant.

How do we understand that failure? I have argued that SDS failed because it was unable to transcend its society's notions of race, of gender, and of nation. It is singularly remarkable that the numerous histories and memoirs of the white New Left do not assess their subject and its failure from the standpoint of race. Most of these narratives discuss race, or rather, trace what SNCC or the Black Panthers did at a given moment. Even the most white centered of the histories and narratives are compelled to acknowledge on some level just how important was the black struggle in the 1960s. The additional problem, however, is to assess the New Left's young activists as white people. Those young people who labored together to produce the Port Huron Statement, who established themselves on the nations' college campuses as a pole that supported the civil rights movement, or opposed a growing war in Asia, were young white people. That is, they were not blank slates receiving information about the world and its injustices, but were historical creations, the creations of a society structured to privilege white people over black, men over women, and the United States and Europe over most of the rest of the world.

What these young white people saw troubled them, deeply. But hundreds of years of white (and male) supremacy could not help but leave their impress on the minds and souls of these activists, their commitment to social change notwithstanding. Thirty years ago James Baldwin reminded us—telling us that we could not "overstate" the case—that "those centuries of oppression are also the history of a system of thought."[1] White supremacy in the United States was not only a structure of privilege and oppression, then, but it was also an elaborately constructed and reconstructed world of illusions; it was a mode of interpreting the world in a manner that always placed white people on top. While black people could afford themselves but few illusions concerning the nature of their country, its institutions, and their identity within that structure, young whites held great illusions on every score. If the struggles of the 1960s laid bare certain of these illusions concerning the nature of the United States and its institutions, young whites struggled with, but ultimately succumbed to, white supremacy's most stubborn, most seductive, most flattering illusion—the final illusion that the world had in some way prepared a place for them, that they had some special destiny: they would pave the way for a better world for all. But so long as this final illusion remained, it would rewrite, reconstruct the other illusions in a manner that would reinforce the illusion—and the practice—of white racial superiority.

People could only make a revolution against this system of white supremacy, against the structure of white supremacy, to the extent to which they were able to recognize and transcend that system's ideological products, products that resided in their brains, in their hearts, in their souls, and in their movements. For a few brief moments, the black movement's strength, coupled with the strength of the Vietnamese rebellion, allowed young white people to grapple with the myths and the illusions with which they had been raised. And it was a noble thing they aspired to: to reunite with the racial "other," which was really to reunite with the alienated self, the humanity in themselves that they had to deny in order to be superior. For those few brief moments when a solidarity with the other could be expressed—a building occupation at Berkeley or Columbia, a taking of the streets in Chicago, a siege of the Pentagon—no other word existed save "liberation." Liberation: a freeing of the self from the lie of inherent superiority and from everything that lie demanded of the person and the culture.

SDS's history from the mid-1960s to mid-1969 is the story of young white people's struggle to understand that they were not a specially favored people destined to free humanity, a struggle to be humble in the face of the great historical drama unfolding before them. On the one side were voices like Robin Brooks—we may be entitled "in keeping with our real merits and numbers" to some share in the rebuilding of the world. But there are "no shortcuts." Or Anne Braden, who insisted that you could not organize white people without placing racism at the center of the agenda, "from the very beginning." Or Carl Oglesby, who recognized that the brutality of Vietnam could not be insulated from American domestic society. Or Noel Ignatin, who understood that white society had built itself on the backs of black Americans and that, whether it was easy or not, organizers could not sidestep that reality. Or Clayton Van Lydegraf, who understood that the pollution of racism had thoroughly dirtied all white people and that white workers neither could be written off for that dirt nor portrayed as though that dirt did not exist.

On the other side were the voices that continually attempted to minimize and marginalize black people's struggles, isolate them, make them particular struggles of no or little necessary relevance to young white people. On the other side were the voices that insisted that black people could be free only if they followed the dictates of this or that white-led "Marxist" party, that they could only be free if they united with white workers or if they united against white workers. On the other side were all the voices of historical arrogance, all the voices that spoke with the great authority and self-confidence of those born to privilege: the voices of PL, of Weatherman, of RYM II and its leading factions.

And in between these two poles stood the great majority of SDSers. Or rather, the struggle between these two poles raged in the breast of each and every SDS member. Even the most arrogant SDSers were occasionally humbled before the magnitude of the struggle, the strength, sacrifice, and humanity of the "other"; even the most humble voices in the organization had their moments of extraordinary arrogance.

In the end, America's white supremacy bested the struggle these young white people waged against it.

How else can we characterize Weatherman when that tendency insisted that the way young whites should follow "black leadership" was to follow Weatherman? Three months after declaring that the Panthers were the vanguard of the revolution, Weatherman still professed a belief in—and to legitimize itself in its own eyes and in the eyes of others, needed—black leadership. But the simple truth was that no organized black activists were good enough to be followed as leaders of the revolution, not Weatherman's revolution. Only Weatherman knew what black leadership meant and knew what was best for black people. How else can we characterize it when a faction of Weatherman sought to carry out militant armed actions in the black community in a manner that would allow black people to construe those actions as coming from "their own"?

Moreover, how different was SDS's designation of the Black Panthers as the vanguard of the revolution from RYM II's designation of five states in the South as the black nation? Both positions involved white people telling black people what they should be struggling for. And for that matter, how do we make sense of the white women's movement and its fear, on the one hand, of inviting Kathleen Cleaver to a women's conference lest she change the issue and, on the other, of its insistence that we "Free Kathleen Cleaver"?

In the 1960s, at the height of the Black Power movement, young white activists understood and, at their best, articulated the notion that the battle against racism and against white supremacy had to be fought both externally and internally—internally, because white supremacist society molded even the identities of young whites, as Baldwin argued. The failure of historians and memoirists to assess the white New Left from the standpoint of this internal struggle against societal notions of race is a measure of the strength and the unexaminedness of white supremacy in our society today. Moreover, this failure is a great disservice to those activists who fought, and lost, that battle. That they lost the battle does not diminish the significance of their having fought it.

Antonio Gramsci, and before him, Frederick Engels, long ago defined the sectarian as one who puts pride of place in what distinguishes him or her from the mass of people, rather than what unites him or her with that mass. When Weatherman surrendered to white supremacy, the organization did not renounce the struggle against white supremacy, but trumpeted it the more strongly. Only it did so now as a sect: what was important to Weatherman activists was not destroying racism, but separating themselves from racists, distinguishing themselves from the mass of "honky bastards." The real problem, however, lay not in separating themselves from other racist white people, but in transforming those people and transforming themselves at the same time. This was the step that Weatherman and the New Left refused to take. They refused that step because they had a grander vision for themselves, and they had that grander vision precisely because that grander vision befitted their upbringing as young white people. And this step—the step of exposing the meaning of white racism, challenging and overturning it—this step remains to be taken by a really New Left.

Neither have historians or memoirists adequately assessed SDS's failure to deal with its male supremacy as a principal source for the New Left's dissolution. Immediately, SDS's male supremacy denied the New Left important and experienced female leadership, leadership that could have strengthened the New Left, educated its base, broadened its approach and its appeal. Indeed, some of the most insightful, powerful, and passionate analysis of the nature of American society, of the meaning of male and female in that society, came from a core of older women, experienced in the movement and brushed aside by younger men asserting their leadership. What a terrible waste it was that the skill and intellect of women like Casey Hayden, Mary

King, Naomi Weisstein, Judith Brown, Beverly Jones, Pam Parker Allen, Marge Piercy, the Bread and Roses women, Robin Morgan, and countless others could not have been unreservedly devoted to building up the antiracist movement and the anti-war movement, alongside the battle for a new way of looking at men and women. How much stronger and healthier both the women's movement and SDS would have been for that cross-fertilization.

Just as important, SDS's attacks on the women's movement as racist and bour-geois encouraged separatist tendencies in the women's movement itself: if the only way that women could participate in the antiracist or antiwar struggle was to allow themselves to be demeaned, well, thanks but no thanks. Thus, SDS drove even those women most open to integrating their concerns with the concerns of others toward a separatist radical feminism, further fragmenting the white movements for social change and reinforcing an outlook of white superiority in both those movements.

To be sure, some women stayed with SDS. It was no accident that Weatherwomen became the loudest voices within SDS against the women's movement. Indeed, it could be no other way. Who better to give legitimacy to and cover up for SDS's male domina-tion than SDS women? At the same time, by playing against the women's movement, a female SDSer could parley the strength of that movement to her own individual advan-tage within SDS, as Brown and Jones had pointed out. Moreover, to a certain extent, it was absolutely necessary for women working in SDS's male environment to condemn the women's movement, and condemn it in the most strident terms. How else to justify one's own participation in SDS?

Still, despite continual SDS attacks launched against the women's movement, the women's liberation movement continued to grow. A new tack became neces-sary: women in SDS (and men, too) would outdo their women's movement sisters in the struggle against male supremacy. So appeared Weatherman's campaign to smash monogamy; so appeared stern "Marxist-Leninist" injunctions about the class nature of women's oppression.

Equally important, women's growing strength within the New Left confronted white male New Leftists with a choice: they would either seriously deal with the male supremacy of the movement and of its leaders, or they would find new means for protecting their little movement fiefdoms. Almost without exception, male movement leaders chose the second course. And since the growing strength of the women's movement continually generated new criticism of male supremacy from women in open, democratic mass organization, male movement leaders deemed mass organization increasingly unreliable. In other words, the women's movement made it increasingly difficult for male strongman—"macher"—leadership in a mass organi-zation like SDS. A new, additional incentive arose then for male movement leaders to develop vanguard sects, sects in which the ability to manipulate Marxist jargon would be the defining characteristic of leadership. Moreover, since America had been endowed with a multitude of talented, intelligent male leaders, each trained from birth believing in his own inherent ability, and since different experiences shaped different people in different ways, it was altogether natural that two, three, many sects would emerge, each committed to the vision of its own set of machers.

Historians and memoirists also have failed to assess adequately the New Left's inability to break definitively with empire and the consequences that that inability held for the New Left's viability.

Vietnam's revolutionaries offered the clearest perspective here. In a political sense, the Vietnamese sought two things: the first, and from the immediate Vietnamese standpoint the most essential, was the unification of the antiwar movement, bringing all those with any opposition to the war together under a slogan of immediate U.S. withdrawal from Vietnam. Second, the Vietnamese wanted the radical antiwar movement to use the war as a means for understanding and exposing the nature of U.S. society, abroad and at home. Here was Nguyen Van Trong's injunction to "carefully study the situation": in order to more effectively oppose the war, Van Trong was asking U.S. radicals to understand the real class nature of the society in which they lived. Why did different sectors behave differently toward the war? In the long term, actually transforming U.S. society was the best guarantee of Vietnam's self-determination.

To be sure, it would be possible to unite the antiwar movement under the broad slogan of immediate withdrawal—and not fundamentally alter the consciousness of a single American. Similarly, it would be possible, and easy, to rant about the class nature of American society, or the evils of American imperialism, and fail to even attempt to draw together the antiwar movement, or educate anyone beyond an already committed base. Taken separately, each position reinforced empire: to unite the antiwar movement without discussing the nature of U.S. society might help end a contest potentially damaging to the United States' long-term imperial interests; it would certainly allow the empire's defenders to write Vietnam off in the liberal manner as a "mistake." But the grounds would be left unchanged for future interventions elsewhere in the world. On the other side, it might be possible to rail against empire without educating or bringing any new people into opposition to that empire. The trick, as Vietnam's revolutionaries understood, was to take on both tasks simultaneously: to foster and use broad opposition to the war as a gateway to fostering a deepened sense of the nature of American society. This job SDSers refused. Weatherman renounced the task most spectacularly, even going so far as to insist that the war was no longer the issue. But even leaving that position aside, Weatherman, its cadre specifically enjoined by the Vietnamese to seek the broadest possibility of unity against the war, insisted that that unity was the revolution. Not for the first time in history, a self-proclaimed revolutionary group promoted a "revolutionary" slogan that actually served to maintain the reaction.

RYM II renounced taking up this dual task also, although RYM II's renunciation was neither so dramatic nor straightforward as was Weatherman's. Some RYM II people, Carl Davidson most notably, took away from the July 1969 Havana meeting with the Vietnamese a clear sense of what the Vietnamese were advocating for radical anti-war activists. But Davidson was in RYM II's minority and isolated from the Avakian forces on the West Coast and the Klonsky forces in Chicago. By and large, both these factions were in a headlong rush to discover sacrosanct Marxist dogma and could not bother themselves with the work of uniting the antiwar movement or using the war's reality as a tool for enlightening those newly joining the antiwar ranks. It was easier to simply issue oracular pronouncements on "class society" than it was to seriously engage people in a discussion about the nature of the war and the society in which they lived. Not surprisingly, then, RYM II Marxists produced theories that duplicated in broad outline the dichotomy that SDS people had been unable to transcend in the mid-1960s: imperialism is what happened abroad, capitalism is what happened at home.

In any case, Weatherman's success in alienating new people from its ranks with window breaking found its complement in RYM II's stolid dogma. Neither approach challenged empire.

The price of the liberation.

Many people told the New Left's young white activists what it would take from them, this liberation: James Baldwin, Malcolm X, Ruby Doris Smith Robinson, Stokely Carmichael, SNCC, the Panthers. Maybe with more time white activists might have taken the counsel to heart. But in the time given, SDSers either could not or did not hear it; either could not or did not want to believe that the price of the liberation was so high. It even seemed that they might pay the price and still lose: Malcolm had been murdered; Rap Brown was constantly in and out of jail; the Panthers were reeling, Fred Hampton and a dozen others mowed down, hundreds more jailed; the Vietnam War continued, its horror ever more visible.

Young whites hesitated before the choice. Could we not "become a part of that suffering and dancing country" without surrendering everything we are, or think we are? they asked, repeatedly.[2] And then it was too late.

What they did not understand, what they would only discover later, painfully, and then often fastly deny, was that although the price of the liberation was high, the price they paid for their privilege was far higher, infinitely higher.

Notes

Introduction

1. Testimony of students Mike York and Fred Kirsch, cited in Fred Halstead, *Out Now: A Participant's Account of the American Movement against the Vietnam War* (New York: Monad Press, 1978), 539.

2. Bernard D. Nossiter, "Thousands of Students Protest War," *Washington Post*, May 6, 1970.

3. Kirkpatrick Sale, *SDS* (New York: Vintage Books, 1973), 36.

4. Paul Booth, "National Secretary's Report," *New Left Notes*, June 17, 1966, 3; Paul Booth, "Letter to SNCC," *New Left Notes*, June 2, 1966, 3.

5. Toni Morrison, *Playing in the Dark: Whiteness and the Literary Imagination* (Cambridge, Mass.: Harvard University Press, 1992), 64.

6. Greg Calvert, "In White America: Radical Consciousness and Social Change," in *The New Left: A Documentary History*, ed. Massimo Teodori (Indianapolis, Ind.: Bobbs-Merrill, 1969), 413–15.

7. SDS, Berkeley, "Proposal for 'BLACK POWER DAY' in Berkeley," October 1966, in Social Protest Collection, Bancroft Library, University of California, Berkeley.

8. SDS, Northern California Regional Office, in Social Protest Collection, Banc mss 86/157, carton 17:4, Bancroft Library (1966).

9. Doug Rossinow, *The Politics of Authenticity, Liberalism, Christianity and the New Left in America* (New York: Columbia University Press, 1998).

10. Errol Henderson, "Shadow of a Clue," in *Liberation, Imagination, and the Black Panther Party: A New Look at the Panthers and Their Legacy*, ed. Kathleen Cleaver and George Katsiaficas (New York: Routledge, 2001), 204.

11. Ruth Rosen, *The World Split Open: How the Modern Women's Movement Changed America* (New York: Penguin Books, 2000), 116, 117, 120; Alice Echols, *Daring to Be Bad: Radical Feminism in America, 1967–1975* (Minneapolis: University of Minnesota Press, 1989).

12. Rosen, *World Split Open*, 134; Echols, *Daring to Be Bad*, 117.

13. Quoted in Echols, *Daring to Be Bad*, 121.

14. Ibid., 133.

15. Rosen, *World Split Open*, 116; Sara Evans, *Personal Politics: The Roots of Women's Liberation in the Civil Rights Movement and the New Left* (New York: Vintage Books, 1979), 105, 108.

16. Echols, *Daring to Be Bad*, 31; Evans, *Personal Politics*, 81.

17. Echols, *Daring to Be Bad*, 63–64.

18. Another characteristic that unites most of the 1960s historiography—liberal and radical—is its white-centeredness. Elizabeth Martinez zeroed in on this white-centeredness in a survey of two dozen books on the 1960s and the New Left. Martinez pointed out that all but a handful of the books wholly ignored Latino and Asian struggles. Most of the authors did refer to the black struggle and even went so far as to credit the size and courage of that movement and its leaders. "You will look long and hard, however," she continues, "for the concept of that movement as *central* or *seminal*, as a catalyst of the 1960s in general. It is seen as germane only to the problems facing African Americans—a 'special interest' group . . . and not as a challenge to the totality of U.S. society." Elizabeth Martinez, *De Colores Means All of Us* (Cambridge, Mass.: South End Press, 1998), 26. More specifically, look at Jon Weiner's argument, for example: "the 60s constituted an explosion of democracy . . . that, in its sweep and intensity, ranks beside the era of Andrew Jackson and the New Deal." SDS, Weiner continues, "occupies the center of this history because it articulated the crucial concept of the decade, 'participatory democracy.'" What perspective guides such a claim? Did SDS accomplish for democracy even a tiny fraction of what the black struggle that overturned segregation accomplished? And was SNCC not developing the basic forms of participatory democracy before SDS articulated the concept? Jon Weiner, "The New Left as History," *Radical History Review* 42 (Spring 1988): 173. Other historians pursue a less overt form of white-centeredness. James Miller, *"Democracy Is in the Streets": From Port Huron to the Siege of Chicago* (New York: Simon and Schuster, 1987), for example, takes the New Left's origins out of the context of the world-historical events unfolding at the time and puts those origins in the thinking and philosophy of this or that white intellectual. Certainly, there is a place for examining such intellectual history, but it is a gross distortion of history to assume that C. Wright Mills, Arnold Kaufman, Tom Hayden, and others developed their ideas separate from the social world in which they lived, or that thousands and tens of thousands of people responded to those ideas simply because those ideas had some transhistoric validity.

19. See, for example, Todd Gitlin, *The Sixties: Years of Hope, Days of Rage* (New York: Bantam Books, 1987). Gitlin repeatedly dismisses black nationalism as "angry," "reckless nationalism," "bombast," and "rage"—never allowing the nationalist voice itself to be heard. Gitlin characterizes the New Left's support for black nationalism as "an orgy of white guilt," and "black militancy held the New Left in thrall" (ibid., 168, 245, 246). For variations on the theme, see also Maurice Isserman and Michael Kazin, *America Divided: The Civil War of the 1960s* (New York: Oxford University Press 2000), 176–78. Tom Hayden's memoir also enters the lists against black nationalism, although somewhat apologetically: "The combined experience of racism, brutality, and official expediency had rusted SNCC's idealism until it gave way to the volcanic hatred and aggression that swells in the lower depths of the human personality. The politics of separatism and violent rhetoric were neither realistic nor humanistic." Tom Hayden, *Reunion: A Memoir* (New York: Collier Books, 1988), 161.

20. Here, Dan Berger, *Outlaws of America: The Weather Underground and the Politics of Solidarity* (Oakland, Calif.: AK Press, 2006), takes its place as the most enthusiastic champion of the New Left and Weatherman specifically. Berger, for example, generally touts a line articulated by the former Weatherman Robert Roth: "Weather's early politics . . . 'represented an insistence on up-front support for Black liberation as a centerpiece for any political movement among white people.'" (102). That Weatherman indeed articulated such politics cannot be questioned. That in its practice Weatherman also disparaged the two leading black nationalist groups of the day, SNCC and the Black Panthers, ignored their organizational advice and criticisms, and promoted a version of black leadership that did not exist in the social life of black people at the time, this, too, cannot be denied. But Berger avoids a deep analysis of this conflict. In varying degrees, Jeremy Varon, *Bringing the War Home: The Weather Underground, the Red Army Faction,*

and Revolutionary Violence in the Sixties and Seventies (Berkeley: University of California Press, 2004), and Ron Jacobs, *The Way the Wind Blew: A History of the Weather Underground* (New York: Verso Press, 1997), both weight their accounts of Weatherman on the side of what the organization was saying about itself, rather than what it actually did, relative to the black and Third World movements of the day. Max Elbaum, *Revolution in the Air: Sixties Radicals Turn to Lenin, Mao and Che* (New York: Verso Press, 2002), follows the same methodology in tracing the history of Weatherman's SDS rival faction, RYM II.

Chapter One. The New Left and the Black Movement

1. One of the central themes of Clayborne Carson, *In Struggle: SNCC and the Black Awakening of the 1960s* (Cambridge Mass.: Harvard University Press, 1981).

2. James Baldwin has described this reality better than anyone: "the black man has functioned in the white man's world as a fixed star, as an immovable pillar: and as he moves out of his place, heaven and earth are shaken to their foundations." James Baldwin, *The Fire Next Time* (New York: Vintage International, 1993), 9.

3. Gene Roberts, "Mississippi Reduces Police Protection for Marchers," *New York Times*, June 17, 1966.

4. *Newsweek*, index for July 4, 1966, to December 26, 1966, listing for "Negroes."

5. Stokely Carmichael, "What We Want," *New York Review of Books*, September 22, 1966, http://www.csulb.edu/~rschmidt/08-StokelyCarmichael-WhatWeWant-NYRB66.htm. The Black Panthers based their policy on the same "internal colonialism" analysis. Robert Allen's *Black Awakening in Capitalist America* (Garden City, N.Y.: Doubleday, 1969) stands as the best elaboration of the internal colonialism thesis.

6. W. J. Rorabaugh, *Berkeley at War, the 1960s* (New York: Oxford University Press, 1989), 41.

7. Stokely Carmichael, *Black Power and Its Challenges. Address to Black Power Day Conference* (Berkeley, Calif.: Academic Publishing, Lecture Transcripts, 1966), 2.

8. Ibid, 7–9. Malcolm X had already defined the same position on whites in his 1965 autobiography. "America's racism is among their own fellow whites. That's where the sincere whites who really mean to accomplish something have got to work." Malcolm X, with Alex Haley, *The Autobiography of Malcolm X* (New York: Grove Press, 1965), 376.

9. Gitlin, *Sixties*, 349; "SDS Statement on SNCC," *New Left Notes*, June 24, 1966, 2.

10. Staughton Lynd, "On White People," *New Left Notes*, August 24, 1966, 18.

11. Quoted in Echols, *Daring to Be Bad*, 39.

12. Sale, *SDS*, 102; James Forman, *The Making of Black Revolutionaries* (New York: MacMillan Press, 1972), 452. Forman contends that very early on, prior to 1962, SNCC's black activists were pushing for white radicals to work in the white community.

13. Hayden, *Reunion*, 120.

14. Richard Rothstein, "Evolution of the ERAP Organizers," in *The New Left: A Collection of Essays*, ed. Priscilla Long, (Boston: Extending Horizon Books, 1969), 280.

15. Sale, *SDS*, 104.

16. Donald Jackson, "An Open Letter to ERAP," *New Left Notes*, August 5, 1966, 3; reprinted from *ERAP Newsletter*, October 5, 1965, 6.

17. Mike James, "ERAP Report JOIN," *New Left Notes*, August 24, 1966, 8.

18. Clarence Walker, discussions with the author. See also Ruth Frankenberg, *White Women, Race Matters: The Social Construction of Whiteness* (Minneapolis: University of Minnesota Press, 1993).

19. See, for example, Robert Allen and Pam Allen, *Reluctant Reformers: Racism and Social Reform Movements in the United States* (Washington, D.C.: Howard University Press, 1974). Socialists, Communists, union organizers, women's suffragists and reformists in general all considered black people as having particular problems that stood in the way of their contributing to improving the human condition.

20. Carol Stevens, "SDS Re-examined at Dec. Conference," *New Left Notes*, January 21, 1966, 1. The excerpt is from a paper by Webb and Booth titled "The Anti-War Movement: From Protest to Radical Politics."

21. Booth, "National Secretary's Report," 3.

22. Booth, "Letter to SNCC," *New Left Notes*, June 10, 1966, 2.

23. Robin Brooks, "Leroi Jones in Atlanta: Black Power and White Liberals," *New Left Notes*, September 2, 1966, 1.

24. Ibid., 3.

25. John Fisher, "At 73, Activist Is Just Starting as Teacher," *Cincinnati Post*, October 24, 1997, www.kypost.com/news/1997/braden102497.html; Anne Braden, "White Organizing and White Racism," *New Left Notes*, June 24, 1966, 1.

26. Braden, "White Organizing," 1, 5.

27. John Saari, "Berkeley, Stanford and Black Power," *New Left Notes*, November 4, 1966, 1.

28. "Black Power Conference," *New Left Notes*, December 9, 1966, 8.

29. Allen Jehlen, "Black Power and Political Strategy," *New Left Notes*, November 11, 1966, 1.

30. Admittedly, scholarly treatments of this question were not available in 1966. But anyone who had read Malcolm X's *Autobiography* was aware of how deeply white America was invested in black urban inner cities.

31. "December Conference & NC," *New Left Notes*, November 18, 1966, 5.

32. Todd Gitlin, "On Organizing the Poor in America," *New Left Notes*, December 23, 1966, 1, 4.

33. Earl Silbar, "Race War and White Radicals," *New Left Notes*, June 12, 1967, 3.

34. Robert Gottlieb, Gerry Tenney, and David Gilbert, "Toward a Theory of Social Change in America," *New Left Notes*, June 22, 1967, 3–6.

35. Malcolm X, *Malcolm X Speaks* (1965; reprint, New York: Pathfinder Press, 1965), 155.

36. Kerner Commission, *Report of the National Advisory Commission on Civil Disorders* (New York: Bantam Books, 1968), 38.

37. Malcolm X, *Malcolm X Speaks*, 155.

38. Ibid., 32, 69, 106–7.

39. Eric Mann, "Newark Riots—NCUP Views," *New Left Notes*, July 24, 1967, 1.

40. Block, "There's a Change Gonna Come," New Left Notes, July 24, 1967, 1.

41. Ibid.; Tom Hayden, *Rebellion in Newark* (New York: Vintage Books, 1967), 4, 68–70.

42. Kerner Commission, *Report*, 95, 100.

43. Ibid., appendix, charts.

44. Marilyn Buck, "In the Interim," *New Left Notes*, August 21, 1967, 7; Floyd Glasby, "Black and White Rebellion," *New Left Notes*, August 21, 1967, 6.

45. Bob Lawson and Mike James, "Poor White Response to Black Rebellion," *New Left Notes*, August 21, 1967, 2.

46. Robert Allen and Pam Allen would subsequently develop this appreciation of race and social reform in their underrated study, *Reluctant Reformers*.

47. Forman, *Black Revolutionaries*, 502.

48. Sale, *SDS*, 375. Sale quotes the resistance leader Stuart McRae in a footnote but fails to comment on the reference to the "summer riots," indeed, pays no special attention anywhere to the impact that the riots had on SDS leaders and members. Sale is quite right when he says that fall 1967's resistance on campuses, for example, in "its extent, [and] its militance ... [was] ... at unexpected heights." But for Sale, this heightened and broadened militance arose from SDS's own internal processes and not from the example and power of black social motion.

49. Quoted in Rorabaugh, *Berkeley at War*, 116.

50. Karen Wald, "The Promise of Oakland," *New Left Notes*, November 6, 1967, 1–2; Sale, *SDS*, 376.

51. Ronald Fraser, *1968: A Student Generation in Revolt* (London: Chatto and Windus, 1988), 134.

52. Sale, *SDS*, 383; Michael Goldfield, "The Washington Siege of '67: Power at the Pentagon," *New Left Notes*, October 30, 1967, 1, 2.

53. "From Protest to Resistance: Students Battle Cops," *New Left Notes*, October 23, 1967, 1.

54. Fraser, *1968*, 134.

55. "Brooklyn College Strike," *New Left Notes*, October 23, 1967, 4.

56. Carl Davidson, "Toward Institutional Resistance," *New Left Notes*, November 13, 1967, 1; Sale, *SDS*, 378.

57. "Blows against the Empire," *Rat*, April 4, 1968, 5; Karen Gellen, "We Made the News Today Oh Boy," *New Left Notes*, February 12, 1968, 7; February 26, 1968, 7; March 4, 1968, 3; April 15, 1968, 3.

58. Davidson, "Toward Institutional Resistance," 3.

59. Randy Furst, "It Was Cold-Blooded Murder," *New Left Notes*, February 26, 1968, 1; Gellen, "We Made the News," March 4, 1968, 3.

60. Ward Churchill and Jim VanderWall, *The COINTELPRO Papers: Documents from the FBI's Secret Wars against Dissent in the United States* (Boston: South End Press, 1989), 92, 110.

61. "Attack on Militants—The Man Moves Hard: Where Are We?" *New Left Notes*, March 11, 1968, 1.

62. Ibid., 1, 8. The article's author probably was Walter "Slim" Coleman, a Chicago SDSer with growing influence in the National Office. In its tone and its concern for the black struggle, it bears Coleman's signature.

63. Noel Ignatin, "Learn the Lessons of U.S. History," *New Left Notes*, March 25, 1968, 4–5. Ignatin based his article on an earlier pamphlet he had written, *White Blindspot* (New York: Osawotomie, 1967), under the pseudonym J. H. Kagin. Noel Ignatin is Noel Ignatiev, the historian. Rather than switch back and forth or use the name Ignatiev, I will use the name that Ignatiev himself used in the 1960s. In a recent interview with the author, Ignatiev indicated that he believed that SDS published "Learn the Lessons" as part of the National Office's counter to PL' growing influence in the organization. Certainly, this may have been a consideration, even a major consideration. But so, too, must have been the reality of growing repression and SDS's disregard for that repression. PL's key program at the time was a program of "fighting racism." Of course, for PL, this meant subordinating race to class and obscuring race's material and structural roots. But countering PL did not necessarily mean countering its Old Left analysis of race. The Left is replete with struggles in which different factions retain virtually identical analyses and split over who will be in charge of "leading." SDS could well have shared PL's line and still have carried out a struggle against PL—ERAP was not significantly different than PL, nor, as we've seen, was the Gottlieb, Gilbert, and Tenney proposal. That SDS's National Office chose to counter PL with Ignatin's line shows that more was at stake for SDS leaders than who would lead SDS and how PL would be countered.

64. "Resolution on Racism," *New Left Notes*, April 8, 1968, 5.

65. Quoted in Sale, *SDS*, 419, where Sale clearly backs Lynd.

66. David Caute, *The Year of the Barricades: A Journey through 1968* (New York: Harper and Row, 1988), 145.

67. Gellen, "We Made the News," April 15, 1968, 3.

68. Sale, *SDS*, 435; James Simon Kunen, *The Strawberry Statement* (New York: Random House, 1969), 14.

69. Mark Rudd, "Columbia: Notes on the Spring Rebellion," in *The New Left Reader*, ed. Carl Ogelsby (New York: Grove Press, 1969), 294–96.

70. "Oakland Police Attack Panthers," *New Left Notes*, April 15, 1968, 1, 7. In early April 1968, *New Left Notes* was reporting that police harassment of the Panthers had intensified eight months previously. The Panthers and the New Left thus had a clear sense of the August 1967 COINTELPRO program, without ever having seen an FBI memo. Of course, at the time, mainstream commentators labeled such charges "paranoid" and condemned Panther "gangsterism" as the real problem. David Hilliard's account of the April 6 events makes it clear, from a Panther source, that the day's events began as an attempted ambush by the Panthers of Oakland police. Cleaver led this attempt, apparently contravening Huey Newton in the matter. Still, the ambush occurred in the context of the growing police repression outlined here—and King's assassination. Moreover, however the attempt began, police killed Bobby Hutton not in a shoot-out, but as he emerged from a building, following police orders, naked and with his arms above his head. David Hilliard and Lewis Cole, *This Side of Glory: The Autobiography of David Hilliard and the Story of the Black Panther Party* (Boston: Little, Brown, 1993), 184–95.

71. Phillip S. Foner, ed., *The Black Panthers Speak* (New York: J. B. Lippincott, 1970), xxi.

72. And not only young blacks. Chicanos in California formed a Panther-like group, the Brown Berets; Puerto Ricans in New York and Chicago founded the Young Lords on Panther-type lines; Native Americans founded the American Indian Movement (AIM); and Asian students founded the I Wor Kuen. SDS organizers even founded a poor white complement to the Panthers—the Young Patriots.

73. Eldridge Cleaver, *Post-Prison Writings and Speeches* (New York: Ramparts Books, 1969), 35–36; reprinted from *Ramparts*, June 15, 1968.

74. All of this is not to deny the many problems of the Panther leadership. See Hilliard and Cole, *This Side of Glory*, and Elaine Brown, *A Taste of Power: A Black Woman's Story* (New York: Doubleday, 1992), for good accounts of both the Panther's strengths and weaknesses. It is not my intention to enter into a discussion of the Panther's many shortcomings here. The Panther leadership, especially, had serious problems with drugs and came to see its "vanguard" role in ways that exempted it from criticism and thus led to irreconcilable splits. Perhaps at the center of these other problems stood the Panther's male supremacy. I discuss the black nationalist movement's male supremacy—and black women's relationship to black nationalism and to the movement's male supremacy—in subsequent chapters. Though these shortcomings ultimately contributed to the Panther's downfall, the U.S. government violently attacked the Panthers not for the Panther's male chauvinism, or even for their drug use, but for their persuasive analysis of U.S. society and their militant defense of the black community.

75. Eldridge Cleaver, *Soul on Ice* (New York: Dell, 1968), 82.

76. Huey Newton, "A Prison Interview," in Oglesby, *New Left Reader*, 227–28, 229, 240. Todd Gitlin, in his *The Sixties: Years of Hope, Days of Rage*, described Newton's prison interview in characteristic fashion: "In a series of prison interviews widely circulated in the movement press, Huey Newton—*primed with reading matter by white leftists*—discoursed fluidly about socialism, anticolonialism, anti-imperialism, and world revolution" (349; my emphasis). People could quite correctly charge Newton

and the Panthers with many things, but needing the white left to shape the Panther rhetoric is not one of those things. Apparently, twenty years later, Gitlin could not conceive of Newton's having a powerful enough mind to have arrived at his understandings of revolution independently of white leftists. In fact, the Panthers "primed" the New Left and shaped the New Left's rhetoric. But even when Gitlin sees evil, whites must be more central to his account than blacks.

77. Oglesby had been SDS president in the 1965–66 school year, had led SDS in its growing understanding of corporate liberalism and imperialism, and had recently completed coauthoring, with Richard Schaull, an important book on the topic, *Containment and Change* (New York: Macmillan, 1967).

78. Bernardine Dohrn, "White Mother Country Radicals," *New Left Notes*, July 29, 1968, 1, 5. Even the title of Dohrn's article is deceptive. "White mother country radicals" was Newton's phrase, apparently indicating additional respect for the Panthers. But the content of the article involved SDS's rejection of the Panther proposal. Ron Jacobs, in *The Way the Wind Blew*, takes SDS at its word—that its goal was to support the Panthers—and fails to see that SDS was professing its support in the context of rejecting the Panther proposal.

79. NIC, "Fifth Party Ticket: Cleaver and Oglesby," *New Left Notes*, September 9, 1968, 3.

80. NIC, "Why Oglesby Won't Run," *New Left Notes*, September 9, 1968, 8.

81. Ibid.

82. Cleaver, *Soul on Ice*, 78. Huey Newton explains the concept more completely in "Prison Interview," 231–33.

83. Baldwin, *Fire Next Time*, 94–95.

Chapter Two. The New Left and the American Empire

1. John F. Kennedy, *A Strategy of Peace* (New York: Harper, 1960), 6.

2. "Port Huron Statement," 1962, http://www.tomhayden.com/porthuron.htm.

3. Nguyen Khac Vien, *Glimpses of United States Neo-Colonialism: United States Neo-Colonialism in South Vietnam*, In *Vietnamese Studies*, no. 31, ed. Nguyen Khac Vien (Hanoi: Xunhasaba, 1971), 20.

4. U.S. Senate, Committee on Foreign Relations, "The United States Government and the Vietnam War: Executive and Legislative Roles and Relationships, Part II, 1961–1964" (Washington, D.C.: Government Printing Office, 1985), http://www.mtholyoke.edu/acad/intrel/pentagon/congress1.htm.

5. Wilfred Burchett, *Vietnam: Inside Story of the Guerrilla War* (New York: International, 1965), 85.

6. Homer Bigart, "United States Helps Vietnam in Test of Strategy against Guerrillas," *New York Times*, March 29, 1962; Ton Vy, "The Staley-Taylor Plan," in *Vietnamese Studies No. 11*, ed. Nguyen Khac Vien (Hanoi: Xunhasaba, ca. 1969), 40–41.

7. Ton, "Staley-Taylor Plan," 30–31.

8. "Colonel Van [*sic*] and General Harkins," *Nation*, October 19, 1963, 230, cited in Eric Norden, *America's Barbarities in Vietnam* (New Delhi: Mainstream, 1966), 29.

9. Sale, *SDS*, 154. Sale argues that the "Part of the way with LBJ" slogan was simply a bone thrown to what even in 1964 was considered SDS's "right wing." Still, it was offered in 1964 and would not have been offered even a year later.

10. Paul Potter, "Name the System," 1965, http://www.sdsrebels.com/potter.htm.

11.. Sale, *SDS*, 188.

12.. Ibid.

242 | Notes to Pages 60–75

13. Clayborne Carson, ed., *The Student Voice, 1960–1965: Periodical of the Student Nonviolent Coordinating Committee* (Westport, Conn.: Meckler, 1990), 35, 43.

14. Marilyn Young, *The Vietnam Wars, 1945–1990* (New York: Harper Perennial, 1991), 333.

15. Stephen Cary, "Three Months in Vietnam," *Progressive* October 1965, 13, cited in Norden, *America's Barbarities*, 21–22.

16. Sale, *SDS*, 195; Carl Oglesby, interview by author, December 9, 2002.

17. It was the first popular radical recounting of the United States' Cold War history. D. F. Fleming, *The Cold War and Its Origins, 1917–1960* (Garden City, N.Y.: Doubleday, 1961), and William Appleman Williams, *The Tragedy of American Diplomacy* (New York: Dell, 1962), had already written Cold War histories that recast the United States as aggressor and sought to understand the basis for this aggression in the United States' economic and political structure. Nevertheless, Oglesby was the person from whom SDS's rank and file learned their Cold War history.

18. Oglesby's emphasis on the interlocking nature of U.S. corporate and political leadership would also become a standard SDS refrain.

19. Carl Oglesby, speech at the November 27, 1965, Washington, D.C., antiwar demonstration; Carl Oglesby, "Liberalism and the Corporate State," *New Left Notes*, January 21, 1966, 2–3.

20. The main Old Left parties—the Communist Party and the Trotskyist Socialist Workers Party— despite ample promptings from their heroes, Marx, Lenin, and Trotsky, and their claims to "scientific" analysis, had never gone so far. Indeed, their sanitized version of the class struggle prohibited them from considering such a sacrilegious notion.

21. Oglesby, "Liberalism," 2–3.

22. Carl Oglesby, "World Revolution and American Containment," *New Left Notes*, April 8, 1966, 3.

23. Ogelsby and Schaull, *Containment and Change*, 137–39.

24. Ibid., 32.

25. All quotes cited from ibid., 53, 65, 66, 68.

26. Ibid., 71.

27. Ibid., 83–96.

28. Ibid., 97–108.

29. Ibid., 110–11.

30. Ibid., 123–29.

31. Ibid., 128.

32. Ibid., 158.

33. Oglesby, "World Revolution," 2–3.

34. Oglesby, "Liberalism," 2–3.

35. Out of the hundreds of references in his book, Oglesby had footnoted exactly one nonwhite political thinker, Kwame Nkrumah, and this reference was a factual, rather than analytic, reference.

36. W. E. B. DuBois, "To the Nations of the World," in *W. E. B. DuBois: A Reader*, ed. David Levering Lewis (New York, 1995), 639–40.

37. Ibid., 645. Important parts of DuBois's work became or were widely available in the early 1960s. *An ABC of Color*, a collection that included DuBois's views of colonialism, racism, and the First World War, was published in 1963; *Black Reconstruction*, a 1935 text, was republished in 1962 and 1964 and contained important insights on the construction of the U.S. empire; and *Souls of Black Folks* (1903), with its insistence that "the problem of the twentieth century was the problem of the color line," was republished in the 1950s and early 1960s.

38. W. E. B. DuBois, *Black Reconstruction* (New York: Athenaeum Press, 1935), 12, 24.

39. Malcolm X, *Malcolm X Speaks*, 49–50.

40. Ibid., 75.

41. Ibid., 124–25.

42. In a still more popular vein, James Baldwin, too, in his 1963 *The Fire Next Time*, also clearly articulated the relationship between Africa and America's black community. Robert Moses, the legendary leader of SNCC's Mississippi organizing project, had also spoken out on the war at Berkeley's 1965 teach-in on the war, and in widely reprinted remarks made the same point.

43. Kim Moody, Fred Eppsteiner, and Mike Flug, "Toward the Working Class (An SDS Convention Position Paper)," *New Left Notes*, July, 29, 1966, 6–8.

44. Gottlieb, Tenney, and Gilbert, "Social Change in America," 3.

45. George C. Herring, *America's Longest War: The United States and Vietnam, 1950–1975* (New York: McGraw-Hill, 1996), 161–62, 168.

46. "Agent Orange Website," http://www.lewispublishing.com/orange.htm.

47. Herring, *America's Longest War*, 169–70.

48. Bertrand Russell, "Appeal to the American Conscience," *New Left Notes*, August 24, 1966, 16–17.

49. Carl Oglesby, "Vietnam: This Is Guernica," *New Left Notes*, September 25, 1967, 4–6.

50. Jeff Shero, "Shero—Our Man in Moscow, from Russia with Love," *New Left Notes*, August 21, 1967, 1.

51. Cathy Wilkerson, "Delegation to Hanoi Returns," *New Left Notes*, December 18, 1967, 4.

52. Cathy Wilkerson, "United States Vietnam STR [*sic*]," *New Left Notes*, January 15, 1968, 2.

53. Wilkerson, "Delegation," 2.

54. Steve Halliwell, "New Leftists Meet with the NLF: A Society in Revolution," *New Left Notes*, October 2, 1967, 5.

55. Sue Munaker, "'In the Belly of the Beast,' Report on the Stockholm Conf.," *New Left Notes*, May 13, 1968, 6.

56. Wilkerson, "Delegation," 4.

57. Jeff Jones, "Report on the Student Mobilization Committee in General and National Student Strike in Particular," *New Left Notes*, November 10, 1967, 3. The smaller and specifically antiwar Student Mobilization Committee against the War did attempt to take up the Vietnamese suggestion and organize a national student strike, much to the consternation of some SDS leaders. Jones, for example, insisted that the Student Mobe was simply trying to co-opt SDS's leadership over the campus antiwar movement.

58. Munaker, "Belly of the Beast," 6.

59. Halliwell, "New Leftists," 1.

60. Todd Gitlin, "The Texture of the Cuban Revolution," *New Left Notes*, February 12, 1968, 4. Back from Cuba, Gitlin passed through Chicago and spoke glowingly of Cuba to 1967 SDS national secretary Greg Calvert. Calvert remarked that "he'd never seen" Gitlin "so free of cynicism." Gitlin *Sixties*, 279.

61. Sale, *SDS*, 124.

62. Progressive Labor Party, "Road to Revolution II," in Progressive Labor Party, *Revolution Today: A Look at the Progressive Labor Movement and the Progressive Labor Party* (Jericho, N.Y.: Exposition Press, 1970), 203; reprinted from *PL Magazine*, December 1966.

63. Sale, *SDS*, 236; "Vietnam Work-In," *New Left Notes*, May 29, 1967, 1, 8. This article, signed by a dozen Chicago-area SDSers, including several PL members and leaders, demonstrated that PL's line—SDS had to broaden its base by going to the working class—was still well within SDS discourse at the time.

64. Mike Klonsky, "The State of SDS," *New Left Notes*, June 24, 1968, 3.

65. Mike Spiegel, "The Growing Development of a Class Politics," *New Left Notes*, June 10, 1968, 4. I discuss Ignatin's refutation of this line in Chapter 1. Ignatin's view first appeared in *New Left Notes* two months earlier.

66. Mark Rudd, "Just a Few Subway Stops from Wall St.," *New Left Notes*, June 10, 1968, 10–11.

Chapter Three. The New Left and Feminism

1. For example, Evans, *Personal Politics* ; Echols, *Daring to Be Bad*; and Rosen, *World Split Open* .

2. Sue Thrasher, "Circle of Trust," in Constance Curry et al., *Deep in Our Hearts: Nine White Women in the Freedom Movement* (Athens: University of Georgia Press, 2000), 222.

3. Theresa Del Pozzo, "The Feel of a Blue Note," in Curry et al., *Deep in Our Hearts*, 191.

4. Sara Evans makes this argument both in her groundbreaking work on the development of radical feminism, *Personal Politics*, and in a 1977 article, "Women's Consciousness and the Southern Black Movement," *Southern Exposure* (Winter 1977) 10–18, which offers a synopsis of her book.

5. Cheryl Lynn Greenberg, *A Circle of Trust: Remembering SNCC* (New Brunswick, N.J.: Rutgers University Press, 1998), 140–41.

6. Evans, "Women's Consciousness," 13.

7. Jo Freeman, "On the Origins of the Women's Liberation Movement," in *The Feminist Memoir Project: Voices from Women's Liberation*, ed. Rachel Blau DuPlessis and Ann Snitow (New York: Three Rivers Press, 1998), 175.

8. Evans, "Women's Consciousness," 16.

9. Emily Stoper, *The Student Nonviolent Coordinating Committee: The Growth of Radicalism in a Civil Rights Organization* (Brooklyn, N.Y.: Carlson, 1989), 260; Forman, *Black Revolutionaries*, 452; Evans, *Personal Politics*, 54.

10. Stoper, *Student Nonviolent Coordinating Committee*, 261–62; Carson, *In Struggle*, 138, 144.

11. Carson, *In Struggle*, 140–48.

12. See Rosen, *World Split Open*; and Evans, *Personal Politics*.

13. Rossinow, *Politics of Authenticity*, 104–6; Hayden, *Reunion*, 40–42; Curry et al., *Deep in Our Hearts*, 19.

14. Casey Hayden, "Fields of Blue," in Curry et al., *Deep in Our Hearts*, 344–53.

15. Sara Evans reproduces the entire "Women in the Movement" position paper in *Personal Politics*.

16. Mary King, *Freedom Song: A Personal Story of the 1960s Civil Rights Movement* (New York: Morrow, 1987), 452. However generously King and others recount Carmichael's response, Carmichael continued to repeat it, without the context, and it became a staple for some sectors of the black nationalist movement. If his statement was originally meant as a comic remark, it took on a life of its own.

17. Cynthia Washington, "We Started from Different Ends of the Spectrum," *Southern Exposure* (Winter 1997): 14.

18. Paula Giddings, *When and Where I Enter: The Impact of Black Women on Race and Sex in America* (New York: William Morrow, 1984), 302; Belinda Robnett, *How Long? How Long? African-American Women in the Struggle for Civil Rights* (New York: Oxford University Press, 1997), 115–17.

19. Evans, "Women's Consciousness," 13.

20. Cynthia Griggs Fleming, *Soon We Will Not Cry: The Liberation of Ruby Doris Smith Robinson* (New York: Rowman and Littlefield, 1998), 101, 156, 153.

21. Ibid., 152.

22. Ibid., 129; King, *Freedom Song*, 452–53.

23. King, *Freedom Song*, 462, 572.

24. Ibid., 460.

25. Evans, "Women's Consciousness," 17–18. Evans says that the "black women who received it ["Memo"] were on a different historic trajectory" and so did not respond to the memo. Echols makes even less of an attempt to understand that Hayden and King were bringing a white agenda into the black movement. She writes, for example, that with the decline of "prefigurative politics"—sociologists' term for politics and organization that allegedly "prefigured" the new egalitarian society—"first in SNCC and later in SDS, the Movement became a less hospitable place for women whose concerns were dismissed as 'personal' or 'apolitical.'" Echols, *Daring to Be Bad*, 33. Black women, as we have seen, were actually becoming a more significant force in SNCC.

26. King, *Freedom Song*, 467.

27. Barbara Omolade extensively discusses the relations between black and white women in "Sisterhood in Black and White," in DuPlessis and Snitow, *Feminist Memoir Project*, 377–408.

28. King, *Freedom Song*, Appendix 3, "A Kind of Memo from Casey Hayden and Mary King to a Number of Other Women in the Peace and Freedom Movements," 571–74.

29. Evans, *Personal Politics*, 162–63.

30. Gitlin, *Sixties*, 370.

31. Paul Booth, "National Program Outlined at Dec. NC for Coming Months," *New Left Notes*, January 21, 1966, 1, 3; "On Roles in SDS," *New Left Notes*, January 28, 1966, 3.

32. Evans, *Personal Politics*, 108–9; Rosen, *World Split Open*, 115–17.

33. Jesse Lemisch and Naomi Weisstein, "Remarks on Naomi Weisstein," http://www.cwluherstory.com/CWLUMemoir/weisstein.html; Amy Kesselman, with Heather Booth, Vivian Rothstein, and Naomi Weisstein, "Our Gang of Four: Friendships and Women's Liberation," http://www.cwluherstory.com/CWLUMemoir/Kesselman.html; Amy Kesselman, with Heather Booth, Vivian Rothstein, and Naomi Weisstein, "Our Gang of Four: Friendships and Women's Liberation," in DuPlessis and Snitow, *Feminist Memoir Project*, 514.

34. Beverly Jones, "Towards Women's Liberation," *Guardian*, January 18, 1969, 9.

35. Kathy McAfee and Myrna Wood, "On Women: Bread and Roses," *Kaleidoscope*, November 1, 1969, 11–12 (originally printed in *Leviathan*, June 1969).

36. Kesselman, "Our Gang of Four," http://www.cwluherstory.com/CWLUMemoir/Kesselman.html.

37. Hayden, "Fields of Blue," 349.

38. Barbara Winslow, "Primary and Secondary Contradictions in Seattle, 1967–1969," in DuPlessis and Snitow, *Feminist Memoir Project*, 244.

39. Marge Piercy, "The Grand Coolie Dam," in *Sisterhood Is Powerful: An Anthology of Writings from the Women's Liberation Movement*, ed. Robin Morgan (New York: Vintage Books, 1970), 482–83 (originally printed in *Leviathan*, November 1969). The Southern Student Organizing Committee (SSOC) published a pamphlet, *Freedom for Movement Girls—Now*, that laid out the reality of movement marriages and relationships still more bitterly than Piercy's account. vanauken, *Freedom for Movement Girls—Now* (Southern Student Organizing Committee, 1969).

40. Piercy, "Grand Coolie Dam," 482–83.

41. Naomi Weisstein, Evelyn Goldfield, and Sue Munaker, "A Woman Is a Sometime Thing, or, Cornering Capitalism by Removing 51% of Its Commodities," in Long, *New Left*, 240–41.

42. Ibid., 248.

43. Liberation News Service, June 28, 1968. Perhaps this cartoon embodied the slogan that one SDS chapter used, or perhaps it inspired the slogan: "The system is like a woman; you have to fuck it to make it change." Sale, *SDS*, 526.

44. Jeff Shero, "Wanna See My Pussy," *Rat*, December 13, 1969, 14.

45. Jane Alpert, *Growing Up Underground* (New York: William Morrow, 1981), 177–78.

46. Jon Jacobson, "Naked Lunch," *Rat*, January 17, 1969, 6.

47. Evans, *Personal Politics*, 141; for a fuller discussion of ERAP, see chapter 6.

48. Quoted in ibid., 146.

49. Quoted in ibid., 150–51.

50. Winslow, "Primary and Secondary Contradictions," 244.

51. Quoted in Evans, *Personal Politics*, 164.

52. For a complete discussion of why women submerged their demands from 1965 to mid-1967, see Echols, *Daring to Be Bad*, 23–50.

53. "Liberation of Women," *New Left Notes*, July 10, 1967, 4.

54. Evans, *Personal Politics*, 191–92.

55. "Liberation of Women," 4.

56. Evans, *Personal Politics*, 192.

57. Beverly Jones and Judith Brown, *Towards a Female Liberation Movement* (Boston: New England Free Press, 1968), 2–4.

58. See Ellen Willis, "Women and the Left," in *Notes from the Second Year* (New York, 1970), for a radical feminist's interpretation of this dichotomy.

59. *New Left Notes*, June 26, 1967, 1, 4.

60. Freeman, "Women's Liberation Movement," 178–80; Echols, *Daring to Be Bad*, 45–49.

61. Freeman, "Women's Liberation Movement," 181–82.

62. Sale, *SDS*, 415.

63. Marilyn Salzman Webb, "Women: We Have a Common Enemy," *New Left Notes*, June 10, 1968, 5.

64. Shulamith Firestone, "The Jeanette Rankin Brigade: Woman Power," in *Notes from the First Year* (New York, 1968); Kathy Amatniek, "Funeral Oration for Traditional Womanhood," in *Notes from the First Year* (New York, 1968).

65. Brown and Jones, *Towards a Female Liberation Movement*.

66. Shulamith Firestone, "The Women's Rights Movement in the U.S.A.: New View," in *Notes from the First Year* (New York, 1968).

67. Elizabeth Martinez, "History Makes Us, We Make History," in DuPlessis and Snitow, *Feminist Memoir Project*, 118.

68. DuBois, *Black Reconstruction*, 30.

69. Baldwin, *Fire Next Time*, 97.

70. Brown and Jones, *Towards a Female Liberation Movement*, 29.

71. Of course, successful anticolonial revolution was not the guarantee of Vietnamese women's liberation; as radical feminists pointed out, successful twentieth-century revolutions had not significantly changed women's subordinate social status.

72. Alice Echols published the transcript of this discussion (*Daring to Be Bad*, 369–77) and discusses the meeting, held at Sandy Springs, Maryland (104–8). Susan Brownmiller, *In Our Time: Memoir of a Revolution* (New York: Dial Press, 1999), 30–34, offers a defense of the radical feminist position.

73. Echols, *Daring to Be Bad*, 369–77.

74. Pam Allen, "Memo to My White Sisters in Our Struggle to Realize Our Full Humanity" (New York: New York Radical Women, 1968), 1–4.

75. I am indebted to Clarence Walker for deepening my understanding of this essential point.

76. Carol Hanisch, "The Personal Is Political," in *Notes from the Second Year* (New York, 1970), 76; Brownmiller, *In Our Time*, 45.

77. Ellen Willis, "Sequel: Letter to a Critic," in *Notes from the Second Year* (New York, 1970), 57 (originally written ca. March/April 1969).

78. Shirley Geok-lin Lim, "'Ain't I a Feminist?': Re-forming the Circle," in DuPlessis and Snitow, *Feminist Memoir Project*, 451–52.

79. Brownmiller, *In Our Time*, 22.

80. Ibid., 35.

81. New York Radical Women, "Miss America Protest Press Release," Liberation News Service, September 2, 1968, D-18.

82. Robin Morgan, "Miss America Goes Down," *Rat*, September 20–October 3, 1968, 4.

83. Marilyn Salzman Webb, "DC Witches Hex United Fruit," *Guardian*, April 26, 1969, 8; Robin Morgan, "Do You Know What's Happening, Mister Jones?" Liberation News Service, July 17, 1969, 9–12; Brownmiller, *In Our Time*, 49–50.

84. Susan Sutheim, "Women Shake Up SDS Session," *Guardian*, June 22, 1968, 6.

85. Sale, *SDS*, 404, 415–16.

86. Bernardine Dohrn and Naomi Jaffee, "The Look Is You," in Teodori, *New Left*, 355–58 (originally printed in *New Left Notes*, March 18, 1968).

87. Doug Rossinow also sees Dohrn's election as the National Office's "tactical response to feminism in the left." Rossinow goes out of his way to portray Dohrn as SDS's own "Vargas Girl," "revolutionary pin-up," and "revolutionary gun-moll." Certainly, ample evidence exists to sustain these characterizations, evidence provided both by her New Left admirers and opponents; however, Dohrn's physical appearance was only one part of her appeal for male SDSers, and perhaps the lesser part of that appeal. Dohrn was an extraordinarily articulate individual. Her answer to women's liberation—her ability to espouse SDS rhetoric without challenging male supremacy—reassured SDS men that they were basically good, that they could have their power over women and not feel guilty about it. And if women objected, it was because they were uptight or not sufficiently committed to black liberation. See Rossinow, *Politics of Authenticity*, 204, 305–6.

88. Noel Ignatin, "Revolutionary Struggle for Women's Liberation," *New Left Notes*, December 23, 1968, 2.

89. Echols, *Daring to Be Bad*, 116.

90. Ibid., 114–19; Gitlin, *Sixties*, 363–64.

91. "International Women's Day," *New Left Notes*, March 1969, 1–4.

92. I am particularly indebted to my conversations with Chude (Pam Parker) Allen for these insights.

Chapter Four. The New Left Starts to Disintegrate

1. A year later, Panther chief of staff David Hilliard would name SDS's rapid growth as a key factor in SDS's arrogance. David Hilliard and Bobby Seale, "Our Enemy's Friends Are Also Our Enemies," *Black Panther*, August 9, 1969, 12.

2. Sale, *SDS*, 263–64.

3. Progressive Labor Party, "Fight Racism: Build a Worker-Student Alliance: Smash Imperialism. Resolution Passed by December 1968 SDS National Council Meeting," *New Left Notes*, January 8, 1969, 4. In subsequent rearticulations of this line, PL would explicitly argue that "all nationalism is reactionary."

4. Thomas Powers, *Diana: Portrait of a Terrorist* (Boston: Houghton Mifflin, 1971), 102.

5. Terry Robbins and Bill Ayers, "Give It a Name/Call It SDS/Join Us," *New Left Notes*, October 7, 1968, 4.

6. Mike Klonsky, "Toward a Revolutionary Youth Movement," *New Left Notes*, December 23, 1968, 3; Howard Machtinger, "Analysis of the Youth Movement," *New Left Notes*, January 22, 1969, 7.

7. Connie Ullman, "San Francisco State Shut Down," *New Left Notes*, November 19, 1968, 1.

8. Sale, *SDS*, 535–36.

9. "We Made the News Today," *New Left Notes*, January 15, 1969, 1; January 29, 1969, 3; February 5, 1969, 1; February 12, 1969, 3; February 21, 1969, 7; February 28, 1969, 7; March 7, 1969, 1; March 20, 1969, 6–7; April 24, 1969, 3.

10. SDS, Southern California Regional Council, "Relationships to Black and Brown Movements," *New Left Notes*, February 28, 1969, 8.

11. "Strike Over but Struggle Goes On. Interview with Tony Miranda, Nesbit Crutchfield and Mason Wong," *Movement*, May 1969, 16–17.

12. Mike Klonsky, "The White Question," *New Left Notes*, March 20, 1969, 12.

13. Brown, *Taste of Power*, 168–70.

14. The New York Panther case was perhaps representative of the scale of the frame-up against the Panthers. Originally, the April bust—which took all the major leaders of the New York chapter off the streets—was accompanied by a huge scare campaign: the Panthers were going to carry out an Easter weekend bombing of New York's major department stores, as well as bombing police stations and, for some unspecified reason, the Bronx Botanical Gardens. Bail was set at $100,000 for each of the twenty-one Panthers, and money could be raised to bail out only a few of the Panthers. The trial itself was the longest trial to date in New York City history and ended twenty-five months after the original arrests. The jury for the trial took four hours—lunch included—to determine that the Panthers were innocent of each count. The *New York Times* celebrated the verdict as proof positive that the Panther claim that they could not receive a fair trial was false.

15. Bill Ayers and Jim Mellen, "Hot Town: Summer in the City, or, I Ain't Gonna Work on Maggie's Farm No More," *New Left Notes*, April 5, 1969, 8.

16. Marilyn Katz and Chicago Regional SDS, "May Day Proposal," *New Left Notes*, March 20, 1969, 10.

17. Les Coleman and Chicago Regional SDS, "The Schools Must Serve the People," *New Left Notes*, March 20, 1969, 4–5.

18. Ed Jennings and Chicago Circle Campus SDS, "The Black Panther Party: Toward the Liberation of the Colony," *New Left Notes*, April 5, 1969, 3.

19. Clayton Van Lydegraf, "Reply to Mellen," *New Left Notes*, June 6, 1969, 8.

20. Julius Lester, "Lester Attacks Panther Resolution as Racist," *New Left Notes*, April 24, 1969, 2 (originally printed in the *Guardian*).

21. Julius Lester, "From the Other Side of the Tracks," *Guardian*, May 10, 1969, 13. Kathleen Cleaver, representing the Panthers, defended SDS against Lester's critique, but in a manner that missed the heart of Lester's criticism. Her argument boiled down to two things: the Panthers really were the vanguard, and SDS could not influence the black community's internal political struggles in any case. Perhaps the

latter point was true, perhaps not. But the real question was the propriety of SDS having done that and the significance of its membership lining up behind the Panthers as the vanguard. Cleaver herself also recognized the curious nature of the resolution, noting that it affirmed the "essentially correct" Black Panther Party program—as though SDS had discerned parts of the program that were incorrect. Kathleen Cleaver, "Kathleen Cleaver Replies to Lester," *New Left Notes*, May 1, 1969, 5–6.

22. Clayton Van Lydegraf, "About Privilege," *New Left Notes*, April 24, 1969, 9.

23. Karin Ashley, Bill Ayers, Bernardine Dohrn, John Jacobs, Jeff Jones, Gerry Long, Howie Machtinger, Jim Mellen, Terry Robbins, Mark Rudd, and Steve Tappis, "You Don't Need a Weatherman to Know Which Way the Wind Blows," *New Left Notes*, June 18, 1969, 3–8. It is generally acknowledged that John Jacobs was the paper's principal author. In addition to its failure to credit the black movement's analysis, the paper also failed to credit Van Lydegraf's "About Privilege" and *The Movement and the Workers* (2nd edition, Eugene, OR: Vision Works Press, 1972), both of which explicitly formulated arguments in terms that strongly would be echoed in "You Don't Need a Weatherman." But while the terms were echoed, Van Lydegraf's larger concerns were bypassed. Moreover, the paper also insisted that because of their central position in the United States, "economically and geo-militarily," black people "could do it alone," that is, take down imperialism without any white help. In an open letter on Weatherman politics written in early 1970, four ex-Weathermen saw the potential for exceptionalist politics stemming from this argument. If blacks "could do it alone," they argued, "whites were reduced to an auxiliary force." Although this auxiliary was unnecessary to the revolution's success, it "would lower the costs of the black revolution. The primary job of white revolutionaries in this view was to organize those whites who could push the struggle ahead as quickly as the blacks." Were Weatherman to emphasize this aspect of its politics, as it increasingly did, the need for serious organizing work, transforming the hearts and minds of masses of white people, would be obviated. Norman Reed, Inessa, Victor Camilo, and Lilina Jones, "It's Only People's Games That You Got to Dodge," in *Weatherman*, ed. Harold Jacobs (Berkeley, Calif.: Ramparts Books, 1970), 421–39.

24. Ashley et al., "You Don't Need a Weatherman," 3–8.

25. Bill Ayers, "A Strategy to Win," in Jacobs, *Weatherman*, 186.

26. Mike Klonsky, Noel Ignatin, Sue Eanet, and Les Coleman, "Revolutionary Youth Movement II," *New Left Notes*, July 8, 1969, 5, 9.

27. Ibid.

28. Mark Rudd, unpublished manuscript (ca. 1988–89), 192, in author's possession.

29. Jack Smith, "SDS Ousts PLP," *Guardian*, June 28, 1969, 11.

30. Evans, *Personal Politics*, 108.

31. On Malcolm's Nation of Islam beliefs about women, see Malcolm X, *Autobiography of Malcolm X*, 226. On his changed view of women, see Malcolm X, *By Any Means Necessary* (New York Pathfinder Press, 1970), 179. Although *By Any Means Necessary* did not appear until 1970, Malcolm's changed position on women was widely noted in the New Left and in the women's movement.

32. Winifred Breines, *The Trouble between Us: An Uneasy History of White and Black Women* (New York: Oxford University Press, 2006), 57–58.

33. Brown, *Taste of Power*, 189–90.

34. Still, as the Panthers increasingly emphasized their "Survival Programs," that is, their community-organizing programs, they debated and sought to change their understanding of the role of black women. Even Eldridge Cleaver, from exile, addressed the question. Verbally, at least, Cleaver's position was more advanced than that of any male SDS leaders. In a July 1969 open letter, Cleaver acknowledged that "we also have a duty to stop inflicting injustices of misuse of women. . . . It is mandatory that all manifestations

of male chauvinism be excluded from our ranks and that sisters have a duty and the right to do whatever they want to do in order to see to it that they are not relegated to an inferior position, and that they're not treated as though they are not equal members of the party and equal in all regards. . . . If we're not careful, it's [male chauvinism] is going to destroy our ranks, destroy our organization, because women want to be liberated just as all oppressed people want to be liberated." Eldridge Cleaver, "Eldridge Cleaver on Women's Liberation," *Guardian*, August 2, 1969, 5. Roberta Alexander, a Panther woman, at the same time asserted that the Panthers were struggling over the question of women's liberation and insisted, again, in advance of most SDS women, that in addition to being oppressed on a class and racial basis, "black women are oppressed by black men. . . . The problem of male supremacy can't be overcome unless it's a two-way street. Men must struggle too." Margie Stamberg, "Women at UFAF and After," *Guardian*, August 2, 1969, 5.

35. Sale, *SDS*, 566–67; Smith, "SDS Ousts PLP," 11; "SDS Convention: The Way It Was," *Old Mole*, July 4–17, 1969, 14; Rudd, unpublished manuscript, 192.

36. Margie Stamberg, "SDS Deals with the Woman Question," *Guardian*, June 28, 1969, 7.

37. Ashley et al., "You Don't Need a Weatherman," 79–80.

38. Ibid., 80–86.

39. Stamberg, "SDS Deals with the Woman Question," 7.

40. Klonsky, "Revolutionary Youth Movement II," 9.

41. RYM II, "Proposed SDS Unity Principles," *New Left Notes*, July 8, 1969, 2.

42. Stamberg, "SDS Deals with the Woman Question," 7.

43. Churchill and VanderWall, *COINTELPRO Papers*, Chapter 5, Part II, 1.

44. Foner, *Black Panthers Speak*, xxvi; "Chronology of Repression," *Old Mole*, December 17–January 8, 1970, 10.

45. Churchill and VanderWall, *COINTELPRO Papers*, Chapter 5, Part II, 21.

46. Arlene Eisen Bergman, "Panther's Struggle Is the People's Struggle," *Movement*, October 1969, 3.

47. "UFAF Conference," *Old Mole*, August 1–14, 1969, 3; Lew Cole, "Volunteers," *Leviathan*, February 1970, 14.

48. NIC, SDS, "NIC Statement on UFAF," *New Left Notes*, July 24, 1969, 2–3.

49. Cole, "Volunteers," 14–17.

50. Old Mole, "UFAF Conference," 19.

51. Susan Stern, *With the Weathermen: The Personal Journey of a Revolutionary Woman* (New York: Doubleday, 1975), 66–67.

52. Seale and Hilliard, "Our Enemy's Friends," 12–13.

53. Detroit Weatherman, "Break on Through to the Other Side," Liberation News Service, August 28, 1969, 6–7.

54. SDS, Motor City, "Break on Through to the Other Side," *New Left Notes*, August 29, 1969, 4; Mike Klonsky, "Why I Quit," *New Left Notes*, August 29, 1969, 2.

55. SDS, Motor City, "Break on Through," 4. In her memoir of the era, Roxanne Dunbar Ortiz recalls discussing the Motor City Nine with a friend, former Chicana SNCC activist and early women's movement activist Betita Martinez. Ortiz, at the time a founding member of Boston's pioneering women's group, Cell 16, wondered why "they say the are part of the women's liberation movement when they don't approve of our existence." Martinez replied: "Sounds like a male idea of what women's liberation should be." Roxanne Dunbar-Ortiz, *Outlaw Woman: A Memoir of the War Years, 1960–1975* (San Francisco: City Lights, 2001), 210–11.

56. "The Steel City 26: SDS Women Vamp on Pittsburgh," Liberation News Service, September 13, 1969, 1–3. Shin'ya Ono best articulated Weatherman's rationale for its actions. Two obstacles stood in the way of white working-class youth's participation in revolution: racism and defeatism. Both these belief systems were deeply ingrained in the psyches of white youth and could not be overcome with a good leaflet or a good rap (as though this is what organizing consisted of); only by seeing other whites actively siding with blacks and Vietnamese could white working-class youth racism and defeatism be overcome. Shin'ya Ono, "You Do Need a Weatherman to Know Which Way the Wind Blows," in Jacobs, *Weatherman*, 232–37. See also "SDS Women Hit Pitt High School," *Guardian*, September 13, 1969, 7.

57. Carl Davidson, "United States Radicals Meet with PRG in Cuba," *Guardian*, August 30, 1969, 6.

58. Reflecting back many years later, former RYM II activist Carl Davidson speculated that the meeting was called precisely because the Vietnamese were concerned that the antiwar movement's radical wing was becoming more and more sectarian. Carl Davidson, interview by author, January 2006.

59. Chicago police found Dohrn's notes in a Chicago Weatherman apartment after the organization went underground. Subsequently, the notes were published in the U.S. Senate Judiciary Internal Security Subcommittee, "The Weather Underground" (Washington, D.C.: Government Printing Office, 1975), 143–46. Dohrn's notes are abbreviated—several sessions do not appear in her notes at all, or are cryptically described. It is certainly possible that the Vietnamese encouraged some SDSers to increase the militancy of their antiwar work. Given the long-term Vietnamese goals, however, it is inconceivable that the Vietnamese would have counseled militancy at the expense of the mass movement, or in contradiction to building that mass movement. That would be Weatherman's contribution alone.

60. Davidson suggested that the Vietnamese were educating the American antiwar radicals in the guise of questioning them about the conditions in the United States. Davidson, interview.

61. Davidson, "United States Radicals," 6.

62. Bernardine Dohrn, interview by author, May 2006.

63. Bo Burlingham, interview by author, February 2006.

64. Weatherman, "Bring the War Home," *New Left Notes*, September 12, 1969, 3.

65. Bill Ayers, *Fugitive Days* (Boston: Beacon Press, 2001), 161. Ayers's account of the Cuba trip had the Weatherman members coming back to the United States more committed to the Vietnamese vision than to the vision of Weatherman leader John Jacobs (CW in Ayers's thinly disguised account). Jacobs, according to Ayers, pulled together a meeting of the returnees, denounced their sentimental journeys and romances, and whipped the Weather cadre into line. As the organization's chief ideologue, Jacobs's vision won out, and the cadre fell into line. While there is probably some truth to this account—Jacobs was the chief ideologue, and Weathermen were swayed by the Vietnamese view—to place so great a responsibility on Jacobs's shoulders alone is to fail to appreciate the social and cultural basis for Weatherman's emergence. Besides, Ayers was himself no babe in the woods intimidated by Jacobs's superior intellect and knowledge of the Marxist classics. On the contrary, Ayers had championed the line of "confrontation politics" and was one of three or four really essential people to Weatherman's formation—something a reader of his memoir might not appreciate.

66. Weatherman, "Bring the War Home," 3. Ron Jacobs offers this account of the meeting with the Vietnamese: "However, Weatherman was told to raise the level of confrontation in the United States in order to help the NLF and North Vietnamese win in Vietnam. . . . Nothing concrete came of the meetings but the inspiration they provided intensified the group's commitment to the struggle of the Vietnamese people and to a revolution in the United States." Jacobs, *Way the Wind Blew*, 51.

67. Kathy Boudin, Bernardine Dohrn, and Terry Robbins, "Bringing the War Back Home, Less Talk, More National Action," *New Left Notes*, August 23, 1969, 6.

68. Ibid.; David Dellinger, *More Power Than We Know: The People's Movement toward Democracy* (Garden City, N.Y.: Anchor Press, 1975), 162–63; Hilliard and Cole, *This Side of Glory*, 258; Gitlin, *Sixties*, 393. Several months later, former SNCC chairman Phil Hutchings answered this charge of "timidity." "The problem with white people," he noted, "is not fighting or violence. (Ask any Indian or black person.) Newark's Tony Imperiale [Italian American fighter for 'white rights'] can get white youth to fight; so can the construction workers in Chicago and Pittsburgh. Whites will fight. The question is for what? And that is a political point, not a military one." Phil Hutchings, "Second Coming," *Guardian*, December 6, 1969, 11. When Weatherman spoke of timidity, it was revealing not a universal about the nature of white people, or white youth, but a characteristic of white middle- and upper-class youth.

69. Klonsky, "Why I Quit," 2.

70. Stern, *With the Weathermen*, 130.

71. Ibid., 127–46; "Weather Report," *Old Mole*, October 14–24, 1969, 14.

72. Carl Davidson and Randy Furst, "Weatherman-SDS Goes It (Very Much) Alone in 'Kick-Ass' Brawl," *Guardian*, October 18, 1969, 4–5; "Weather Report," 14; Tom Thomas, "The Second Battle of Chicago 1969," in Jacobs, *Weatherman*, 203; Ono "You Do Need a Weatherman," 228–274; "Chicago: Weathereport," *Rat*, October 29–November 12, 1969, 16; Hayden, *Reunion*, 360–61; Stern, *With the Weathermen*, 127–46.

73. Stern, *With the Weathermen*, 127–46; "Weather Report," 14; Thomas, "Second Battle of Chicago," 203.

74. Thomas, "Second Battle of Chicago," 203; Ono, "You Do Need a Weatherman," 260–63.

75. Thomas, "Second Battle of Chicago," 222; "Chicago: Weathereport," 16.

76. "Chicago: Weathereport," 16; Thomas, "Second Battle of Chicago," 223; Ono, "You Do Need a Weatherman," 271–74; Weatherman, "Chicago 69," *Fire*, October 21, 1969, n.p. The Black Panther newspaper acknowledged that during the action itself, police withdrew from the black community, but only to return, with a vengeance, after the National Guard was called out. On Friday, October 10, the last evening of Weatherman's action, Chicago police killed two black Chicagoans. "Fascism in Chicago," *Black Panther*, October 25, 1969, 2. Lynn French, a member of the Chicago Panthers at the time, recalled that following these killings, a small Panther contingent went to Weatherman's headquarters to criticize the white radicals. Fred Hampton, who did most of the talking, criticized the Weathermen for their irresponsible actions. French insisted that "we were never into aggressively provoking anything with the police. We were really angry, we thought they were really irresponsible." It seemed to the Panthers that, as they had predicted prior to the Days of Rage, Weatherman's actions *had* brought down increased repression in the black community. French remembers that this criticism session grew heated and wound up with the Panthers physically confronting the Weathermen present. Panther leaders Elaine Brown and David Hilliard also recall, in their respective memoirs of the period, that Weatherman's actions, in Brown's words, "brought down all hell on the black community," just as Fred Hampton had predicted. Brown, *Taste of Power*, 198; Hilliard and Cole, *This Side of Glory*, 258.

77. Eugene Charles, "SDS: A Need for Revolutionary Line," *Black Panther*, October 18, 1969, 3.

78. Ayers, "Strategy to Win," 3.

79. Hayden, *Reunion*, 360.

80. Klonsky, "Revolutionary Youth Movement II," 5, 9.

81. The Illinois Panther criticism of the Days of Rage reiterated this point. In a discussion between Illinois Black Panther Party deputy chairman Fred Hampton and Weathermen leader Mark Rudd, the Panther newspaper reported that Rudd insisted that SDS "was the vanguard of the White community." The *Black Panther* characterized Rudd's contention as "a racist (white-skin chauvinism) statement. There

is only one vanguard for all communities, The Black Panther Party. The one ruling class oppresses both communities, as a result, there can only be one vanguard to lead the assault on that ruling class." Charles, "SDS," 3. In a February 1969 interview with Bernardine Dohrn, SNCC's James Forman had argued the same thing: "it is absolutely essential for whites to be prepared to accept the question of black leadership." Bernardine Dohrn, "NLN Talks to James Forman," *New Left Notes*, February 28, 1969, 12. The black revolutionary union movements that emerged in 1969 and gained SDS's support in various locales similarly asserted, in the words of Dodge Revolutionary Union Movement leader John Watson, that "black workers are the vanguard of the revolutionary movement." Watson bemoaned the great difficulty that SDSers had in appreciating this truth. "Revolutionary Black Workers," *New Left Notes*, May 30, 1969, 6.

82. Randy Furst, "Millions Join Oct. 15 War Protest," *Guardian*, October 25, 1969, 4–5; Tom Wicker, "Dissent: Deepening Threat of a Sharply Divided Nation," *New York Times*, November 16, 1969.

Chapter Five. Reasserting the Centrality of White Radicals

1. "Moratorium," *Helix*, October 23, 1969, 8.

2. Halstead, *Out Now*, 480.

3. Jack Rosenthal, "Protest Organizers Call for an Immediate Cease-Fire," *New York Times*, November 15, 1969.

4. Halstead, *Out Now*, 467–70. In an unpublished memoir Rudd wrote twenty years after the event, the former SDS leader acknowledged that at the Mobe conference he had "sneeringly dismissed all counterarguments. Anybody who proposed a broader action, with less militancy and violence, was a 'liberal.'" Rudd, unpublished manuscript, 201.

5. Wallace Turner, "More Than 100,000 on Coast Demonstrate in Moderate Vein," *New York Times*, November 16, 1969; "Seize the Time," *Movement*, January 1970, 2.

6. Halstead, *Out Now*, 509.

7. John Herbers, "250,000 War Protesters Stage Peaceful Rally in Washington," *New York Times*, November 16, 1969.

8. David Rosenbaum, "Tear Gas in Capital Halts March on Saigon Embassy," *New York Times*, November 15, 1969.

9. Ibid. In Seattle, twenty-five Weathermen broke from a crowd of 4,000 to trash the office windows of some major airlines as well as a restaurant on the march route. Seattle's underground newspaper, *Helix*, offered a tart commentary on the action: "In a statement prepared and delivered to French and English correspondents [in Paris], the North Vietnamese representative . . . called the breaking of two windows in the 'Minute Chef' restaurant in downtown Seattle 'an act which will have a great deal of influence on the Vietnamese peoples' struggle for national liberation.'" "Dispatch," *Helix*, November 20, 1969, 13.

10. John Kifner, "Tear Gas Repels Radicals' Attack," *New York Times*, November 16, 1969; Gitlin, *Sixties*, 395; Abe Peck, "There WAS Violence at the Justice Department," *Rat*, December 6–20, 1969, 6.

11. Weatherman, "Washington November 15, 1969," *Fire*, November 21, 1969, n.p.

12. Weatherman, "Then There's Us," *Fire*, November 21, 1969, n.p.

13. A Weatherwoman, "Inside the Weather Machine," *Rat*, February 6, 1970, 5, 25.

14. Mark Naison, *White Boy* (Philadelphia: Temple University Press, 2002), 128–29.

15. Ibid., 121.

16. Stern, *With the Weathermen*, 168–69. Ron Jacobs, in his account, *The Way the Wind Blew*, puts a cheerful face on Weatherman's smash monogamy program. Jacobs stresses Weatherman's words and sees

the organization's practice as deviating from the ends Weatherman proclaimed: "Weather's opposition to monogamy was based on the belief that it prevented members from taking risks and that the desire to protect the relationship would cause a failure of will. Doing away with traditional forms of monogamy was not necessarily a bad idea and formed part of a strategy to end male supremacist attitudes in the organization, but the authoritarian manner in which it was undertaken caused much useless dissension and emotional stress." Jacobs, *Way the Wind Blew*, 46. In fact, this is backward: smashing monogamy was about retaining male supremacy in the organization, and the "authoritarian manner" simply reflected that end. Most of Jacobs's account follows this same pattern of reading Weatherman's motivations from its words, rather than putting those words in the context of the actual struggles being raised within the movement and between the black movement and the women's movement, on the one hand, and the New Left, on the other.

17. Stern, *With the Weathermen*, 187. In his memoir, Rudd admitted that men in the Weather Bureau quickly grasped "the possibilities in abolishing couples: besides being politically correct, it would make more women available to us!... For me it meant freedom to approach any woman in any collective. And I was rarely turned down, such was the aura and power of my position of leadership.... I could have almost any of these beautiful, strong revolutionary women I desired. I was not the only male member who took advantage of the situation—I can't think of any that didn't." Rudd, unpublished manuscript, 213.

18. Bread and Roses Collective, "Weatherman Politics and the Women's Movement," in Jacobs, *Weatherman*, 335–36.

19. Piercy, "Grand Coolie Damn," 16–19, 22.

20. Robin Morgan, "Goodbye to All That," *Rat*, February 6–23, 1970, 6.

21. Piercy, "Grand Coolie Damn," 18.

22. Bay Area Revolutionary Union, *The Red Papers* (San Francisco: Bay Area Revolutionary Union, 1969), 6. Max Elbaum's history of the "New Communist Movement," *Revolution in the Air*, uncritically touts RU's promoting of women's liberation. Elbaum fails to see that RU was raising women's liberation precisely to defend its own male supremacy. Elbaum, *Revolution in the Air*, 96.

23. Dunbar-Ortiz, *Outlaw Woman*, 298–300.

24. Kathy McAfee and Marcia Salo, "A Caucus-Race and a Long Tale," *Leviathan*, May 1970, 15–18.

25. Ibid., 18–20.

26. Morgan, "Goodbye to All That," 6–7. Todd Gitlin's 1987 book, *The Sixties: Years of Hope, Days of Rage*, is not so far removed from Gitlin's 1970 persona. He characterizes both Morgan's "Goodbye" and Piercy's "Grand Coolie Dam" as "diatribe[s]." Gitlin, *Sixties*, 373.

27. The author can himself testify to the varieties of untreated diseases that Weathermen suffered through in the early winter of 1970. So common were these diseases that they earned their own nickname: "weathercrud."

28. Morgan, "Goodbye to All That," 7.

29. Beulah Richardson, "A Black Woman Speaks" (ca. late 1960s), in author's possession. Thanks to Chude (Pam Parker) Allen for sharing the poem with me.

30. Kathleen Cleaver, interview by author, January 2006.

31. "I Might Have Killed 10 or 15," *Helix*, December 4, 1969, 12.

32. Subsequently, buried away in reports and lawyers' statements or on the inside pages of the newspapers, this conclusion would be further substantiated. Colonel Oran K. Henderson, facing charges of covering up My Lai, insisted that "every unit of brigade size has its Mylai hidden some place." "Colonel Says Every Large Combat Unit in Vietnam Has a Mylai," *New York Times*, May 25, 1971.

33. "My Lai," *Life*, December 5, 1969, 36–45.
34. Clark Kissinger, "Top Illinois Panthers Murdered," *Guardian*, December 13, 1969, 9, 11.
35. Ibid.; "Boom Lowers on Chicago Panthers," Liberation News Service, June 14, 1969, 2; Clark Kissinger, "Raid Chicago Panther Office," *Guardian*, June 14, 1969, 3.
36. Kissinger, "Top Illinois Panthers Murdered," 9, 11; "When All the Cops Are Criminals: Coroner's Jury Finds Hampton Killing 'Justifiable,'" Liberation News Service, January 24, 1970, 2; Clark Kissinger, "5,000 Honor Murdered Panthers," *Guardian*, December 20, 1969, 4.
37. Kissinger, "Top Illinois Panthers Murdered," 11.
38. Karen Wald, "Interview with James Baldwin," Liberation News Service, February 18, 1970, 15.
39. Ayers, *Fugitive Days*, 141.
40. From Ayers's memoir, *Fugitive Days*, the reader would not know that Ayers himself had been elected one of SDS's three national officers in June 1969. Neither would the reader know what happened to SDS. It simply disappears from Ayers's narrative.
41. "SDS Weatherman War Council: Year of the Fork?" *Fifth Estate*, January 22–February 4, 1970, 14.
42. Rudd, unpublished manuscript, 248–49.
43. A Weatherwoman, "War Report," *Rat*, February 24, 1970, 7.
44. Lynn French, who was circulation manager for the *Black Panther* newspaper in Chicago and later was the party's fund-raiser, professed amazement at the pedestal that Weatherman created for Hampton at Flint: "They treated him with disrespect when he was alive. So we were all pretty amazed." French also recalled that, "in terms of real relationships, I think we had more real relationships with the RYM II people than we did with them [the Weathermen].... With the Weatherpeople, they would show up, to talk to Fred or talk to [Panther leader Bobby] Rush. ... They were going to talk to the top and I never felt that they showed any respect to the women in the Party or any desire to know who we were." Lynn French, interview by author, January 2006.
45. Not surprisingly, Dohrn had cleared her proclamation of Manson as revolutionary hero with the Weather Bureau. In other words, this was not an off-the-cuff remark—the picture of Sharon Tate in the gallery of enemies confirmed this as well. Nor was it a joke, as Dohrn and Ayers have later claimed. Howard Machtinger, "Clearing Away the Debris: New Left Radicalism in 1960s America" (Master's thesis, San Francisco State University, 1995), 188.
46. "SDS Weatherman War Council," 14. Later, Dohrn and others would insist that she simply had been joking.
47. Stern, *With the Weathermen*, 205.
48. Tibor Kalman, "Homemade Weather Guide," *Rat*, January 7–20, 1970, 5.
49. "SDS Weatherman War Council," 12.
50. Stern, *With the Weathermen*, 203.
51. Weather Bureau, "Everyone Talks About the Weather," in Jacobs, *Weatherman*, 446–47.
52. Larry Grathwohl, "Terroristic Activity Inside the Weatherman Movement. Hearings before the Subcommittee to Investigate the Administration of the Internal Security Act and Other Internal Security Laws of the Committee on the Judiciary, United States Senate, Ninety-third Congress, Second Session. Part 2" (Washington, D.C.: House Internal Security Subcommittee, 1974), 132.
53. Former New York Weatherman, interview by author, May 2006.
54. Fred Hampton, "They Killed a Revolutionary but They Can't Kill the Revolution," *Movement*, January 1970, 12.

55. Critiques of those white New Leftists, Weatherman in the first place, who labeled the Panthers "revisionist" can be found in Cole, "Volunteers," 15, and Bergman, "Panther's Struggle," 3, among other places. My own recollections from the time and from an April 28, 2003, discussion with another former Columbia University SDS activist also corroborate this as a Weatherman line. Anonymous source, interview by author, May 2006; Lewis Cole, interview by author, May 2006; Varon, *Bringing the War Home*, 155.

56. Louis Segal, letter to the author, November 23, 2001, in author's possession. Max Elbaum refers to this same kind of action: "Talking glibly about (although never actually implementing) tactics such as assassinating police officers in minority communities in order to bring down repression and thus radicalize more people of color—an outright racist position despite its ultrarevolutionary guise—didn't win many friends among radicals of any color either." Elbaum, *Revolution in the Air*, 71. In preparing this book, I spoke with half a dozen former Weathermen, most of whom could not recall either the notion that the Panthers were revisionist or the corollary for that position—that Weatherman would inspire a new black vanguard through its anonymous actions in the black community. I can only conclude that this was not a consolidated Weatherman line. Nonetheless, this position was the logical conclusion of Weatherman's politics, consistent with the notion that Weatherman would stimulate a Third World revolutionary upsurge that would destroy U.S. imperialism, and this position was articulated in different parts of the Weathermen organization prior to, and possibly for a short time after, the town house explosion.

57. Reed et al., "It's Only People's Games," 436.

58. Eldridge Cleaver, "On Weatherman," in Jacobs, *Weatherman*, 295; reprinted from the *Berkeley Tribe*, November 7, 1969. The *Black Panther* republished Cleaver's article on November 22, 1969.

59. In *Outlaws of America*, Dan Berger finesses Weatherman's handling of its differences with Hampton and the Panthers by insisting that "by 1969 fissures within the group [the Panthers] were becoming more apparent," and pointing to the fact that while Hampton condemned the Days of Rage, the New York Panthers "largely cheered Weather's militancy" (108). It is true that the New York Panthers sided with Cleaver in the Black Panther Party split, but this split occurred well after the Days of Rage. More to the point, the New York Panther leaders, scattered about New York City's prison system during the summer and fall of 1969, were in no position to communicate with each other, much less support Weatherman in its feud with Fred Hampton. Berger also entirely leaves out of his account Weatherman's earlier rejection of the Panther UFAF program. It is also true that from time to time, other well-known black leaders, SNCC's James Forman and Rap Brown, for example, called for white radical retaliation for crimes committed against the black community. However, SNCC, like the Panthers, had taken a clear organizational position that whites needed to be organizing in white communities against the racism there. The two positions do not necessarily contradict each other—but Weatherman renounced both the Panthers' and SNCC's formal organizational position, making the two positions contradictory.

60. "Home of Justice Murtaugh [*sic*], Panther 21 Judge, Is Bombed," Liberation News Service, February 25, 1970, 16.

61. Bernardine Dohrn and the Weather Underground, "New Morning, Changing Weather," in *The Weather Eye: Communiques from the Weather Underground, May 1970–May 1974*, ed. Jonah Raskin (New York: Union Square Press, 1974), 28; *The Weather Underground*, directed by Sam Green and Bill Siegel (2003).

62. Rudd, unpublished manuscript, 202, 260.

63. Ibid., 259.

64. Dohrn and the Weather Underground, "New Morning," 28.

65. Carl Davidson, "Women Lead Founding of RYM," *Guardian*, December 20, 1969, 7.

66. Ibid.

67. Sale, *SDS*, 621.

68. Federal Bureau of Investigation, Atlanta Office, "Microfilm FBI Files on SDS and the Weather Underground" (1971).

69. Bay Area Revolutionary Union, *Red Papers*, 3–9. Max Elbaum (*Revolution in the Air*, 97) interprets RU's insistence that "a 'major section of the leadership' must and would come from people of color" as an advance for white activists, rather than a retreat.

70. Elbaum, *Revolution in the Air*, 102.

71. Phil Hutchings, "Second Coming: Marxism and Black Power," *Guardian*, January 17, 1970, 11; Phil Hutchings, "Second Coming: Movement Relations—Blacks and Whites," *Guardian*, March 7, 1970, 11.

72. Elbaum, *Revolution in the Air*, 106; Sojourner Truth Organization, "Editorial," *Urgent Tasks*, May 1977, 2.

73. "The Official National Strike Call," Liberation News Service, May 6, 1970, 20a.

74. Jeff Gerth, "Slaughter at Kent State," Liberation News Service, May 6, 1970, 1–2.

75. Carl Davidson, "Antiwar Movement Explodes," *Guardian*, May 9, 1970, 3, 6; "On Strike!" Liberation News Service, May 9, 1970, 1; "Nine Days in May," Liberation News Service, May 16, 1970, 11–24; Rod Such, "Millions Protest against Cambodia Invasion throughout the U.S.," *Guardian*, May 23, 1970, 6–7.

76. Davidson, "Antiwar Movement Explodes," 3, 6.

77. The Weathermen, of course, later claimed credit for this upsurge of militancy: Weatherman had set the precedent, they claimed, during the Days of Rage. But as we've seen, militant activity against ROTC, war research, and the like had been on the rise since the fall of 1967. Moreover, no necessary contradiction existed here either between the organizing and educating that the Vietnamese had projected for the antiwar movement and the militancy displayed in May 1970 and earlier. But Weatherman did renounce organization, and thus rejected the Vietnamese vision. And even if it were true that Weatherman set the precedent followed by the May 1970 events, the loss of SDS as a center for educating and organizing masses of people had a tremendous debilitating effect on the movement.

78. Rudd, unpublished manuscript, 276.

79. "6 Blacks Slain in Augusta," *Guardian*, May 23, 1970, 5; "Avenge the August Seven," *Miami Daily Planet*, June 8, 1970, 8.

80. "2 Blacks Slain in Jackson," *Guardian*, May 23, 1970, 5; "Jackson Police Fire on Students," *New York Times*, May 15, 1970; Roy Reed, "Blacks Start Wide Protest on Police Killings in South," *New York Times*, May 18, 1970.

81. Reed, "Blacks Start Wide Protest."

82. Julius Lester, "Aquarian Notebook," *Liberation*, June 1970, 39.

83. Such, "Millions Protest," 7.

Conclusion

1. James Baldwin, "No Name in the Street," in *Collected Essays* (New York: Modern Library, 1998), 405.

2. Baldwin, *Fire Next Time*, 96.

Bibliography

"Agent Orange Website." http://www.lewispublishing.com/orange.htm.

Allen, Pam. "Memo to My White Sisters in Our Struggle to Realize Our Full Humanity." New York: New York Radical Women, 1968.

Allen, Robert, and Pam Allen. *Reluctant Reformers: Racism and Social Reform Movements in the United States.* Washington, D.C.: Howard University Press, 1974.

Alpert, Jane. *Growing Up Underground.* New York: William Morrow, 1981.

Amatniek, Kathy. "Funeral Oration for Traditional Womanhood." In *Notes from the First Year.* New York, 1968.

Aronowitz, Stanley. "On the Line." *Guardian,* June 28, 1969.

Ashley, Karin, Bill Ayers, Bernardine Dohrn, John Jacobs, Jeff Jones, Gerry Long, Howie Machtinger, Jim Mellen, Terry Robbins, Mark Rudd, and Steve Tappis. "You Don't Need a Weatherman to Know Which Way the Wind Blows." *New Left Notes,* June 18, 1969.

"Attack on Militants—The Man Moves Hard: Where Are We?" *New Left Notes,* March 11, 1968.

Ayers, Bill. *Fugitive Days.* Boston: Beacon Press, 2001.

———. "A Strategy to Win." *New Left Notes,* September 12, 1969.

Ayers, Bill, and Jim Mellen. "Hot Town: Summer in the City, or, I Ain't Gonna Work on Maggie's Farm No More." *New Left Notes,* April 5, 1969.

Baldwin, James. *The Fire Next Time.* New York: Vintage International, 1993.

———. "No Name in the Street." In *Collected Essays.* New York: Modern Library, 1998.

Bay Area Revolutionary Union. *The Red Papers.* San Francisco: Bay Area Revolutionary Union, 1969.

Berger, Dan. *Outlaws of America: The Weather Underground and the Politics of Solidarity.* Oakland, Calif.: AK Press, 2006.

Bergman, Arlene Eisen. "Panther's Struggle Is the People's Struggle." *Movement,* October 1969.

"Black Power Conference." *New Left Notes,* December 9, 1966.

Block, Steve. "There's a Change Gonna Come." *New Left Notes,* July 24, 1967.

"Blows against the Empire." *Rat,* April 4, 1968.

"Boom Lowers on Chicago Panthers." Liberation News Service, June 14, 1969.

Booth, Paul. "Letter to SNCC." *New Left Notes,* June 2, 10, 1966.

———. "National Program Outlined at Dec. NC for Coming Months." *New Left Notes,* January 21, 1966.

———. "National Secretary's Report." *New Left Notes,* June 17, 1966.

Boudin, Kathy, Bernardine Dohrn, and Terry Robbins. "Bringing the War Back Home, Less Talk, More National Action." *New Left Notes,* August 23, 1969.

Braden, Anne. "White Organizing and White Racism." *New Left Notes,* June 24, 1966.

Bread and Roses Collective. "Weatherman Politics and the Women's Movement." In *Weatherman,* ed. Harold Jacobs. Berkeley, Calif.: Ramparts Press, 1970.

Breines, Winifred. *Community and Organization in the New Left: 1962–1968.* South Hadley, Mass.: Praeger, 1982.

———. *The Trouble between Us: An Uneasy History of White and Black Women.* New York: Oxford University Press, 2006.

———. "Whose New Left?" *Journal of American History* (September 1988).

"Brooklyn College Strike." *New Left Notes,* October 23, 1967.

Brooks, Robin. "Leroi Jones in Atlanta: Black Power and White Liberals." *New Left Notes,* September 2, 1966.

Brown, Elaine. *A Taste of Power: A Black Woman's Story.* New York: Doubleday, 1992.

Brownmiller, Susan. *In Our Time: Memoir of a Revolution.* New York: Dial Press, 1999.

Buck, Marilyn. "In the Interim." *New Left Notes,* August 21, 1967.

Burchett, Wilfred. *Vietnam: Inside Story of the Guerrilla War.* New York: International, 1965.

Calvert, Greg. "In White America: Radical Consciousness and Social Change." In *The New Left: A Documentary History,* ed. Massimo Teodori. Indianapolis, Ind.: Bobbs-Merrill, 1969.

Carmichael, Stokely. *Black Power and Its Challenges. Address to Black Power Day Conference.* Berkeley, Calif.: Academic Publishing, Lecture Transcripts, 1966.

———. "What We Want." *New York Review of Books,* September 22, 1966. http://www.csulb.edu/
~rschmidt/08-StokelyCarmichael-WhatWeWant-NYRB66.htm.

Carson, Clayborne. *In Struggle: SNCC and the Black Awakening of the 1960s.* Cambridge, Mass.: Harvard University Press, 1981.

———, ed. *The Student Voice, 1960–1965: Periodical of the Student Nonviolent Coordinating Committee.* Westport, Conn.: Meckler, 1990.

Caute, David. *The Year of the Barricades: A Journey through 1968.* New York: Harper and Row, 1988.

Charles, Eugene. "SDS: A Need for Revolutionary Line." *Black Panther,* October 18, 1969.

"Chicago: Weathereport." *Rat,* October 29–November 12, 1969.

"Chronology of Repression." *Old Mole,* December 17–January 8, 1970.

Churchill, Ward, and Jim VanderWall. *The COINTELPRO Papers: Documents from the FBI's Secret Wars against Dissent in the United States.* Boston: South End Press, 1989.

Cleaver, Eldridge. "Eldridge Cleaver on Women's Liberation." *Guardian,* August 2, 1969.

———. "On Weatherman." In *Weatherman,* ed. Harold Jacobs. Berkeley, Calif.: Ramparts Press, 1970.

———. *Post-Prison Writings and Speeches.* New York: Ramparts Books, 1969.

———. *Soul on Ice.* New York: Dell, 1968.

Cleaver, Kathleen. "Kathleen Cleaver Replies to Lester." *New Left Notes,* May 1, 1969.

Cole, Lew. "Volunteers." *Leviathan,* February 1970.

Coleman, Les, and Chicago Regional SDS. "The Schools Must Serve the People." *New Left Notes,* March 20, 1969.

"Curry, Constance, Joan Browning, Dorothy Dawson Burlage, Penny Patch, Theresa Del Pozzo, Sue Thrasher, Elaine DeLott Baker, Emmie Schrader Adams, and Casey Hayden. *Deep in Our Hearts: Nine White Women in the Freedom Movement.* Athens: University of Georgia Press, 2000.

Davidson, Carl. "Antiwar Movement Explodes." *Guardian*, May 9, 1970.

———. "Toward Institutional Resistance." *New Left Notes*, November 13, 1967.

———. "U.S. Radicals Meet with PRG in Cuba." *Guardian*, August 30, 1969.

———. "Why SDS Expelled PL." *Guardian*, July 24, 1969.

———. "Women Lead Founding of RYM." *Guardian*, December 20, 1969.

Davidson, Carl, and Randy Furst. "Weatherman-SDS Goes It (Very Much) Alone in 'Kick-Ass' Brawl." *Guardian*, October 18, 1969.

Davis, Rennie, and Staughton Lynd. "On NCNP." *New Left Notes*, September 4, 1967.

"December Conference & NC." *New Left Notes*, November 18, 1966.

Dellinger, David. *More Power Than We Know: The People's Movement toward Democracy*. Garden City, N.Y.: Anchor Press, 1975.

Del Pozzo, Theresa. "The Feel of a Blue Note." In Constance Curry et al., *Deep in Our Hearts: Nine White Women in the Freedom Movement*. Athens: University of Georgia Press, 2000.

Densmore, Dana. "A Year of Living Dangerously." In *The Feminist Memoir Project*, ed. Rachel Blau DuPlessis and Ann Snitow. New York: Three Rivers Press, 1998.

Detroit Weatherman. "Break on Through to the Other Side." Liberation News Service, August 28, 1969.

"Dispatch." *Helix*, November 20, 1969.

Dohrn, Bernardine. "NLN Talks to James Forman." *New Left Notes*, February 28, 1969.

———. "White Mother Country Radicals." *New Left Notes*, July 29, 1968.

Dohrn, Bernardine, and Naomi Jaffee. "The Look Is You." In *New Left: A Documentary History*, ed. Massimo Teodori. Indianapolis, Ind.: Bobbs-Merrill, 1969.

Dohrn, Bernardine, and the Weather Underground. "New Morning, Changing Weather." In *The Weather Eye: Communiques from the Weather Underground, May 1970–May 1974*, ed. Jonah Raskin. New York: Union Square Press, 1974.

DuBois, Ellen Carol. "Dare to Struggle, Dare to Win." *Radical History Review* (Winter 1991).

DuBois, W. E. B. *Black Reconstruction*. New York: Athenaeum Press, 1935.

———. *W. E. B. DuBois: A Reader*. Ed. David Levering Lewis. New York: Henry Holt, 1995.

Dunbar-Ortiz, Roxanne. *Outlaw Woman: A Memoir of the War Years, 1960–1975*. San Francisco: City Lights, 2001.

Echols, Alice. *Daring to Be Bad: Radical Feminism in America, 1967–1975*. Minneapolis: University of Minnesota Press, 1989.

Elbaum, Max. *Revolution in the Air: Sixties Radicals Turn to Lenin, Mao and Che*. New York: Verso Press, 2002.

Evans, Sara. *Personal Politics: The Roots of Women's Liberation in the Civil Rights Movement and the New Left*. New York: Vintage Books, 1979.

———. "Women's Consciousness and the Southern Black Movement." *Southern Exposure* (Winter 1977).

Fanon, Frantz. *Toward the African Revolution*. New York: Grove Press, 1969.

"Fascism in Chicago." *Black Panther*, October 25, 1969.

Federal Bureau of Investigation, Atlanta Office. "Microfilm FBI Files on SDS and the Weather Underground." 1971.

Federal Bureau of Investigation Director. "Counterintelligence Program; Black Nationalist—Hate Groups; Internal Security." Washington, D.C.: Federal Bureau of Investigation, 1967.

Firestone, Shulamith. "The Jeanette Rankin Brigade: Woman Power." In *Notes from the First Year*. New York, 1968.

———. "The Women's Rights Movement in the U.S.A.: New View." In *Notes from the First Year*. New York, 1968.

Fleming, Cynthia Griggs. *Soon We Will Not Cry: The Liberation of Ruby Doris Smith Robinson*. New York: Rowman and Littlefield, 1998.

Foner, Philip S., ed. *The Black Panthers Speak*. New York: J. B. Lippincott, 1970.

Forman, James. *The Making of Black Revolutionaries*. New York: MacMillan Press, 1972.

Frankenberg, Ruth. *White Women, Race Matters: The Social Construction of Whiteness*. Minneapolis: University of Minnesota Press, 1993.

Fraser, Ronald. *1968: A Student Generation in Revolt*. London: Chatto and Windus, 1988.

Freeman, Jo. "On the Origins of the Women's Liberation Movement." In *The Feminist Memoir Project: Voices from Women's Liberation*, ed. Rachel Blau DuPlessis and Ann Snitow. New York: Three Rivers Press, 1998.

"From Protest to Resistance: Students Battle Cops." *New Left Notes*, October 23, 1967.

Furst, Randy. "It Was Cold-Blooded Murder." *New Left Notes*, February 26, 1968.

———. "Millions Join Oct. 15 War Protest." *Guardian*, October 25, 1969.

Gellen, Karen. "We Made the News Today Oh Boy." *New Left Notes*, February 12, 26, 1968, March 4, 1968, April 15, 1968.

Gerth, Jeff. "Slaughter at Kent State." Liberation News Service, May 6, 1970.

Giddings, Paula. *When and Where I Enter: The Impact of Black Women on Race and Sex in America*. New York: William Morrow, 1984.

Gitlin, Todd. "On Organizing the Poor in America." *New Left Notes*, December 23, 1966.

———. "Potentials of the Poor." *New Left Notes*, June 22, 1967.

———. *The Sixties: Years of Hope, Days of Rage*. New York: Bantam Books, 1987.

———. "The Texture of the Cuban Revolution." *New Left Notes*, February 12, 1968.

Glasby, Floyd. "Black and White Rebellion." *New Left Notes*, August 21, 1967.

Goldfield, Michael. "The Washington Siege of '67: Power at the Pentagon." *New Left Notes*, October 30, 1967.

Gottlieb, Robert, Gerry Tenney, and David Gilbert. "Toward a Theory of Social Change in America." *New Left Notes*, June 22, 1967.

Grathwohl, Larry. "Terroristic Activity Inside the Weatherman Movement. Hearings before the Subcommittee to Investigate the Administration of the Internal Security Act and Other Internal Security Laws of the Committee on the Judiciary, United States Senate, Ninety-third Congress, Second Session. Part 2." Washington, D.C.: House Internal Security Subcommittee, 1975.

Greenberg, Cheryl Lynn. *A Circle of Trust: Remembering SNCC*. New Brunswick, N.J.: Rutgers University Press, 1998.

Haber, Al. "Radical Education Project—Draft for Discussion and Comment." *New Left Notes*, March 25, 1966.

Halliwell, Steve. "New Leftists Meet with the NLF: A Society in Revolution." *New Left Notes*, October 2, 1967.

Halstead, Fred. *Out Now: A Participant's Account of the American Movement against the Vietnam War*. New York: Monad Press, 1978.

Hampton, Fred. "They Killed a Revolutionary but They Can't Kill the Revolution." *Movement*, January 1970.

Hanisch, Carol. "The Personal Is Political." In *Notes from the Second Year*. New York, 1970.

Hayden, Casey. "Fields of Blue." In Constance Curry et al., *Deep in Our Hearts: Nine White Women in the Freedom Movement*. Athens: University of Georgia Press, 2000.

Hayden, Tom. *Rebellion in Newark*. New York: Vintage Books, 1967.

———. *Reunion: A Memoir*. New York: Collier Books, 1988.

Henderson, Errol. "Shadow of a Clue." In *Liberation, Imagination, and the Black Panther Party: A New Look at the Panthers and Their Legacy*, ed. Kathleen Cleaver and George Katsiaficas. New York: Routledge, 2001.

Herring, George C. *America's Longest War: The United States and Vietnam, 1950–1975*. New York: McGraw-Hill, 1996.

Hilliard, David, and Lewis Cole. *This Side of Glory: The Autobiography of David Hilliard and the Story of the Black Panther Party*. Boston: Little, Brown, 1993.

Hilliard, David, and Bobby Seale. "Our Enemy's Friends Are Also Our Enemies." *Black Panther*, August 9, 1969.

"Home of Justice Murtaugh [*sic*], Panther 21 Judge, Is Bombed." Liberation News Service, February 25, 1970.

Hutchings, Phil. "Second Coming." *Guardian*, December 6, 1969.

———. "Second Coming: Marxism and Black Power." *Guardian*, January 17, 1970.

———. "Second Coming: Movement Relations—Blacks and Whites." *Guardian*, March 7, 1970.

Ignatin, Noel. "Learn the Lessons of U.S. History." *New Left Notes*, March 25, 1968.

———. "Revolutionary Struggle for Women's Liberation." *New Left Notes*, December 23, 1968.

"I Might Have Killed 10 or 15." *Helix*, December 4, 1969.

"International Women's Day." *New Left Notes*, March 1969.

Isserman, Maurice. "Where Have All the Convict Heroes Gone, Long Time Passing." *Radical History Review* (Winter 1996).

Isserman, Maurice, and Michael Kazin. *America Divided: The Civil War of the 1960s*. New York: Oxford University Press, 2000.

Jackson, Donald. "An Open Letter to ERAP." *New Left Notes*, August 5, 1966.

Jacobs, Harold, ed. *Weatherman*. Berkeley, Calif.: Ramparts Press, 1970.

Jacobs, Ron. *The Way the Wind Blew: A History of the Weather Underground*. New York: Verso Press, 1997.

Jacobson, Jon. "Naked Lunch." *Rat*, January 17, 1969.

James, Mike. "ERAP Report JOIN." *New Left Notes*, August 24, 1966.

Jehlen, Allen. "Black Power and Political Strategy." *New Left Notes*, November 11, 1966.

———. "The NCNP Convention . . . William Pepper's Lonely Hearts' Club Band." *New Left Notes*, October 9, 1967.

Jennings, Ed, and Chicago Circle Campus SDS. "The Black Panther Party: Toward the Liberation of the Colony." *New Left Notes*, April 5, 1969.

Jones, Beverly. "Towards Women's Liberation." *Guardian*, January 18, 1969.

Jones, Beverly, and Judith Brown. *Towards a Female Liberation Movement*. Boston: New England Free Press, 1968.

Jones, Jeff. "Report on the Student Mobilization Committee in General and National Student Strike in Particular." *New Left Notes*, November 10, 1967.

Kagin, J. H. *White Blindspot*. New York: Osawotomie, 1967.

Kalman, Tibor. "Homemade Weather Guide." *Rat*, January 7–20, 1970.

Katz, Marilyn, and Chicago Regional SDS. "May Day Proposal." *New Left Notes*, March 20, 1969.

Kennedy, John F. *A Strategy of Peace*. New York: Harper, 1960.

Kerner Commission. *Report of the National Advisory Commission on Civil Disorders*. New York: Bantam Books, 1968.

Kesselman, Amy, with Heather Booth, Vivian Rothstein, and Naomi Weisstein. "Our Gang of Four: Friendships and Women's Liberation." 1998. http://www.cwluherstory.com/CWLUMemoir.

———. "Our Gang of Four: Friendships and Women's Liberation." In *The Feminist Memoir Project: Voices from Women's Liberation*, ed. Rachel Blau DuPlessis and Ann Snitow. New York: Three Rivers Press, 1998.

King, Mary. *Freedom Song: A Personal Story of the 1960s Civil Rights Movement*. New York: Morrow, 1987.

Kissinger, Clark. "5,000 Honor Murdered Panthers." *Guardian*, December 20, 1969.

———. "Raid Chicago Panther Office." *Guardian*, June 14, 1969.

———. "Top Illinois Panthers Murdered." *Guardian*, December 13, 1969.

Klonsky, Mike. "The State of SDS." *New Left Notes*, June 24, 1968.

———. "Toward a Revolutionary Youth Movement." *New Left Notes*, December 23, 1968.

———. "The White Question." *New Left Notes*, March 20, 1969.

———. "Why I Quit." *New Left Notes*, August 29, 1969.

Klonsky, Mike, Noel Ignatin, Sue Eanet, and Les Coleman. "Revolutionary Youth Movement II." *New Left Notes*, July 8, 1969.

Kunen, James Simon. *The Strawberry Statement*. New York: Random House, 1969.

Lawson, Bob, and Mike James. "Poor White Response to Black Rebellion." *New Left Notes*, August 21, 1967.

Lemisch, Jesse, and Naomi Weisstein. "Remarks on Naomi Weisstein." 1997. http://www.cwluherstory.com/CWLUMemoir/weisstein.html.

Lester, Julius. "Aquarian Notebook." *Liberation*, June 1970.

———. "From the Other Side of the Tracks." *Guardian*, May 10, 1969.

———. "Lester Attacks Panther Resolution as Racist." *New Left Notes*, April 24, 1969.

"Liberation of Women." *New Left Notes*, July 10, 1967.

Lim, Shirley Geok-lin. " 'Ain't I a Feminist?': Re-forming the Circle." In *The Feminist Memoir Project*, ed. Rachel Blau DuPlessis and Ann Snitow. New York: Three Rivers Press, 1998.

Lipsitz, George. "The Possessive Investment in Whiteness." *American Quarterly* 47, no. 3 (1995).

Lynd, Staughton. "On White People." *New Left Notes*, August 24, 1966.

Machtinger, Howard. "Analysis of the Youth Movement." *New Left Notes*, January 22, 1969.

———. "Clearing Away the Debris: New Left Radicalism in 1960s America." Master's thesis, San Francisco State University, 1995.

Malcolm X. *By Any Means Necessary*. New York: Pathfinder Press, 1970.

———. *Malcolm X Speaks*. 1965. Reprint, New York: Grove Weidenfeld, 1990.

Malcolm X, with Alex Haley. *The Autobiography of Malcolm X*. New York: Grove Press, 1965.

Mann, Eric. "Newark Riots—NCUP Views." *New Left Notes*, July 24, 1967.

Martinez, Elizabeth. *De Colores Means All of Us*. Cambridge, Mass.: South End Press, 1998.

———. "History Makes Us, We Make History." In *The Feminist Memoir Project*, ed. Rachel Blau DuPlessis and Ann Snitow. New York: Three Rivers Press, 1998.

McAfee, Kathy, and Marcia Salo. "A Caucus-Race and a Long Tale." *Leviathan*, May 1970.

McAfee, Kathy, and Myrna Wood. "On Women: Bread and Roses." *Kaleidoscope*, November 1, 1969.

Miller, James. *"Democracy Is in the Streets": From Port Huron to the Siege of Chicago.* New York: Simon and Schuster, 1987.

Moody, Kim, Fred Eppsteiner, and Mike Flug. "Toward the Working Class (An SDS Convention Position Paper)." *New Left Notes,* July 29, 1966.

"Moratorium." *Helix,* October 23, 1969.

Morgan, Robin. "Do You Know What's Happening, Mister Jones?" Liberation News Service, July 17, 1969.

———. "Goodbye to All That." *Rat,* February 6–23, 1970.

———. "Miss America Goes Down." *Rat,* September 20–October 3, 1968.

Morrison, Toni. *Playing in the Dark: Whiteness and the Literary Imagination.* Cambridge, Mass.: Harvard University Press, 1992.

Munaker, Sue. " 'In the Belly of the Beast,' Report on the Stockholm Conf." *New Left Notes,* May 13, 1968.

"My Lai." *Life,* December 5, 1969.

Naison, Mark. *White Boy.* Philadelphia: Temple University Press, 2002.

Newton, Huey. "A Prison Interview." In *The New Left Reader,* ed. Carl Oglesby. New York: Grove Press, 1969.

New York Radical Women. "Miss America Protest Press Release." Liberation News Service, September 2, 1968.

Nguyen, Khac Vien. *Glimpses of United States Neo-Colonialism: United States Neo-Colonialism in South Vietnam.* In *Vietnamese Studies,* No. 31, ed. Nguyen Khac Vien. Hanoi: Xunhasaba, 1971.

Nguyen, Van Ba. "United States Aggression in Vietnam." In *Vietnamese Studies,* No. 12, ed. Nguyen Khac Vien. Hanoi: Xunhasaba, 1966.

NIC. "Fifth Party Ticket: Cleaver and Oglesby." *New Left Notes,* September 9, 1968.

———. "Why Oglesby Won't Run." *New Left Notes,* September 9, 1968.

NIC, SDS. "NIC Statement on UFAF." *New Left Notes,* July 24, 1969.

"Nine Days in May." Liberation News Service, May 16, 1970.

Norden, Eric. *America's Barbarities in Vietnam.* New Delhi: Mainstream, 1966.

"Oakland Police Attack Panthers." *New Left Notes,* April 15, 1968.

O'Brien, Jim. *American Leninism in the 1970s.* Boston: New England Free Press, 1978.

"The Official National Strike Call." Liberation News Service, May 6, 1970.

Oglesby, Carl. "Liberalism and the Corporate State." *New Left Notes,* January 21, 1966.

———. "An Open Letter: Dear McCarthy Supporters." *New Left Notes,* August 19, 1968.

———. "Vietnam: This Is Guernica." *New Left Notes.*

———. "World Revolution and American Containment." *New Left Notes,* April 8, 1966.

———, ed. *The New Left Reader.* New York: Grove Press, 1969.

Oglesby, Carl, and Richard Schaull. *Containment and Change.* New York: Macmillan, 1967.

Omolade, Barbara. "Sisterhood in Black and White." In *Feminist Memoir Project: Voices from Women's Liberation,* ed. Rachel Blau DuPlessis and Ann Snitow. New York: Three Rivers Press, 1998.

Ono, Shin'ya. "You Do Need a Weatherman to Know Which Way the Wind Blows." In *Weatherman,* ed. Harold Jacobs. Berkeley, Calif.: Ramparts Press, 1970.

"On Roles in SDS." *New Left Notes,* January 28, 1966.

"On Strike!" Liberation News Service, May 9, 1970.

Ortiz, Roxanne Dunbar. *Outlaw Woman: A Memoir of the War Years.* San Francisco: City Lights Books, 2002.

Painter, Nell Irvin. "Slavery and Soul Murder." In *Black on White: Black Writers on What It Means to Be White*, ed. David Roediger. New York: Schocken Books, 1998.

Payne, Charles. *I've Got the Light of Freedom: The Organizing Tradition and the Mississippi Freedom Struggle*. Berkeley: University of California Press, 1995.

Peck, Abe. "There WAS Violence at the Justice Department." *Rat*, December 6–20, 1969.

Piercy, Marge. "The Grand Coolie Dam." In *Sisterhood Is Powerful: An Anthology of Writings from the Women's Liberation Movement*, ed. Robin Morgan. New York: Vintage Books, 1970.

"Port Huron Statement." 1962. http://www.tomhayden.com/porthuron.htm.

Potter, Paul. "Name the System." 1965. http://www.sdsrebels.com/potter.htm.

Powers, Thomas. *Diana: Portrait of a Terrorist*. Boston: Houghton Mifflin, 1971.

Progressive Labor Party. "Fight Racism: Build a Worker-Student Alliance: Smash Imperialism. Resolution Passed by December 1968 SDS National Council Meeting." *New Left Notes*, January 8, 1969.

———. "Road to Revolution II." In *Revolution Today: A Look at the Progressive Labor Movement and the Progressive Labor Party*. Jericho, N.Y.: Exposition Press, 1970.

Reed, Norman, Inessa, Victor Camilo, and Lilina Jones. "It's Only People's Games That You Got to Dodge." In *Weatherman*, ed. Harold Jacobs. Berkeley, Calif.: Ramparts Press, 1970.

"Resolution on Racism." *New Left Notes*, April 8, 1968.

"Revolutionary Black Workers." *New Left Notes*, May 30, 1969.

Richardson, Beulah. "A Black Woman Speaks." Ca. late 1960s. In author's possession.

Robbins, Terry, and Bill Ayers. "Give It a Name/Call It SDS/Join Us." *New Left Notes*, October 7, 1968.

Robnett, Belinda. *How Long? How Long? African-American Women in the Struggle for Civil Rights*. New York: Oxford University Press, 1997.

Roediger, David. *The Wages of Whiteness*. New York: Verso Press, 1991.

Rorabaugh, W. J. *Berkeley at War, the 1960s*. New York: Oxford University Press, 1989.

Rosen, Ruth. *The World Split Open: How the Modern Women's Movement Changed America*. New York: Penguin Books, 2000.

Rossinow, Doug. "The New Left in the Counterculture: Hypotheses and Evidence." *Radical History Review* 67 (Winter 1997).

———. *The Politics of Authenticity, Liberalism, Christianity and the New Left in America*. New York: Columbia University Press, 1998.

Rothstein, Richard. "Evolution of the ERAP Organizers." In *The New Left: A Collection of Essays*, ed. Priscilla Long. Boston: Extending Horizon Books, 1969.

Rudd, Mark. "Columbia: Notes on the Spring Rebellion." In *The New Left Reader*, ed. Carl Oglesby. New York: Grove Press, 1969.

———. "Just a Few Subway Stops from Wall St." *New Left Notes*, June 10, 1968.

———. Unpublished manuscript. Ca. 1988–89. In author's possession.

Russell, Bertrand. "Appeal to the American Conscience." *New Left Notes*, August 24, 1966.

RYM II. "Proposed SDS Unity Principles." *New Left Notes*, July 8, 1969.

Saari, John. "Berkeley, Stanford and Black Power." *New Left Notes*, November 4, 1966.

Sale, Kirkpatrick. *SDS*. New York: Vintage Books, 1973.

SDS, Berkeley. "Proposal for 'BLACK POWER DAY' in Berkeley." October 1966. In Social Protest Collection, Bancroft Library, University of California, Berkeley.

SDS, Motor City. "Break on Through to the Other Side." *New Left Notes*, August 29, 1969.

SDS, Northern California Regional Office. In Social Protest Collection (Banc mss 86/157), carton 17:4, Bancroft Library, University of California, Berkeley, 1966.

SDS, Southern California Regional Council. "Relationships to Black and Brown Movements." *New Left Notes*, February 28, 1969.

"SDS Convention: The Way It Was." *Old Mole*, July 4–17, 1969.

"SDS Statement on SNCC." *New Left Notes*, June 24, 1966.

"SDS Weatherman War Council: Year of the Fork?" *Fifth Estate*, January 22–February 4, 1970.

"SDS Women Hit Pitt High School." *Guardian*, September 13, 1969.

Segal, Louis. Letter to the author, November 23, 2001. In author's possession.

"Seize the Time." *Movement*, January 1970.

Shero, Jeff. "Shero—Our Man in Moscow, from Russia with Love." *New Left Notes*, August 21, 1967.

———. "Wanna See My Pussy." *Rat*, December 13, 1969.

Silbar, Earl. "Race War and White Radicals." *New Left Notes*, June 12, 1967.

"6 Blacks Slain in Augusta." *Guardian*, May 23, 1970.

Smith, Barbara. " 'Feisty Characters' and 'Other People's Causes.' " In *The Feminist Memoir Project*, ed. Rachel Blau DuPlessis and Ann Snitow. New York: Three Rivers Press, 1998.

Smith, Jack. "SDS Ousts PLP." *Guardian*, June 28, 1969.

Sojourner Truth Organization. "Editorial." *Urgent Tasks*, May 1977.

Spiegel, Mike. "The Growing Development of a Class Politics." *New Left Notes*, June 10, 1968.

Stamberg, Margie. "SDS Deals with the Woman Question." *Guardian*, June 28, 1969.

———. "Women at UFAF and After." *Guardian*, August 2, 1969.

"The Steel City 26: SDS Women Vamp on Pittsburgh." Liberation News Service, September 13, 1969.

Stern, Susan. *With the Weathermen: The Personal Journey of a Revolutionary Woman*. New York: Doubleday, 1975.

Stevens, Carol. "SDS Re-examined at Dec. Conference." *New Left Notes*, January 21, 1966.

Stoper, Emily. *The Student Nonviolent Coordinating Committee: The Growth of Radicalism in a Civil Rights Organization*. Brooklyn, N.Y.: Carlson, 1989.

"Strike Over but Struggle Goes On. Interview with Tony Miranda, Nesbit Crutchfield and Mason Wong." *Movement*, May 1969.

Such, Rod. "Millions Protest against Cambodia Invasion throughout the U.S." *Guardian*, May 23, 1970.

Sugrue, Thomas. *The Origins of the Urban Crisis: Race and Inequality in Postwar Detroit*. Princeton, N.J.: Princeton University Press, 1996.

Sutheim, Susan. "Women Shake Up SDS Session." *Guardian*, June 22, 1968.

Tate, Sonsyrea. *Little X, Growing Up in the Nation of Islam*. San Francisco: Harper SanFrancisco, 1997.

Teodori, Massimo, ed. *The New Left: A Documentary History*. Indianapolis, Ind.: Bobbs-Merrill, 1969.

Thomas, Tom. "The Second Battle of Chicago 1969." In *Weatherman*, ed. Harold Jacobs. Berkeley, Calif.: Ramparts Press, 1970.

Thrasher, Sue. "Circle of Trust." In Constance Curry et al., *Deep in Our Hearts: Nine White Women in the Freedom Movement*. Athens: University of Georgia Press, 2000.

Ton, Vy. "The Staley-Taylor Plan." In *Vietnamese Studies*, No. 11, ed. Nguyen Khac Vien. Hanoi: Xunhasaba Press, ca. 1969.

"2 Blacks Slain in Jackson." *Guardian*, May 23, 1970.

"UFAF Conference." *Old Mole*, August 1–14, 1969.

Ullman, Connie. "San Francisco State Shut Down." *New Left Notes*, November 19, 1968.

U.S. Senate, Committee on Foreign Relations. "The U.S. Government and the Vietnam War: Executive and Legislative Roles and Relationships, Part II, 1961–1964." Washington, D.C.: Government Printing Office, 1985. http://www.mtholyoke.edu/acad/intrel/pentagon/congress1.htm.

U.S. Senate Judiciary Internal Security Subcommittee. "The Weather Underground." Washington, D.C.: Government Printing Office, 1975.

vanauken. *Freedom for Movement Girls—Now*. Southern Student Organizing Committee, 1969.

Van Lydegraf, Clayton. "About Privilege." *New Left Notes*, April 24, 1969.

———. "Reply to Mellen." *New Left Notes*, June 6, 1969.

"Vietnam Work-In." *New Left Notes*, May 29, 1967.

Wald, Karen. "Interview with James Baldwin." Liberation News Service, February 18, 1970.

———. "The Promise of Oakland." *New Left Notes*, November 6, 1967.

Washington, Cynthia. "We Started from Different Ends of the Spectrum." *Southern Exposure* (Winter 1997).

Weather Bureau. "Everyone Talks About the Weather." In *Weatherman*, ed. Harold Jacobs. Berkeley, Calif.: Ramparts Press, 1970.

Weatherman. "Bring the War Home." *New Left Notes*, September 12, 1969.

———. "Chicago 69." *Fire*, October 21, 1969.

———. "Then There's Us." *Fire*, November 21, 1969.

———. "Washington November 15, 1969." *Fire*, November 21, 1969.

"Weather Report." *Old Mole*, October 14–24, 1969.

A Weatherwoman. "Inside the Weather Machine." *Rat*, February 6, 1970.

———. "War Report." *Rat*, February 24, 1970.

Webb, Marilyn Salzman. "DC Witches Hex United Fruit." *Guardian*, April 26, 1969.

———. "Women: We Have a Common Enemy." *New Left Notes*, June 10, 1968.

Weiner, Jon. "The New Left as History." *Radical History Review* 42 (Spring 1988).

Weisstein, Naomi, Evelyn Goldfield, and Sue Munaker. "A Woman Is a Sometime Thing, or, Cornering Capitalism by Removing 51% of Its Commodities." In *The New Left: A Collection of Essays*, ed. Priscilla Long. Boston: Extending Horizon Books, 1969.

"We Made the News Today." *New Left Notes*, January 15, 29, 1969, February 5, 12, 21, 28, 1969, March 7, 20, 1969, April 24, 1969.

"When All the Cops Are Criminals: Coroner's Jury Finds Hampton Killing 'Justifiable.'" Liberation News Service, January 24, 1970.

Wilkerson, Cathy. "Delegation to Hanoi Returns." *New Left Notes*, December 18, 1967.

———. "U.S. Vietnam STR [*sic*]." *New Left Notes*, January 15, 1968.

Williams, William Appleman. *The Tragedy of American Diplomacy*. New York: Dell, 1962

Willis, Ellen. "Sequel: Letter to a Critic." In *Notes from the Second Year*. New York, 1970.

———. "Women and the Left." In *Notes from the Second Year*. New York, 1970.

Winslow, Barbara. "Primary and Secondary Contradictions in Seattle, 1967–1969." In *Feminist Memoir Project*, ed. Rachel Blau DuPlessis and Ann Snitow. New York: Three Rivers Press, 1998.

Young, Marilyn. *The Vietnam Wars, 1945–1990*. New York: Harper Perennial, 1991.

Interviews

Chude Allen, December 2001

Bo Burlingham, February 2006

Kathleen Cleaver, January 2006

Lewis Cole, May 2006
Rev. Walter (Les) Coleman, January 2006
Carl Davidson, January 2006
Bernardine Dohrn, May 2006
Former New York Weatherman, May 2006
Lynn French, January 2006
Noel Ignatiev, March 2002
Martin Kenner, May 2006
Mike Klonsky, January 2006
Julius Lester, January 2006
Russ Neufeld, May 2006
Carl Ogelsby, December 2002
Mark Rudd, January 2006

Index

Hoover, J. Edgar, 39, 206

"Hot Town: Summer in the City, or, I Ain't Gonna Work on Maggie's Farm No More" (Ayers and Mellen), 176, 182; acknowledgment of black movement's significance, 153–54; practical implementation of (summer 1969), 173; resolution's projected goals, 154; Weatherman paper elucidates Hot Town organizing philosophy, 161

Hutchings, Phil: white-centeredness of New Left (1969–1970), 221–22; white youth and violence, 252n68

Hutton, L'il Bobby, 44

I Wor Kuen, 240n72

IDA (Institute for Defense Analysis), 94

Ignatin, Noel, 157, 229, 244n65; background of, 148; formation of STO, 222; leader of one of the tendencies within RYM II, 219; resolution on women's liberation, 135–37; sees his rise to influence within SDS stemming from struggle with PL, 239n63; white skin privilege introduced to SDS by, 40–41

imperialism, 14, 171, 186, 217, 220; anti-imperialism as defining context for RYM faction politics, 150, 153, 154; black understandings of imperialism, 73–78; efforts at integrating imperialism and domestic class analysis, 78–81, 92–93; imperial division of labor in New Left, 10, 77; Potter refuses to name system, 58; on RU, 220; on RYM II, 162–63; on Van Lydegraf, 158–59; Weatherman, on, 159–62, 176. See also American empire

imperialist division of labor, 81

India, 74

industrial proletariat: RYM II reemphasizes centrality of, 162–63, 186–87, 219; Tenney, Gottlieb, and Gilbert argue against the centrality of, 80–81. See also U.S. multinational working class; white working class

integration, 16, 18

International War Crimes Tribunal, Stockholm, 82–84

Iran, 62

Isserman, Maurice, historiography, 15, 236n19

"It's Only People's Games That You Got to Dodge" (Norman Reed, Inessa, Victor Camilo, Lilina Jones): significance of black people doing it "alone," 249n23; on Weatherman's racism, 214

Jackson State University, 225

Jacobs, Ron: historiography, 15; smash monogamy, on, 253n16; taking Weatherman at its word, 236-37n20, 241n78; on Weatherman's Havana meeting with Vietnamese, 251n66

Jaffee, Naomi: critiques Weatherman's community organizing, 167; "The Look Is You," 133–34

Jamaica, 70

James, Mike, 175; black urban rebellions and, 35; confronted on male supremacy, 113; organizing methods in Chicago JOIN project, 22

Japan, 71

Jeanette Rankin Brigade, 119, 121, 130

Jehlen, Allen, 28

Jesse James Gang, 161, 163, 166–67; formation and politics of, 148–49

JJ (Jacobs, John), 148, 157, 197; background of, 149; bringing Weather cadre back in line following Havana meeting with Vietnamese, 180; principal author of Weatherman paper, 249n23; promises big turnout for Days of Rage, 182; smashing monogamy in Seattle collective, 196

Johnson, Lyndon, 52, 57, 58, 62, 107, 180

JOIN (Jobs or Income Now) (Chicago ERAP project): black urban rebellions and, 35; gender roles in, 112–13; organizing strategy, 22–23

Jones, Beverly, 141, 200, 231; on male reception of women in the movement, 108–9; Towards a Female Liberation Movement, 122–24

Jones, Jeff, 170, 243n57; scuttling SDS, 186

Jones, LeRoi, 25–27, 141

Karenga, Ron, 141, 164

Katz, Marilyn, 140

Kaufman, Arnold, 236n18

Kazin, Michael, historiography, 236n19

Kennedy, Jacqueline, 204

Kennedy, John F., 62, 63; understandings of Third World, 54–56; Vietnam policy, 54–56

Made in the USA
Lexington, KY
14 March 2014